E-MAIL SECURITY
How to Keep Your Electronic Messages Private

E-MAIL SECURITY

How to Keep Your Electronic Messages Private

BRUCE SCHNEIER

John Wiley & Sons, Inc.
New York • Chichester • Brisbane • Toronto • Singapore

Publisher: Katherine Schowalter
Editor: Paul Farrell
Managing Editor: Robert Aronds
Copyeditor: Karen Cooper
Composition: Pronto Design & Production, Inc.

This publication is designed to provide accurate and authoritative information in regard to the subject matter covered. It is sold with the understanding that the publisher is not engaged in rendering professional services. If legal, accounting, medical, psychological, or any other expert assistance is required, the services of a competent professional person should be sought. ADAPTED FROM A DECLARATIONS OF PRINCIPLES OF A JOINT COMMITTEE OF THE AMERICAN BAR ASSOCIATION AND PUBLISHERS.

In no event will the publisher or author be liable for any consequential, incidental, or indirect damages (Including damages for loss of business profits, business interruption, loss of business information, and the like) arising from the use or inability to use the protocols and algorithms in this book,even if the publisher or author has been advised of the possibility of such damages.

Some of the protocols and algorithms in this book are protected by patents and copyrights. It is the responsibility of the reader to obtain all necessary patent and copyright licenses before implementing in software any protocol or algorithm in this book. This book does not contain an exhaustive list of all applicable patents and copyrights.

Some of the protocols and algorithms in this book are regulated under the United States Department of State International Traffic in Arms Regulations. It is the responsibility of the reader to obtain all necessary export licenses before implementing in software for export any protocol or algorithm in this book.

Trademarks
Many words in this publication in which the Author and Publisher believe trademark or other proprietary rights may exist have been designated as such by use of Initial Capital Letters. However, in so designating or failing to designate such words, neither the Author nor the Publisher intends to express any judgment on the validity or legal status of any proprietary right that may be claimed in the words.

Library of Congress Cataloging-in-Publication Data
Schneier, Bruce, 1963—
     E-mail security : how to keep your electronic messages private / Bruce Schneier
        p.   cm.
     Includes index.
     ISBN 0-471-05318-X
     1. Electronic mail systems. I. Title.
HE6239.E54S36 1995
005.7'1369—dc20   94-33251
                                                              CIP

Printed in the United States of America

10 9 8 7 6 5 4 3 2 1

Dedication

To Karen

Contents in Brief

Foreword

by William Murray

Let me tell you about my day. This morning, before I even awoke, my computer called up three of my E-mail boxes and downloaded my mail. It connected to two on-line services and downloaded my news, including the scores of my favorite teams and the quotes on all the stocks that I own or follow. When I went to the office, I plugged my computer into the local area network (LAN) and checked another E-mail box. Since the voice-mail icon on my phone was blinking, I checked my voice-mail and returned two calls. One of them was a request from a colleague for information. I asked him whether he preferred it by fax or E-mail. Since he was going to have to operate on the information, he said he preferred it by E-mail. However, his client's phone system was difficult for him to connect to so my computer sent it directly to his client's fax. I felt guilty that he was going to have to transcribe and a little concerned that he might make an error. He assured me that it was not a problem: He had character recognition software that would automatically convert the facsimile image to text.

During the day, I got a call from a potential business ally. He wanted a copy of the documentation for my alliance program. I asked him what form he would like to have it in and was happy to find that his word processor was able to import documents prepared by my word processor. However, since we did not share a mail system that would enable us to transfer the binary files with bit-for-bit integrity, we decided to use the Internet. Since Internet mail deals only in ASCII, we decided to encode the files into a single package using a public code called PKZIP and then convert that into an ASCII file using another public code called UUENCODE. This was simpler than it might sound; I opened a window, marked the files to be included in the zip file, and then dropped the zip file on the UUENCODE icon.

Later in the day, I received an E-mail message from the CEO of a company on whose board of directors I serve. When I looked in the in-basket, I noted that the file was encrypted using a secret code. When I clicked on the decrypt icon, I was prompted for the pass phrase protecting my public key. After I supplied it, I was assured that the message really did originate with the CEO. I returned to the in-basket, and found the clear text of the message.

After I got off from my afternoon plane, checked into my hotel room, and plugged my computer into the data-port on the telephone in the room, I checked my voice-mail to find that one of the secretaries had sent a fax to my fax mailbox. Two clicks later, the fax began to appear on my screen. Before going to bed, I connected to a shopping service to order a new piece of software; they asked if I would like a confirmation by E-mail. I used another service to pay my VISA® card bill; the payment order was carried by E-mail.

To recap, I have more phones than I can count—including a hand-held cellular phone, seven phone numbers, a fax mailbox, two voice mailboxes, an answering machine, an answering service, and seven E-mail boxes. I also share two secretaries. I communicate with colleagues, clients, family, friends, and even strangers. I do not intend to suggest that it is easy or convenient. No one should have more than one phone, phone number, mailbox, or mail handler. One should not have separate phones for voice, data, and facsimile. I suspect that it will get worse but hope that eventually it will get better.

Ten years ago I could have done none of these things. Some of them have become possible only within the last few months. I have dealt only with those services or capabilities that I used on a given day. I admit that I use far more than most people of my generation, but the coming generations will use all of them as routinely as we use pen, paper, and telephone.

You may well ask if, in fact, all these things that I have mentioned are really E-mail. While this is certainly a legitimate question, I insist that the similarities are more important than the differences. All involve the binary encoding of a file or message for later delivery to a distant mailbox. In the short run the receiving hardware and software depend in part upon the nature of the final presentation to the user. However, this is more likely an accommodation to the originating than to the receiving technology. By the time this appears in print, IBM will have announced In-Touch™ to compete with PersonaLink® from AT&T. These services will provide a single mailbox for facsimile, voice mail, electronic messaging, and other information such as I have described.

Written language gave humankind the ability to make a mark, to record across both time and distance. Such language is a major repository of culture. To make a mark across distance is to have power and influence. It permits coordination of activity across large spaces and populations. The infrastructure to do that is called mail.

Mail as we know it dates back to ancient Persia. While often a function of a powerful government, mail has also been a church, a university, and a commercial function. It has been closely tied to transportation and has been exploited and changed with every advance in transportation technology. It was one of the first uses for the coach, the railroad, and for aviation.

Government has wanted to control mail for reasons of state security, revenue, and patronage. Since the times of the Roman Empire this has been justified, in part, by government's role in road building. However, control of mail has also been used to justify government intervention into other areas.

Oliver Cromwell's government justified its postal franchise in part by the need to prevent "many dangerous and wicked designs which have been and are daily contrived against the welfare of this Commonwealth, the intelligence whereof cannot well be communicated but by letter of escript." Except for the archaic language, this could be the current President of the United States justifying why his Attorney General should be given the right to consent to telephone technology.

Nowhere has mail been more politicized than in the United States. For much of the United States' history, mail was a mechanism for getting votes and paying political favors. The right to appoint postmasters was a major perquisite of office. From the administration of Andrew Jackson, until the Postal Reform Act of 1970, the Postmaster General was a member of the President's cabinet. He was often the chairman of the President's party and was frequently the President's chief political functionary. In rural America, farmers often had a greater interest in postal service than in agricultural policy. Some have argued that rural free delivery had as much influence on American culture as the newspaper, the cinema, and the radio.

Modern mail, as we know and love it, can best be dated from the invention and introduction of the adhesive postage stamp only 150 years ago. This one invention did a great deal for both mail and commerce. However, the price and the conventions that went with the penny stamp were also important. For example, the fact that the stamp was independent of distance contributed a lot.

Security has been an issue in mail from ancient times, when most important mail originated with the sovereign and when it was not uncommon to cut out the tongue of the king's messenger. Security is still important today. Early writing, narrowly held within the scribe, mandarin, and clerical classes, was a security mechanism in itself. However, by Roman times literacy had become so wide-spread that it was necessary to introduce primitive codes and ciphers.

Security in mail deals first with reliable delivery to the addressee. In addition to snow, rain, heat and gloom of night, threats have included mailbox pilferage, train robbery, and employee theft. Likewise, reliable delivery necessitates evidence or confidence that the mail was delivered.

Mail security means delivery to the addressee only, that is with confidentiality. The modern standard for confidentiality in mail is the single white envelope, wherein almost all commercial mail moves. A combination of culture, law, and potential evidence that the envelope has been tampered with act to protect confidentiality. Only a tiny portion of mail requires higher security than that. For that portion two envelopes, leather or canvas pouches with lead seals, or even a special courier with a brief case handcuffed to his or her wrist are used.

The United States postal system has enjoyed a good reputation for security, even if that reputation is somewhat at odds with the record. This reputation results, in part, from the fact that most of the mail ultimately gets through, and in part from the attention paid to public relations by the postal service. The U. S. postal service likes to brag that diamond merchants routinely send their goods by mail. Of course, to the merchant, diamonds are simply a commodity with no unique, sentimental, intrinsic or other non-economic value.

Prior to the modern national postal service, much of the mail did not get through. The user's response to this was to send important messages multiple times by multiple paths. Of course, this increased the probability that the contents of the message would be disclosed.

The Postal service's response was to offer optional and premium priced services. For example, in the United States, first class mail includes a "return to sender" service if the message is undeliverable as addressed. Optional secure delivery services include the return receipt, registered and certified mail, and insured mail. The return receipt provides evidence that the message was received by the addressee or his agent. Registered mail ensures that the service keeps an audit trail or registry for the handling of the message. Certified mail provides a representation by the service, as opposed to a receipt from the addressee, that the message was delivered. Finally, insured mail provides a financial remedy for property, as opposed to simply notification, that mail is lost or stolen by the service.

Today there are dozens of systemic security problems in the U.S. mail system. These include problems that are local to the postal system, such as pilferage by postal employees in illegal cooperation with law enforcement and national security authorities. They include problems with outsiders such as theft of checks and credit cards from mailboxes. They include all kinds of mail fraud. These last are often aggravated by lax security practices of large users, such as failure to confirm name and address changes. They include abuses by nation states. While these abuses are more rampant in some states than others, the power of the state invites abuse; all governments abuse their powers to some degree, usually in the name of law and order.

While systemic, these problems have not destroyed the trust necessary for the continued use of the system. In part, users do not recognize the risk, in part they accept it, and in part they compensate by using alternatives or precautions. In general, however, the security problems are not sufficiently severe to damage the system.

Few technologies hold the promise of electronic mail. Mail has risen, and fallen, in importance with civilization. It has flourished when civilization has flourished and has languished when civilization has ebbed. As with most such things, it is difficult to establish a cause and effect relationship. It might not even be useful to do so. It is sufficient to know that mail and civilization are related. As we enter into a new technological era, it will be a good thing for each if the other flourishes.

Almost all implementations to date of E-mail can be described as toy technology. They have been fun, even interesting, but they have not been serious. While they have grown rapidly, they still carry only a very small quantity of message traffic. Few such systems were seriously expected to succeed. They were not designed for success. Indeed most can hardly be said to have been designed at all. They were simply initiated and elaborated. Most have succeeded beyond the wildest hopes of their originators or sponsors.

This should not really surprise anyone, least of all students of technology. Much of the paper mail system was not designed either; it just grew. Indeed, this is part of its beauty. Services were added, developed, and introduced slowly, sometimes in response to need, and sometimes in response to technological developments that altered the economics. For example, while most first class mail today moves by air, and while mail was one of the first applications of aviation, for its first 50 years, air mail was a premium priced service.

The E-mail system is growing in much the same manner. It is growing by connection of many systems to one another. It is growing by exploitation of telephone, facsimile, and even paging system technologies. It is growing by using these other systems as the delivery mechanisms of last resort. It is growing as the result of thousands of small commercial ventures in cooperation with a few large ones. It is growing as the result of the favor of end-users. It is growing because its users, both individual and institutional, enjoy an economic advantage over non-users.

To date, the role of government in E-mail has been limited. In the United States, government sponsored the Internet, the infrastructure for connecting other networks together. They have sponsored much basic research. In other countries, government has simply been indifferent. However, E-mail is not a government function as yet. It is much more a cooperative and collaborative effort. The present infrastructure is the result of connection of peer systems without any central authority. It is governed more by custom and agreement, both formal and informal, than by any law or regulation.

While individuals in government see the value of the present arrangement and are favorably disposed toward it, government as an institution is threatened. I first knew that the coup against Gorbachev had failed when I got a message from a correspondent in Moscow assuring me that he was okay, thanking me for my expression of concern, and requesting tanks. Not only is government threatened but so is the very idea of the nation state.

To the extent that E-mail proves to be important, we can expect to see many attempts on the part of government to coopt it in much the same way that they have coopted the paper mail system. The excuses that it will use to do so will be related to security. It will repeat the claim of Cromwell's government and will create whatever evidence is required to convince the people of the validity of the claim. Arguments to the contrary notwithstanding, the real motive will be to maintain political control and influence.

Today it seems clear that electronic mail will be important. However, in a way, this is simply speculation. Little evidence exists and it is inconclusive. On the other hand, the economics are changing rapidly. By the end of the century we are likely to have a billion transistors or switches on a single chip. The material and replication cost of the chip will be tiny. Most of the cost will be in the information and the capital. Such systems feed on their own success. The greater the number of units produced, the lower the cost; the lower the unit cost, the higher the demand.

This kind of knowledge will greatly expand the capacity or bandwidth of the ether, of copper, and of glass. The cost of the computer is plummeting while its functionality is increasing. In less than 50 years, it has fallen in price from the tens of millions of dollars to the low hundreds and risen in numbers from the tens to the tens of millions. There seems to be little doubt that both trends will continue.

The power and value of a communication medium grows with the number of potential connections, and with the speed of the message. The telephone has given us the ability to exchange information almost instantaneously but only synchronously and only among a limited number of people at a time. For the most part, it leaves no permanent record. Radio and television have been both synchronous and one-to-many. Electronic mail is asynchronous and many-to-many. While the toy systems of today are limited to text, those of tomorrow promise the limitless exchange of mixed voice, sound, image, moving image, and data.

The cultural impact of successful E-mail is potentially greater than that of the telephone and will rival that of paper.

Security, that is, confidential, reliable, and known delivery is essential to the success of E-mail. In other words, people will not use a mail system that they cannot trust to deliver their messages. While many of their messages could go on a postcard, they will not use a system in which all messages must go on a postcard. While they may not seal all of their envelopes, they will not use a system in which there are no envelopes. While they trust the postman, they will not use a system in which they must trust the postman. While they will use a toy system for some applications, they expect a mature and robust one for most applications.

The fundamental mechanism for providing security for binary encoded messages in an open network is encryption. It enables us to emulate all of the controls that we have historically relied upon. Public-key cryptography enables us to emulate not only envelopes but also signatures. While we have the necessary primitive structures, we do not yet have the necessary infrastructure.

In addition to media for recording messages, a mail system must have an infrastructure for carrying messages and distributing them. It must have trucks, planes, post offices, an addressing system, and zip codes. Likewise, a system of logical envelopes and signatures must have an infrastructure for naming and distributing encryption keys.

As electronic mail evolves from a toy system to an infrastructure system, a number of problems must be solved. While security may not be the most significant of these, it is by no means the least. The Internet is the laboratory where these problems are researched and prototype solutions are conceived. This book deals with how this will be done.

In conducting these experiments, I hope that the analog of the traditional system is adhered to. Most of what users know about security and control in a mail system has been learned from the paper model. To the extent that the system follows this model, it will exploit the habits of users. To the extent that it fails to operate in the manner that users habitually expect, it will cause user error.

To the extent that the security expectations of users are not met, the ultimate success of the system is put at risk. To the extent that the public becomes anxious or concerned, the intrusion of government is invited and justified.

About the Author

Bruce Schneier is President of Counterpane Systems, a cryptography and computer security consulting firm in Oak Park, Illinois. He is a contributing editor to both *Dr. Dobb's Journal* and *Computer and Communications Security Review*, and a monthly columnist for the Computer Security Institute Newsletter. In addition to being a frequent lecturer, Bruce is the author of two other computer books, *Applied Cryptography* and *Protect Your Macintosh*. He can be reached by electronic mail at **schneier@counterpane.com**.

Part **I**

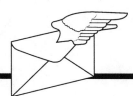

Privacy and Electronic Mail

Chapter 1

The Problem

The State of Electronic Mail

The world of electronic mail is the world of postcards. Messages travel from machine to machine open and available, just like the messages on the back of postcards. As those postcards move through the network, anyone on a machine that handles them can read the messages. People may choose not to, or they may not have the access privileges to do so easily, but the only security anyone has is based on the honesty, ignorance, and indifference of those at the intermediate points. And even worse, the sender of the message has no control over what those intermediate points are. They can be universities, competing companies, foreign governments—whatever.

E-mail networks are *decentralized* systems. Imagine that Alice wants to send a message to Bob. (Throughout this book we'll be using Alice to represent the sender of a piece of electronic mail, and Bob to represent the receiver. There's nothing special about these names. It's just tradition.) Alice writes her message on her computer and sends it to Bob, with his address at the top. The message flows through the system, going from one machine to another. When a machine gets the message, the machine reads it (or, at least, the machine reads the header), figures out if the message is for anyone who has an account on that machine, and then sends it off to another machine if it isn't. The other machine does the same, and so on. Eventually the message reaches the correct machine and is placed in Bob's electronic-mail file. The next time Bob logs on, he reads the message.

In reality, the various networks work a bit more intelligently. Electronic mail (or e-mail) doesn't bounce randomly from one machine to another, hoping to find its destination. The different computers on the Internet have routing tables. When a computer receives a piece of e-mail that is for someone on another computer, it knows enough to look up that computer on the routing table and to send it in the general direction of that computer. Even so, look at the routing information next time you receive a piece of electronic mail; it probably passed through quite a few intermediaries between its source and its destination.

The scary thing is that any of these intermediaries can easily read your e-mail. Imagine that Eve, an eavesdropper, is sitting at one of these intermediary machines on the Internet. (Eve will represent the eavesdropper throughout this book. Again, it's tradition.) She can be the system administrator, a clever hacker, or, if the security on the machine is poor enough, a regular user. In any case, the world is an open book to her. She can sit at her terminal and see every electronic mail message that passes through the machine, no matter whom it is addressed to. She can print out a message if she likes. She can show it to her friends. She can post it on the net. She can send a copy to *The New York Times*. And if she's halfway clever, she can alter the message in transit.

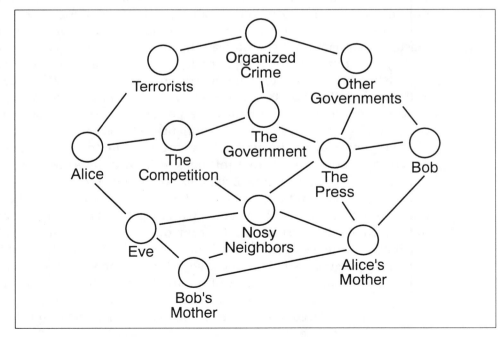

Figure 1.1 Who can read your mail.

Alice and Bob have no control over who reads their e-mail in transit. It doesn't matter that their mail is marked confidential, that their computers are in locked rooms, or that they both have been subjected to rigorous psychological screening and have been selected for their discretion. By sending a message over the Internet to Bob, Alice is trusting the security of every machine the message will pass through (see Figure 1.1). By sending a message over the Internet to Alice, Bob is making the same leap of faith.

I've been singling out the Internet in this example, but the other electronic mail systems are no better. CompuServe, GEnie, America Online, AppleLink, MCIMail: messages sent over all these networks are also like postcards, and can be read by anyone who can get to the appropriate level of the network.

Envelopes for Electronic Mail

If electronic-mail messages are postcards, what we want are letters in envelopes (see Figure 1.2). Like electronic-mail messages, letters are routed through lots of intermediate points. You drop a letter in a mailbox, a postal worker collects the mail and brings it to the local post office, there it is routed to its destination through a variety of post offices and transport vehicles, and eventually a postal

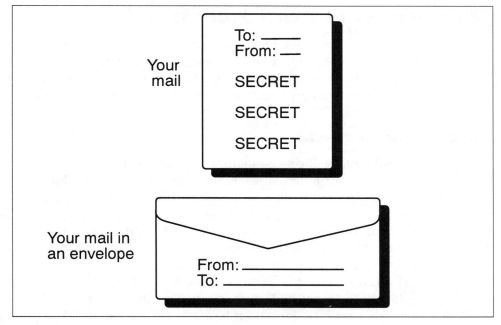

Figure 1.2 Mail and envelopes.

worker delivers it into the mailbox of the intended recipient. A dozen different people might handle a letter as it travels through the system, but none of them can read the letter. It is protected inside an envelope.

We can't put electronic-mail messages into envelopes. (Well, we could put a floppy disk in an envelope, but that would defeat the point.) But we have an analogy for them. We can use strong encryption as our "envelope."

Electronic-mail security programs, such as Pretty Good Privacy (PGP) and implementations of the Privacy Enhanced Mail (PEM) standard, do exactly that. By encrypting her electronic mail so that only Bob can read it, Alice ensures that Eve cannot read her message—even if Eve intercepts it in transit. By adding a digital signature to her electronic mail, Alice can ensure that Bob knows who sent the message; Eve cannot substitute one message for another and claim it came from Alice.

So, these electronic-mail security programs are better than physical envelopes. Eve can open envelopes, either surreptitiously or publicly, and read their contents. Eve can intercept an envelope in transit, open it and read the message, and replace it with another message in another envelope. Eve can't do this in the digital world. The combination of encryption and a digital signature provides an "envelope" that Eve cannot tamper with.

Who Wants to Read Your Mail?

I've said that anyone who wants to can read your electronic mail, as well as remote logon sessions, ftp downloads, real-time conversations, and anything else you do on the net. But who would want to? The answer depends on who you are, what you are doing, and who may be interested in it.

Foreign Governments

The military intelligence organizations of major governments are the most sophisticated of potential eavesdroppers. Reading other individuals' mail is their job. Since the beginning of the Cold War they have spent billions of dollars a year collecting, compiling, and analyzing intelligence data on each other. Just because the Cold War is over, don't think that these organizations are not still at it. Computer transmissions are just a part of that overall collection effort, but are an important part.

This is not to say that if you are not involved in defense, you are safe from military intelligence collection efforts. The lines between military and corporate espionage have long been blurred; many commercial technologies have military applications. The militaries of several countries routinely target civilian companies in other countries for spying, and think nothing of passing the information they collect on to competing companies in their own country. France and Japan are the best-known offenders, but there are undoubtedly others. The National Security Agency has been accused of, in at least one instance, intercepting a telephone call between two European countries and passing on marketing information to a U.S. competitor. As the post-Cold War world continues to evolve, large military intelligence communities need new reasons to justify their existence. Industrial spying by military intelligence organizations is likely to increase.

Your Own Government

Domestic governments are often interested in spying on their own citizens. This is obviously true in totalitarian regimes like China, North Korea, and Cuba, but it is true of other countries as well. The government of France prohibits encryption on civilian communications circuits unless a copy of the encryption key and algorithm is given to the authorities. The governments of both Taiwan and South Korea have been known to request that companies remove encryption from voice, data, and facsimile telephone connections. Even the United States has a long, sordid history of conducting illegal wiretaps. Any country that would, without a court order, tap the telephones of Martin Luther King Jr. could easily justify reading its citizens' electronic mail messages. And the fact that electronic mail doesn't yet have the same Constitutional protection as paper mail makes it even easier.

Within the U.S., many government organizations might be interested in reading private e-mail conversations. The FBI might be looking for criminals, people starting fringe political parties, people who don't floss regularly, or other unsavory characters. Child pornographers are particularly popular targets. The DEA might be looking for drug dealers. (The "War on Drugs" seems to be a good excuse for a whole lot of questionable law enforcement ideas.) The IRS might be looking for tax cheats. There's also the Treasury Department, the Bureau of Alcohol, Tobacco, and Firearms, the CIA: if you're doing something even remotely interesting, somewhere in the bowels of Washington, DC there is a government acronym that wants to know about it.

Business Competitors

Businesses might spy on rival companies. They could potentially be interested in customer lists, employee directories, marketing plans, financial data . . . almost anything. The Coca-Cola Company might pay dearly to know

Pepsi's new advertising plan; Ford might be similarly interested in the designs for next year's Chevrolet models. Stockbrokers might be very interested in data that may eventually affect a company's stock price. A salesman might be very interested in the customer database of a rival salesman, perhaps even of another salesman in the same company.

Reporters

Investigative reporters would certainly be interested in private electronic-mail conversations between public individuals: politicians, corporate leaders, entertainers, and others. Remember when Washington, DC's *City Paper* collected and published data on Supreme Court nominee Robert Bork's videotape rental records? Remember when reporters broke into Tonya Harding's electronic mailbox? Although there have not yet been any public instances of reporters actually going so far as to publish some-one's electronic-mail messages, it is bound to happen soon. How would a Senate candidate feel if his college-age postings to **alt.beer** were reprinted in the newspaper? (Consider that the next time you flame someone on the net.)

Criminals

Criminals can get some valuable data from electronic mail, as well. Police have long known that people monitor cellular phone channels, listening for credit card numbers. There's no reason why they can't look for the same thing among the electronic mail messages moving back and forth across the networks. Some companies are already opening up shop on the Internet, offering various consumer goods for sale by credit card. It would be easy to set up an automatic program to scan the mail feed into a computer, looking for credit card numbers. If commerce on the Internet ever takes off, this prac-tice will undoubtedly become more widespread.

Friends and Family

And finally, colleagues, friends, and family are possible spies. These are not sophisticated spies, but they may very well be the most interested. Some companies explicitly reserve the right to read all e-mail sent by their employ-ees, whether work-related or personal. A worker in an office might be very interested in the personal electronic-mail correspondence of a co-worker, for no other reason than nosiness. A family member might have the same motivation. If someone is carrying on an illicit love affair, keeping correspondence private could be very important. If someone is planning a surprise birthday party, it is less so.

The Collection Problem

The biggest problem with reading someone's e-mail is finding it among the sea of other electronic mail messages. It's a small needle inside an enormous haystack.

Consider the National Security Agency. (I am just singling them out as an example. There are certainly other possible threats.) One of its jobs is to monitor computer data flowing into and out of the United States, as well as data flowing between other countries. (They may very well monitor electronic mail messages flowing from one point in this country to another, but that's not supposed to be their job. At least, I don't think that is supposed to be their job. I don't really know; almost everything about the NSA is classified.)

This is a task of Herculean proportions. In 1994, gigabytes of computer data flow in and out of our borders every day: that's a billion messages a month. This includes electronic mail, Usenet newsgroups, remote logons, ftp downloads, real-time "chat" conversations, and everything else. Storing this amount of data on computer tape is a massive problem, let alone reading and analyzing it (see Figure 1.3).

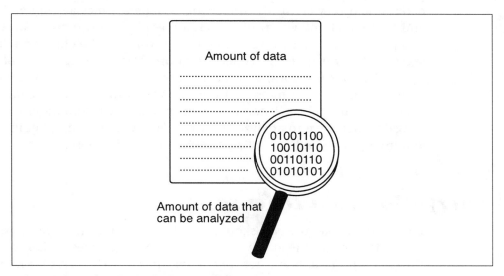

Figure 1.3 The collection problem.

It is widely assumed (again, anyone who knows isn't talking) that computers sift through the data in real time, looking for interesting information. Using one technique or another, the NSA has tapped the data lines in and out of the country. (Again, this is assumed—but it's a good assumption.) This enormous data stream is fed into large computers, whose job is to look for the data that the NSA might be interested in. Maybe the computers look for certain key words. An electronic-mail message containing the words "nuclear," "cryptography," or "assassination" might be stored on tape for further analysis. Certainly "shoot the President" is a string to look for.

There are other collection techniques that the NSA computers might use. They might look for data from particular people, or from particular organizations. They might look for data with a particular structure. They might have artificial intelligence software that does things I can't even comprehend. The NSA has a lot of money to throw at this problem, and they've been working on it for a long time.

The important point is that they have to do this in real time. There are just too much data to save it all. The best they can hope for is to collect as much data in a day as can be analyzed in a day. They can't collect any more, because more is coming the next day. Data collection is like a never-ending treadmill—if they fall behind, they will never catch up.

Collection is useless without analysis, and that is what comes next. Analysis is far more complicated than collection. Unless the NSA has more advanced computing resources than I can imagine, they need people for this part. People have to read those "interesting" electronic-mail messages to determine if they are really interesting. Maybe the message saying "nuclear" and "assassination" was really about a science fiction movie. For a while it was popular to add a string of interesting words at the end of all your messages, just to frustrate this collection effort. Maybe the mention of blowing up the UN was frivolous, and maybe it was a message from one terrorist to another. Maybe that message from an American high-tech company was innocuous, and maybe it was a foreign spy passing information back home.

Again, they have to analyze all of the day's data in a day, because more is coming right behind it. It's like drinking from a fire hose.

Encryption as a Defense

Encryption makes the NSA's job difficult on several fronts. The most obvious is that they cannot read the various electronic messages. This is only true if the encryption method is secure enough that the NSA can't break it; I'll talk more about what that means in Chapter 2. If the NSA can't break the encryption method, they can only do traffic analysis (explained below).

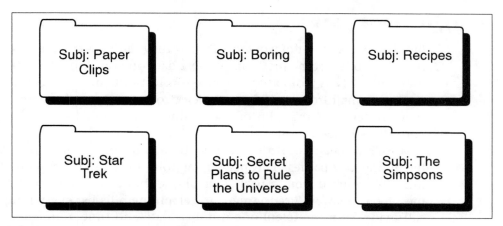

Figure 1.4 Find the interesting e-mail.

If the NSA can break the encryption method, then it is just a matter of allocating the resources necessary to break it. Maybe that means five minutes of time on a Pentium or PowerPC computer before the NSA can read the message; maybe that means several hours of time on a Cray III. Whatever is required, if the NSA wants to spend the computing resources, it will read the message.

However, this is only really true if encryption is not widespread. Remember the collection problem. There is an enormous amount of data flowing through the Internet every day—far too much to examine it all. The NSA has "interesting stuff" checkers: computer programs that sift through all the data and cull out the specific things that might warrant closer examination (see Figure 1.4). These programs could easily collect encrypted messages, and then route those messages to another computer program for further analysis. However, this only works if only a very small percentage of messages are encrypted. If 80 percent of all electronic mail traffic, ftp downloads, remote logon sessions, Usenet posts, and so on are routinely encrypted, there is no way that the NSA's computers will have the time to break them all—if they *can* be broken.

And even worse, the interesting stuff checkers have a lot harder time deciding which messages to ignore and which are worth breaking. If only a few messages a day are encrypted, then those are obviously interesting messages. But if *everyone* routinely encrypts messages, even people chatting with their friends, the NSA can't tell the interesting encrypted messages from the innocuous encrypted messages. There's just too much data flowing through the net, and not enough computing power to bring to bear on the problem. Encryption, even poor encryption, can quickly make the collection problem insurmountable.

Traffic Analysis

But the NSA isn't out of work yet. Even if they can't read your electronic mail, they can collect some pretty impressive data on you through traffic analysis.

Traffic analysis looks at who you send electronic mail to, who you receive electronic mail from, how long the electronic mail messages are, and when they are sent. There's a lot of good information buried in that data, if you know how to look for it.

Most European countries do not itemize telephone bills like American telephone companies. European telephone bills list how many "message units" were used from a particular phone, but not where and when these message units were used. American telephone bills list every long-distance call made from the telephone number: date and time, number called, and duration of the call. The American system makes it easier to spot errors and to catch your children making hundreds of calls to 1-900-HI-SANTA, but it also gives the telephone company information about your calling patterns (see Figure 1.5). Do you make a lot of long-distance calls to Montana? Then maybe you are interested in these Montana vacation packages. Do you order from catalogs frequently? Then you should be on this mailing list. Do

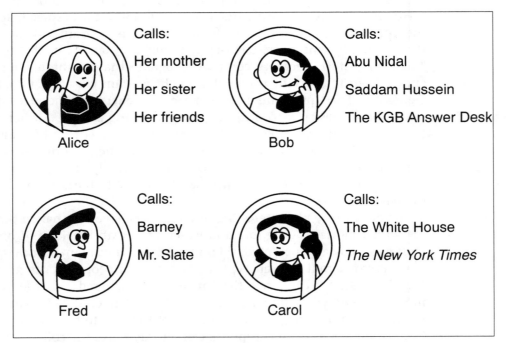

Figure 1.5 Intelligence from phone records.

you call the Suicide Prevention Hotline regularly? Then maybe a prospective employer should hire someone else. Or Tax Cheats Anonymous? Maybe the IRS is interested.

During World War II the Nazis used detailed calling records to round up the friends of suspected enemies of the state. Many European countries believe it is worth the loss of an itemized telephone bill to prevent that from ever happening again.

Similar analyses are possible by examining electronic-mail messages. Even if the message is encrypted, the header clearly states who the message is from, who it is to, when it was sent, and how long it is. There are anonymous remailing services that purport to hide who a message is from (see Chapter 7), but I am suspicious of the security of these services. They may prevent the average Internet user from knowing where a particular piece of electronic mail came from, but I'll bet they don't fool a sophisticated eavesdropper like the NSA for a minute.

Imagine that Eve is interested in Alice, a suspected terrorist. Alice encrypts all her e-mail, so Eve can't read the contents of her messages. However, Eve collects all the information she can on Alice's traffic patterns. Eve knows the electronic-mail addresses of everyone Alice regularly corresponds with. She often sends long messages to someone called Bob, who always immediately responds with a very short message. Perhaps she is sending him orders, and he is confirming receipt of those orders. One day there is a big jump in the volume of electronic-mail traffic between Alice and Bob. Perhaps they are planning something. Then, there is silence. No mail flows between the two of them. The next day, a government building is bombed. Is this enough evidence to arrest both of them? Perhaps not in the United States, but certainly in countries with weaker concepts of personal freedom.

Terrorists are not the only ones with something to fear from traffic analysis. Would the FBI start investigating people for drug use simply because they corresponded over e-mail with a convicted—or even just a suspected—drug dealer? Does a company, after receiving information that an employee is regularly corresponding with an electronic-mail address in a competitor's offices, have grounds to fire that employee? What if the company receives information that the employee is posting to **alt.sex.abuse.recovery**? What would a jealous person think after learning that his or her spouse was corresponding regularly with a potential rival? Traffic analysis is an important intelligence tool, and its implications on personal privacy are significant.

Additionally, keep in mind that most laws that protect personal privacy don't cover traffic analysis. The U.S. government can't tap a telephone without a warrant, but there's no law to stop government agents from getting all the traffic information about the telephone that they want.

Spoofing

Spoofing is another security problem on computer networks. It is the problem of one person impersonating another. Whether the impersonation is intended as a joke, a means to discredit or disgrace someone, or as a means to defraud someone, it is a problem (see Figure 1.6).

Every month or so a particular type of message is posted to a variety of Usenet newsgroups. The message might have a subject line that reads, "I am a child molester and I'm proud of it," or it might have some sexist or racist slogan. The body of the message isn't any better. Then, anywhere from ten minutes to a day later, there is another posting from the same person apologizing for the first posting. The first posting was a forgery, the second posting says. It was a prank—don't believe any of it.

Even so, some damage is already done. Many people see the first posting and, not knowing that it is a forgery, believe the purported sender to be whatever the posting claims him to be. They send an angry reply. They write a scathing letter to his system administrator demanding his account be revoked. They report him to the police, or to some political action group. If they know him, they may avoid his presence. They may further damage his reputation by spreading the story to even more people. (This is particularly bad as those other people are even less likely to see the retraction.)

Maybe Eve wants to smear Alice. She writes an incriminating electronic mail message, puts Alice's name on the bottom and forges Alice's header on top (it's not hard for a skilled hacker to fake a message header). Then Eve sends a copy to *The New York Times*.

Figure 1.6 Spoofing.

There are other, less overt, ways to do damage by impersonating someone else. Imagine that Alice and Bob are collaborating via electronic mail on some project. Eve sends a message to Alice, purporting to be from Bob. In it, "Bob" claims that he has moved, and notes his new electronic mail address. Alice doesn't know better, and changes her address directory. Now Eve can correspond with Alice, pretending to be Bob. If Eve is really clever, she can simultaneously convince Bob that she is Alice. Then, Eve can have conversations with both of them, passing messages through most of the time and only changing them on occasion. Eve can thwart whatever project Alice and Bob are working on through judicious use of misinformation. If Alice and Bob don't communicate face-to-face or over the telephone regularly, Eve can keep this ruse up for a long time.

It can get even simpler. Eve could get an account in the name of a known, but not too well-known, reporter. She could promise Alice publicity in exchange for some information. Alice trusts the name on the "From" line of the header, and is tricked into revealing whatever information Eve wants.

Spoofing can be prevented with something called a digital signature. A written signature provides proof of authorship of (or, at least, agreement with) a physical document. A digital signature provides the same for an electronic document. With this sort of digital authentication, Alice can always check to make sure a document is actually from the person it is purported to be from. No one can send an incriminating posting purportedly from Alice. Alice can always check who really sent a piece of e-mail she received. And no one can pretend to be Alice to someone else and hope to get away with it.

Making Security Work

There are several things we can do to keep our digital connections secure. The simplest and easiest is to regularly use encryption and digital signatures. By regularly, I mean all the time. Encrypt and sign all of your correspondence, even when the content doesn't warrant secrecy. To do otherwise only invites trouble.

Currently, almost no one encrypts his or her e-mail. It's inconvenient to do so. Unfortunately, the side effect is that anyone who uses encryption immediately attracts attention. Remember those interesting stuff checkers that the NSA uses to monitor electronic mail? When one of these checkers sees an encrypted message go from the United States to another country, a red flag goes up. If the message is encrypted, it must be interesting. Even if the NSA can't break the encryption scheme and read the message, they can record who the message was from and to, when it was sent, and its length.

Strength in Numbers

If everyone were to regularly use encryption, there would be no red flags. No one in the post office stares at a sealed envelope, wondering what is so private that it can't be written on a postcard. Envelopes are the rule; no one thinks twice about them. If encrypted electronic mail were the rule, no one would suspect the average correspondent of having something to hide.

In the same way, digital signatures should be the rule. At this writing, almost no one signs his or her digital correspondence. Again, it's a hassle and it takes time to do. A digitally signed message is sure to arouse suspicion: What is so important about this piece of electronic mail that it has to be signed? If every message is routinely signed, then a signed message won't even warrant a comment.

The way to make security ubiquitous is to make it transparent. If it is just as easy for someone to send signed and encrypted e-mail as it is for her to send unsigned and unencrypted mail, then she is more likely to choose the former. No one wonders if someone might think she has something to hide as she reaches for an envelope. Likewise, no one will think that she is somehow engaging in skulduggery as she encrypts her correspondence. Signed and encrypted correspondence will be commonplace, yet another example of the triumph of personal privacy over Big Brother government.

Strength in Software

The tools to make security transparent are not here yet, but they are starting to show their faces on the horizon. The two security programs discussed in this book, Pretty Good Privacy (PGP) and implementations of the Privacy Enhanced Mail (PEM) standard, go a long way towards making strong security easy to use.

PGP and PEM are comprehensive electronic-mail security programs. (Actually, PGP is a program and PEM is a standard. There are programs that implement the PEM standard.) They handle encryption and digital signatures. They have a whole key infrastructure to ensure that people can send secure messages to each other. They work on a variety of hardware platforms, with a variety of mail software, and over a variety of networks. They are what this book is about.

However, before we examine what PGP and PEM do, how they work, and how they compare with each other, we need to talk about how cryptography works. When you understand the tools you can understand the programs.

Chapter 2

Encryption

The Basics of Encryption

The aim of encryption is to turn an otherwise intelligible message into gibberish, so that anyone who intercepts the message can't read it. This sounds easy, but the catch is that the intended recipient of the message has to turn the gibberish back into a readable message. The science of doing this sort of thing is called *cryptography*.

Remember our players: Alice is the sender, Bob is the receiver, and Eve is the eavesdropper. Alice wants to send a message to Bob. She takes the message, also called the *plaintext*, and encrypts it. The encrypted message is called the *ciphertext*. Alice then sends the ciphertext to Bob. Eve, who intercepts the ciphertext in transmission, can't read it. But Bob, who receives the ciphertext, is able to decrypt it and recover the plaintext message.

How does this work? How is Bob able to decrypt the message while Eve cannot? To understand how this works, you have to understand how encryption works.

Algorithms

Encryption is based on two things: an algorithm and a key. An algorithm is a mathematical transformation. It transforms plaintext into ciphertext, and it transforms ciphertext back into plaintext. When Alice encrypts a message, she uses an encryption algorithm to transform the plaintext into ciphertext. When Bob decrypts a message, he uses the corresponding decryption algorithm to transform the ciphertext back into plaintext. See Figure 2.1.

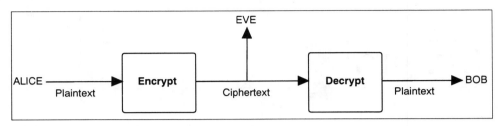

Figure 2.1 Encryption and decryption.

Until 1883, the security of this operation was based on keeping the algorithm secret. If Eve knows the algorithm, she can decrypt the ciphertext just as easily as Bob. But if Alice and Bob keep the details of the algorithm to themselves, Eve won't know what to do. The best she can do is to try to figure out what the algorithm is. This is called *cryptanalysis*, and there was a whole lot of it going on during World War I and WW II.

Trying to keep the algorithm a secret creates problems. One, it is not easy to do. The military organizations of the world spend a lot of time and energy keeping their algorithms secret, and still details leak across borders. If the algorithm is embedded in a piece of military hardware—a tactical radio, for example—eventually the enemy will capture or steal one and reverse-engineer the algorithm. If the algorithm is in a commercial piece of software, it only takes a few hours for a clever programmer to disassemble the program and reverse-engineer the algorithm. And once those details have become public, the security of that communication system is lost forever.

Two, if this type of system is going to work for everyone, then every pair of people needs their own unique algorithm. If there are 100 people in a network, there must be almost 5,000 different algorithms, each person has to know 100 of them, and he has to keep all of them secret from everyone else! Designing an encryption algorithm that is secure from cryptanalysis is a difficult task; designing 5,000 of them is absurd.

Keys

We can get around these problems with the second basis of cryptography: the key. A key is a random bit string—sometimes a number, sometimes an ASCII value, or sometimes a word or phrase—that is used in conjunction with an algorithm. An algorithm can take any one of a large number of possible keys. Each different key causes the algorithm to work in a slightly different way (see Figure 2.2). Only two people with the identical key can encrypt and decrypt messages. Someone with one key cannot decrypt messages encrypted with a different key.

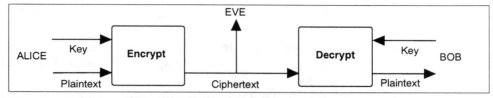

Figure 2.2 Encryption and decryption with key.

When Alice encrypts a message, she uses an encryption algorithm and a key to transform the plaintext into ciphertext. When Bob decrypts a message, he uses the corresponding decryption algorithm and the exact same key to transform the ciphertext back into plaintext. Eve, who does not have the key, cannot decrypt the message.

Think of a lock. The world doesn't need a new lock design for every front door. It is enough to have one lock design, and hundreds of thousands of different keys. Even if two people are using identical locks, they cannot open the other's door unless they have the same key.

The important aspect of this process is that the security of the system rests entirely within the key. If Eve does not have the exact key that Alice and Bob are using, she cannot decrypt the message. We assume that Eve has complete knowledge of the algorithm. We assume that Eve has a copy of the software that Alice and Bob are using to encrypt messages. (If it is mass-market software, this is a perfectly reasonable assumption.) We can even assume that Eve knows what Alice and Bob are encrypting. But without the key, Eve cannot decrypt the message.

Now, the encryption process is much easier. Alice and Bob don't have to keep an algorithm secret; they only have to keep a particular key secret. This key might only be 20 or 30 digits, and a whole lot easier to keep secret than an entire software program. They can choose an algorithm, one that has been published and is known to be secure, and not have to design their own. If their message key is compromised, it only compromises the messages encrypted with that key, not all messages encrypted with that algorithm. They can change the key and keep on encrypting messages; they don't have to recall all the software and design a new algorithm. And an entire network of users can communicate securely with one another using just one algorithm and many different keys.

Modern Encryption Algorithms

This is where encryption is today. We encrypt messages using algorithms that are public and known—DES, IDEA, etc.—and secret keys. Assuming those algorithms are secure, then messages encrypted with them are as secure as the key.

Assuming those algorithms are secure. . . That assumption turns out to be one of the hardest problems in cryptography. Encryption is easy to explain, but much harder to do securely.

I don't think it's possible to count the number of hours that have gone into designing secure algorithms. And those hours pale in comparison to the vast number of hours that have gone into analyzing and testing to see if those algorithms are really secure. It's a complex and subtle game of making and breaking, but that is how the science progresses.

Since the beginning of this century, much of the work in designing secure algorithms has gone on behind the electrified fences and door alarms of military security agencies. In the United States much of the work has been done by the NSA; in England, by the GCHQ. France has its DGSE, and the Soviet Union had the KGB. These agencies spent billions of dollars designing algorithms for their own use, and trying to break algorithms used by opposing militaries. It's all done in secret; these organizations don't publicize their results. Therefore, I have no idea how good they are or how successful they have been.

My guess, though, is that they are very good. Take the NSA, for example. Their budget is classified, but rumored to be on the order of $20 billion per year. They are known to be the largest employer of mathematicians in the world and the largest purchaser of computer hardware in the world. The first two Cray computers off the assembly line rolled directly into their basement. While the academic world was just beginning to figure out how to do cryptography with computers, they were designing and using algorithms that were based on principles that no one else knew about. Time and again they have proven to be 10 to 15 years ahead of "the state of the art."

From the end of World War I to the mid-1970s, most advanced cryptographic research took place in military agencies. Since then, however, there has been a shift. In the last 20 years, academic mathematicians, programmers, and cryptographers have been reinventing the way secure algorithms are designed, and today, it is arguable, the "cutting-edge" of cryptographic research is found outside the military. A good dozen cryptography and computer security conferences are held every year. Universities world-wide have research labs. There are journals, theses, and books. And the vast majority of this research is available to the public.

What all this public research has given us is a handful of algorithms that are believed to be secure. "Believed" is the key word in that sentence. In cryptography, it is only possible to prove that an algorithm is insecure; there has never been invented a practical algorithm that is provably secure. (An exception is a one-time pad, which will be discussed below.) You can only say that no one can break the algorithm, *yet*. You can say that these particular people, all intelligent cryptographers, have spent thousands of man-hours trying to break the algorithm, and they have not succeeded. You can say that there is no known attack that can break the algorithm. But you cannot say that someone won't figure out how to break the algorithm tomorrow. You can't even say that one of those military agencies mentioned above doesn't already know how to break the algorithm, because if they did they would not go public about it.

For the most part, the encryption algorithms used in electronic-mail security programs are all published algorithms, and they have undergone years of public scrutiny. While this doesn't prove anything, it does instill some confidence in the algorithms.

Attacks Against Algorithms

The job of a cryptanalyst is to find weaknesses in an algorithm that allow him to recover plaintext messages without the key. (Actually, he can also exploit weaknesses in the implementation of the algorithm, weaknesses in the security program that uses the algorithm, and any other weakness he finds, but this chapter is about algorithms.) Exploiting a weakness is called an attack. There are several broad classifications of attack:

A *ciphertext-only attack*. A cryptanalyst has some ciphertext encrypted with an algorithm. He does not know the plaintext or the key, but he knows the algorithm. His job is to find the corresponding plaintext.

A *known plaintext attack*. A cryptanalyst has some ciphertext encrypted with an algorithm, and the corresponding plaintext. He does not know the key, but he knows the algorithm. His job is to find the key, so that he can decrypt additional ciphertext encrypted with the same algorithm and the same key.

A *chosen plaintext attack*. A cryptanalyst gets to choose a piece of plaintext to be encrypted with an algorithm. He knows that plaintext and the corresponding ciphertext, but does not know the key. He knows the algorithm. His job is to find the key, so that he can decrypt additional ciphertext encrypted with the same algorithm and the same key.

All attacks are possible in real life, and an algorithm should be secure against all three (see Figure 2.3). The first attack is the most common; it corresponds to Eve intercepting an encrypted message between Alice and Bob and trying to decrypt it without knowing the key.

Figure 2.3 Attacks against algorithms.

The second attack is harder, but still common. A cryptanalyst might get a copy of some plaintext by some other means, and intercept the corresponding ciphertext in transmission. He may know something about the format of the encrypted message: It is a WordPerfect file, for example, or it has a standard Internet message header, or it is a TIFF image. All of these formats have some predefined bytes. Later in this chapter I will talk about a brute-force attack that requires only 8 bytes of known plaintext in order to work. ("Work" means that it will find the key eventually. However, it may take so long that the universe collapses first.) In the real world, it isn't hard to find these 8 bytes.

The third attack is even harder, but still possible. The cryptanalyst has to dupe Alice into encrypting a message of his own choosing, one that is designed to facilitate cryptanalysis. Maybe he can sneak into Alice's office and use her equipment. Maybe Alice has an automatic remailer that sends an encrypted copy of all messages received to a particular location, or that sends an encrypted copy back as a receipt. Chosen-plaintext attacks were used extensively in World War II. In any case, because this attack is possible, an algorithm should be secure against it.

Brute-Force Attack

The most obvious way to break an algorithm is to try every possible key. This is a known-plaintext attack, and requires a very small hunk of ciphertext and an equally small hunk of corresponding plaintext in order for it to work. You set up a computer program to try and decrypt the ciphertext with every possible key, one after the other, until the resultant plaintext equals the correct plaintext. When this happens, you have found the key and can use it to decrypt the rest of the ciphertext message.

This attack is always possible; there is no way to prevent it. The best one can do is to make the attack so expensive, both in time and money, that no one would even consider launching it. And how expensive is too expensive? It depends.

The algorithms listed below take an arbitrary key of a fixed length: 56 bits, 112 bits, 128 bits, etc. Each of those bits can be either a 1 or a 0. This means that there are 2^{56} possible 56-bit keys. This is about 1 trillion. Similarly, there are 2^{64} possible 64-bit keys, and 2^{112} possible 112-bit keys. Table 2.1 summarizes this for a number of different key lengths.

Notice that it's easy to calculate the total number of possible keys for a given key length. For a key of length n, the total number of possible keys is 2^n.

We can also estimate how many different possible keys a cryptanalyst can test in an hour. Table 2.2 looks at attacks by specialized hardware and attacks by the fastest software machines. Both guesses assume that the cryptanalyst has $1 million to spend on equipment. In the hardware case, he builds a specialized machine designed to break a particular algorithm. In the software case, he uses a general-purpose computer.

Since the number of keys that have to be tested far exceeds the amount of time necessary to test any single key, these numbers can be examined inde-

TABLE 2.1: Key Lengths and Number of Possible Keys

Length in Bits	Possible Keys
40	$2^{40} = 10^{12}$
56	$2^{56} = 10^{16}$
64	$2^{64} = 10^{19}$
80	$2^{80} = 10^{24}$
112	$2^{112} = 10^{33}$
128	$2^{128} = 10^{38}$

pendent of algorithm. Sure, an algorithm that is twice as fast can be broken twice as fast, but that is hardly relevant when time means millions of years to break either. Some algorithms are designed to take a long time to change keys, which further frustrates brute-force cryptanalysis, though that will be ignored for the purposes of this overview.

Both columns include current numbers plus estimates for the future. Future estimates assume that computing power, both hardware and software, increases by a factor of 10 every five years.

Realize that these numbers can be scaled directly with the addition or subtraction of money. For example, if in 1995 you can build a machine that can test 10^{16} keys in one hour for $1 million, then you can build a machine that can test ten times the number of keys in an hour (10^{17}) for $10 million. And

TABLE 2.2: Efficiency of Brute-Force Attacks with $1 Million Worth of Equipment

Year	Number of Possible Keys Tried Per Hour	
	Hardware	Software
1995	$2^{54} = 10^{16}$	$2^{40} = 10^{12}$
2000	$2^{57} = 10^{17}$	$2^{44} = 10^{13}$
2005	$2^{60} = 10^{18}$	$2^{47} = 10^{14}$
2010	$2^{64} = 10^{19}$	$2^{50} = 10^{15}$
2015	$2^{67} = 10^{20}$	$2^{54} = 10^{16}$
2020	$2^{70} = 10^{21}$	$2^{57} = 10^{17}$
2025	$2^{74} = 10^{22}$	$2^{60} = 10^{18}$
2030	$2^{77} = 10^{23}$	$2^{64} = 10^{19}$

TABLE 2.3: Length of a Hardware Brute-Force Attack Given $1 Million in Equipment						
	Length of Key in Bits					
Year	**40**	**56**	**64**	**80**	**112**	**128**
1995	.2 sec	3.6 hrs	38 days	7,000 yrs	10^{13} yrs	10^{18} yrs
2000	.02 sec	21 min	4 days	700 yrs	10^{12} yrs	10^{17} yrs
2005	2 ms	2 min	9 hrs	70 yrs	10^{11} yrs	10^{16} yrs
2010	.2 ms	13 sec	1 hr	7 yrs	10^{10} yrs	10^{15} yrs
2015	.02 ms	1 sec	5.5 min	251 days	10^{9} yrs	10^{14} yrs
2020	2 mcs	.1 sec	31 min	25 days	10^{8} yrs	10^{13} yrs
2025	.2 mcs	.01 sec	3 sec	2.5 days	10^{7} yrs	10^{12} yrs
2030	.02 mcs	1 ms	.3 sec	6 hrs	10^{6} yrs	10^{11} yrs

you can build a machine that can test one-tenth the number of keys in an hour (10^{15}) for $100,000.

Putting these two tables together tells us how long it will take to break a key of a given length during a given year, given a budget of $1 million. Again, these tables are independent of algorithm. One algorithm could be broken in a factor of four faster or slower than another, but key length is a much more important consideration. Table 2.3 summarizes this for hardware, and Table 2.4 does the same for software.

Remember that these results all scale with more or less money. For example, if in 1995 you can build a machine that can break a 64-bit key in 38 days for $1 million, then you can build a machine that can break the same key at ten times the speed (4 days) for $10 million. And you can build a machine that can break the key at one-tenth the speed (1 year) for $100,000.

These results indicate that a 64-bit key is barely enough for today's security needs, let alone the security needs of the future. An 80-bit key is sufficient for the short term, but not for the very long term. If you are really concerned about the security of your data, use a key of at least 112 bits.

Keep in mind when reading this analysis that it is ludicrous to estimate computing power 35 years from now. Breakthroughs in some science-fiction technology could make these tables look like a joke in the future. Conversely, physical limitations unknown at the present time could make them unrealistically optimistic.

TABLE 2.4: Length of a Software Brute-Force Attack Given $1 Million in Equipment

	Length of Key in Bits					
Year	40	56	64	80	112	128
1995	33 min	3 yrs	1000 yrs	10^7 yrs	10^{17} yrs	10^{22} yrs
2000	3.3 min	115 days	100 yrs	10^6 yrs	10^{16} yrs	10^{21} yrs
2005	20 sec	15 days	10 yrs	700,000 yrs	10^{15} yrs	10^{20} yrs
2010	2 sec	1.5 days	1 yr	70,000 yrs	10^{14} yrs	10^{19} yrs
2015	.2 sec	3.6 hrs	38 days	7,000 yrs	10^{13} yrs	10^{18} yrs
2020	.02 sec	21 min	4 days	700 yrs	10^{12} yrs	10^{17} yrs
2025	2 ms	2 min	9 hrs	70 yrs	10^{11} yrs	10^{16} yrs
2030	.2 ms	13 sec	1 hr	7 yrs	10^{10} yrs	10^{15} yrs

The other caveat here is that these calculations assume the best way to break a given algorithm is through a brute-force attack. If there is another, easier, way to break an algorithm, it doesn't matter how long the key is. This is why choosing a secure algorithm is so important.

DES

DES, the Data Encryption Standard, is an international standard encryption algorithm. It is the most widely used encryption algorithm in the world, at least for nonmilitary applications. DES was developed by IBM in the early 1970s. Adopted in 1976 as a federal encryption standard by the National Bureau of Standards, or NBS (now the National Institute of Standards and Technology, or NIST), DES was later renamed DEA-1, as an international encryption standard. Since then it has seen application in almost every form of digital communication and storage. It has been widely analyzed by cryptographers around the world and, although it has some weaknesses, it remains the algorithm of choice for many applications.

DES is something called an *iterated block cipher*. "Cipher" is just another name for an encryption algorithm. A "block cipher" is an encryption algorithm that encrypts data in block-size chunks. DES has an 8-byte block size. This means that the algorithm accepts 8 bytes of plaintext and spits out 8 bytes of ciphertext. If the message is longer than 8 bytes—most messages are—the algorithm encrypts the message 8 bytes at a time. At the other end, the algorithm decrypts the ciphertext in 8-byte chunks. "Iterated" means the algorithm consists of a simple function repeated over and over again. DES has 16 iterations. As a general rule, more iterations, or rounds, provides greater security. However, DES is constructed in such a way that 16 iterations make the algorithm as secure as it is going to get; adding more iterations doesn't add much to the algorithm's security.

A Brief History of DES

DES had its genesis in another algorithm called Lucifer, developed at the IBM Thomas Watson Laboratories in Yorktown Heights, New York during the early 1970s. When the NBS issued a request for candidate algorithms for their proposed federal encryption standard in 1974, IBM submitted a variant of Lucifer. The NSA helped evaluate the algorithm, IBM gave the world a nonexclusive, royalty-free license for the algorithm, and the NBS proposed the algorithm as its standard.

The proposal was met with immediate suspicion. Many cryptographers were leery of the NSA's "invisible hand" in the development of the algorithm. Both the NBS and IBM repeatedly stated that the NSA did not have a hand in developing the algorithm, but that did not assuage fears. The U.S. Senate Select Committee on Intelligence, with full top-secret clearances, poked their noses into the matter in 1978. They exonerated NSA from any improprieties, but the cryptographic community remained suspicious.

The reason for all the suspicion was that the design process of the algorithm was classified. During the design of both Lucifer and DES, IBM developed some cryptanalytic techniques that the NSA didn't want to become public. To many cryptographers, the design choices—orders of operations, values of particular constants, uses of the key—seemed arbitrary and mysterious.

The most mysterious of all were the algorithm's S-boxes. These weird mathematical things are arrays of constant values, which seemed to have some sort of structure behind them. Cryptographers wanted to know why the constants were chosen to be what they were, and not some other values. IBM, the NBS, and the NSA all refused to talk. Did the NSA put a "trap door" into the algorithm that made it easier for them, and only them, to break the algorithm? Did they deliberately weaken the algorithm? What were they hiding?

As it turns out, they were hiding a powerful cryptanalytic technique called *differential cryptanalysis*. This technique has been invented at least three times during the course of history: by the NSA (though they won't say when), by IBM during the development of Lucifer and DES in the early 1970s, and finally by two Israeli cryptographers, Eli Biham and Adi Shamir, in the 1990s.

Those two cryptographers made the technique public. It turned out that DES was optimized against differential cryptanalysis. Those mysterious S-boxes made such an attack all but useless. Change the values in the boxes and differential cryptanalysis will probably break the modified algorithm easily. In fact, any minor change in the inner workings of DES weakens the algorithm. Far from adding a trap door or deliberately weakening the algorithm, IBM and the NSA made sure the algorithm was as secure as it could be. They made DES secure against an attack that the public would not discover for another fifteen years.

Less mysterious, but even more worrisome to cryptographers, was the choice of key size. The original Lucifer algorithm had a 128-bit key. DES, when it was proposed as a federal standard, had a 56-bit key. Although 56 bits were more than enough security against cryptanalysts with mid-1970s computer technology, many cryptographers argued for a longer key length. Their arguments centered around the future possibility of brute-force attacks, as discussed above.

Attacks on DES

In 1979, cryptographers Whitfield Diffie and Martin Hellman argued that a massively-parallel special-purpose DES-breaking computer could recover a key from a single plaintext/ciphertext pair—that's 8 bytes of ciphertext and 8 bytes of corresponding plaintext—in 24 hours; the machine would cost somewhere between $20 million and $50 million to build. The cost of this machine progresses steadily downward as computers become more powerful. In 1993, a similar argument by Michael Wiener put the cost for a machine capable of recovering a key in three and a half hours at $1 million.

Recent cryptanalytic advances have yielded attacks against DES that are in theory more efficient than brute force, but in practice more difficult. Differential cryptanalysis, mentioned above, can recover a DES key 512 times faster than brute force, but differential cryptanalysis requires 2^{55} blocks of known plaintext or 2^{47} bytes of *chosen* plaintext to work. That's a message so long that it can't fit on 1.8 million CD-ROM disks. That's a message so large that it takes 30,000 years to transmit it over a 9600 bps modem link. That's a message so long that we don't have to worry about it.

Linear cryptanalysis, invented by Mitsuru Matsui of Mitsubishi Electronics in Japan, is even more efficient than differential cryptanalysis. However, it is another known-plaintext attack requiring more plaintext than a message is likely to provide. The attack needs 2^{43} bytes of plaintext and corresponding ciphertext to work: only 117,000 CD-ROMs worth of data. Some researchers, most notably Martin Hellman, are trying to combine techniques from both linear and differential cryptanalysis to create an even more powerful attack. Others are investigating such esoteric variants as "higher-order differential cryptanalysis." So far, no results apply to the full 16-round DES.

A brute-force attack is still the most efficient way to break DES. It only requires one ciphertext block and the corresponding plaintext block, and the time, money, and desire to implement the cracking machine.

DES is no longer secure enough to protect data from the most powerful of adversaries. The 56-bit key is just too short. However, $1 million is a lot of money for someone to spend to read your e-mail.

There are two e-mail security packages discussed in detail in this book: Privacy Enhanced Mail (PEM) and Pretty Good Privacy (PGP). PEM specifies the use of DES. PGP does not.

Modes of DES

DES, and in fact any block algorithm, can operate in one of several modes. The three modes you're likely to see in software are Electronic Codebook (ECB) mode, Cipher Block Chaining (CBC) mode, and Cipher Feedback (CFB) mode.

Electronic Codebook mode is the simplest. Remember that DES encrypts data 8 bytes at a time. ECB treats each 8-byte block independently. Eight bytes of plaintext in; eight bytes of ciphertext out. Eight bytes of ciphertext in; eight bytes of plaintext out.

This means that if you have a message that has two identical 8-byte blocks in the right locations, the resultant ciphertext will have two identical 8-byte blocks in the same locations. While a cryptanalyst may not be able to decrypt these blocks, he could use this information to his advantage.

Imagine that a bank is using DES-encrypted e-mail to transmit information about account deposits. Eve might be able to figure out which ciphertext blocks correspond to her name, and substitute those blocks for the blocks corresponding to other people's names on other messages. Even though Eve cannot read any of the messages, she can watch her bank balance increase at the expense of all the other depositors. This attack, and others like it, is a serious vulnerability of ECB mode.

Cipher Block Chaining (CBC) mode prevents this kind of attack (it's called a block-replay attack) by making ciphertext blocks depend on each other. If Eve tries to replace one block with another, or even change the order of a pair of blocks, she will be detected. CBC also makes other forms of analysis more difficult.

Cipher Feedback (CFB) mode also makes ciphertext blocks depend on each other, frustrating Eve's cryptanalytic attempts. The type of feedback is different, but the results are the same.

Both CBC and CFB require a variable in addition to the key, a variable called an "initialization vector," or IV. The IV is 8 bytes long, and does not have to be kept secret.

The trade-off between ECB and the other modes is in error propagation. ECB mode has minimal error propagation. If there is a single bit error in the ciphertext transmission, only one 8-byte block of the decrypted plaintext will be wrong. CBC mode garbles the 8-byte block and a portion of the next 8-byte block. CFB has similar error propagation characteristics. Transmission errors don't seem to be much of a problem in modern electronic-mail systems, so this doesn't seem to be something to really worry about. And even if transmission errors were a problem, they are better off handled with error-correcting codes.

PEM specifies the use of DES in CBC mode for data encryption, and PGP uses the IDEA algorithm in CFB mode for data encryption.

Triple-DES

Triple-DES is a simple variant of DES: encrypt the message with DES three times, one after the other. If you use a different key for each encryption, the result is an algorithm that is far more secure than DES. PEM has an option for triple-DES. (There's a proof that double-DES is no more secure than single DES, subject to many caveats, but it is far more complicated than this space allows for. Just realize that the designers of PEM knew what they were doing when they specified triple-DES instead of double-DES.)

Actually, it's a little more complicated than that. There are several ways to implement triple-DES. And the method of implementation has considerable implications on its security. The designers of PGP and PEM have paid attention to the public analysis on the topic, and they have both implemented triple-DES correctly.

One version of triple-DES, the version used in PEM, is called EDE mode. EDE stands for encrypt-decrypt-encrypt. In PEM it is called DES-EDE. DES-EDE encrypts a plaintext block with DES and one key, decrypts it with DES and a second key, and re-encrypts it with DES and the first key (see Figure 2.4). Decryption is the reverse: first decrypt the ciphertext with DES and the first key, then encrypt it with DES and the second key, and finally, re-encrypt it with DES and the first key.

DES-EDE has a 112-bit key: two independent 56-bit keys. This is long enough to make a brute-force attack infeasible. It is resistant to both differ-

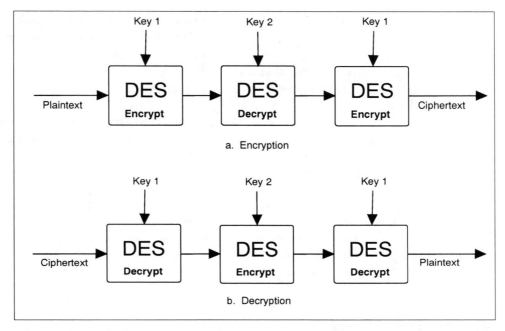

Figure 2.4 Triple-DES.

ential cryptanalysis and linear cryptanalysis. It is, as far as anyone who is telling knows, completely secure against any attack in the near future.

It is also about half as fast as regular DES. (It is not one third as fast because of some clever tricks the programmers use when they implement it.)

IDEA

IDEA is the International Data Encryption Algorithm. It was invented in 1991 by James Massey and Xuejia Lai of ETH Zurich, in Switzerland. (Actually, the algorithm is Xuejia Lai's Ph.D. thesis. This should give you some idea how hard designing a secure algorithm really is: The design and analysis of a good algorithm is worthy of a doctorate.) The algorithm is structured along the same general lines as DES. It is an iterated block cipher, with a 64-bit block size and a 128-bit key size. It has only 8 iterations, compared with DES's 16, but each IDEA iteration works as if it were a double-DES iteration. On most microprocessors, a software implementation of IDEA is faster than a software implementation of DES.

IDEA has a key length over twice that of DES; its key length is even longer than the one used in triple-DES. And it is much faster than triple-DES. On the other hand, IDEA is a very new algorithm. Remember that it took cryptographers fifteen years of studying DES to invent differential cryptanalysis, something that the NSA knew about all along. Who can tell what the NSA knows about now that allows them to break IDEA? I suppose we will eventually discover those tricks somewhere around the year 2000.

However, there is more mathematical theory built into IDEA than there was in DES. IDEA is based on something called "mixing operations from different algebraic groups." Regardless of what that means, it gives cryptographers some measure of confidence that the algorithm is secure. On the other hand, there could always be a discovery tomorrow that could break it. That is also true of DES.

There are no assurances in the security business. IDEA is a good-looking algorithm, but it is new. Ten years from now we will all consider it an amazing feat of security or an impressive failure. I would bet on the former, but I recognize that it is a bet.

PGP 2.0 and later versions use the IDEA algorithm in CFB mode.

One-Time Pads

A one-time pad is the only encryption scheme that can be proven to be absolutely unbreakable. It is used extensively by spies because it doesn't require any hardware to implement and because of its absolute security. For many years, the hotline between Moscow and Washington was encrypted with a one-time pad.

The algorithm requires the generation of many sets of matching encryption key pads. Each pad consists of a number of random key characters. These key characters are chosen using some truly random process. They are *not* generated by any kind of cryptographic key generator. Each party involved receives matching sets of pads. Each key character in the pad is used to encrypt one and only one plain text character, then the key character is never used again. Any violation of these conditions negates the perfect security available in the one-time pad.

Neither PGP nor PEM uses one-time pads. Why? Because it isn't practical. The number of random key pads that need to be generated must be at least equal to the volume of plaintext messages to be encrypted, and these key pads must somehow be exchanged ahead of time. This might work for some low-speed applications (a WORM drive has 250 megabytes, which translates to about 2400 bps), but it is impractical in modern high-speed communications systems.

Other Algorithms

There are lots of other algorithms out there in the world. The military organizations of the world use various encryption algorithms, some good and some bad, for all sorts of purposes; they're not talking about them. PGP 1.0 used an algorithm called Bassomatic. Phil Zimmermann invented the algorithm himself, and it underwent no peer review. Recognizing that he was much better off using an established algorithm from the public literature, Zimmermann replaced Bassomatic with IDEA in PGP 2.0 and later.

FEAL, which stands for Fast Encryption Algorithm, was invented by Akihiro Shimizu and Shoji Miyaguchi of NTT Japan. It's been broken, so it is unlikely you'll see it used in a product. LOKI is another algorithm, invented by some cryptographers in Australia. Some secure-computer being hyped in Germany uses it. Khufu and Khafre were invented by Ralph Merkle of Xerox Parc. I recently wrote an algorithm called Blowfish; it is far too early to make any judgments about its security. There are countless others, most of them so obscure that you'll never see nor hear of them. And there are proprietary algorithms, which you might hear vague mention of in some products.

You're very likely to hear of Skipjack, though. Skipjack is the NSA-invented algorithm that is in the U.S. government's Clipper and Capstone chips. (Those are the chips with a key escrow mechanism that allows the government to listen to your private telephone calls, if they have either a warrant or the chutzpah to ignore the law.) The government has refused to release details of the Skipjack algorithm or to allow any implementations of the algorithm in software, so it is very unlikely you'll see it in any e-mail security program.

There's also RC2 and RC4. These are proprietary algorithms invented by Ron Rivest, a cryptographer at MIT who also works for RSA Data Security, Inc. These algorithms have been given special export approval by the U.S. government—if their key lengths are 40 bits or less. No one has proposed using either of the algorithms for PGP or for PEM, but they are used in several e-mail products like Lotus® Notes and Apple®'s Open Collaboration Environment (AOCE). The exportable version of these products uses 40-bit keys; possibly domestic versions of the same programs use longer key lengths, but probably not.

The details of RC2 and RC4 have not been officially made public, so there is no reason to trust them to same degree as DES or IDEA. RC4 was released to the Internet in September 1994. Anyone who wants a copy can get it via anonymous ftp from ftp.ox.ac.uk. RSA Data Security, Inc. claims that they have been analyzed by several cryptographers and that none of them has found any weaknesses. I believe their claims, but I would still be skeptical about using the algorithm. Despite what anyone will tell you, there is no substitute for public scrutiny by skilled cryptographers.

Choosing an Algorithm

Keep two things in mind when choosing an algorithm: security and speed. They are all that really matter.

Table 2.5 summarizes security. If security is your primary concern, choose triple-DES. Triple-DES is believed to be so strong that no organization on the planet can even hope to break it. Again, no one can prove this or state this definitively, but there is a lot of evidence to support this claim.

DES is still a good choice if you are not concerned about long-term security, or security from major governments. The NSA probably has a DES-cracking machine in their basement. The governments of Russia, China, England, France, Germany, Japan, and Israel probably have similar machines. If you think that the intelligence services of those countries have more important things to decrypt with their machines than your personal correspondence, then you're probably safe with DES.

Remember to use DES in either Cipher Block Chaining mode or in Cipher Feedback mode, and not in Electronic Codebook mode. The difference in security is well worth any additional processing time.

The benefit of choosing DES or triple-DES over a newer algorithm is simple: DES has been extensively studied. Since the algorithm was proposed in the mid-1970s, hundreds of people have spent hundreds of hours attempting to cryptanalyze it. They have made some headway, but everything we know about DES says that it is as secure as the length of the key. And that triple-

TABLE 2.5: Security of Different Algorithms

Algorithm	Key Length	Best Attack	Comments
DES	56 bits	Brute force	Brute-force attack feasible
Triple-DES	112 bits	Brute force	Brute-force attack infeasible
IDEA	128 bits	Brute force	Still a new algorithm
RC2	Variable	Unknown	Details of algorithms are unknown
RC4	Variable	Unknown	Details of algorithms are unknown

DES is as secure as the length of a double key.

IDEA seems to be a good algorithm, but it doesn't have nearly as long a track record. It was only invented in 1991. Yes, it has been analyzed extensively since then, but to nowhere near the same degree. All evidence points to IDEA being secure, and I feel somewhat confident recommending it for long-term security.

I don't recommend RC2 and RC4. Those algorithms are too new, and they haven't been analyzed by enough people. Furthermore, their secrecy makes me leery. Unfortunately, some products for export use these algorithms and no others. If that's the case, you have no choice. But realize that exportable versions of these algorithms only have 40-bit keys, and that the government can easily break them. Probably, so can anyone else who is sufficiently competent and interested.

And finally, beware of proprietary algorithms. If the history of cryptography has taught us anything, it is that encryption is a subtle art. The only way to adequately test the security of an algorithm is through peer review. The author has to put the algorithm under public scrutiny, and let his colleagues attempt to cryptanalyze it. Anyone who claims to have invented an unbreakable algorithm without going through this process is either a genius or a fool, and the latter is much more likely than the former. Some vendors will claim that keeping the details of their algorithm secret increases its security. Do not believe that, either. The security of a good algorithm rests in the key, not in the details of the algorithm. If a vendor does not want to make his algorithm public, it is probably because he knows that the algorithm cannot withstand public scrutiny. "Trust me; I'm with the government" just doesn't cut it.

Speed is the other consideration. Triple-DES is the slowest of the three algorithms. It is over twice as slow as DES. On a 33MHz SparcStation, you can encrypt about 296 Kbits per second using triple-DES. DES isn't terribly fast, either. Expect an encryption rate of 487 Kbits per second on the same machine. IDEA is faster: 520 Kbits per second. RC2 and RC4 are supposedly faster than IDEA, but I don't like reprinting claims that I cannot independently verify.

However, none of these encryption rates is really slow. Given a message of 10 kilobytes, the slowest algorithm (triple-DES) can encrypt it in a few seconds. Larger files will, of course, take longer. But if you can wait for a data compression algorithm to compress a file, you have time for an encryption algorithm to make it secure.

And in electronic-mail security programs like PGP and PEM, which use public-key cryptography for key management, the time required to encrypt the key is much greater than the time required to encrypt the message. This is true unless the message is very large. What this means is, for a typical electronic-mail message, there is no noticeable difference in the time required to encrypt a message with DES, triple-DES, or IDEA.

Another, more minor, consideration is patents and licenses. DES and triple-DES are in the public domain. Anyone, including the Russians, Libyans, North Koreans, and drug cartels, can use those algorithms. IDEA is patented, and requires a license for commercial use. RC2 and RC4 are unpatented, but trade secrets. Blowfish is unpatented and in the public domain.

Choosing Encryption Keys

The security of an encryption algorithm is based on the security of the key. It is not based on the secrecy of the algorithm, the inaccessibility of the ciphertext, or even the inaccessibility of the plaintext. Assuming that the algorithm is a good one, its security is no more or no less than the security of the key.

What this means is that an upper limit on the time required to break an algorithm is the time required to launch a brute-force attack. But you know that. You've already chosen an algorithm that is resistant to a brute-force attack, or at least resistant to a brute-force attack by a likely adversary in a reasonable period of time.

But good key security points out another vulnerability to worry about. Imagine that you're using an algorithm, IDEA for example, that takes a 128-bit key. A brute-force attack against IDEA takes upwards of 10^{18} years; long enough not to matter for any possible application. However, in this imaginary implementation of IDEA the user picks his own encryption key, in the same way that he might pick a password. The user could pick any 128-bit key—there are over 10^{38} of them—but he is far more likely to pick a key that corresponds to an easy-to-remember word.

If you assume that the typical dictionary contains 200,000 words, and multiply that by 100 to account for proper nouns, slang words that don't appear in a dictionary, combinations of words, and odd capitalizations, you have a potential "dictionary" of 2 million likely keys. A hardware machine can do a brute-force search against these keys in minutes; a software implementation will take hours.

This is an example of a successful cryptanalytic attack, not against the algorithm, but against the key generation method. The solution is to not allow users to generate their own keys, but to let the electronic-mail encryption program do it.

The reasoning here is that a computer doesn't know one key from another, so it will do a much better job of picking a random key. This sounds good, but having a computer generate a random key is not an easy task. Convincing a computer, which is really good at doing the same things over and over again, to do something it will never do again is not easy. I will talk about the various tricks these programs use to generate random numbers in Chapter 7.

Encryption: How We Used to Do It

Symmetric encryption, the kind used in DES, IDEA, and the other algorithms discussed above, is based on the concept of a shared secret. Both Alice and Bob know a secret that no one else does: the encryption key. Alice encrypts the message using the key. Bob decrypts the message with the same key. Eve, who doesn't know the key, cannot decrypt the message.

This is the way cryptography has worked since it was invented. But the system has several drawbacks. Let's look at the drawbacks before describing how modern e-mail security protocols get around them.

First, Alice and Bob must have met in secret and agreed on a secret key sometime before Alice encrypts her message. This can be difficult if Alice and Bob live far from one another and don't trust either the mails or the telephone. This is impossible if Alice and Bob have never heard of each other before Alice wants to send the message.

Second, Alice and Bob must save their secret key in some secure location until they need it. Remember, the only thing keeping Eve from being able to read Alice's mail is that secret key. If Bob stores the key in his telephone book, Eve might sneak into his office at night and copy it down.

Third, Alice and Bob have to share a different key with everybody they want to send secure messages to. If Alice has a hundred people with whom she wishes to communicate securely, she needs 100 different secret keys. The keys have to be different so that each conversation will be private. The keys must be agreed upon in advance. And the keys have to be stored securely. This can be a logistical nightmare.

And fourth, there is a problem proving who sent which message. When Bob receives a message from Alice, he knows she sent it because she is the only other person who knows their shared secret key. The same is true for Alice; she knows that any message she receives that is encrypted in the key she shares with Bob is from Bob. But what if there is a court case, and Bob wants to prove that a message he received is in fact from Alice? He can't. Since both Alice and Bob share the same secret key, any message he maintains came from Alice could just as easily have been encrypted by him. All he can prove to a third party is that the message has been encrypted by either

Alice or Bob; he cannot prove anything further.

Fortunately, modern electronic mail security protocols solve all of these problems.

Encryption: How We Do It Today

Each electronic mail message is encrypted with its own unique key. This means that each time you send an encrypted e-mail message with either PGP or PEM, that security program generates a random key and uses it to encrypt the message.

There are a lot of benefits to this scheme. First, the disclosure of any single encryption key compromises just one message. If Alice and Bob use the same secret key to encrypt all of their correspondence over the course of a month, then the key becomes very valuable. If Eve were to get her hands on it, she could read all the messages encrypted with that key. However, if Alice and Bob use a new key each time they send a message, then Eve can only decrypt one message if she were to get her hands on that particular key.

Second, Alice and Bob do not have to store the secret key. If they are using the same key over and over, they have to keep it in some secure location lest Eve learn it. If they are using a key only once, they don't have to store it for very long. Alice has to store it only as long as it takes her to encrypt the message. Bob has to store it only as long as it takes him to decrypt the message. Afterwards they can destroy the key, and with it any chance of Eve finding the key and decrypting the message.

And third, unique message keys make the problem of a network full of users easier. If Alice generates a new encryption key every time she sends a message, it is just as easy for her to send a message to two people as it is for her to send two messages to one person.

Unique message keys also make the resultant implementation more secure. Recall that differential cryptanalysis and linear cryptanalysis both require massive amounts of ciphertext and corresponding plaintext to discover the encryption key. Changing the key with each message makes amassing this data difficult or impossible. And it means that learning the key used to encrypt one message doesn't help at all in decrypting the next message.

At first glance, this scheme might seem to create more problems than it solves. How does Bob know the secret key used to encrypt Alice's message to him? She created it just before encrypting the message. She didn't meet with him beforehand and agree on a secret key. And even if she did, that key would only be good for one message. What about an ongoing communication—can we really expect Alice and Bob to meet in secret every time they have a new message to send to each other? Why don't they just hand each other the messages when they meet in secret?

This problem has been solved, but it required a whole new branch of cryptography. It's called public-key cryptography, and it will be discussed in the next chapter.

Chapter **3**

Key Management

Why Key Management?

Key management is the hardest part of cryptography. It's easy to choose a secure encryption algorithm. It's easy to implement the algorithm in CBC mode to increase security. It's easy to encrypt data on one end and decrypt data on the other. What's hard is managing the key. In the last chapter, I mentioned the potential security problems inherent in allowing people to choose their own key. These problems pale next to those that arise in key distribution.

Before Alice can send an encrypted message to Bob, they have to agree on a key. They can meet beforehand and agree on a key. Or Alice can generate the key herself and send it to Bob by some secure courier. Then, they have to either store the key somewhere until it is needed, and risk theft, or remember the key until it is needed, and risk forgetfulness. Historically, military intelligence organizations have been far more successful attacking another country's key management mechanisms than their encryption algorithms. The Walker spy ring provided the Soviet Union with copies of U.S. Navy encryption keys for years. It didn't matter how good the Navy's algorithms were; the Soviets could read everything.

Thankfully, there is a better solution than Alice and Bob meeting in a dark alley. Modern electronic-mail security programs allow Alice to send an encrypted message to Bob without having to agree on a secret key beforehand. Moreover, the programs allow Alice to send an encrypted message to Bob even if they have never met. Even if they don't know each other. Even if they don't trust each other. This marvel is possible due to something called *public-key cryptography*.

Public-Key Cryptography

Remember that conventional encryption algorithms, like DES and IDEA, are based on the concept of a shared key. Alice encrypts a message using a key, and Bob decrypts the ciphertext with the identical key to recover the message. If Alice and Bob do not share a key, they cannot communicate.

Public-key cryptography is different. There are two different keys: one for encryption and another for decryption (see Figure 3.1). They come in pairs; a specific encryption key works with a specific decryption key. And you can't derive one key from the other, so someone with the encryption key cannot decrypt messages.

This is how the system works in real life: Bob, and everyone else who wants to communicate securely, generates an encryption key and corresponding decryption key. (Don't worry about how he generates the pair. I'll talk about that later.) He keeps the decryption key secret; this is called his private key. He publishes the encryption key; this is called the public key.

The public key is public. Anyone can get a copy of it. In fact, everyone is encouraged to get a copy of it. He e-mails it to his friends, posts it on bulletin boards, publishes it in his plan file or in a phone directory, whatever. He even gives a copy to Eve. When Alice wants to send a message to Bob, first she finds Bob's public key. She encrypts her message in his public key, and sends it to him.

When Bob receives the message, he decrypts it with his private key. He knows his own private key, so he can easily do this. Eve, who has intercepted the message in transmission, does not know Bob's private key. She knows Bob's public key, but that does not help her decrypt the message. She can't read Bob's mail. Even Alice, who encrypted the message with Bob's public key, cannot decrypt it.

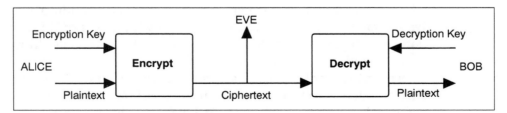

Figure 3.1 Encryption and decryption with public-key cryptography.

The beauty of this system is that anyone, even someone Bob has never met, can pull Bob's public key off a database and send him encrypted mail. There is no need for them to meet beforehand, and they need not share a secret. Anyone can send Bob an encrypted message.

This is an important point. Think of the system as a mailbox: anyone can drop mail through the slot (encrypt messages with the public key). Only the authorized recipient, with the key to the mailbox (the private key) can open the box and read the mail (decrypt the messages).

How It Really Works

In the previous section, I simplified matters some. Electronic-mail security programs don't really work in the way I described; I left out a step.

Public-key cryptography algorithms, the ones that generate key pairs, are cumbersome and complicated. No one uses them to encrypt entire electronic mail messages; it would take much too long. (There are also security problems with encrypting messages directly using public-key cryptography, but that topic is a bit too advanced for this book.) E-mail security programs use public-key cryptography for key management.

Remember the message-encryption programs that generate a new secret key every time they encrypt a message? That key is used with a conventional algorithm, like DES or IDEA, to encrypt the message. Then, that key is encrypted using public-key cryptography. The public-key algorithm is only used for key distribution.

An example might make things clearer. Alice is using PEM: DES for message encryption and RSA for key management. (You'll learn about how RSA works in a little bit.) She wants to send an encrypted message to Bob. This is what she does (see Figure 3.2):

1. Alice writes the message.
2. Alice generates a random encryption key.
3. Alice encrypts the signed message and the random encryption key with a conventional algorithm, such as DES.
4. Alice gets Bob's public key.
5. Alice encrypts the random encryption key and Bob's public key with a public-key algorithm, such as RSA.
6. Alice concatenates the encrypted message to the encrypted key to get the final, secure, message.
7. Alice e-mails this encrypted message to Bob.

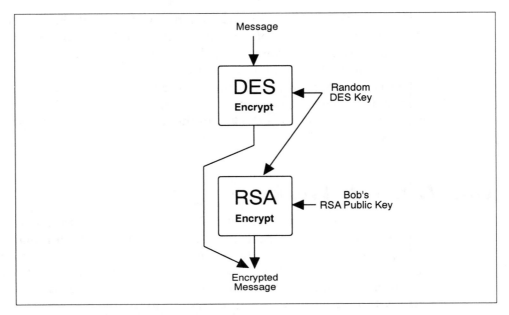

Figure 3.2 Encryption of electronic mail.

Bob also has PEM. He has received an encrypted message from Alice. This is what he has to do (see Figure 3.3):

1. Bob separates the encrypted message from the encrypted key.
2. Using a public-key algorithm and his private key, Bob decrypts the key.
3. Using a conventional algorithm and the decrypted key, Bob decrypts the message.
4. Bob reads the decrypted message.

This sequence is secure from Eve. She can, of course, intercept the message in transmission. However, she does not know Bob's private key, so she cannot decrypt the secret key. She either has to break DES to recover the message, or break RSA to recover the key (and then recover the message). Either way, her chances look pretty bleak.

This may look like a complicated procedure, but remember that the various electronic-mail security programs take care of the details. All Alice has to do is indicate that she wishes to send an encrypted message to Bob, and the program does the rest. It generates the secret key, encrypts the message, finds Bob's public key, encrypts the secret key, concatenates them together, and ships the whole thing off to Bob. On the receiving end, Bob's program makes the decryption operation just as easy.

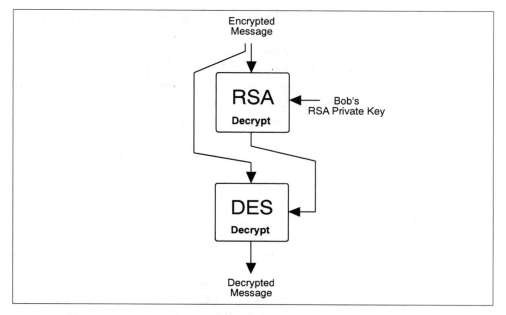

Figure 3.3 Decryption of electronic mail.

Public-Key Algorithms

Many different public-key algorithms have been invented. Here's an overview, with discussion of those that you are likely to see in use, either in current or future versions of PGP or PEM.

RSA

RSA is a public-key cryptography algorithm. It is called RSA after its inventors: Ron Rivest, Adi Shamir, and Len Adleman. RSA uses prime numbers: numbers that are evenly divisible only by 1 and themselves. The premise behind RSA is that it is easy to multiply two prime numbers to get a third number, but very hard to recover the two primes from that third number. This is known as "factoring." For example, the prime factors of 3,337 are 47 and 71. Generating the public key involves multiplying two large primes; anyone can do it. Figuring out the private key from the public key involves factoring a large number. If the number is large enough, then no one can do it in anything resembling a reasonable length of time.

Actually, I'm leaving a whole lot of mathematics out of that explanation. It's not important. What is important is that the security of RSA is dependent on the difficulty of factoring large numbers. (By large, I'm talking about primes of 300 digits or more.)

All right, that too, is technically a lie. No one has proven mathematically that the security of RSA is dependent on the difficulty of factoring large numbers. It is only conjectured. Everyone believes that the only way to break RSA is to factor the large number, but it is always possible that someone could discover a way to break RSA without doing so. Factoring will always break RSA; the trick is to make the factoring problem so hard that it is infeasible.

Think of the situation as analogous to that of conventional algorithms and brute-force attacks: a brute-force attack is always possible and represents an upper limit for the time necessary to break the algorithm; however, it is always possible that a more efficient attack will be found. Similarly, it is always possible to launch a factoring attack against RSA, and that attack represents an upper limit for the time necessary to break the algorithm. However, it is always possible that someone will invent a more efficient attack against RSA, one that will not involve factoring.

Honestly, there's not much chance of it. Most cryptographers think that there is no other way to break RSA. A lot of mathematical theory stands behind this belief; it's not blind faith. The only trick is choosing a number large enough so that there is no hope in factoring it. I'll talk about this very important choice soon.

ElGamal

ElGamal is another public-key algorithm used for key management. Its mathematics are different from RSA's, but much of the general flavor is the same. The algorithm involves mathematical manipulation of large numerical quantities. Its security comes from something called the *discrete logarithm problem*, which is pretty much the same as the factoring problem. (In fact, any advances in the discrete logarithm problem can generally be applied to the factoring problem, and vice versa.) And there is no guarantee that there isn't a better way of breaking ElGamal that doesn't involve discrete logarithms, but everyone suspects not.

Currently no electronic-mail security program uses ElGamal, but I have heard talk of adding it to a version of PEM. If you see it, don't worry. It is no more or less secure than RSA. It is based on the same mathematical theory as RSA: the theory of finite fields. It is, in theory, possible for one to be broken and not the other, but not very likely. In an electronic-mail security program, the only real reason to choose one over the other is to avoid patent violations.

Other Public-Key Algorithms

There are other public-key algorithms, but you will probably never see them in an electronic-mail security program. One common algorithm is Diffie-Hellman, which allows two parties to interactively exchange a secret key over an insecure communications channel. This was one of the first public-key algorithms invented, but it is not really suited for electronic mail, where one party sends a message to another. It is more useful for a secure telephone conversation, where two parties use Diffie-Hellman to agree on a secret key to encrypt the conversation.

Knapsack algorithms (called that because they are based on something known as the knapsack problem) were once popular for public-key cryptography, but they have all been broken. And there are other, even more obscure, algorithms. (There are also public-key algorithms that can only be used for digital signatures, and not for key management. DSA, the Digital Signature Algorithm, is one of those; see Chapter 4.)

Choosing a Public-Key Algorithm

For all practical purposes, there isn't any difference between RSA and ElGamal. They are both equally secure, they both take about the same amount of time to encrypt and decrypt, and they both work in pretty much the same way.

Not that you really have much choice. Both PGP and PEM use RSA.

Choosing a Key Length

The security of any public-key algorithm, whether based on the difficulty of factoring large numbers or the difficulty of taking discrete logarithms of large numbers, depends on the size of those large numbers. If the number is small enough, you have no security. If the number is large enough, you have security against all the computing power in the world working from now until the sun goes nova.

You have a choice of key length, and it is an important choice. What follows is an analysis of different key lengths and their susceptibility to factoring, both today and in the near future.

We do not analyze modulus size in the same way as we do for key length with the conventional algorithms, such as DES or IDEA. Breaking RSA does not involve trying every possible key to see if it works; breaking RSA involves trying to factor a product of two primes, called the modulus. Several fast-

TABLE 3.1: MIPS-years Required to Factor a Number	
Digits	**MIPS-years**
100	74
150	1,000,000
200	4,000,000,000
250	2,000,000,000,000
300	10^{14}
350	10^{16}
400	10^{18}
450	10^{19}
500	10^{21}

factoring algorithms are in the academic literature. These algorithms are all very complicated, and require massive computer resources to mount.

Using a branch of mathematics called complexity theory, it is possible to figure out how much computing power the fastest of these algorithms requires to factor a number of a given length. This is summarized in Table 3.1.

The analysis is given in MIPS-years. "MIPS" means "million instructions per second"; a "MIPS-year" is a year's worth of them. This measure of computing power is independent of hardware; it works equally well measuring machines from supercomputers to subnotebooks.

For example, it would require one million MIPS-years to factor a 150-digit number, and two trillion MIPS-years to factor a 250-digit number. And the times go up from there.

A 1-MIPS computer operating for a year equals a MIPS-year. This does not mean that a 1-MIPS computer is required; it is just as effective to have two $\frac{1}{2}$-MIPS computers operating for a year, or ten 10-MIPS computers operating for a hundredth of a year.

What does this mean? Well, today the cost of a MIPS-year is about $10. (You can buy a 10-MIPS computer for about $500; if you assume that the computer will have a useful life of five years, that translates to $10 per MIPS.) If we assume that computing power increases by a factor of ten every five years, Table 3.2 shows how much a MIPS would cost in the future.

This table can be turned inside out to show how many MIPS can be bought for a dollar in future years. In 1995, you could buy 0.1 MIPS for $1. In 2010, you could buy 100 MIPS for a dollar; in 2025 you could buy 100,000. (Note that these are constant dollars; I am ignoring inflation.)

TABLE 3.2: Cost of a MIPS in a Given Year

Year	Cost
1995	$10
2000	$1
2005	$0.10
2010	$0.01
2015	$0.001
2020	$0.0001
2025	$0.00001
2030	$0.000001

Taking the above information in Table 3.3, we can determine how much money it will cost to factor a number of a given size, in a given year.

Some implementations use bit lengths instead of digits. Figure that about 332 bits equals 100 digits. Table 3.4 can help with conversion.

Again, remember that extrapolating computing power this far into the future is ridiculous. These numbers are meant to be a rough guide . . . nothing more.

The algorithms used to factor large numbers can be easily spread over a number of different computers. These computers don't even have to be co-located; significant results in factoring have been done by computers that communicate with each other via electronic mail.

These statistics suggest that 512-bit numbers are too insecure to use for public-key cryptography. Use 1024-bit numbers.

TABLE 3.3: Cost to Factor a Number

Year	Number of Digits							
	100	150	200	250	300	350	400	450
1995	$740	$10M	$40B	$20T	$10^{15}	$10^{17}	$10^{19}	$10^{20}
2000	$74	$1M	$4B	$2T	$300T	$10^{16}	$10^{18}	$10^{19}
2005	$7.40	$100K	$400M	$200B	$30T	$10^{15}	$10^{17}	$10^{18}
2010	$0.74	$10,000	$40M	$20B	$3T	$200T	$10^{16}	$10^{17}
2015	$0.07	$1,000	$4M	$2B	$300B	$20T	$10^{15}	$10^{16}
2020	free	$100	$400K	$200M	$30B	$2T	$100T	$10^{15}
2025	free	$10	$40K	$20M	$3B	$200T	$10T	$200T
2030	free	$1.00	$4K	$2M	$300M	$20T	$1T	$20T

TABLE 3.4: Conversion between Bits and Digits

Bits	Digits
332	100
386	116
498	150
512	154
664	200
830	250
996	300
1024	308
1162	350
1328	400
1494	450

PGP supports three different RSA key lengths: 384-bit (casual grade), 512-bit (commercial grade), and 1024-bit (military grade). PEM can support a variety of different RSA key lengths.

Remember that even though this analysis centered around the factoring problem, upon which the security of RSA rests, these exact same numbers can be used to measure the security of algorithms based on the discrete logarithm problem (ElGamal).

Generating a Public and Private Key

Generating keys for a public-key algorithm is not as easy as generating keys for a conventional algorithm. For a conventional algorithm, all you need is a random string of bits of the correct length. For a public-key algorithm, you need prime numbers. You need to combine them in particular ways. And you need them to be very large.

Fortunately, generating large random primes is much easier than factoring them. Several fast algorithms do this quickly and easily, and one of those is implemented in any e-mail security program that uses the RSA algorithm.

These prime-number generation routines use probabilistic tests to generate primes. This means that the routines generate numbers that are very probably, but not definitely, prime. (Another option would have been to use a deterministic prime generation routine, which generates numbers that are definitely prime.) Probabilistic prime generation algorithms are a whole lot faster than deterministic ones so they are used in e-mail security programs. The enormous increase in speed is more than worth the bit of doubt.

And it is only a little bit of doubt. Before you worry about whether or not your private key is based on a number that isn't really prime, keep in mind that the odds of this happening are extremely small. It is unlikely that anyone out there has a false prime generated by this method. It is far more likely that you will be hit by lightning during the next thunderstorm than it is for you to get a false prime.

More difficult is generating random numbers that are used to generate the primes. If there is a flaw in the algorithm that generates the random numbers, then that flaw might be exploitable by an adversary to break the system. This is a tough problem, and the designers of the various programs have put a lot of effort into getting it right.

Imagine what would happen if the program didn't do random-number generation correctly. The program might only generate 10 million possible public-key/private-key pairs. This would be large enough so that no two users would have the same key, but small enough for a computer to search them all. Even though the program used RSA and DES, breaking the system would be easy.

Chapter 4

Authentication

What Is Authentication?

When you receive an electronic-mail message, how do you know it is from the person who purported to send it? You don't. Sure, the message has a header on it, but that header can be faked. It is easy for a not-so-skilled hacker to pretend that his message came from anyone he likes and from anywhere he likes, and do it well enough that you will be fooled. It is wise never to completely trust the "From" line on any e-mail message.

Electronic-mail security programs can guarantee, or authenticate, that a given message is actually from the person whose name appears on that "From" line. This is sometimes known as "data origin authentication" and is done with something called a *digital signature*. Before looking at the digital equivalent, let's look at handwritten signatures.

Authentication on Paper

Handwritten signatures on documents have long been used as proof of authorship of, or at least agreement with, the contents of the document. What is it about the signature on a document and the act of signing that is so compelling?

1. The signature is unforgeable. The signature proves that the signer deliberately signed his name to the document.

2. The signature is authentic. The signature can convince the recipient of the document that the signer did indeed sign his or her name to it.

3. The signature is not reusable. The signature is written on the document, and cannot be moved to a different document. In other words, an unscrupulous person cannot move a signature on one document to a completely different document.

4. The signed document is unalterable. After the document is signed, it cannot be altered. This is not really true, but if a typewritten and signed letter has substantive handwritten changes in the body, someone is going to get suspicious.

5. The signature cannot be repudiated. The signature and the document are physical things. The signer cannot later claim that he or she didn't sign it.

Actually, this isn't necessarily true for handwritten signatures: Forgery is possible, signatures can be photocopied from one document and put on another, documents can easily be altered after signature, and people deny that they signed something all the time. But this is the idea.

It's even worse on computers. Simply attaching a bitmap of a handwritten signature to a computer document won't work. The document could easily be altered after the signature is attached, and no one would be able to detect it. Even worse, the signature could easily be copied onto other documents.

Digital Signatures

A digital signature is a sequence of bits appended to a digital document (see Figure 4.1). Like a handwritten signature, its authenticity can be verified. But unlike a handwritten signature, it is unique to the document being signed. Someone's handwritten signature looks pretty much the same, time after time. That person's digital signature looks different for each different document she signs.

```
Version: 2.5

iQBVAgUBLdezEVUFZvpKACuaOfMynsL9NDE7hAQGRhAH+QGmJpp9ToWEJB+1OFGb
wsk3ydpMyFTb/YhoZbHbw/H268zIrFoCcm24UITcBiIcuSBgIbzgqQ==
=EbV1
```

Digital signatures are another application of public-key cryptography. If you remember, public-key cryptography uses a public and a private key. Anyone can encrypt messages with Bob's public key, but only Bob can decrypt messages with his private key.

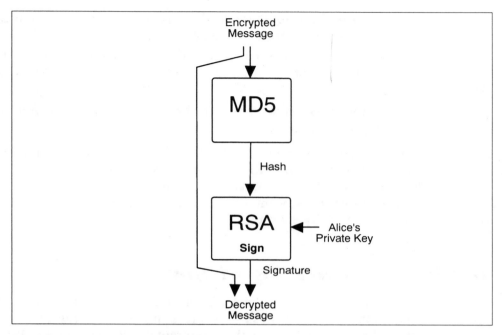

Figure 4.1 Signing electronic mail.

There's another thing you can do with public-key cryptography. You can reverse the roles of the public and private key. Alice could encrypt her message with her private key and send it to Bob. This is not secure communication. Bob, or anyone else for that matter, could decrypt the message with Alice's public key and read it. (Remember, her public key is public. It is widely available.) But no one else has Alice's private key. No one else could have encrypted it, and this authenticates the message's origin.

This is a central idea, and is worth discussing in some depth. Only Alice knows her private key, so only she can encrypt the message. Everyone knows Alice's public key, so anyone can decrypt the message. By encrypting the message with her private key, she is effectively signing the message. She is doing something to the message that only she can do. When Bob decrypts the message with Alice's public key, he verifies her signature, which authenticates the message's origin. For the decryption to produce a readable message, it must have been signed by Alice's private key. Anyone can verify Alice's signature.

Digital signatures satisfy the five criteria for paper signatures I listed earlier:

1. The signature is unforgeable; only Alice knows her private key.

2. The signature is authentic; when Bob verifies the signature with Alice's public key he knows that she signed (encrypted) it.

3. The signature is not reusable; the signature on one document cannot be transferred to any other document.

4. The signed document is unalterable; any alteration to the document (whether or not it has been encrypted) and the signature is no longer valid.

5. The signature cannot be repudiated. Bob doesn't need Alice's help to verify her signature.

There is one important simplification in the above explanation: signing isn't really encrypting with the private key, and verification isn't really decrypting with the public key. The math is generally more complicated. You'd best just think of these authentication operations as signing and verification, and be done with it.

Digital Signature Algorithms

Just as many different public-key algorithms do key management, many different public-key algorithms do digital signatures. I will only discuss those that you are likely to see in use, either in current or future versions of PGP or PEM.

RSA

In addition to encrypting keys (see Chapter 3), the RSA public-key algorithm can also be used to generate digital signatures. The mathematics are the same whether you use RSA for key management or digital signatures: there is a public and a private key, and the security of the system is based on the difficulty in factoring large numbers. Both PGP and PEM use RSA for digital signatures.

DSA

DSA is the Digital Signature Algorithm. (There is also a Digital Signature Standard, or DSS. The standard implements the algorithm—it's just a difference in terminology, really.) It is a public-key algorithm, but can only be used for digital signatures.

DSA was invented at the NSA, and it is patented by the government. (Whether or not this patent is valid is not clear; see Chapter 8 for details.) NIST has approved DSA as a federal digital signature standard.

When DSA was first proposed, RSA Data Security, Inc. and companies that had already licensed the RSA algorithm launched a smear campaign against it. They alluded to a possible "trap door" which would allow the government to break DSA. They complained about the speed of the algorithm, the fact that it cannot be used for encryption, and the size of the key.

The only real security issue is the size of the key. When the standard was first proposed, the key size was 512 bits—too small. The final standard allows for keys up to 1024 bits—more than enough for anyone's security needs.

DSA gets its security from the discrete logarithm problem. The mathematics are very different from RSA, but security is similar for similar-sized keys. Although exceptions are theoretically possible, it is likely that any great advance in breaking RSA will also yield a similar advance in breaking DSA, and vice versa. There is no security advantage in using one algorithm over the other.

Occasionally speed and efficiency comparisons between the two algorithms are published. Not surprisingly, those published by RSA Data Security, Inc. show that RSA is better than DSA, and those published by NIST show that DSA is better than RSA. With RSA, it takes much longer to sign a message than to verify a signature. With DSA, both the signing and verification operations take the same amount of time. In reality, these differences are minor; for the purposes of an electronic-mail security program they are negligible.

Currently no electronic-mail security program uses DSA, but I have heard talk of using it for digital signatures in a version of PEM (the same version that will use ElGamal instead of RSA for key management). Again, don't worry if you see it; it's just as secure as RSA.

Choosing a Key Length

This is an important decision. Look at Chapter 3, where I discuss key lengths for public-key algorithms. The analysis is exactly the same here. The tables tell us that 1024-bit keys are required for any long-term security.

How It Really Works

The real world is, as always, more complicated. The complication is analogous to the problem of using public-key cryptography for message encryption: Public-key algorithms are cumbersome and complicated, and it takes far too long to sign an entire message. The way electronic-mail security programs use digital signatures is by taking a digital "fingerprint" of the document, and signing that fingerprint.

This fingerprinting function is called a one-way hash function. (See the next section, "One-Way Hash Functions," for details.) A one-way hash function takes an arbitrary-length message and outputs a fixed-length fingerprint of that message. The fingerprint is a unique mathematical function of the message, and is long enough so that the chance of two different messages having the same hash value is astronomically small.

So, the electronic-mail security program uses a one-way hash function to generate a hash value of the document to be signed, and then uses a public-key cryptography digital-signature algorithm to sign the hash value.

An example might make things clearer. Alice is using PEM: MD5 as a one-way hash function, and RSA for digital signatures. (You'll learn about how MD5 works in a little bit.) She wants to send a signed message to Bob. These are the steps she has to go through:

1. Alice writes the message.
2. Alice generates a one-way hash of the message, using a one-way hash function, such as MD5.
3. Alice signs the hash value with a public-key digital signature algorithm, such as RSA, and her private key.
4. Alice concatenates the message and the signature to get a new, signed, message.
5. Alice e-mails this signed message to Bob.

On Bob's end, he can read the message without doing any work. But he wants to verify Alice's signature. These are the steps he has to go through (see Figure 4.2):

1. Bob separates the message from the signature.
2. Using a one-way hash function, Bob computes the hash value of the message.

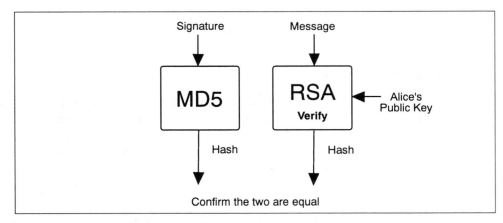

Figure 4.2 Verifying signed electronic mail.

3. Bob gets Alice's public key.

4. Using a public-key digital-signature algorithm and Alice's public key, Bob decrypts Alice's signature.

5. Bob compares Alice's decrypted signature with the hash value of the message. If they are the same, Bob has verified Alice's signature and accepts the message as genuine. If they are different, Bob rejects the signature.

Eve cannot forge Alice's signature. Eve does not know Alice's private key, so she cannot sign "Alice" on a message. Eve cannot take a signature from a valid message signed by Alice and attach it to a new message; when Bob tries to verify the signature he will realize that the two hash values are different and the signature isn't valid.

This might look like a complicated procedure, but remember that e-mail security programs take care of the details. All Alice has to do is indicate that she wishes to send a signed message, and the program takes care of the rest. It generates the one-way hash value, signs the hash, concatenates the message and the hash together, and ships the whole thing off to Bob. On the receiving end, Bob's program makes the verification operation just as easy.

One-Way Hash Functions

A one-way hash function converts an arbitrary-length message into a fixed-length hash. This is another one of cryptography's tricks. Like an encryption algorithm, a one-way hash function converts a plaintext message into gibberish. However, unlike an encryption algorithm, there is no way to go backwards with a one-way hash function. With the correct key, one can always decrypt ciphertext encrypted with an encryption algorithm; it is impossible to reverse a one-way hash function to get the original input from the output value.

This is an important difference: An encryption algorithm does not destroy any information. For any given ciphertext (and a key), there is only one correct plaintext that could have produced that ciphertext. A one-way hash function destroys information. For any given output of a one-way hash function, several messages could have produced that output.

Another difference between encryption algorithms and one-way hash functions is that one-way hash functions do not have a key (see Figure 4.3). No secrecy is involved in the one-way hash function; the security is in the lack of ability to go the other way. This property makes it a useful way to identify a message.

Think of a one-way hash function as a fingerprint. Just as a fingerprint uniquely identifies an individual, a one-way hash function uniquely identifies an arbitrary-length message. At least, that's the idea. Technically it's a lie.

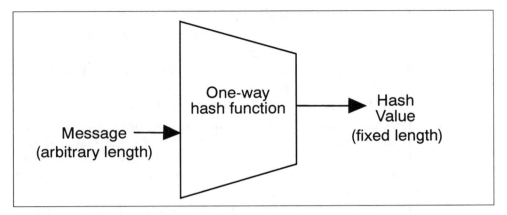

Figure 4.3 One-way hash function.

One-way hash values are usually small: 16 or 20 bytes. Messages can be large, very large. It's a simple matter to show that an infinite number of different messages will hash to the same one-way hash value. But remember, the chances of any two messages hashing to the same value are minute enough to be negligible.

Showing that there is an arbitrarily large number in one thing, but finding two messages that hash to the same value is another. This is where really clever mathematicians come in. One-way hash functions are designed so that it is infeasible to create a message that hashes to a particular value, or to create two different messages that hash to the same value.

TABLE 4.1: Time Needed to Mount a $1 Million Hardware Brute-Force Attack to Find a Message That Hashes to a Particular Value		
	Length of Hash in Bits	
Year	**64**	**128**
1995	38 days	10^{18} years
2000	4 days	10^{17} years
2005	9 hours	10^{16} years
2010	1 hour	10^{15} years
2015	5.5 min	10^{14} years
2020	31 sec	10^{13} years
2025	3.1 sec	10^{12} years
2030	.3 sec	10^{11} years

TABLE 4.2: Time Needed to Mount a $1 Million Hardware Brute-Force Attack to Find Two Messages That Hash to the Same Value

	Length of Hash in Bits			
Year	64	128	160	256
1995	19 days	38 days	7,000 yrs	10^{18} years
2000	2 days	4 days	700 yrs	10^{17} years
2005	4.7 hours	9 hours	70 yrs	10^{16} years
2010	28 min	1 hour	7 yrs	10^{15} years
2015	2.8 min	5.5 min	251 days	10^{14} years
2020	17 sec	31 sec	25 days	10^{13} years
2025	1.7 sec	3 sec	2.5 days	10^{12} years
2030	.2 sec	.3 sec	6 hours	10^{11} years

This is good. If Eve were able to create two messages that hash to the same value she could create an innocuous message for Alice to sign, and an incriminating message stating that Alice owes Eve $1 million. Alice would sign the innocuous message. Then Eve could take the signature and append it to the incriminating message. Now, since both messages hash to the same value, Eve has Alice's valid signature on the incriminating message.

Eve could always try a brute-force attack against a one-way hash function. That is, she could hash message after message, looking for one that hashes to a particular value, or two that hash to the same value. The success rate of this attack depends on the length of the hash value.

Tables 4.1 and 4.2 look at attacks by specialized hardware; attacks by the fastest computers are either 1,000 times slower or 1,000 times more expensive. Since the number of messages that have to be tested far exceeds the amount of time necessary to test any single message, these numbers can be examined independent of the one-way hash function. All tables include estimates for 1995 and the future, and all assume a hacker can spend $1 million. Future estimates assume that computing power, both hardware and software, increases by a factor of 10 every five years. It can get either ten times faster or ten times cheaper.

It is much easier to find two messages that hash to the same random value than it is to find a message that hashes to a given value. This is called the "birthday paradox."

How many people have to be in the same room before there is a 50 percent chance that one of them shares your birthday? The answer is 183. All right, how many people have to be in the same room before there is a 50 percent chance that two of them share the same birthday? The answer is surprisingly low: 23. So, how many random 64-bit hash values do you have to generate to find one that hashes to a particular value? 2^{64} (10^{19}). How many random 64-bit hash values do you have to generate to find two that hash to the same value? 2^{32} (4 billion).

Using at least a 128-bit hash value is essential for security, and a 160-bit hash value is better. Anything less is asking for trouble.

Of course, this whole analysis assumes that there is no better attack against the one-way hash function. Like most everything else in cryptography, no one can prove that a one-way hash function is secure against all but a brute-force attack. All we can do is invent functions, subject them to public scrutiny and peer review, and hope for the best.

MD5

MD5 is a one-way hash function invented by Ron Rivest of MIT, who also works for RSA Data Security, Inc. "MD" stands for "Message Digest," and the algorithm produces a 128-bit hash value for an arbitrary-length input message.

MD5 was first proposed in 1991, after some cryptanalytic attacks were discovered against Rivest's previous MD4 one-way hash function. The algorithm is designed for speed, simplicity, and security. Of course, the details of the algorithm are public, and have been analyzed by a variety of cryptographers.

A weakness in part of MD5 has been discovered, but so far it has not affected the overall security of the algorithm. However, the fact that it only produces a 128-bit hash value is more worrisome; I prefer a one-way hash function that produces a longer value.

Both PGP and PEM use MD5 as a one-way hash function.

SHA

SHA is the Secure Hash Algorithm, a one-way hash function invented at the NSA. It produces a 160-bit hash value from an arbitrary-length message.

The inner workings of SHA are very similar to those of MD4, indicating that the cryptographers at the NSA took the MD4 algorithm and improved on its security. In fact, the weakness in part of the MD5 algorithm mentioned above, discovered after SHA was proposed, does not work against SHA.

Currently, there are no known cryptanalytic attacks against SHA except for a brute-force attack. And its 160-bit value makes a brute-force attack infeasible. Of course, there's no proof that someone couldn't figure out how to break SHA tomorrow.

Neither PGP nor PEM currently uses SHA, but I expect that both will offer it, at least as an option, before long.

MD2 and MD4

MD4 is a precursor to MD5, and was also invented by Ron Rivest. After some security weaknesses were discovered in MD4, Rivest wrote MD5. MD4 was part of the original PEM specifications, but is no longer used.

MD2 is a simplified one-way hash function, and produces a 128-bit hash. It is an option in PEM; I recommend against using it because it is generally believed to be less secure.

Other One-Way Hash Functions

There are other one-way hash functions in the literature. Snefru and N-Hash have been broken; stay away from any program that uses them. Haval hasn't, but it isn't used very much. RIPE-MD was developed for the European Community. And there are a whole pile of one-way hash functions based on block algorithms like DES and IDEA, some secure and some not very secure.

Using a One-Way Hash Function as an Encryption Algorithm

It is possible to modify a one-way hash function for use as an encryption algorithm. This is not a trivial modification. Remember the big difference between an encryption algorithm and a one-way hash function: With a one-way hash function, it is impossible to go the other way and recover the original message from the hash value.

But there are ways to convert one-way hash functions into encryption algorithms. The resultant encryption algorithm is as strong as the original one-way hash function. I have heard rumors of SHA being modified in this way for use in a future version of PGP. I think it's a good idea.

Digital Signatures and Encryption

Encryption provides security and confidentiality, and digital signatures provide proof of authenticity and origination, but a user does not have to choose between the two. There's no reason that she can't use both encryption and digital signatures together. In fact, that is what both PGP and PEM do. Encryption provides privacy; digital signatures provide authentication. Together they provide security against both eavesdropping and tampering.

Think of the series of operations necessary to secure a message as layers of an onion. At the center is the message. Around the message is a digital signature. Around the digitally signed message is encryption. Around encryption is whatever else your e-mail program needs: uuencoding to allow the message to pass through various networks, routing information so the message gets to its destination, etc. Any compression is done as close to the actual message as possible, even before the digital signature.

PGP puts the authentication step (the digital signature) inside the encryption step. This means that only someone who can correctly decrypt the message can verify the digital signature. It could just as easily have been done the other way around, but this method makes traffic analysis a little more difficult. The message's originator is hidden by the encryption. Eve can neither decrypt the messages she intercepts nor verify the signatures. If authentication were outside encryption, Eve could verify signatures even though she could not read the messages' contents.

PEM doesn't use the onion approach. It does encryption and authentication sort of side-by-side. Eve can verify a signature even though she can't read the message. Yes, this is less secure. No, I have no explanation as to why PEM does things this way, but I point out that it was designed by committee.

The Steps: Encrypting and Signing a Message

Let's put everything together. Alice wants to send a secure message to Bob, both encrypted and signed—here's what happens. (Actually, her electronic mail security software goes through this process. Most of it is transparent to her.)

1. Alice writes the message.
2. Alice generates a one-way hash of the message, using a one-way hash function such as MD5.
3. Alice signs the hash value with her signature (her private key put through a digital signature algorithm, such as RSA.)
4. Alice concatenates the message and the signature to get a new, signed, message.
5. Alice generates a random encryption key, to be used to quickly encrypt the signed message.

6. Alice uses the random encryption key to encrypt the signed message with a conventional algorithm, such as DES.

7. Alice gets Bob's public key from someplace like a key server.

8. Alice encrypts that random encryption key with Bob's public key and a public-key algorithm, such as RSA.

9. Alice concatenates the encrypted message to the encrypted key to get the final, secure, message.

10. Alice e-mails this secure message to Bob.

Although there are considerable differences in the details, both PGP and PEM work this way.

The Steps: Verifying and Decrypting a Message

At the other end, Bob wants to read Alice's message. Before he can do so, his electronic-mail security program must go through the following steps:

1. Bob separates the encrypted message from the encrypted random key.

2. Using a public-key algorithm and his private key, Bob decrypts the random encryption key.

3. Using a conventional algorithm, such as DES, and the decrypted key, Bob decrypts the message.

4. Bob separates the message from Alice's signature.

5. Using a one-way hash function, Bob computes the hash value of the message.

6. Bob gets Alice's public key from someplace like a key server.

7. Using a public-key digital signature algorithm, such as RSA, and Alice's public key, Bob decrypts Alice's signature.

8. Bob compares Alice's decrypted signature with the hash value of the message. If they are the same, Bob has verified Alice's signature and accepts the message as genuine. If they are different, Bob rejects the signature.

Even if you forget these details, the important thing to remember is that a good electronic-mail security program uses conventional encryption, public-key cryptography key management, one-way hash functions, and digital signatures. Every one of those things is required, and the overall security of the system is only as good as the weakest link.

Chapter 5

Certificates

The Identification Problem

There's still a major problem with this whole key management process, one that I have conveniently ignored until now. The problem is that of identification.

In order for Alice to send Bob an encrypted message, or for Alice to verify Bob's signature, Alice needs Bob's public key. If you remember, one of the great benefits of public-key cryptography is that Alice and Bob don't have to meet in secret and exchange keys. So, how does Alice get Bob's public key?

Maybe she can send him unencrypted electronic mail and ask him for it. He can send it to her unencrypted, and then they're in business. To see why this won't work, imagine that Eve is pretending to be Bob, trying to fool Alice.

Alice sends an unencrypted message to "Bob," asking for his public key. Eve, pretending to be Bob, sends Alice her own public key. Alice, thinking she has received Bob's public key, encrypts her secret message to Bob in Eve's public key. Eve can now intercept and decrypt Alice's messages to Bob.

The same problem arises if Alice gets Bob's key from a public-key server somewhere on the network. Eve could break into the server and place her key under Bob's name. Alice, thinking she is getting Bob's public key from the server, actually gets Eve's. And then Alice, thinking she is encrypting a message that only Bob can read, actually encrypts a message that only Eve can read.

After Eve intercepts and reads the message, she can re-encrypt it using Bob's real public key and send it onward to Bob. If she forges the message headers so that it looks as if it were coming from Alice's machine, Bob won't know

Figure 5.1 Eve pretending to be Alice.

that anything is wrong (see figure 5.1). Why should he? The message is encrypted with his public key and signed by Alice's private key. It came from Alice's machine. It really was written by Alice to him. Even if they talk later in person, they won't notice any funny business that indicates that Eve has read the message.

If Eve wants to, she can send phony messages purporting to come from Bob. Remember, for Alice to check Bob's signature, she needs his public key. Where does she get it?

From the public-key server. But this is the same public-key server that Eve has broken into. When Alice gets Bob's public key, she actually gets Eve's key with Bob's name attached to it. When she verifies "Bob's" signature, it comes up valid.

The fundamental problem is that Alice has no way of verifying that a given key is really Bob's. Public-key cryptography gives Alice a way of sending a message to a given public key, or ensuring that a message was signed by a given public key, but it contains no mechanisms for associating a key with a person. Alice has no way of confirming the identity behind a key.

To prevent this type of abuse, we need a system that prevents tampering with public keys. If Eve tries to substitute her key for Bob's, we want it to be immediately obvious to Alice and everyone else. This sounds like a job for digital signatures and, in fact, our solution will make use of them.

Certificates

A certificate is a message, but it is a special message. It consists of someone's name, his e-mail address, and his public key (see Figures 5.2 and 5.3).

```
—-BEGIN PGP PUBLIC KEY BLOCK—-
Version: 2.5

9QUqAi3L864AAAEEAKRe8jdLLL4PDQSsliTKQOyTkmQCN8BFBm7cO3RC9Ol5PP9K
j/RtnsdxpY1jF23HR+x54LrOpi8ig6HEmFMTtW7wkMwTiXVVWuNByRjSMgz8jvrn
ylkJrrOd54ZKyXBTw/D7AL7u4qxAAURMMO/tIOCPAgNMxiANUWqretPEWCZE9sLb
tCFDb2xpbiBQbl4LmNzLmRlLmVkdT6JAJUCHVtYiA8Y29saW5BbnBRAtyxCUZXmE
uMepZtOBxTlT5ocGNzyE8mkZXvbmoSOm7sdAeiyA/4tNXz6loqEwyMv65TMGtqsd
6GnjHoeanP8lrkQz/anrzAHJMBOaZOV68ZyhaXpc2e7EVut4ZiaVBvHfKT7aCLAK
hC5uiA/1diwLXhC8OoHwKqZDT+uNnJLLdlAzrJiOaELAzXXeOvtMXopmq4kAYAIF
EC3L/BnKPaH9hle2HehjGIiOmQ+Zcqn8wEBXWgCWMgIh8Lsww5pFHRFbAnL3pOhw
tLdoGm6lqWbe4pWNv6Go13t9p+1GmTh+RrnGoZ4njDSTULxDpKUtq6rs3Mlg+IkA
1QIFEC3LXLwEEgFKpxQvWLqI2+zgPw+wC+7uKsQEBDZkEAJYkHK5nO2Gxz33rPDa
OeT6+RYMDTaFTVNRbRznvwNTDcQXVsnyPg5yGdRIcr/1vzTqX7CwNpCuIMPnWuGf
gSEP7vjm832gm4vQboJiQ+zzvfdh5te4ag6jobCN1PVyqIIxIV5S8iPv64+53qoS
WJ6BNDq9
=Wjfi
—-END PGP PUBLIC KEY BLOCK—-
```

Figure 5.2 A sample certificate.

(Actually, it consists of a lot more things, as we shall soon see.) And to ensure that it has not been tampered with, the certificate has been signed by someone trustworthy. Exactly what "someone trustworthy" means will be left for the next section. For now just assume that someone trustworthy exists, and that he spends all day signing certificates.

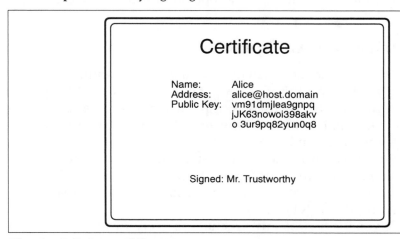

Figure 5.3 A certificate.

When you first receive someone's certificate, your security program checks the digital signature. Assuming that it verifies the signature correctly, you then accept the certificate as genuine. You trust that the public key belongs to the person named, that his address is as it is named, and that other information included with the certificate is valid.

This prevents Eve from tampering with certificates. If Eve substitutes her public key for Bob's in Bob's certificate, then the signature would no longer be valid. Alice will immediately recognize Eve's foul play.

So, who is this trusted person who signs certificates? It is a certification authority.

Certification Authorities

A certification authority is a trusted individual (or individuals, or organization, or whatever) who signs certificates. It is important that he be trusted. If you get a certificate signed by a certification authority, your trust in the certificate depends on your trust in the authority. If you trust the authority to only sign valid certificates, then you will trust that the certificate is valid. If you don't trust the authority, then you have no reason to trust his signature on a certificate.

PGP and PEM have completely different philosophies regarding trust and certification authorities; this is probably the chief difference between the two. PEM defines trust in terms of a hierarchy: You trust the person over you (your superior), and people under you trust you. PGP defines trust in a more distributed manner: You trust your friends. (Actually, if you really wanted to, you could make PGP behave like PEM and PEM behave like PGP, but each is designed for its particular philosophy of trust.)

PEM Certification Authorities

PEM has a hierarchical system of certification authorities. Think of the world as a pyramidal organization; everyone has a boss. At the top of the pyramid is the supreme boss—insert your particular deific reference. (In real life it is more likely to be someone who actually has a digital signature.) Under him are lesser bosses, and so on.

When Alice creates her public-key/private-key pair, the PEM software turns her public key into a certificate. Then, she gets the certificate signed by her boss, whose certificate is signed by her boss's boss, whose certificate is signed by her boss's boss's boss.

Everyone is part of this structure, so every two people share at least one

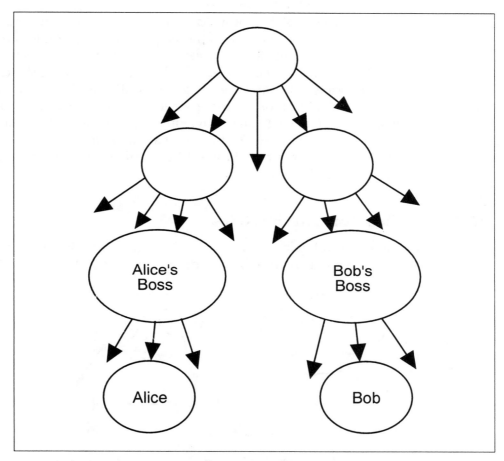

Figure 5.4 Hierarchical certificate certification.

common signature up their chain of authentication (see Figure 5.4). For example, assume Bob also has a certificate. If Alice and Bob share the same boss, then both certificates will be signed by all the same people. If Alice and Bob have different bosses, but both of their bosses share the same boss, then their certificates will have all the same signatures but one. If Alice and Bob work in different divisions in different offices in different cities, then they might share only the signature of the supreme boss.

For messages between companies, there is a whole hierarchy of trusted organizations, empowered to sign certificates for other organizations. And at the top, a single trusted authority called the Internet Activities Board (IAB) empowers all these trusted organizations. Trust flows downward from this single authority to everyone else.

When Alice gets Bob's certificate, she checks to see where she and he share a common boss. Then, she verifies the signature chain leading to that boss. (She knows the boss's public key, because it is part of her own certificate.) If the signature chain is valid, she knows she can trust Bob's certificate. This works only because Alice and Bob are guaranteed to share at least one boss.

PEM's system is ideal for situations where there is a hierarchical organizational structure, like companies, governments, militaries, etc. There, everyone has a boss. It is less useful when you have a lot of unrelated individuals, some of whom may not have bosses. PGP's system is much better suited for these situations.

PGP Certification Authorities

PGP uses a distributed system of certification authorities (see Figure 5.5). Every PGP user is a certification authority. Alice, as a PGP user, certifies those

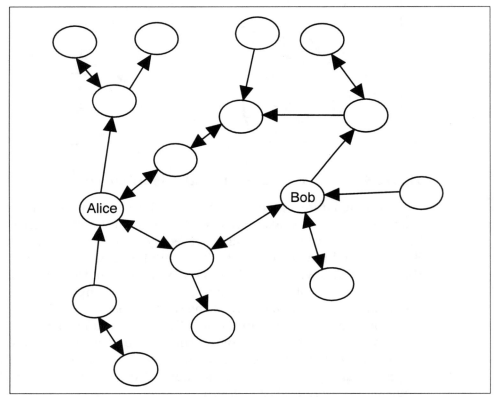

Figure 5.5 Distributed certificate certification.

keys she knows are valid. They could be the keys of her friends, her co-workers, or her relatives. Whatever the case, she is acting as a notary public, affixing her signature to those certificates that she knows are correct.

PGP certificates can have more than one authority certifying their validity. In fact, it is better for a certificate to have multiple certifications. This indicates that many people attest that the certificate is valid. Unlike PEM, no single certifying authority that everyone trusts exists. PGP users rely on a vast web of certifying authorities, each of whom a few people trust.

When Alice gets Bob's public key, she checks the signatures on the certificate. If the certificate is signed by someone whose public key she already has, then she knows to trust the validity of Bob's certificate. If the certificate is signed by someone whose public key is signed by someone whose public key she already has, then she might trust Bob's certificate less. If the certificate is not signed by anyone she has ever heard of, then she has no reason to trust Bob's certificate as being genuine.

This is the major drawback to the PGP system of certifications: When you get someone's certificate, there is no guarantee that you will trust it. With PEM it is always possible to trace the hierarchy of certifying authorities to the top; not so with PGP.

Certifications and methods for certifying are very convoluted, both for PGP and for PEM. I will discuss them more in the chapters on the different programs.

Distributing Certificates

Since neither PGP nor PEM certificates can be altered without detection, it makes sense to distribute them as widely as possible. The great value of electronic-mail security programs is that Alice can send Bob a secure message, even if they have never met. This means that Alice has to be able to get Bob's key. If Bob only sends his certificate to his friends, Alice might never get it. If he posts it on bulletin boards, adds a reference to it in his **.sig** file, adds it to his **.plan** file, sends it to special key servers, or publishes it in electronic mail telephone books, it is more likely to be available. Alice can just look Bob's name up and get his key.

There are no security problems with this. Bob doesn't care who has his public key. The principles of public-key cryptography prevent anyone from using this key to read his mail or to forge his signature. The mechanics of certificates prevent anyone from tampering with his key, or substituting one key for another. Bob wants everyone, even people he has not met yet, to be able to send him encrypted messages and to verify his signature on messages he sends.

PGP Key Servers

There are several PGP key servers on the Internet. These are databases of PGP public keys. You can post your public key on the server; you can query the server for other public people's public keys. It's easy.

You communicate with the key servers by electronic mail. The key server supports a number of commands, and you tell the server what you want on the subject line. For example, if you want the help file, send the server a message with the subject line: HELP. Don't put anything in the message body; the server will just ignore it.

If you want to add your public key to the server, send the server the key with the subject line: ADD. If you want to get someone else's public key, send the server a message : GET followed by the user ID of the person. For example, to get my public key, type the subject line:

```
GET schneier@counterpane.com
```

Again, don't put anything in the message body. The key server will ignore it.

There are other commands that the key servers support. And some key servers even allow you to get public keys via anonymous ftp.

Here's a list of PGP key servers active at the time of this writing. There may be more by now:

```
pgp-public-keys@pgp.mit.edu
pgp-public-keys@cs.tamu.edu
pgp-public-keys@demon.co.uk
pgp-public-keys@phil.utmb.edu
pgp-public-keys@chao.sw.oz.au
pgp-public-keys@proxima.alt.za
pgp-public-keys@dsi.unimi.it
```

Chapter 6

Keeping Your Private Key Private

Your Private Key

The strength of your electronic-mail security program is wholly dependent on the secrecy of your private key. That private key identifies you; it is the piece of knowledge that only you know. If you tell that key to someone else, she will be able to impersonate you. She will be able to read private e-mail addressed to you. She will be able to sign e-mail so that other people believe that it is from you. She will, for all intents and purposes on the net, be you.

Do not tell your private key to anyone. Not your boss. Not your spouse. Not even your mother. It does not matter how much easier it would make things, or how much you trust the other person. This is not a question of trust; it is a question of identity. Giving away your private key is akin to giving away your identity. Don't do it.

And don't make it possible for someone to steal your private key. Don't write it down . . . anywhere. Don't save it in a computer file. Keep it in your memory; make it a part of you.

Private Keys—The Reality

Actually, you will probably never know your private key. Your electronic-mail security program will generate one randomly for you—remember, it is a large number made up of large prime numbers—and store it, encrypted, on a disk. What you do have to remember is a password or pass phrase that unlocks the private key. (A pass phrase is like a password, but it can be an entire phrase or sentence and not a single word.) This is the thing that you should never write down and never divulge. This password or pass phrase will allow someone else to go to your computer and impersonate you.

Choosing a Password or Pass Phrase

It's a real bad idea to choose a password or pass phrase that is easy to guess. The first thing Eve will do when she tries to break into your electronic-mail security program is to try a bunch of easy passwords. If yours is one of them, she will get in. Remember that passwords and pass phrases are subject to the same kinds of dictionary attacks discussed in Chapter 2.

Tips

Here are some tips for picking a password that is not easy to guess:

Don't pick passwords that are your name or the name of anyone close to you (pets included).

Don't pick passwords that are important dates, such as your birthday.

Don't pick passwords that are any number associated with you, such as your Social Security number or your car license plate number.

Don't pick passwords that name the street you live on, the model car you drive, or any other word that can be easily traced to you.

Don't pick passwords from what is obviously visible when you are sitting at your computer. The model of the computer and the title of the poster in front of your desk are both bad passwords.

Don't pick passwords that are single words, or passwords that are simple transformations of single words. For example, single words with a number on the end, single words with "i" replaced by "1" or "o" replaced by "0", or single words with varied capitalization.

Don't pick short passwords. Your password should be as long as possible—eight characters is really too short. If you can use a pass phrase, it should be an entire sentence or phrase.

Pick a mix of letters, numbers, and punctuation marks. Vary capitalization.

Why Is This Such a Big Deal?

Imagine that Alice and Bob have been sending secure messages back and forth to each other for years using PGP. Somehow, Eve manages to get the encryption key for one of those messages. She can now read it, and knows what it says. This is damaging, but it's only one message.

Now imagine that Eve got her hands on Alice's PGP pass phrase, and thereby has her private key. Now, Eve can read every message that Bob (or anyone else, for that matter) ever sent to Alice. She can impersonate Alice in correspondence to Bob or anyone. This is significantly worse than the compromise of just one message; the amount of damage Eve can do is enormous.

Private keys are so important because they remain unchanged from message to message, from year to year. Their secrecy is critically important to proving the authenticity of a message. Their compromise means the possible loss of everything that was ever encrypted with that key. Don't compromise your private key.

PGP supports arbitrary-length pass phrases.

Key Revocation

Unfortunately, you can never make security entirely people-proof. Eventually, someone somewhere will lose their private key, forget their pass phrase, write it down somewhere, or accidentally tell it to someone else.

If someone else has your private key, he can impersonate you. He can read electronic mail encrypted with your public key; he can send messages signed by your private key. Unless you can kill that person or otherwise render him incapable of using a computer, you have no choice but to invalidate your public-key/private-key pair.

This is called key revocation, and both PGP and PEM have mechanisms to handle it. Basically, you send a message to everyone in the universe saying that your private key has been stolen, and not to encrypt any messages with the public key or to trust any messages signed by the private key.

This is an enormous hassle, and in an ideal world it would never happen. But in the real world it does.

Chapter 7

Odds and Ends

Generating Random Numbers

Both PGP and PEM use lots of random numbers. They need random numbers when they generate a public-key/private-key pair. They need a random encryption key every time they encrypt a message.

These random numbers have to be random. If they are not, if there is even a slight bias in the randomness, a cryptanalyst can use that bias to help break your messages. Remember that brute-force attacks are based on trying every possible key until the analyst finds the correct one. If your random-number generator only generates some of the possible keys, or generates some keys much more frequently than others, then a brute-force attack will be much more effective.

PGP gets the random numbers needed to create your public-key/private-key pair based on your typing characteristics. That is, the PGP random-number generator uses the time interval between successive keystrokes to generate its random numbers. For random encryption keys, PGP uses the IDEA encryption algorithm as a random-number generator. Whether or not this is a good idea depends on the security of IDEA. However, if you use IDEA to encrypt your data, there's no additional security problem with using IDEA to generate random numbers.

Random-number generation is not part of the PEM specification, but the various programs that use PEM use their own methods to generate random numbers. There is no standard.

None of these tricks is perfect, and honestly, if there is a fatal flaw in either PGP or PEM that allows government intelligence organizations such as the NSA to break messages, this is where it lies.

Compression

If your messages are long, it is a good idea to compress them before transmission. Compression reduces the number of bits required to store a message, making the message smaller (sometimes considerably so). Compression techniques are reversible, and no data is lost. At the other end, the message is expanded again, and the expanded message will be identical to the original.

The reason compression works is because most messages are highly redundant. English messages are encoded using an 8-bit ASCII code, even though there are only about 100 standard characters on a keyboard. Graphic images generally have a whole lot of white space, or at least repeat the same color over and over again. These files are saved on a computer in ways suited for efficient storage and retrieval, but not necessarily for space efficiency.

So, compression makes data files smaller. This makes them easier to send through the network. It also makes the encryption operation faster; there is less data to encrypt. And it increases security.

Redundancies in the plaintext is one of the wedges that cryptanalysts use to break algorithms. By eliminating redundancies through compression, you will make the cryptanalyst's job much harder. He will have less data to work with, and the data he does have will be more random.

This isn't terribly important. You've already chosen an algorithm that is secure against all kinds of cryptanalytic attacks. It should be strong even if there are redundancies in the plaintext. But every bit of security helps.

If you use compression, remember to compress before you encrypt. This means that you have to compress your message before running it though your e-mail security program. (PGP has a compression option built in; it takes care of getting the order right.) The reason is that an encrypted message—at least, a message encrypted with a good encryption algorithm—cannot be compressed. The ciphertext is indistinguishable from random bits, and there are no redundancies.

Compression comes before encryption, never after.

File Encryption

Electronic-mail security programs will protect your e-mail in transit, but they won't necessarily protect your electronic mail when it is stored on your computer. And that's where it is most vulnerable.

If Eve is after your secrets, she can try one of two things. She can try a cryptographic attack against your electronic-mail security program, and read your mail in transmission. Or she can try what is known as a "black bag" attack: she can break into your home or office and read your mail while it is sitting on your desk. Given that both PGP and PEM are very secure programs, the latter is much easier.

Bob, the recipient of the mail messages, can thwart Eve by storing all mail in encrypted form, and never printing out copies. Alice, the sender, has other problems. When she encrypts a message to Bob, only he can read it; she no longer can. In order for her to save a secure copy, she needs to encrypt it so that only she can read it.

It's probably easiest for both Alice and Bob to use some sort of encryption program that encrypts all the data on their hard disk drive. Many such programs are available for a variety of computer architectures; most of them are lousy. Make sure the encryptor you buy implements full DES (or better yet, triple-DES), has good key-management mechanisms (there should be no way to recover the plaintext if you forget the key), and has some mechanism to make it easy to use a secure password (that is, it has some mechanism for hashing an arbitrary-length pass phrase into a key).

This is not a book about computer security, so these topics will have to be put aside. Don't forget about them, though. The overall security of your computer system is only as strong as the weakest part. Closing one security hole just means that your adversaries will look for another.

File Erasure

Generally, when you delete a file you only delete the file name from the directory. The actual bits that make up the file remain on the hard disk, perhaps with some trivial modification, until overwritten by another file. Many utility programs—Norton Utilities is the most popular for PCs and Macs—can recover deleted files. To erase a file so these software packages cannot read it, you have to physically write over all of the bits on the disk. To delete a file so that adversaries with electron-tunnelling microscopes can't recover it, you have to do even more. (See Figure 7.1.)

Many utility programs can erase files so that file-recovery utilities can't bring them back. They overwrite the file multiple times. If you are concerned about the security of your data, use one of them.

If you are concerned about an adversary with considerably more resources than a file-undelete program, you have to do even more work to completely

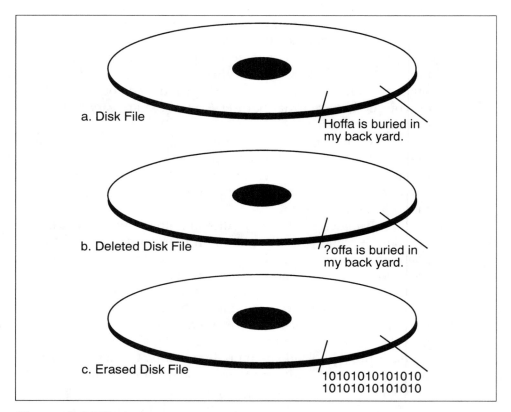

a. Disk File

Hoffa is buried in
my back yard.

b. Deleted Disk File

?offa is buried in
my back yard.

c. Erased Disk File

10101010101010
10101010101010

Figure 7.1 File erasure.

erase your files. The Department of Defense recommends overwriting a deleted file not once, but three times. Any fewer and someone with special-purpose
equipment can read the overwritten bits. Most file erasure programs support
overwriting files in accordance with Department of Defense specifications.

Recent experiments at NIST with electron-tunnelling microscopes suggest
even that might not be enough. The only way to securely erase magnetic
media is to physically destroy it: burn it, shred it, feed it to your pet tiger.

And here's another thing to worry about: The virtual memory features of
many state-of-the-art operating systems mean that your computer can write
memory to disk at any time. Even if you are careful never to save a sensitive file, you never know when the computer might decide to swap the data
onto disk. If you are clever, you might be able to write a word processor that
doesn't allow the system to use virtual memory on it. It's easier to find a
utility that erases all the free space on your hard disk. Use it.

This is not a book about file erasure, so I'll leave the topic. Remember it,
though. It is important.

Trojan Horses

Electronic-mail security programs can protect the security of your correspondence as it travels through the network. But you have to trust the program. You have to trust the computer you work on. And you have to trust everyone who has access to that program and that computer.

Imagine that the NSA is out to read your mail. For whatever reason, they have targeted you as someone worth spying on. And they have a budget to do it right.

You use PEM, so they can't read your mail in transit. You use a good file encryptor on your home machine and a good file-erasure program, so they can't read your mail in your computer. They can't break triple-DES; they can't break RSA. But they can break into your home and your office. And this is what they will do.

They will turn your computer on and replace your copy of PEM with a Trojan Horse: their own, slightly-modified, copy of PEM. This new copy looks and feels exactly like the PEM you know, but it has a trap door built into it. Maybe this new version of PEM surreptitiously mails a plaintext copy of every message you encrypt to a certain address. Maybe this new version of PEM has a modified key-generation routine, that generates one of only 1,000 possible keys. Maybe it has one of dozens of other slight modifications that will let NSA agents read your mail quickly and easily.

And you have no way of knowing whether or not this is true. You have no way of checking to see whether or not this has already happened.

This is a paranoid scenario, but it illustrates an important point: In the end, you can't get any real security with software products. Unless the computer is locked away where the agent cannot get to it, he will be able to rig the computer so that you think it is secure, but it really isn't.

If your electronic-mail security program has some sort of checksum feature, the NSA will modify that too. If you carry your electronic-mail security program in your shirt pocket, the NSA will write a program that sits on your computer and waits until you load that floppy. Or maybe they will switch floppies while you are asleep. Unless your encryption is embedded in the computer's hardware where someone cannot modify it, you are at risk.

Now, let's step back to a more reasonable level of paranoia. Unless the intelligence services of several major governments are after you, you don't have to worry about this sort of thing. Mounting this sort of attack requires a lot of time, money, and personnel; it is unlikely you will be singled out.

You should, however, think about the integrity of the software package you are using. It is very expensive for the NSA to break into your home and switch your copy of PGP with a modified one, but it would be very cost-effective if they could do that with a single master copy of the program. Then, everyone who downloads the program will have the modified version.

What can you do? Well, if you are a programmer, you can get a copy of the source code to one of these programs and check it for trap doors yourself. This is not to say that the NSA isn't clever enough to make their trap doors so subtle that you couldn't find them, but it's a place to start. If you are an excellent programmer with a lot of free time, you can recode the whole thing from scratch. If, however, you are just a normal person who wants some privacy, you have no choice but to trust the programs you are using. It's not a very satisfying answer, but it's the best I can do.

Anonymous Remailers

Anonymous remailers are not a part of either PGP or PEM, but they are an important part of e-mail security. The purpose of these remailers is to take privacy one level further. Remember traffic analysis? Eve may not be able to read the encrypted mail that you are sending, but she is still able to know who you send mail to. This gives her information on who you correspond with, how frequently, and what size messages you send.

To counter this type of attack, you can use a third party whose function is simply to remail your message with his return address on it instead of yours.

There are two different types of remailers. The first type only accepts plaintext remailing headers. This means that you send a message to the remailer, and the unencrypted message contains the follow-on address, where you'd like the message sent. The remailer strips off your return address and sends the message on. This is useful only if your goal was to prevent the person to whom you are sending mail from learning your identity. It would do nothing for the problem of net eavesdroppers learning to whom you are sending mail.

The second type of remailer accepts encrypted remailing headers. With this type of remailer, you encrypt your message twice. First, you encrypt it in the public key of the person ultimately receiving the message. You then add the remailing header and encrypt it again using the public key for the remailer that you are using. When the remailer receives your message, the system will recognize that the header is encrypted and will use its private key to decrypt the message. The remailer can now read the forwarding information, but because the body of the message is still encrypted in the key of another party, no one else can read your mail. The remailer simply sends the message to its proper destination. At its ultimate destination, the recipient uses her private key to decrypt this encryption and reads the message.

Remailer Programs

Since this process of multiple encryption and remailing headers can get quite involved, several programs are available to simplify the process. Ftp to **soda.berkeley.edu** and examine the directory **/pub/cypherpunks/remailers** for the available remailing programs. Table 7.1 is a table of remailer addresses.

```
TABLE 7.1: Remailer Addresses
```

hh@pmantis.berkeley.edu[1]
hh@cicada.berkeley.edu[1]
hh@soda.berkeley.edu[1]
nowhere@bsu-cs.bsu.edu[1]
remail@tamsun.tamu.edu[1]
ebrandt@jarthur.claremont.edu[2]
hal@alumni.caltech.edu [Fwd: hfinney@shell.portal.com][2]
elee7h5@rosebud.ee.uh.edu[2]
hfinney@shell.portal.com[2]
remailer@utter.dis.org[2]
0x@uclink.berkeley.edu [Fwd: hh@soda.berkeley.edu][1]
remailer@rebma.mn.org[2]
remail@extropia.wimsey.com[3]

[1]: Remailer accepts only plaintext headers.
[2]: Remailer accepts both plaintext and encrypted headers.
[3]: Remailer accepts only encrypted headers.

The following former Cypherpunk remailers are no longer in service. Either a message stating that the system had been shut down was received, or the test message was returned due to an invalid address and no test message was returned after three attempts.

```
phantom@mead.u.washington.edu [Shutdown message returned]
remail@tamaix.tamu.edu [Mail returned, invalid address]
```

Here's how to send a message to a Cypherpunks remailer: The first non-blank line in the message must start with two colons (::). The next line must contain the user-defined header **Request-Remailing-To: <destination>**. This line must be followed by a blank line. Finally, append your message. As an example, if you wanted to send a message to me via a remailer, you would compose the following message:

```
::
Request-Remailing-To: schneier@counterpane.com
```

```
[body of message]
```

You would then send the above message to the desired remailer. Note the section labeled "body of message" may be either a plaintext message, or a PGP message addressed to the desired recipient. To send the above message with an encrypted header, use PGP to encrypt the entire message shown above to the desired remailer. Be sure to take the output in armored text form. In front of the BEGIN PGP MESSAGE portion of the file, insert two colons (::) as the first non-blank line of the file. The next line should say "Encrypted: PGP". Finally the third line should be blank. The message now looks like this:

```
::
Encrypted: PGP
```

```
—-BEGIN PGP MESSAGE—-
Version 2.3a
[body of PGP message]
—-END PGP MESSAGE—-
```

You would then send the above message to the desired remailer just as you did in the first case with a nonencrypted header. Note that it is possible to chain remailers together so that the message passes through several levels of anonymity before it reaches its ultimate destination.

Complete Anonymity

There is another type of remailer on the Internet, one not run by the Cypherpunks. It is in Finland (which means the NSA almost certainly collects traffic to and from it), and its address is **anon.penet.fi**.

The syntax for sending mail through this remailer is different from the Cypherpunk remailers. For example, if you wanted to send mail to me (**schneier@counterpane.com**) through **anon.penet.fi**, you would send the mail to **schneier%counterpane.com@anon.penet.fi**. (Note that the @ sign in my Internet address is changed to a %.

Unlike the Cypherpunk remailers, **anon.penet.fi**, directly supports anonymous return addresses. Anybody using the remailer is assigned an anonymous id of the form **an?????**, where **?????** is an arbitrary number representing that user. To send mail to someone when you only know his or her anonymous address, address your mail to **an?????@anon.penet.fi**, replacing the question marks with the userid you are interested in.

Do not use your mailer's automatic reply with this service; if you do, you will inadvertently reveal your secret **an?????**. I've seen this done several times.

This is amazingly cool. Not only can you send someone a message hiding your identity, but you can also preserve your anonymity in a reply.

For additional information on **anon.penet.fi**, send a blank message to **help@anon.penet.fi**. You will receive complete instructions on how to use the remailer, including how to obtain a pass phrase on the system and how to post to newsgroups anonymously.

The anonymous remailers aren't perfect. Imagine that Eve is watching one of the encrypted remailers closely, and collects every message going in and going out. She can't read any messages, but she can read the headers: she knows who they are from, where they are going, and their size. At 12:00, she records a message going to the remailer from Alice. At 12:01, she records another message, of about the same size, going out to Bob. It doesn't take a rocket scientist to figure out that Alice just sent an anonymous message to Bob.

Even if the remailers are very busy, with hundreds of messages going in and out every minute, Eve can make very good guesses about who is talking to whom. Remailers prevent traffic analyses from arbitrary places in the network; they do not prevent traffic analysis of the remailers themselves.

There are ways to help solve this problem: The remailer should standardize message sizes, send bogus messages to random people on the Internet, and store messages for a random amount of time in order to uncorrelate messages received from messages sent. And, at the same time, people who use anonymous remailers should send bogus messages to them regularly, to disguise when they send out real messages.

TEMPEST

Your computer radiates data. It radiates from the monitor; it radiates into your AC power line. With the right equipment, a sophisticated eavesdropper can read what you are writing on your computer from hundreds of feet away: perhaps from a van parked outside your home or office. Needless to say, encryption doesn't do much good if the plaintext is available this way.

TEMPEST is a U.S. military standard for electromagnetic shielding of computer equipment. Normal, off-the-shelf computers are not built to TEMPEST specifications. They can easily be monitored. The military buys TEMPEST equipment—it's specially built and shielded not to radiate.

If you are worried about keeping your data secure from major governments, no encryption program alone will protect you. The government could just set up a monitoring van outside your home and read everything that you are doing on your computer.

The expensive solution is to buy a TEMPEST computer. Manufacturers advertise in government computer magazines: *Government Computer News*, *Federal Computer Week*, and *Defense Electronics*. These computers are not cheap; figure $10,000 for a top-of-the-line PC clone.

A cheaper solution is to use a laptop computer run on batteries. No emissions are fed back into the power lines, and the amount of power being fed to the display and being consumed by a laptop is much less than the typical home computer and monitor. This provides a much weaker signal for snoopers to monitor. In addition, a laptop computer has the advantage of not being anchored to one location. Anyone trying to monitor your emissions would have to follow you around, maybe making herself a little more obvious.

Remember, a laptop does not meet TEMPEST specifications, so it is still not safe. It is just a bit safer than the standard personal computer.

Chapter 8

Patents, Governments, and Export Laws

Patents

Public-key cryptography is patented at every turn. The basic concepts of public-key cryptography fall under a patent issued to Whitfield Diffie, Martin Hellman, and Ralph Merkle:

> M.E. Hellman, W. Diffie, and R.C. Merkle
> "Cryptographic Apparatus and Method"
> U.S. Patent #4,200,770
> Date awarded: 29 April 1980

This patent is controlled by a company called Public-Key Partners (At least for now. The "partners" are currently suing each other.) Public-Key Partners is a consortium of four entities: RSA Data Security, Inc., the purveyors of the RSA algorithm; Cylink, Inc., developers of cryptography hardware; Massachusetts Institute of Technology, who patented the RSA algorithm; and Stanford University, who patented the original Diffie-Hellman algorithm. Public-Key Partners also controls the RSA algorithm patent:

> R. Rivest, A. Shamir, and L. Adleman
> "Cryptographic Communications System and Method"

U.S. Patent #4,405,829

Date awarded: 20 September 1983

Public-Key Partners controls three other public-key cryptography patents, and they use these patents to claim royalties from anyone using any form of public-key cryptography in the United States. (For example, the ElGamal algorithm is unpatented, but Public-Key Partners claims that the general idea falls under their patents anyway.) Whether or not these patents are broad enough to cover all of that is debatable, but so far it has never been questioned in court. I doubt this will ever happen for a few reasons. One, Public-Key Partners will spend a lot of money defending their only asset. Two, giant companies such as Microsoft, IBM, Apple, DEC, Sun, AT&T, and Novell, who employ more lawyers than you can comfortably comprehend, decided to license the patent rather than fight Public-Key Partners in court. And three, the Diffie-Hellman patent will expire in April 1997. After that, people can use a variety of public-key encryption and digital-signature algorithms royalty-free; it's easier to wait than fight.

This is only a concern in the U.S. RSA is not patented in any other country. People here can use PGP or PEM for free.

The free version of PGP does not use RSA in violation of the patent. It is distributed by MIT, who can legally distribute the algorithm. ViaCrypt, who sells a commercial implementation of PGP, has a license to use the RSA algorithm. PEM uses an RSA implementation called RSAREF, which can be used royalty-free by individuals. Commercial versions of PEM are also available; the vendors have taken care of royalty issues themselves.

DSA has been patented by the U.S. Government:

D. Kravitz

"Digital Signature Algorithm"

U.S. Patent #5,231,668

Date Awarded: 27 July 1993

The status of this patent has been questioned. Public-Key Partners claims that it infringes on one of their patents (Schnorr, U.S. Patent #4,995,082). I don't think there is any credence to this claim, but that would never stand in the way of the American legal system. Heaven alone knows what the eventual outcome of this will be.

The IDEA algorithm is patented, both in the United States and abroad. The U.S. patent is:

J.L. Massey and X. Lai

"Device for the Conversion of a Digital Block and the Use of Same"

U.S. Patent #5,214,703

Date Awarded: 25 May 1993

The patent holders of IDEA have allowed individual users of PGP to use the algorithm royalty-free. ViaCrypt has a license to sell PGP with the IDEA algorithm.

DES was patented by IBM, but the patents have long expired, and anyway IBM gave the world a royalty-free license. Triple-DES is unpatented.

I know of no other patents that affect either PGP or PEM. However, given the rough-and-tumble world of U.S. patents, someone may make a claim of infringement tomorrow.

Standards

DES is a government encryption standard, at least until 1997 or 1998. Sometime around then the official certification of DES will run out. NIST claims that they will not recertify DES again. However, they've said that before. These are NIST documents that specify DES; they are free for the asking:

NBS FIPS PUB 46-1

"Data Encryption Standard"

National Bureau of Standards

U.S. Department of Commerce

January 1988

NBS FIPS PUB 74

"Guidelines for Implementing and Using the NBS Data Encryption Standard"

National Bureau of Standards

U.S. Department of Commerce

April 1981

NBS FIPS PUB 81

"DES Modes of Operation"

National Bureau of Standards

U.S. Department of Commerce

December 1980

Even though the security of DES erodes with the continuing increases in available computing power, there's nothing around to replace it. Hardware-only algorithms like Skipjack won't work, because users need software encryption solutions. Industries that use DES heavily, like the banking industry, will probably convert from DES to triple-DES and be done with it.

DSS is a government digital signature standard. It's not being used much for two reasons. One, it is very new. Two, no one is sure how the patent issues are going to resolve themselves. NIST has these documents that specify DSS and SHS:

NIST FIPS PUB 186

"Digital Signature Standard"

National Institute of Standards and Technology

U.S. Department of Commerce

May 1994

NIST FIPS PUB 180

"Secure Hash Standard"

National Institute of Standards and Technology

U.S. Department of Commerce

April 1993

The DSS is a mandatory standard for the federal government.

The National Security Agency

The NSA is the official intelligence-gathering organization of the United States. President Truman created the agency in the late 1940s. Its mission is to eavesdrop on the world's communications, looking for things of interest to the United States. At the same time, the NSA works to prevent other governments from doing the same thing to the United States. And while the CIA is prohibited by its charter from engaging in any spying activities on U.S. soil, the NSA isn't hindered by such niddling prohibitions.

The NSA conducts research in cryptography, designing secure algorithms for the United States military and designing cryptanalytic techniques to listen in on the communications of other nations. Its budget is classified, but rumored to be in excess of $20 billion, and they undoubtedly possess cryptographic expertise years ahead of the state of the art in academia. If nothing else, they have a lot of people employed in full-time research, and they have been working at it a lot longer than everyone else has. They can probably break many of the encryption algorithms proposed in academia.

The academic community's experiences with differential cryptanalysis and DES (see Chapter 2) are an excellent example of the NSA's expertise. In the mid-1970s, IBM discovered the techniques of differential cryptanalysis, and ensured that DES was secure against them. NSA classified IBM's research, and for 15 years the world had no idea why the algorithm was structured the way it was. Only after Biham and Shamir rediscovered differential cryptanalysis did we learn that DES was already optimized against it. And both IBM and the NSA claim that differential cryptanalysis was discovered even before the mid-1970s, inside the depths of the NSA. IBM discovered it a second time—Biham and Shamir a third. (Whether or not differential cryptanalysis was independently discovered any other times, by other nations' military intelligence organizations, is still an open question.)

The NSA probably has a machine to break DES. In fact, they probably have built several. Maybe they can break IDEA: Who knows? They may be able to break MD5, but almost certainly can't break SHA. I doubt they can break RSA or DSA. It is rumored that they use RSA in some of their own equipment, and they themselves proposed DSA for signing official U.S. documents.

Remember, though, that all of this is speculation. We have no proof of anything. Maybe their research isn't as advanced as they like people to think. Maybe they can break RSA. Maybe they're omnipotent, and don't have to bother with cryptanalysis at all.

The National Institute of Standards and Technology

This is NIST, formerly the National Bureau of Standards (NBS). NIST is part of the Department of Commerce, and supposedly is involved in the nonmilitary cryptographic needs of the country.

The Computer Security Act of 1987 gives NIST the authority to issue computer security standards, and to make them either optional or mandatory for the federal government. They have no authority to make standards mandatory for industry, although of course the mere existence of a government standard gives it considerable momentum within private industry.

NIST is responsible for making DES a standard. They've issued a plethora of standards regarding DES: the algorithm, different modes of operation, and key-management compatibility. Eventually they'll be the ones responsible for replacing DES with something else, when the public finally gets tired of DES's small key size. NIST is also responsible for the Digital Signature Algorithm (and the associated Digital Signature Standard), the

Secure Hash Algorithm (and the associated Secure Hash Standard), and the Clipper chip.

Opinions are mixed regarding the relationship between NIST and the NSA. Some believe that never the twain shall meet: the NSA is chartered with military cryptography, and should not have anything to do with civilian cryptography. Some believe that since the NSA has the expertise, it is perfectly reasonable for NIST to go to them for advice.

So far NIST has not proposed a standard for secure electronic mail. This would be a perfectly reasonable thing for them to do, and the only logical explanation for them not doing it is because the NSA doesn't want to encourage a proliferation of good cryptography on computer networks.

RSA Data Security, Inc.

Who are these guys, anyway? They're the company that markets the RSA algorithm. If you use the algorithm in the United States and don't pay them royalties, they are likely to be annoyed with you. If you are a major company, expect a letter from their lawyers. If you are a humble user, they'll probably leave you alone. If you run a bulletin board and distribute PGP, they may or may not bother you.

RSA Data Security, Inc. is a major partner in Public-Key Partners. They sell a variety of public-key encryption software products. They have a royalty-free implementation of the RSA algorithm available free for the asking, as long as you don't make any money from the code.

Opinions are mixed as to whether RSA Data Security, Inc. is the evil empire or just another American company trying to make a buck. Certainly they can't be held responsible for the state of the patent system in this country. If the company's officers didn't try to protect their patent rights with as much fervor as possible, they would be doing a disservice to their owners. They're a private company, by the way. On the other hand, they have done their damndest to stop the distribution of PGP. It hasn't worked. Figure they deserve at least some credit for failing.

Exporting Cryptography from the United States

Don't think for a minute that something as seditious as encryption has escaped the notice of the U.S. government. There are no rules limiting either the import or use of cryptography within the U.S., but there are significant laws restricting the export of cryptography.

According to the U.S. government, cryptography is a weapon. As such, it is covered under the same export rules that cover M-16 rifles, F-16 fighter planes, and Tomahawk cruise missiles. If you export cryptography without the proper approvals, you can be arrested as an international arms trafficker. Unless spending time in a federal penitentiary is part of your career path, pay attention to the rules.

The rules are set by the Department of State, Office of Defense Trade Controls. They have a document called the ITAR, the International Traffic in Arms Regulations. In it you'll find all the rules that you must follow if you want to legally export weapons. Much of it is legal mumbo-jumbo. Only a very small part of it relates to cryptography. I advise that you don't read it; it will only give you a headache. If you are planning on exporting cryptography, have a professional read it for you.

In practice, the rules regarding cryptography are simple enough: You can't export any encryption product that is any good. Of course the government never states the rule this way, but that's effectively what it is. If a product uses a lousy encryption algorithm that the NSA can break, they will let you export it. If a product uses DES, IDEA, RSA, or any other algorithm that the NSA can't break (or, at least, won't admit that they can break), you can't export it.

Special provisions have been made for the export of RC2 and RC4 encryption algorithms, provided that the key lengths are 40 bits or less. (Don't let anyone fool you; this means that the NSA can break RC2 and RC4 with a 40-bit key. If this were not so, they would never let the algorithms out of the country.) No one has suggested putting either of these algorithms in any electronic-mail security programs.

This means that neither PGP is PEM is exportable—legally. However, the net is very fluid; it is next-to-impossible to prevent them from being exported. Both programs have snuck out of the country, and are widely available on bulletin boards around the world. In fact, much of the current PGP development is being done outside the country, far from the reach of both the U.S. export laws and the U.S. patent laws.

But be warned. If you live outside the U.S., get your copies from a bulletin board outside the U.S. Don't ask someone inside the U.S. to send it to you. If you live inside the U.S., don't send a copy outside the country.

Yes, the laws are stupid, but it's not worth the risk.

Other Governments

Not every country has cryptography laws as bizarre as the United States. Most countries are perfectly reasonable about these things. If anything, they restrict use. There are some exceptions, though.

The Canadian government maintains significant export restrictions on cryptography that are similar to the United States'. Check with the Export Controls Division of the Special Trade Relations Bureau of the Department of External Affairs in Ottawa. Importing cryptography is not controlled.

France requires a license to import cryptography, and it has export restrictions as well. Even worse, the French government may require users of cryptography to deposit a copy of the key with them. This is true for DES-based cryptography, and may also apply to algorithms that may be as strong or stronger.

The United Kingdom, Italy, Japan, and the Netherlands have no import controls on cryptography, and no export controls on public-domain or mass-market cryptography software.

Germany has no import controls, but it does control export of both mass-market and public-domain encryption software.

And as far as I know, the following countries have no import or export controls on cryptography: Australia, Belgium, Brazil, India, Mexico, Russia, Saudi Arabia, South Africa, Spain, Sweden, and Switzerland.

As a final warning, remember that this is not a legal guide, and that I am not a lawyer. Always consult the government in question before you do something that might land you in jail.

Part **II**

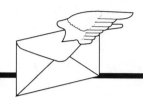

Achieving
Electronic-Mail
Privacy

Chapter 9

Requirements and Features

What do we want out of an electronic-mail security program? The quick answer is that we want it to be secure and easy to use. The long answer is quite a bit more complicated.

Requirements

Let's look at what we need an e-mail security program to provide:

- Confidentiality
- Data origin authentication
- Message integrity
- Nonrepudiation of origin
- Key management

Providing these features requires a certain toolbox. On the sender's end, we need:

Public-key encryption. The whole point of these programs is to be able to communicate securely with people without having to exchange secret keys with them first. Public-key cryptography is the only way to do this.

Digital signatures. This is the only way to provide authentication and message integrity. Again, public-key cryptography is the only way to efficiently do this.

On the receiver's end, we need:

- Public-key decryption
- Digital signature verification

Additionally, we need an entire infrastructure of public keys, so that any random Alice can send an encrypted message to any random Bob, without having to meet with him first. We need to generate and distribute keys, and some way to revoke keys that are lost or stolen.

And we need it all in an easy-to-use package that interoperates with all of the net mail systems already in existence. We need electronic-mail security to become second nature, so that everyone does it as a matter of course.

Security

First and foremost, an electronic-mail security program has to be secure. Otherwise, there's no point in using it. And as we have seen in Part I, security is a whole lot more than choosing a couple of good cryptographic algorithms.

The Chain

Security is like a chain; it is only as strong as the weakest link. In an electronic-mail security program, there are a lot of links to worry about:

- Conventional (secret-key) algorithms for data encryption (e.g.: DES)
- Public-key algorithms for key management (e.g.: RSA)
- Public-key algorithms for digital signatures (possibly a different algorithm than the one used for key management) (e.g.: RSA, DSA)
- One-way hash functions, for use with digital signatures (e.g.: SHA, MDS)
- Random-number generation, for use in generating keys for the conventional (secret-key) algorithm
- Prime-number generation, for use in generating public and private keys
- Storage of private and secret keys
- Key management procedures
- Thorough file erasure
- User interface

This isn't even an exhaustive list. If the government is going to eavesdrop on your communications, it won't be by breaking IDEA or triple-DES. They are going to exploit some weakness in an obscure section of your electronic-mail security program.

The algorithms are the easiest things to design securely. Cryptography is a mature academic discipline; several algorithms in the published literature have been analyzed by many people and are generally considered secure. Conservatives choose triple-DES; those more willing to take risks can either choose IDEA or one of several others. Implementing the algorithm without errors is harder, but still easy.

Preferences

The conventional cryptographic algorithm should support a key length of at least 112 bits. The public-key algorithm should support a key length of at least 1024 bits.

Key generation is a lot harder than choosing and implementing an algorithm. Random-number generation on a personal computer is an enormous headache. Computers are supposed to be able to do the same task over and over again. Asking them to generate a random number is like asking them to produce a wrong, and variable, answer. It is possible, but it's very difficult.

Key management is also difficult. There are a lot of possible attacks against keys, and a good system has to take them all into account. The system has to guard against false keys substituted for good ones, keys that are stolen, old keys being saved for later reuse, and perhaps a dozen other types of attacks.

Traffic analysis should be made as difficult as possible. This is a very complex problem. Except in a few specific ways, it cannot be solved solely by an electronic-mail security program.

This list isn't meant to be exhaustive, but just a reminder as to how arduous a task designing an electronic-mail security program is. Security is an elusive goal. It is much easier to break a security program than it is to prove that it can't be broken. It might be possible to prove that a given person cannot break it with a given set of resources in a given time, but that says nothing about another person with more resources and more time. Or, if that other person is the NSA, with more knowledge.

Flexibility

A good electronic-mail security program is flexible. It should allow users to send unsigned encrypted messages, signed but unencrypted messages, and signed and encrypted messages. The program should encrypt messages for storage. It should make it possible to send messages to a single receiver, or to multiple receivers.

The program should be available on all sorts of platforms. The world has no use for a MS-DOS-only or a UNIX-only security program. People who use one operating system should be able to send secure messages to people who use another system.

It is probably impossible to write one program that does everything, but it is a worthy goal. The more flexible a program is, the more useful it is. The more useful a program is, the more nearly ubiquitous it will become. The ultimate goal of any electronic-mail security program is to be ubiquitous.

Adaptability

If there's one thing we've learned from cryptography, it is that algorithms that seem secure one day can be proven insecure the next. And even if DES doesn't end up broken tomorrow, there will always be users who prefer another algorithm. Some users might be willing to sacrifice security for speed (perhaps their messages must remain secure for just minutes). Other users might be willing to take extra time for a slower, and stronger, algorithm.

Any good e-mail security program should allow for a variety of different algorithms. Some users might prefer DES, others might prefer IDEA, and others might prefer triple-DES. If the world wakes up one day and learns that one algorithm has been broken, it should be a simple matter to switch to another. It is a fine line to walk, allowing for a variety of different algorithms and having a cacophony of incompatible algorithms, but it is an important consideration.

At a minimum, I feel that an electronic-mail security program should allow for the following algorithms:

       Data Encryption Algorithm:

           Triple-DES

       Key Management Algorithm:

           ElGamal

       One-Way Hash Function:

           SHA

       Digital Signature Algorithm:

           ElGamal

Other possible algorithms, although in my opinion less ideal choices, are:

Data Encryption Algorithm:

DES

IDEA

Key Management Algorithm:

RSA

One-Way Hash Function:

MD5

Digital Signature Algorithm:

RSA

DSA

I prefer seeing ElGamal to RSA because of patent issues; ElGamal will enter the public domain in 1997. The various public-key algorithms—RSA, ElGamal, and DSA—should support keys of at least 1024 bits. I prefer triple-DES to DES because it is more secure. DES is reaching the end of its cryptographic lifetime. I prefer to see something that will be secure for a long time. I prefer triple-DES to IDEA because triple-DES has been analyzed much more extensively than IDEA. IDEA may be a good algorithm, but the smart money bets on the older, better-analyzed algorithm.

I prefer ElGamal to RSA because the patent on the former will expire in 1997. At that point, people can use it in electronic-mail security programs without any worry of patent infringement. There is, however, no security reason to choose one algorithm over the other. DSA may become a standard for digital signatures, but right now the patent and licensing issues are too muddled to make it a definitive choice.

And finally, I prefer SHA to MD5 because SHA has a longer hash value and seems to be more secure.

User Interface

If you asked an Air Force fighter pilot whether or not he wanted a new piece of equipment in his plane, he would say: "Only if it takes up no space, uses no power, and adds lift to the aircraft." Computer security is a lot like that. People want it, but only if it has no memory requirements, doesn't affect system performance, and is transparent to the user. Unfortunately, that is impossible.

Even so, we want our electronic-mail security program to get as close as possible to that goal. Sending a signed and encrypted electronic-mail message should be the default option in any program. The user should have to do extra work to send the message unsigned and unencrypted, signed and unencrypted, or to send it unsigned and encrypted. (Of course, any security program should support these options—there are valid reasons for wanting to do all three of them.)

The program should be able to produce encrypted messages that pass through all e-mail systems unchanged, and should be able to decrypt messages at the receiving end that have been through a variety of e-mail gateways. In general, this should be done with as little user intervention as possible; in the ideal case, with no user intervention.

A good user interface is even harder to achieve than good security. (Although, in the balance, I would prefer a secure program with a poor user interface over an insecure program with a good user interface.) The world of the net is filled with different computers, operating systems, mail programs and users. Everyone has his own preferences, and it is virtually impossible to make one program work well in every environment.

Chapter 10

Privacy Enhanced Mail (PEM)

PEM isn't a product, it's a standard. Technically it's a draft Internet standard, but that's a misnomer. The Internet community has learned that the way you avoid the endless debates that precede the adoption of a standard is to call it a draft—forever. PEM is a proposed standard that defines message encryption and authentication procedures in order to provide privacy-enhanced mail (PEM) services for electronic mail transfer on the Internet. It is most commonly used in conjunction with the Internet's Simple Mail Transfer Protocol (SMTP), but can be used with any electronic mail scheme (such as X.400).

PEM is intended to be compatible with a wide range of key management approaches. It has mechanisms for using conventional (secret-key) cryptography or public-key cryptography for key management (as was discussed in Chapter 3). However, since all the readily available PEM implementations use public-key cryptography for key management, that's what I'll spend most of my time on here.

The PEM specifications can be found in four Internet RFCs, reprinted in Appendix B:

> RFC 1421, Part I: Message Encryption and Authentication Procedures. This document defines message encryption and authentication procedures. These are used to enhance privacy in electronic-mail transfers on the Internet.

RFC 1422, Part II: Certificate-Based Key Management. This document defines a supporting key-management architecture and infrastructure, based on public-key certificate techniques. This provides information about the keys and how they were generated to message originators and recipients.

RFC 1423, Part III: Algorithms, Modes, and Identifiers. This document provides definitions, formats, references, and citations for cryptographic algorithms and any associated information.

RFC 1424, Part IV: Key Certification and Related Services. This document describes three services that support PEM: key certification, certificate revocation list (CRL) storage, and CRL retrieval.

"RFC" stands for "Request for Comment." The acronym belies the importance of these documents. They are not mere proposals, but are more like actual standards. (As I said above, by calling them RFCs, the documents can have the effect of standards without all of the tedious meetings, arguments, and lowest-common denominator thinking that generally surround standards organizations.)

These RFCs come from the PEM Working Group, which is part of the Internet Engineering Task Force (IETF). The IETF is, in turn, part of the Internet Architecture Board (IAB). The IAB oversees architectural issues that affect the Internet.

The final documents were published in 1993; work on the project began in 1985 as an activity of the Privacy and Security Research Group of the IAB. Much of the information in this chapter was taken from "Internet Privacy Enhanced Mail," Steven T. Kent, *Communications of the ACM*, v. 36, n. 8 (Aug 1993), pp. 48-60. It's a good technical introduction to PEM.

The PEM Environment

PEM is designed to work with existing electronic-mail systems, primarily the e-mail systems used in the Internet. (PEM also works on Compuserve, America Online, GEnie, Delphi, and most other bulletin board networks.) As such, PEM was designed to fit into existing mail system architectures. PEM messages can be created with text editors, and most mail systems don't destroy PEM messages in transit. (This could be a problem. A mail system that, for example, added space characters at the left margin would cause PEM to think that the message was tampered with in transit, and would cause PEM to decrypt it incorrectly.)

PEM is useful for a variety of security applications, in a variety of contexts, and on a variety of hardware and software platforms. The major features of PEM's design are that:

- PEM is not restricted to a particular host or operating system, but rather allows interoperability among a broad range of systems. PEM does not depend on any features of either the mail software, the operating system, the hardware, or the network.
- PEM is compatible with normal, nonsecure electronic mail. PEM has no effect on mail processing in the network.
- PEM is compatible with a range of mail systems, protocols, and user interfaces.
- PEM operations can be performed on personal computers as well as on large systems. (This is important; sometimes you may not trust a shared system with your privacy.)
- PEM supports privacy protection of e-mail addressed to mailing lists.
- PEM is compatible with a variety of key-management approaches, including (but not limited to) manual distribution, centralized key distribution based on symmetric (also known as secret-key or conventional) cryptography, and the use of public-key certificates.

Designing an electronic-mail security program with all these features is a major undertaking, and the result succeeds on all counts.

PEM Security Features

PEM provides all essential security features for e-mail users:

- Confidentiality
- Data origin authentication
- Message integrity
- Nonrepudiation of origin
- Key management

Not all of PEM's security features are necessarily part of every message. PEM messages automatically incorporate authentication, integrity, and nonrepudiation; however, confidentiality is an optional feature. It is not possible to send a PEM message without the digital signature that provides authentication of origin.

Confidentiality protects the contents of the e-mail message against unauthorized disclosure. No one other than the authorized recipient of the message can read the message. The message is protected while it is in transit—from wiretapping, misdelivery, and collection—and while it is in the recipient's mailbox waiting for the recipient to read it. After that, it is no longer necessarily protected. The recipient, of course, can do as he wishes with the unprotected message.

Data origin authentication (sometimes called originator authentication) permits someone—who could be either the authorized recipient of the message or even nonauthorized eavesdroppers who intercept the message—to verify digital signatures and reliably determine the identity of the sender. The sender is the person who *sent* the message, and may be someone entirely different from the person who *wrote* the message. For example, in the case of forwarded messages, the authentication feature identifies the forwarder of the message and not the original sender.

Message integrity gives the authorized recipient of the message (as well as nonauthorized eavesdroppers) assurance that the message has not been modified in transit. The message that the recipient received is identical to the message that the sender sent. PEM's message integrity feature is called "connectionless" because it makes no difference in what order messages are received. Other e-mail security implementations provide message integrity, but only when the messages received by the recipient are in exactly the same order as they are sent by the sender.

Authentication and message integrity are really two parts of the same thing. Together they tell the recipient who wrote the message. Nothing is gained by knowing that the message was not tampered with in transit if you don't know who actually sent it. And there is no point in knowing that a message originally came from a particular person, if you have no assurance that the message was not modified in transit.

Nonrepudiation of origin is a feature that allows someone to verify the identity of the original sender of a forwarded message. That is, Alice can send Bob a message. Bob can take that message and send it on to Carol. Using PEM's authentication and integrity features, Carol can verify that Bob sent her the message. However, using PEM's nonrepudiation feature, Carol can also verify that Alice sent the original message to Bob.

Cryptographic Algorithms

PEM can use a variety of cryptographic algorithms: public-key algorithms for key management, conventional algorithms for data encryption, and public-key digital signature algorithms and one-way hash functions for digital signatures. "Can use" is important; PEM does not require any particular algorithms.

PEM provides the means to identify which algorithms are used for each message for each recipient. Currently a particular suite of algorithms are identified for use by PEM, but the standard allows for the use of different algorithms. The designers hope that new algorithms will also be grouped into suites; otherwise there could easily be too many different combinations of algorithms used by different people. A given sender and receiver might not have the same algorithms. It is certainly possible for an implementation of PEM to allow users to switch among algorithms.

The current suite of encryption algorithms, defined in RFC 1423 (see Appendix B) are:

> Data Encryption Algorithm:
>> DES in Cipher Block Chaining mode
>
> Key-Management Algorithms:
>> DES in Electronic Codebook mode
>>
>> DES in Cipher Block Chaining mode
>>
>> RSA
>
> Message Integrity Check Algorithms:
>> RSA and MD2
>>
>> RSA and MD5
>
> Digital Signature Algorithms:
>> RSA and MD2
>>
>> RSA and MD5

DES has a 56-bit key, and PEM's triple-DES uses two DES keys for a total key length of 112 bits. The standard does not specify key lengths for the RSA keys; the level of security is up to the different implementations.

It is possible to use PEM without public-key cryptography at all. That is, you could use DES for key management. Of course, if you do, you lose the benefits of using public-key cryptography which we saw in Chapter 3. All of the key-management problems that public-key algorithms like RSA solve come back to haunt anyone who uses this option. Even so, it is an option. If your particular implementation of PEM has a DES option for key management, I recommend ignoring it and sticking with RSA as a key-management algorithm.

In addition to specifying cryptographic algorithms, the PEM standards provide a framework for public keys and public-key certification. This framework will be discussed in detail later on in the chapter.

Types of Messages

There are three different types of PEM messages:

- MIC-CLEAR
- MIC-ONLY
- ENCRYPTED

Each type of message offers the user a different combination of features.

A MIC-CLEAR message provides integrity and authentication, but no confidentiality. The message is sent unencrypted. Anyone can read the message, but PEM users will also be able to verify the authenticity of the message. This option is useful for sending messages to a Usenet newsgroup, for example. Both PEM and non-PEM users can read the message, and the authentication is there for PEM users to verify the signature if they wish.

A MIC-ONLY message is the same as a MIC-CLEAR message, but has an additional encoding step. This encoding allows PEM messages to pass through various electronic-mail gateways: It is similar to the "uuencode" command in UNIX. Some electronic-mail gateways might modify the signature information of a PEM message in a way that invalidates the integrity and authenticity checks (perhaps by adding carriage-returns or indenting lines). A MIC-ONLY message prevents this.

Finally, an ENCRYPTED message has all the features of a MIC-CLEAR message—integrity, authentication—with the addition of confidentiality. Only the intended recipients of an ENCRYPTED message can read it. Eavesdroppers cannot read the message, but they can use PEM to verify the origination and integrity of the message. ENCRYPTED messages also have the same encoding as MIC-ONLY messages.

A PEM Message

To create a PEM message (actually, a normal message protected by PEM), you have to go through a series of steps. Basically, two different sources of data go into a PEM message: message header and message content. The message header becomes part of the electronic-mail header of the final message. (The mail header is what your mailer uses to send your mail to its destination. The message header is what PEM uses.) This remains unencrypted, and largely bypasses PEM processing. It is used by the electronic-mail program to deliver the message to its intended recipient.

PEM specifies a particular line separating this header from the PEM message. The line appears:

```
- - - - BEGIN PRIVACY-ENHANCED MESSAGE - - - -
```

Then comes the PEM message. Figure 10.1 shows an encrypted message using symmetric key (or secret key) management, Figures 10.2 and 10.3 shows an authenticated and encrypted message using public-key key management, and Figure 10.4 shows an authenticated (but unencrypted) message using public-key key management.

The rest of this section explains the message formats, line by line. Feel free to skip it if you don't want to get bogged down in the details.

```
---- BEGIN PRIVACY-ENHANCED MESSAGE ----
Proc-Type: 4,ENCRYPTED
Content-Domain: RFC822
DEK-Info: DES-CBC,F8143EDE5960C597
Originator-ID-Symmetric: schneier@chinet.com,,
Recipient-ID-Symmetric: schneier@chinet.com,ptf-kmc,3
Key-Info: DES-ECB,RSA-
MD2,9FD3AAD2F2691B9A,B70665BB9BF7CBCDA60195DB94F727D3
Recipient-ID-Symmetric: pem-dev@tis.com,ptf-kmc,4
Key-Info: DES-ECB,RSA-
MD2,161A3F75DC82EF26,E2EF532C65CBCFF79F83A2658132DB47

LLrHBOeJzyhP+/fSStdW8okeEnv47jxe7SJ/iN72ohNcUk2jHEUSoH1nvNSIWL9M

8tEjmF/zxB+bATMtPjCUWbz8Lr9wloXIkjHU1BLpvXROUrUzYbkNpkOagV2IzUpk

J6UiRRGcDSvzrsoK+oNvqu6z7Xs5Xfz5rDquUcM1K1Z6720dcBWGGsDLpTpSCnpot
dXd/H5LMDWnonNvPCwQUHt==
---- END PRIVACY-ENHANCED MESSAGE ----
```

Figure 10.1 Example encapsulated message using symmetric (secret-key) cryptography.

```
---- BEGIN PRIVACY-ENHANCED MESSAGE ----
Proc-Type: 4,ENCRYPTED
Content-Domain: RFC822
DEK-Info: DES-CBC,BFF968AA74691AC1
Originator-Certificate:

MIIB1TCCAScCAWUwDQYJKoZIhvcNAQECBQAwUTELMAkGA1UEBhMCVVMxIDAeBgNV

BAoTF1JTQSBEYXRhIFN1Y3VyaXR5LCBJbmMuMQ8wDQYDVQQLEwZCZXRhIDExDzAN

BgNVBAsTBk5PVEFSWTAeFw05MTA5MDQxODM4MTdaFw05MzA5MDMxODM4MTZaMEUx
```

Figure 10.2 Example encapsulated ENCRYPTED message using Public-key cryptography.

CzAJBgNVBAYTAlVTMSAwHgYDVQQKExdSU0EgRGF0YSBTZWN1cml0eSwgSW5jLjEU

MBIGA1UEAxMLVGVzdCBVc2VyIDEwWTAKBgRVCAEBAgICAANLADBIAkEAwHZH17i+

yJcqDtjJCowzTdBJrdAiLAnSC+CnnjOJELyuQiBgkGrgIh3j8/xOfM+YrsyFlu3F

LZPVtzlndhYFJQIDAQABMAOGCSqGSIb3DQEBAgUAAlkACKrOPqphJYwlj+YPtcIq

iWlFPuN5jJ79Khfg7ASFxskYkEMjRNZV/HZDZQEhtVaU7Jxfzs2wfX5byMp2X3U/
5XUXGx7qusDgHQGs7Jk9W8CWlfuSWUgN4w==
Key-Info: RSA,

I3rRIGXUGWAF8js5wCzRTkdhO34PTHdRZY9Tuvm03M+NM7fx6qc5udixps2LngO+
wGrtiUm/ovtKdinz6ZQ/aQ==
Issuer-Certificate:

MIIB3DCCAUgCAQowDQYJKoZIhvcNAQECBQAwTzELMAkGA1UEBhMCVVMxIDAeBgNV

BAoTF1JTQSBEYXRhIFN1Y3VyaXR5LCBJbmMuMQ8wDQYDVQQLEwZCZXRhIDExDTAL

BgNVBAsTBFRMQOEwHhcNOTEwOTAxMDgwMDAwWhcNOTIwOTAxMDclOTU5WjBRMQsw

CQYDVQQGEwJVUzEgMB4GA1UEChMXU1NBIERhdGEgU2VjdXJpdHksIEluYy4xDzAN

BgNVBAsTBkJldGEgMTEPMAOGA1UECxMGTk9UQVJZMHAwCgYEVQgBAQICArwDYgAw

XwJYCsnp6lQCxYykNlODwutF/jMJ3kL+3PjYyHOwk+/9rLg6X65B/LD4bJHtO5XW

cqAz/7R7XhjYCmOPcqbdzoACZtIlETrKrcJiDYoP+DkZ8klgCk7hQHpbIwIDAQAB

MAOGCSqGSIb3DQEBAgUAA38AAICPv4f9Gx/tY4+p+4DB7MV+tKZnvBoy8zgoMGOx

dD2jMZ/3HsyWKWgSFOeH/AJB3qr9zosG47pyMnTf3aSy2nBO7CMxpUWRBcXUpE+x

EREZd9++32ofGBIXaialnOgVUnOOzSYgugiQO77nJLDUjOhQehCizEs5wUJ35a5h
MIC-Info: RSA-MD5,RSA,

Figure 10.2 (con't.)

```
UdFJR8u/TIGhfH65ieewe2lOW4tooa3vZCvVNGBZirf/7nrgzWDABz8w9NsXSexv
 AjRFbHoNPzBuxwmOAFeAOHJszL4yBvhG
 Recipient-ID-Asymmetric:
MFExCzAJBgNVBAYTAlVTMSAwHgYDVQQKExdSU0EgRGFOYSBTZWN1cml0eSwgSW5j
 LjEPMAOGA1UECxMGQmVOYSAxMQ8wDQYDVQQLEwZOT1RBU1k=,
 66
 Key-Info: RSA,

O6BS1ww9CTyHPtS3bMLD+LOhejdvX6Qv1HK2ds2sQPEaXhX8EhvVphHYTjwekdWv
 7xOZ3Jx2vTAhOYHMcqqCjA==

qeWlj/YJ2Uf5ng9yznPbtDOmYloSwIuV9FRYx+gzY+8iXd/NQrXHfi6/MhPfPF3d
 jIqCJAxvld2xgqQimUzoS1a4r7kQQ5c/Iua4LqKeq3ciFzEv/MbZhA==
 ---- END PRIVACY-ENHANCED MESSAGE ----
```

Figure 10.2 (con't.)

```
    ---- BEGIN PRIVACY-ENHANCED MESSAGE ----
  Proc-Type: 4,MIC-ONLY
  Content-Domain: RFC822
  Originator-Certificate:

MIIB1TCCAScCAWUwDQYJKoZIhvcNAQECBQAwUTELMAkGA1UEBhMCVVMxIDAeBgNV

BAoTF1JTQSBEYXRhIFN1Y3VyaXR5LCBJbmMuMQ8wDQYDVQQLEwZCZXRhIDExDzAN

BgNVBAsTBk5PVEFSWTAeFw05MTA5MDQxODM4MTdaFw05MzA5MDMxODM4MTZaMEUx

CzAJBgNVBAYTAlVTMSAwHgYDVQQKExdSU0EgRGFOYSBTZWN1cml0eSwgSW5jLjEU

MBIGA1UEAxMLVGVzdCBVc2VyIDEwWTAKBgRVCAEBAgICAANLADBIAkEAwHZH17i+

yJcqDtjJCowzTdBJrdAiLAnSC+CnnjOJELyuQiBgkGrgIh3j8/xOfM+YrsyF1u3F

LZPVtzlndhYFJQIDAQABMAOGCSqGSIb3DQEBAgUAA1kACKrOPqphJYw1j+YPtcIq
```

**Figure 10.3 Example encapsulated MIC-ONLY message using
Public-key cryptography.**

```
iWlFPuN5jJ79Khfg7ASFxskYkEMjRNZV/HZDZQEhtVaU7Jxfzs2wfX5byMp2X3U/
   5XUXGx7qusDgHQGs7Jk9W8CW1fuSWUgN4w==
Issuer-Certificate:

MIIB3DCCAUgCAQowDQYJKoZIhvcNAQECBQAwTzELMAkGA1UEBhMCVVMxIDAeBgNV

BAoTF1JTQSBEYXRhIFN1Y3VyaXR5LCBJbmMuMQ8wDQYDVQQLEwZCZXRhIDExDTAL

BgNVBAsTBFRMQOEwHhcNOTEwOTAxMDgwMDAwWhcNOTIwOTAxMDc1OTU5WjBRMQsw

CQYDVQQGEwJVUzEgMB4GA1UEChMXU1NBIERhdGEgU2VjdXJpdHksIE1uYy4xDzAN

BgNVBAsTBkJldGEgMTEPMAOGA1UECxMGTk9UQVJZMHAwCgYEVQgBAQICArwDYgAw

XwJYCsnp61QCxYykN1ODwutF/jMJ3kL+3PjYyHOwk+/9rLg6X65B/LD4bJHtO5XW

cqAz/7R7XhjYCmOPcqbdzoACZtI1ETrKrcJiDYoP+DkZ8k1gCk7hQHpbIwIDAQAB

MAOGCSqGSIb3DQEBAgUAA38AAICPv4f9Gx/tY4+p+4DB7MV+tKZnvBoy8zgoMGOx

dD2jMZ/3HsyWKWgSFOeH/AJB3qr9zosG47pyMnTf3aSy2nBO7CMxpUWRBcXUpE+x

EREZd9++32ofGBIXaialnOgVUnOOzSYgugiQO77nJLDUjOhQehCizEs5wUJ35a5h
   MIC-Info: RSA-MD5,RSA,

jV20fH+nnXHU8bnL8kPAad/mSQ1TDZ1bVuxvZAOVRZ5q5+Ej15bQvqNeqOUNQjr6
   EtE7K2QDeVMCyXsdJ1A8fA==

LSBBIG11c3NhZ2UgZm9yIHVzZSBpbiBOZXN0aW5nLgOKLSBGb2xsb3dpbmcgaXMg
       YSBibGFuayBsaW51Og0KDQpUaG1zIG1zIHRoZSBlbmQuDQo=
----- END PRIVACY-ENHANCED MESSAGE -----
```

Figure 10.3 (con't.)

Fields

Here's an explanation of the message header: The first field of the message header is "Proc-Type," and identifies the type of processing performed on the message whether MIC-CLEAR, MIC-ONLY, or ENCRYPTED. The "ENCRYPTED"

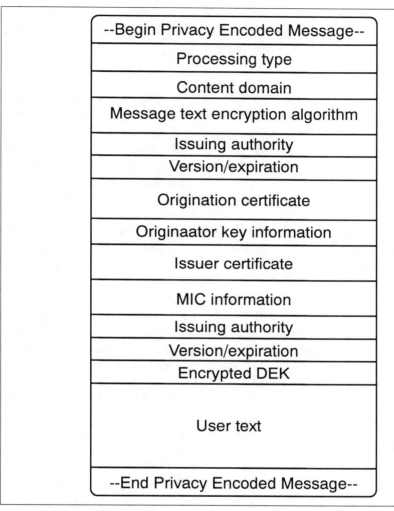

Figure 10.4 A PEM message (asymmetric case).

specifier signifies that the message is encrypted and authenticated. The "MIC-ONLY" and "MIC-CLEAR" specifiers indicate that the message is signed, but not encrypted. MIC-CLEAR messages are not encoded, and can be read using non-PEM software. MIC-ONLY messages must be transformed to a human-readable form before being read, so PEM software is needed. A PEM message is always signed; it is optionally encrypted.

The next field, "Content-Domain," has nothing to do with security. It specifies the type of canonicalization used in the mail message. This will be discussed in the next section.

The "DEK-Info" field specifies information pertaining to the Data Exchange Key (DEK), the encryption algorithm used to encrypt the text and any parameters associated with that algorithim. Only one algorithm is currently specified: DES in CBC mode. Look for "DES-CBC." The subfield that follows DES-CBS specifies the Initialization Vector (IV) used by the algorithm. Other algorithms may be specified by PEM in the future; their use will be noted in the DEK-Info and other fields which identify algorithms.

For messages with symmetric (secret-key) key management (key management using DES), the next field is "Originator-ID-Symmetric." It has three subfields. The first subfield identifies the sender by a unique electronic mail address. The second subfield is optional, and identifies the authority that issued the interchange key. The third subfield is also optional; it is the Version/Expiration subfield.

Continuing with the symmetric key management case, the next fields deal with the recipients. Each recipient has two fields: "Recipient-ID-Symmetric" and "Key-Info." The "Recipient-ID-Symmetric" field has three subfields; it identifies the receiver in the same way that "Originator-ID-Symmetric" identified the sender.

The "Key-Info" field, with its four subfields, specifies the key management parameters. The first subfield specifies the algorithm used to encrypt the DEK. Since the key management in this message is symmetric, the sender and receiver have to share a common key. This is called the Interchange Key (IK), and is used to encrypt the DEK. The DEK can either be encrypted using DES in Electronic Codebook Mode—denoted by "DES-ECB"—or triple-DES: denoted by "DES-EDE," for DES-Encrypt-Decrypt-Encrypt. The second subfield specifies the MIC algorithm. It can either be MD2, denoted by "RSA-MD2"; or MD5—denoted by "RSA-MD5." The third subfield is the DEK, encrypted with the IK. The fourth field is the MIC, also encrypted with the IK.

For messages with public-key (asymmetric) key management (RSA), the headers are different. After the "DEK-Info" field is the "Originator-Certificate" field. The certificate follows the X.509 standard. The next field, with its two subfields, is "Key-Info." The first subfield specifies the public-key algorithm used to encrypt the DEK; currently PEM only supports RSA. The next subfield is the DEK, encrypted in the originator's public key. This is an optional field, intended to permit the originator to decrypt his own message in the event that it is returned by the mail system. The next field, "Issuer-Certificate," is the certificate of whoever signed the Originator-Certificate.

Continuing with the asymmetric key management case, the next field is "MIC-Info." The first subfield specifies the algorithm under which the one-way hash (called a MIC) was computed. The second subfield specifies the algorithm under which the MIC was signed. The third subfield consists of the MIC, signed by the sender's private key.

Still continuing with asymmetric (or public-key) key management, the next fields deal with the recipients. There are two fields for each recipient: "Recipient-ID-Asymmetric" and "Key-Info." The "Recipient-ID-Asymmetric" field has two subfields. The first identifies the authority that issued the receiver's public key; the second is an optional Version/Expiration subfield.

The "Key-Info" field specifies the key management parameters. The first subfield identifies the algorithm used to encrypt the message; the second subfield is the DEK, encrypted with the receiver's public key.

Sending a PEM Message

Sending a PEM message involves four steps:

1. Canonicalization
2. Message integrity and originator authentication
3. Encryption (optional)
4. Transmission encoding (optional)

As a user, you really don't have to worry about the steps and how they work. Just tell the PEM program what type of message you are sending and, if you are using encryption, who you are sending the message to, and the program does the rest. The rest of this section is for those interested in peeking at PEM's inner workings.

Every PEM message does not follow each step. A MIC-CLEAR message only follows steps 1 and 2. A MIC-ONLY message follows steps 1, 2, and 4. An ENCRYPTED message follows steps 1 through 4.

Canonicalization

This first step translates the message from whatever representation the particular word processor or mail program uses to a common representation, one that is standard across every platform and every machine on the network. A message sent by Alice from one computer might be received by Bob using a completely different computer platform. The PEM standard wants to make sure that Bob can read Alice's message.

For example, different computers handle new lines differently: MS-DOS uses a carriage-return and a line-feed, while the Macintosh just uses a line feed. (Many MS-DOS programs can handle a line-feed only or a carriage-return only, but virtually no Macintosh programs can handle carriage-return and line-feed. Go figure.) Sometimes tabs are converted to spaces as files transfer from one computer to another. If canonicalization were omitted, then every computer would have to implement specialized translation features for every other type of computer. Translating every computer's output into a standard representation avoids this problem.

E-mail systems often do this sort of thing anyway, but PEM has to do it first. The reason is that the various PEM security features—authentication and encryption—require the message to be unchanged in transmission. Any changes to the message content that occur after the digital signature is created will invalidate the signature. And if the message is modified after encryption, it will not decrypt correctly at the other end: The message will be just as unintelligible to the receiver as it would be to an eavesdropper.

PEM allows for different canonicalization transformations for different messaging environments. (This is what the "Content-Domain" field in the PEM message format is for.) On the Internet, you will be using the same canonicalization employed by the Simple Mail Transfer Protocol (SMTP), the same one that you normally use for electronic mail. This transformation is specified in RFC 822. Currently, it is the only transformation specified in the PEM documents.

Message Integrity and Originator Authentication

Now we're starting to deal with security. This step begins with the calculation of the hash value (called a MIC). This is the code that tells the receiver that the message has not been modified in transit.

The PEM standard allows for a choice of MIC algorithms; currently two are specified in the PEM documents. The particular algorithm used is specified in the PEM header. I recommend using MD5 and ignoring MD2; MD5 is much more secure.

The MIC is calculated based on the canonicalized version of the message, so that it can be verified in any computing environment. (Remember, if PEM didn't do it this way, the MIC might be invalid solely on the basis of differences between computers.) This value is stored in the PEM header.

To provide both authentication of the sender and integrity of the message (and to support nonrepudiation with proof of origin), the MIC must be protected in some manner that binds it to the message originator. That is, there must be something about the MIC that shows that it was created by the same person who created the message, and not by someone else.

If this were not done, spoofing attacks would be successful. Remember spoofing? Alice sends a message to Bob. Bob modifies the message and sends it to Carol, but claims that it comes unmodified from Alice. With some message integrity algorithms, Bob's tampering would go unnoticed by Carol; she would believe that the message was sent, unmodified, by Alice. PEM's algorithms prevent this; if Bob were to try it, the MIC would be invalid and Carol would know that the message was not sent by Alice.

Digital Signatures

Digital signatures solve this problem. The MIC is signed by the message sender. This digital signature can be verified by any receiver—and any eavesdropper—but cannot be forged. Thus in the above example, Bob would not be able to forge Alice's signature in the message he is trying to fool Carol with.

Again, the PEM format allows for a variety of digital signature algorithms, and the particular algorithm used is specified in the "MIC-INFO" field. Currently, the standard only specifies the use of the RSA algorithm. Future versions of PEM might also allow for DSA.

To allow the receiver to verify the MIC value and the identity of the sender, the PEM header must include the sender's public-key certificate. (This assumes that the sender is using public-key cryptography, which is a reasonable assumption.) This certificate will be used by the receiver to verify the signature. The sender must also include one or more Issuer-Certificates in the header; these will be used to verify the sender's certificate. (This will be discussed in more detail in the section on verifying certificates.) PEM implementations will automatically include all the certificates necessary to verify the MIC value.

Note that just because the sender signed the MIC doesn't mean that it is secure. Anyone—the authorized receiver, an eavesdropper—can verify the signature and recover the MIC. This information does not allow an eavesdropper to work backwards and reconstruct the message, but it does give her some information.

Imagine that Eve has intercepted a message from Alice. It is encrypted, so she can't read the contents. However, she can make a guess at the contents and then try to verify the signature. If her guess is correct, then the verification is successful. If her guess is incorrect, then the verification is unsuccessful. If there are only a few possible messages, Eve can use this trick to figure out what they are—without having to decrypt the message.

PEM solves this potential problem. If the message is encrypted, then the MIC is also encrypted (using the same key). Now, Eve cannot verify candidate messages.

Also, since the value of the MIC is usually binary, it could have the same representation problems as the message. To prevent these problems, it is encoded for transmission with the same algorithm as is an encrypted message. (This will be discussed in a few paragraphs.)

Encryption

The third step is encryption. It is optional; PEM only encrypts messages if the type is "ENCRYPTED." The PEM standards can support multiple encryption algorithms, but currently specify just one: DES in Cipher Block Chaining mode. The algorithm is specified in the "DEK-Info" field of the message header, along with any data that the algorithm needs. "DES-CBC" specifies DES in Cipher Block Chaining mode, and the string of characters afterward specifies the Initialization Vector (IV).

Encryption is itself a multi-stage process. First, the message is padded so that it is a multiple of eight blocks long. (Remember, DES processes data in 8-byte blocks.) Then a unique random-encryption key is generated, as well as a unique and random IV. Finally, the message is encrypted using the key and IV.

The message has been encrypted, but it is encrypted with a random key that only the sender knows. In order for her to transfer that key to the receiver, she needs to use public-key cryptography. Using the RSA algorithm, she encrypts the message encryption key with the receiver's public key. (Again, it is possible to use other algorithms, but RSA is currently the only algorithm defined in the PEM documents for this purpose.) In this way, the random message-encryption key is protected so that only the authorized receiver can read it. The encrypted key is in the "Key-Info" field, and the name of the authorized receiver is in the "Recipient-ID-Asymmetric" field.

Even if the message has multiple receivers, it is encrypted only once. A copy of the message-encryption key is encrypted once for each authorized recipient. Each copy of the message-encryption key is protected so that only one authorized receiver can read it. In such a case, there would be multiple "Recipient-ID-Asymmetric" fields in the PEM header, each followed by a different "Key-Info" field. Each pair of these PEM header fields provides the information required for a receiver to decrypt the message.

The information in the "Recipient-ID-Asymmetric" field is the name of the person who issued the receiver's public-key certificate and the serial number of that certificate, a combination that uniquely identifies the recipient.

PEM also allows for key distribution without public-key cryptography—although I know of no instances where this is being used. In this case, the message is still encrypted with a random message-encryption key, and the key is encrypted with a conventional algorithm once for each recipient. If different recipients use different key-distribution algorithms, PEM can handle this as well. There is no reason why each Key-Info field has to be encrypted in the same way.

Encoding

The last step involved in sending a PEM message is encoding it for transmission. This step is optional; only ENCRYPTED and MIC-ONLY messages are encoded. Most electronic-mail systems are designed to handle text messages and not binary messages. An encrypted message is binary, and hence may be inadvertently modified in transit. Any modification will make the message decrypt to nonsense at the receiving end, and so must be encoded to avoid transmission problems.

The specific encoding scheme is another PEM parameter, and can be modified. Currently PEM supports an encoding scheme that transforms the (optionally) encrypted message into a 6-bit alphabet. This encoding is compatible with the SMTP canonicalization in the first step, and is also compatible with most electronic-mail gateways to the Internet. If the message has been encrypted, this encoding transforms the 8-bit binary ciphertext into a form that can be transmitted over the Internet without modification.

Even if the message has not been encrypted, this encoding step is important. It ensures—well, it doesn't ensure, but it makes it pretty likely—that the message will not be modified as a result of transmission. Such modification generally goes unnoticed in normal messages, but it will invalidate integrity and authentication in PEM messages. A change as little as one bit of the message content would cause the MIC check to fail at the receiving end. As I said previously, MIC-CLEAR messages are not encoded.

And that's it. The PEM message is then encapsulated so that it won't get modified by the mail system while in transit, and sent to its destination or destinations, via whatever electronic-mail program you are using.

Receiving a PEM Message

Receiving and processing a PEM message is an equally complicated undertaking. Luckily, the PEM implementations take care of all the details; the user doesn't really have to worry about any of these steps.

When PEM software receives a PEM message, it first scans the message to find the PEM message boundary, and then looks through the PEM header to find out which version of PEM was used to process the message. Then it proceeds to deal with the message.

Decoding

If the message is of either type ENCRYPTED or MIC-ONLY, the first step is to invert the encoding step at the sender's end. If the message is encrypted, the 6-bit encoding is inverted back into 8-bit ciphertext. If the message is not encrypted, then the 6-bit encoding is inverted back to the canonical plaintext.

Decrypting

If the message is of type ENCRYPTED, PEM has to decrypt the message. The receiver's PEM software scans the PEM header to locate the Recipient-ID-

Asymmetric field that uniquely identifies him. (Remember, in the case of multiple receivers, there may be multiple Recipient-ID-Asymmetric fields, one for each authorized receiver.) Then the recipient examines the next field, the Key-Info field. The first subfield here specifies the message-encryption algorithm used, and the second subfield is the encrypted key. Assuming public-key cryptography is being used for key distribution, the receiver uses his private key to decrypt the encrypted key to recover the message-encryption key.

The DEK-Info field, which appears earlier in the PEM header, specifies the encryption algorithm, mode, and any necessary parameters. Since the only mode PEM currently supports is DES in CBC mode, the recipient can now use the message key he just decrypted with the IV in the DEK-Info field to decrypt the message text.

After decryption, the message content is now at the same processing status as a MIC-ONLY or a MIC-CLEAR message. The rest of the section applies to all three message types.

Verifying Message Integrity and Authenticity

The receiver first checks the PEM header to determine which MIC algorithm and signature algorithm is used for this message. (Remember, the receiver doesn't do this manually; his software does it automatically.) Assuming that the sender used RSA as a digital signature algorithm (a good assumption), the receiver gets the public key of the sender from the originator certificate field and decrypts the signed MIC value.

Finally, the receiver computes the MIC on the canonical form of the message, and then compares this value with the value he just decrypted. If they match, then the message has been authenticated. If they do not, the receiver knows that the message has either been deliberately tampered with or has been mangled in transmission.

To really identify the sender, the receiver must examine not only the sender's certificate, but also the certificates of the person that certified the sender, the certificate of the person that certified that person, etc. The PEM standards allow including all of those certificates with the message, but that doesn't always happen in practice. It would make messages far too long. Instead people are expected to save certificates locally for use later.

Translation

Finally, after verifying message integrity and authenticity, the canonical form of the message is translated into whatever representation is proper for the receiver's system, and is then displayed for the receiver to read. The receiver's PEM system informs him that the message integrity has been verified, and it displays the authenticated sender's identity. This displayed identity should include both the originator's name from his certificate, and an indication of the policy under which that certificate was validated (see the section on X.509 public-key certificates). Note that this identity is independent of the identity contained within the message; i.e., the value in the "From" field. It will usually be the same, but it does not have to be.

Message Disposition

After the receiver has read the PEM message, he has a number of options. He can store the message in decrypted, decanonicalized form, with none of the PEM headers. He can store the message in decrypted, canonical form, along with the PEM header fields needed for signature verification: MIC-Info, Originator-ID-Asymmetric, Originator-Certificate, and Issuer-Certificate. This form of storage works if the receiver wants to forward a signed message to a third party, and also provides protection against modification while the message is being stored. If the receiver wants to protect the confidentiality of the message, he can choose to save the message in encrypted form.

X.509 Public-Key Certificates

A public-key certificate is a specialized data structure used to securely bind a public key to a bunch of attributes. This identifies Alice as a person with a public key. Her certificate is her public key, her name, and some other information about her, all collected together and signed by a trusted person (a Certification Authority, or CA, in PEM lingo). Anybody else in the PEM universe can verify the CA's signature and be assured that the key belongs to Alice.

PEM uses certificates that conform to the X.509 standard. These certificates bind a public key to a directory name (also known as a unique Internet address), and identify the issuer of the certificate. The whole thing is signed much like a regular PEM message—the canonicalization rules are different. The following paragraphs explain the different parts of the certificate in detail.

The "Version" field differentiates between successive versions of the certificate format. The initial value identifies the 1988 version, the only version adopted by PEM to date. Sometime in the future a new certificate version may be defined; until then, this field is always "0".

The "Serial Number" field uniquely identifies this certificate among those issued by a particular issuer. This provides a quick and easy way of identifying a certificate relative to an issuer.

The "Signature" field identifies the digital signature algorithm used to sign the certificate. Right now, two signature algorithms are defined: RSA with MD2, and RSA with MD5. (Also, the size of the RSA key is variable.) This field also specifies any parameters the algorithms require.

The "Issuer" is the name of the person who signed the certificate. The "Subject" is the name of the person whose certificate this is. The "Validity" field contains a pair of dates: the certificate is valid only after the first date and before the second.

And finally, the subject's public key is in the "Subject Public Key Info" field.

The issuer signs this whole construct, using the signature algorithm specified in the "Signature" field and his own private key. Then he attaches his signature to the end of the construct. That's the certificate.

To validate the certificate, all a user has to do is to verify the issuer's signature, much in the same way that a receiver verifies the signature on an incoming message.

A user, Bob, still needs to trust that signature. If you remember, Bob's problem with getting Alice's public key is that he needs a way to be sure that it actually belongs to Alice, and not to someone who is trying to fool him. This certificate protocol ensures that Bob trusts Alice's public key, but only as much as he trusts the public key of Alice's issuer. Now, the issuer also has a certificate, and for Bob to trust that he has to trust the public key of Alice's issuer's issuer. And so on, up the chain of issuers.

In the PEM world, there is one common issuer that sits at the top of every chain. Eventually, Bob will find that issuer, or a lower common issuer that both Alice and Bob share. Presumably Bob already trusts this issuer, since the issuer is also in Bob's certification path. Bob can then validate the signatures back down the chain to Alice.

Certificate Revocation

A certificate, like a credit card, does not remain valid forever. The "Validity" field specifies exactly when it expires. It may also be revoked by the issuer if the binding between the subject and the public key is no longer valid. For example, the "Subject" field may identify the subject as holding a particular job in a company. If he changes jobs, then the certificate is no longer valid. Or, the subject may have defrauded the issuer into signing a bogus certificate. Or, the subject's private key may be compromised. Or, the issuer's private key

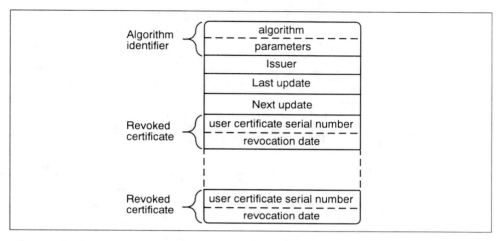

Figure 10.5 PEM certificate revocation list.

may have been compromised. Whatever happened, there must be a mechanism where a key is marked as no longer valid.

PEM has special mechanisms to handle certificate revocation. The PEM specification defines a Certificate Revocation List (CRL) to spread information about revoked certificates (see Figure 10.5). (The X.509 specification for public-key ˜ertificates also defines a CRL, but the PEM definition is slightly different.) A CRL is a special message, signed by its issuer. It consists of the issuer's name, the date the CRL is generated, and a sequence of pairs, each consisting of a certificate serial number and a date at which the certificate was revoked. This CRL is spread far and wide across the net.

So, when a receiver validates a certificate, he has to check that the certificate is not listed on a CRL. This is similar to a merchant checking a credit card against a "hot list" of bad numbers.

The PEM Public-Key Certification Framework

The PEM certification framework conforms to the CCITT X.509 standard (as do the certificates themselves). The framework is very general, incorporating everything from strictly hierarchical systems to distributed systems (PGP-like systems could conform to this standard, but its rigid hierarchy is contrary to the flavor of PGP). PEM's certification framework is a subset of the X.509 standard; it is hierarchical, but with some modifications to deal with the real world.

PEM's certification framework accommodates a wide range of trust policies, but imposes constraints to facilitate uniformity across mail systems. In particular,

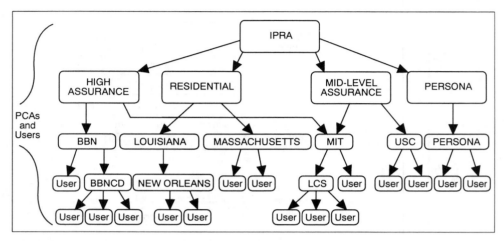

Figure 10.6 PEM certification hierachy.

the framework permits automated certificate validation with minimal user interaction, yet it ensures that users can easily interpret the results.

The framework is based on the concept of a certification authority (CA). According to the X.509 documents, a CA is "an authority trusted by one or more users to create and assign certificates." In PEM, CAs are the people who sign certificates.

These CAs are organized in a single tree (see Figure 10.6). At the top is the Internet PCA Registration Authority (IPRA); it will operate under the auspices of the Internet Society, a nonprofit, professional organization that promotes use of Internet technology around the world. The IPRA not only will provide that common reference point from which all certification chains stem, it also will set policy for PEM certifications.

The IPRA will issue certificates to a second tier of entities, called Policy Certification Authorities (PCAs). The IPRA will be responsible for registering the PCAs. Each PCA must file a document describing its policies with the IRPA. The IRPA will then sign and distribute that statement; any user will be able to get a signed copy of the policy statement of any PCA.

The IPRA will have other functions, as well. (Actually, this entity does not exist yet, but the idea is that it will operate under the auspices of the Internet Society.) It will make sure that all PCA and CA names are unique, and will manage all certificate revocation lists.

There is only one IPRA, but there are several PCAs. Each PCA can have different policies for the registration of users. One may require a government ID before registration; another may only require a name. The goal is for there to be a small number of different PCAs, each with a substantially different policy. In this way, different users can have different certification strengths.

PCAs, in turn, issue certificates to CAs. Three different types of CAs are identified for PEM:

Organizational. This is the obvious one. Company A is allowed to issue certificates for its employees. This grouping includes companies, government organizations, academic institutions, and professional societies.

Residential. Alternatively, users may receive certificates based on where they live. A CA might be run by a local government, and would issue certificates to anyone living in a certain geographical area.

Personal. Finally, users could register just based on a name (perhaps even a pseudonym). Of course, the user would also have to get an anonymous or aliased mailbox, but this type of certification would allow users to remain anonymous while still taking advantage of the security features of PEM.

CAs issue certificates to other CAs, or to individuals. This is where the majority of certification goes on. There is only one IPRA and only a few PCAs, but there can be an enormous number of CAs. It is possible for a single CA to be certified by a number of PCAs (perhaps a CA wishes to issue certificates based on the policies of two different PCAs).

Names

Everyone in the PEM world has a name, called a *distinguished name* (DN). The name is distinguished not because it is important, but because it is unique. PEM doesn't use a person's Internet address as his name; it follows the X.500 directory standard.

The X.500 directory standard provides a format for not only naming individuals, but also organizations, roles, devices, mailing lists, and so forth. There may be applications where an organization may wish to send and receive secure mail without having to be tied to a particular individual. Or a database on the Internet may want to digitally sign electronic-mail messages. Or a particular office within an organization may wish to be able to sign mail. (For example, the treasurer of an organization may wish to sign digital checks.) The X.500 directory standards permit all of this.

Think of the naming convention as a tree. At the base is a broad attribute: the country the distinguished name lives in. Further attributes refine the DN further: the state or province, the city, the organization, the legal name, etc.

For example, my DN might be expressed as:

{C = US, S = Illinois, L = Chicago, O = Counterpane Systems, CN = Bruce Schneier}

Here "C" represents the country name, "S" represents the state or province name, "L" the locality name, "O" the organization name, and "CN" the common name of the entity. In this example, the entity is a person—me. The entity could possibly be a job title: for example, "Treasurer." The ANSI X.520 standard lists a number of attributes that can be used to construct a DN, as well as rules for creating new attributes as needed.

RIPEM

Riordan's Internet Privacy Enhanced Mail (RIPEM) is an implementation of Privacy Enhanced Mail (PEM). The current version of RIPEM does not implement the entire PEM standard, but it is still a very useful electronic-mail security program. RIPEM allows your e-mail to have the four security facilities provided by PEM: message encryption, called disclosure protection (optional), and originator authenticity, message integrity measures, and nonrepudiation of origin (always).

RIPEM is not really a complete implementation of PEM, because PEM specifies certificates for authenticating keys, which RIPEM does not handle on all platforms at this time. They have already been added to the Macintosh version, and will be added to other versions.

RIPEM was written primarily by Mark Riordan. Most of the code is in the public domain, except for the RSA code, which is a library called RSAREF licensed from RSA Data Security, Inc.

The current version of RIPEM is 1.2a; the current version of the Macintosh port of RIPEM is 0.8b1.

RIPEM is available via anonymous ftp to citizens and permanent residents in the U.S. from **rsa.com**; find the **rsaref/directory** and read the **README** file for info. Note that the non-RSAREF portion of RIPEM is not a product of RSA Data Security, Inc. They are merely helping distribute it.

RIPEM, as well as some other crypt stuff, has its "home site" on **ripem.msu.edu**, which is open to nonanonymous ftp for users in the U.S. and Canada who are citizens or permanent residents. To find out how to obtain access, ftp there, change directory to **pub/crypt/**, and read the file **GETTING_ACCESS**. For convenience, binaries for many architectures are available as well as the full source code.

RIPEM uses the library of cryptographic routines RSAREF, which is considered a munition and thus is export-restricted from distribution to persons who are not citizens or permanent residents of the U.S or Canada. No export license has been obtained (nor would one likely be granted unless the key were shortened to 512 bits and the secret-key algorithm were changed to something weaker than DES). The author requests in the **README** file that this law not be violated:

> #Please do not export the cryptographic code in this distribution
>
> #outside of the USA or Canada. This is a personal request from me,
>
> #the author of RIPEM, and a condition of your use of RIPEM.
>
> #I don't agree with US export restrictions, but I intend to comply.

Note that RSAREF is not in the public domain, and a license for it is included with the distribution. You should read it before using RIPEM.

The standard RIPEM has been ported to MS-DOS, Macintosh, OS/2, Windows NT, and many UNIX systems including NeXT, SunOS, Solaris, ULTRIX, AIX, HP/UX, Irix, MPIS RISC/os, V/88, Apollo, SCO, 386BSD, Linux, and ESIX. In addition to the standard Macintosh port, a particularly nice version written by Raymond Lau (author of StuffIt) is available.

RIPEM works with most e-mail programs. How easy and clean the user interface will be depends on the sophistication and modularity of the mailer, though. The user's guide, included with the distribution, discusses ways to use RIPEM with many popular mailers, including Berkeley, mush, elm, and MH. Code is also included in elisp to allow easy use of RIPEM inside GNU Emacs.

For a remote user to be able to send secure mail to you, she must know your public key. For you to be able to confirm that the message received came from her, you must know her public key. RIPEM allows for three methods of key management: a central server, the distributed finger servers, and a flat file. All three are described in the RIPEM user's guide, which is part of the distribution. None of them provides perfect security. The PEM standard calls for key management by certificates; this addition to RIPEM is planned, but the hierarchy of certifying authorities is still developing and thus few people have certificates yet.

RIPEM was originally created with no connection to RSA Data Security, Inc. other than its use of the RSAREF library, and for no reason other than its author's desire to see widespread use of public-key cryptography. However, after the ball started rolling, people at RSA Data Security, Inc. got interested. RIPEM was a competitor to PGP, and the company had no love for PGP. RSA Data Security, Inc. decided to carry RIPEM on its ftp site, and some people there started making their own RIPEM keys. RSA Data Security, Inc.'s and RIPEM's developers share the goal of improving RSAREF; its performance has been enhanced substantially by various optimizations, including hand-hacking critical portions in assembler, and improvements are continuing. RIPEM even won the "Best Application Built on RSAREF in 1992" award.

RIPEM/SIG

RIPEM/SIG is a variant of RIPEM 1.2 with encryption and decryption taken out. In effect, RIPEM/SIG only permits MIC-CLEAR and MIC-ONLY messages; ENCRYPTED messages are not supported.

RSA Data Security, Inc. has obtained a U.S. State Department Commodities Jurisdiction ruling determining that RIPEM/SIG is exportable from the USA. At this writing, RIPEM/SIG is undergoing a classification to determine what countries it may not be exported to. (The worst case is that RIPEM/SIG may not be exported to such countries as Libya, Iraq, and North Korea. The best case is that it can be exported everywhere.)

RSA Data Security, Inc. has granted a free license to users worldwide of RIPEM/SIG for any purposes other than direct commercial services, such as selling the software itself or selling a service directly based on the program's functions. You are allowed to use the software at a commercial location or on commercial computer systems. Use for personal communication, or even corporate communications, is also permitted. These rights will be clarified in a new RSAREF license and new RSA software, to be available by the time this book is printed. For a license to use RIPEM/SIG to deliver commercial services, contact RSA Data Security, Inc. for terms.

I believe that RIPEM/SIG is the only U.S.-exportable signature software in the world available for free to U.S. users. (Non-U.S. users are not bound by RSA Data Security, Inc.'s U.S. patents, but would be bound by copyright laws.)

RIPEM/SIG is built from RIPEM 1.2a sources; thus, RIPEM/SIG source code is not exportable. The executables are exportable. Mark Riordan has compiled RIPEM/SIG for several popular architectures and has placed the executables on **ripem.msu.edu**, available for anonymous ftp from **/pub/crypt/ripem/ripemsig/binaries**. Other USA and Canada citizens are welcome to obtain the RIPEM 1.2a source distribution and create and export executables for other platforms.

Remember, RIPEM/SIG does not have any encryption capabilities; it does not provide for any confidentiality. It is only available in executable form, so it would be difficult to add encryption capabilities to the program. RIPEM/SIG might be great for authentication, but an eavesdropper would get as much benefit from RIPEM/SIG as the legitimate users.

TIS-PEM

TIS-PEM is a reference implementation of PEM. It was written for UNIX by Trusted Information Systems, Inc. For information, write to:

Trusted Information Systems, Inc.
3060 Washington Rd (Rt 97)
Glenwood, MD 21738

RPEM

RPEM stands for Rabin Privacy Enhanced Mail. It was similar to RIPEM, but used a different public-key algorithm (not RSA) in an attempt to avoid the patents on public-key systems. It was written by Mark Riordan, who later wrote RIPEM.

Its distribution was halted when, contrary to the beliefs of many (including Rabin), Public Key Partners (PKP) claimed that their patents were broad enough to cover the algorithm employed. This claim is not universally accepted, but was not challenged for pragmatic reasons.

RPEM is not really used anymore. It is not compatible with RIPEM or PGP.

Chapter 11

Pretty Good Privacy (PGP)

PGP is an electronic-mail security program. It's available free of charge on the net. It works on a variety of hardware platforms. It's relatively easy to use. It uses public key cryptography, and gives users privacy and authentication. And it requires no complicated infrastructure to work. Since it was first introduced in 1991, PGP has spread around the world and is currently one of the most popular electronic-mail security programs.

PGP version 1 was defined and developed by Philip Zimmermann in June 1991. Version 2.0, released in the fall of 1992, was developed by a whole lot of people worldwide, and was coded outside the U.S. to avoid patent and export laws. In the summer of 1993 version 2.3a was released, a more robust, feature-rich version.

PGP was written without permission from RSA Data Security, Inc., the patent holder of the RSA algorithm. Starting with version 2.5, PGP used demonstration code from RSA Data Security, Inc. to avoid patent violations. Version 2.5, as well as the subsequent version 2.6, was released by the Massachusetts Institute of Technology, who holds the PGP patent. MIT's formal announcement of version 2.6 stated that "PGP 2.6 is being released by MIT with the cooperation of RSADSI." This means that all parties consider PGP version 2.6 to be noninfringing and can be legally used for personal, noncommercial use.

For commercial use, ViaCrypt sells PGP version 2.7. This version is also fully licensed, and legal for all uses.

At the time of writing, the current versions of PGP are 2.6.2 and 2.7, although that could change at any time. PGP version 3.0 is currently in the design stage.

PGP is a product, not a standard. It does not interoperate with any other security product, either PEM or non-PEM, but it has been ported to a wide variety of hardware platforms.

PGP Security Features

PGP provides a variety of security features for electronic mail:

- Confidentiality
- Data origin authentication
- Message integrity
- Nonrepudiation of origin

Although PGP is designed to automatically provide confidentiality, authentication, and integrity for all messages, it is possible to send a PGP-protected message without providing confidentiality. It is also possible to send a PGP-protected message without providing for authentication or integrity.

Confidentiality protects the contents of the e-mail message against unauthorized disclosure. No one other than the authorized receiver of the message can read the message. The message is protected—from wiretapping, misdelivery, and collection—while it is in transit and while it is in the recipient's mailbox waiting to be decrypted. After that, it is no longer necessarily protected. The receiver, of course, does whatever he wants with the unprotected message.

Data origin authentication permits the authorized receiver of the message to reliably determine the identity of the sender. Only an authorized receiver can authenticate it; an eavesdropper who intercepts the message cannot authenticate the sender. (She can, of course, read the return address on the message. If the sender uses an anonymous remailer, then this will give the eavesdropper no information.)

Note that the sender is the person who sent the message, which may be different from the person who wrote the message. For example, in the case of forwarded messages, the authentication feature identifies the forwarder of the message and not the original sender.

Message integrity gives the authorized receiver of the message assurance that the message has not been modified in transit. The message received is identical to the message that the sender sent. Only the authorized receivers of the message can check its integrity; an eavesdropper who intercepts the message cannot. This feature is called "connectionless" because it does not depend on the ordering of the received messages; some systems provide integrity, but only by assuming that the messages are received by the receiver in exactly the same order as they are sent by the sender. PGP does not assume this.

Authentication and integrity are really two parts of the same thing. Together they tell the receiver who wrote the message. There is no point in knowing that the message was not tampered with in transit if you don't know who it came from. And there is no point in knowing that a message originally came from a particular person, if you have no assurance that the message was not modified in transit.

Nonrepudiation is the feature that allows one person to forward a message to another person, who can then verify the identity of the original sender. That is, Alice can send Bob a message. Bob can take that message and send it on to Carol. Using PGP's authentication and integrity features, Carol can verify that Bob sent her the message. By checking the authentication and integrity of the original message, Carol can verify that Alice sent the original message to Bob.

If the original message was encrypted, Bob must first decrypt it before sending it on to Carol. However, he can then re-encrypt it using Carol's public key.

The PGP Environment

PGP is designed to work within existing electronic mail systems, primarily those used on the Internet. Although the program is not integrated with any mail program or text editor, it can be used with all of them. There are a number of PGP add-on products that facilitate use of PGP within certain environments. Since these are all public domain, they vary greatly in quality.

Cryptographic Algorithms

PGP uses public-key cryptography for key management and digital signatures, conventional (secret-key) cryptography for data encryption, and a one-way hash function for digital signatures.

PGP version 2 uses the following algorithms:

Data Encryption Algorithm:
    IDEA in Cipher Block Chaining mode

Key-Management Algorithm:

RSA

Message Integrity Check and Digital Signature Algorithm:

MD5 and RSA

PGP's RSA keys can be one of three lengths:

- Casual grade (384 bits)
- Commercial grade (512 bits)
- Military grade (1024 bits)

I've heard some talk about adding a 2048-bit "Alien grade" key length, but nothing has happened along those lines yet.

The 384-bit key should only be used for testing, and not for encrypting actual messages. Keys of this length can be broken, though it takes a whole lot of work. The 512-bit key might possibly be breakable by the NSA and similar organizations, and with every year that possibility becomes more and more likely. You're secure against most adversaries with a 512-bit key, but it's getting chancy. (Remember, your public-key/private-key pair is likely to remain unchanged for years.) The 1024-bit keys are not breakable by anyone, barring some major advance in mathematics that someone is not telling us.

If you are concerned about your security, choose a 1024-bit key. If you are not too worried about security, choose a 512-bit key. If you fall somewhere in between, I recommend choosing the longer key. PGP isn't that much slower with the longer key length, and it's better to be safe than sorry.

Version 1 of PGP used a home brew algorithm called Bassomatic for data encryption and MD4 as a one-way hash function. Neither of these algorithms is used any more in PGP. They are both less secure than their replacements.

Types of Messages

PGP's primary purpose is to send secure messages: signed and encrypted. PGP also allows sending messages that are only signed.

Encrypted messages can only be read by the intended receiver. Using public-key cryptography, the sender does not have to exchange a secret key with the receiver. If the sender has the receiver's public key, then she can send him a message.

Encrypted PGP messages can be addressed to one receiver or several receivers.

PGP can also be used to send signed but unencrypted messages. These messages are in the clear: Anyone can read them. Also, anyone who has the sender's public key can verify the integrity and authentication of the message. This type of security is useful for messages posted to Usenet newsgroups.

Although PGP is primarily designed for electronic-mail security, it is also possible to use the program as a stand-alone file encryptor. PGP has an option to encrypt a file using the IDEA algorithm and a given key. This option allows you to encrypt files to store on your hard disk, but in theory the encrypted file can be sent across the network without bothering to use PGP's public-key cryptography key management (just remember, the receiver must have the same IDEA key in order to decrypt it). Also remember that it isn't enough to delete the unencrypted file from your disk after you encrypt it; good security mandates using a file-erasure program.

A PGP Message

The underlying data structures in PGP messages are all in binary. Therefore, they are very efficient. This means when you look at a PGP message, it is very hard to pick out any interesting details. There is no header information, as there is in PEM.

A *packet* is a digital envelope with data inside. A PGP file is the concatenation of one or more packets. In addition, one or more of the packets in a file may be transformed using encryption, compression, or encoding.

A packet consists of a type field, a length field, and the contents of the packet itself. Any other characteristics of the packet are determined by the type of the packet. Note that packets may be nested: One digital envelope may be placed inside another. For example, a packet encrypted with secret-key cryptography contains another packet, which in turn might be a compressed data packet.

This means that when you see a PGP message, you don't have much information about it. The outer packet contains an RSA keyid, RSA-encrypted key, and encrypted message. The keyid tells you what key to use to decrypt the message. Only after you decrypt the message can you see the packets inside; then you will then be able to extract the random encryption key. Figure 11.1 is a PGP message.

Sending a PGP Message

Sending a PGP message consists of four steps (see Figure 11.2).

- Signing (optional)
- Compression
- Encryption (optional)
- Transmission encoding (optional)

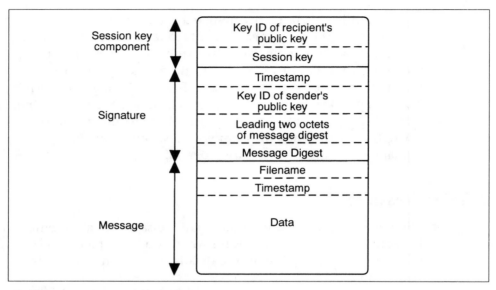

Figure 11.1 A PGP message.

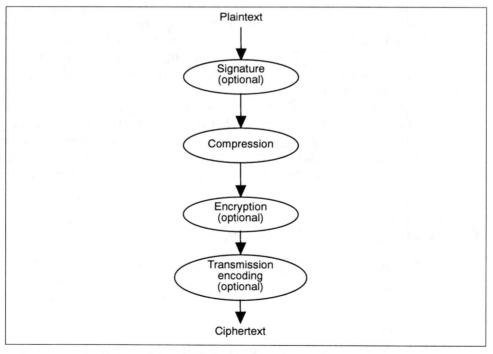

Figure 11.2 Preparation of a PGP message.

As a user, the details of each of these steps don't really concern you. All you have to do is tell PGP whether you want the message signed, whom you want it encrypted to, and whether you want it encoded. PGP handles all the details, which are given here only for those interested in its inner workings.

Signing

PGP messages can be digitally signed by the sender. Signatures are optional; the sender does not have to sign her message. There are cases where a sender might not want to sign her message. If she is sending mail through an anonymous remailing service, for example, she would not want to sign the message.

PGP signatures allow the receiver to verify both the identity of the sender and that the message has not been tampered with in transit. If Alice sends a message to Bob, Bob can verify her signature and be sure that the message came from Alice. If Alice posts a message to a newsgroup, anyone reading the message can verify that she posted it (and that no one else has modified it).

PGP's digital signature involves the use of the MD5 hash function and the RSA public-key encryption algorithm. To create a digital signature, first PGP generates the MD5 hash value of the message. Then PGP encrypts the hash using the sender's private key. And finally, the encrypted hash is prepended to the message.

Although digital signatures usually are found attached to the message or file that they sign, this is not always the case. PGP also supports detached signatures. A detached signature may be stored and transmitted separately from the message it signs. This is useful in several contexts. A user may wish to maintain a separate signature log of all messages sent or received.

Detached signatures are also useful when more than one party must sign a message, such as a legal contract. Each person's signature is independent and therefore is applied only to the message. That is, both Alice and Bob sign just the message; the second signer does not sign the first signature. Otherwise, signatures would have to be nested, with the second signer signing both the document and the first signature, and so on.

Compression

After signing, PGP compresses the message. This compression reduces the size of the message. However, the very act of reducing the size of the message eliminates any redundancies in the plaintext; this cannot but hinder cryptanalysis. The compression algorithm is the same one used in the public-domain compression program ZIP 2.0. Figure that compression will reduce the length of a text message by about one-half.

Note that PGP compresses the message after applying the signature but before encryption. The signature is compressed along with the rest of the message.

Encryption

PGP provides confidentiality by encrypting messages to be transmitted or data files to be stored locally using the IDEA conventional (secret-key) encryption algorithm. Encryption is optional; PGP does not require the sender to encrypt her messages. This may be useful when a sender wants to post a message to a public forum, like a Usenet newsgroup; she wants anyone to be able to read the message. In this case, she would not use encryption.

PGP uses the IDEA encryption algorithm in Cipher Block Chaining mode to encrypt messages. Encryption is a multi-stage process, similar to the process used in PEM. First, the message is padded so that it is a multiple of 8 bytes long. (IDEA encrypts data in 8-byte blocks.) Then, PGP generates a message encryption key and an IV. These keys are random and unique to each message; PGP generates a random 128-bit IDEA key and a random 64-bit IV every time it encrypts a new message. Finally, the message is encrypted using the message encryption key and the IV.

Still, PGP isn't finished with encryption. The message is encrypted using the IDEA algorithm and a random message encryption key. PGP encrypts this key using the RSA algorithm and the public key of the receiver. If there is more than one receiver, PGP encrypts multiple copies of this key, one with each receiver's public key.

PGP can both encrypt and sign a single message. First, a signature is generated for the message and prepended to the message. Then, the message plus signature is encrypted using a random encryption key. Finally, the random encryption key is encrypted using RSA and prepended to the encrypted block. Note that the digital signature is encrypted along with the message. It is impossible to verify the signature on an encrypted message without decrypting it first.

Transmission Encoding

With PGP, at least part of the block to be transmitted is encrypted. If a detached signature is used, then the hash is encrypted (with the sender's private key). If encryption is used, the message plus signature (if present) are encrypted (with a one-time conventional key). Thus, part or all of the resulting block consists of a stream of arbitrary bytes. However, many electronic-mail systems only permit the use of ASCII text blocks. To accommodate this restriction, PGP converts the raw 8-bit binary stream of ciphertext to a stream of printable ASCII characters.

The scheme used for this purpose is radix-64 conversion. Each group of three octets of binary data is mapped into four ASCII characters. This format also appends a code to detect transmission errors. This is the same encoding algorithm as is used in PEM.

Radix-64 conversion increases the length of the message by one-third. Remember that PGP previously compressed the message by about one-half, so the final compressed and encoded message is still only two-thirds the length of the original message.

Receiving a PGP Message

Receiving a PGP message involves unraveling everything done by the sender. Happily, the PGP software handles everything. First, the software looks to see which PGP version was used by the sender. Each version of PGP is always compatible with itself and at least one version in either direction. Thus, PGP 2.6 can decrypt and verify messages created with (at least) PGP 2.5 and can create messages that can be decrypted and verified with (at least) PGP 2.7. At the time of this writing, the current version of the free PGP is 2.6.1 and the current version of the commercial PGP is 2.7.

Transmission Decoding

If the message is encoded for transmission, it is decoded from ASCII back into 8-bit ciphertext.

Decrypting

PGP determines if the message is encrypted. If it is, PGP attempts to decrypt it. First, the software looks at the packet (or packets) that contain the encrypted random encryption key, to see if it can decrypt the message. (Remember, there may be multiple receivers, or a single receiver may have multiple public keys.) Assuming PGP is able to, it decrypts the random encryption key using the receiver's private key. Then, it decrypts the message using the random encryption key.

Remember that encryption is an optional step. If the original PGP message was not encrypted, no decryption is necessary.

Signature Verification

PGP determines if the message is signed. If it is, PGP decrypts the hash value using the sender's public key. Then, it generates a new hash value for the received message and compares it to the decrypted hash value. If the two match, the message is accepted as authentic. This is also an optional step; without a signature, there is nothing to verify.

Message Disposition

After the receiver has read the PGP message, he has a number of options. He can store the message in decrypted form without the signature attached. He can store the message in decrypted form with the signature information. This form of storage is appropriate if the receiver wants to forward a signed message to a third party, and also provides protection against modification while the message is being stored. If the receiver wants to protect the confidentiality of the message, he can choose to save the message in encrypted form.

Segmentation and Reassembly

Some e-mail systems have restrictions on message size. Some don't allow messages longer than 50,000 characters. To save the grief of breaking a long message into parts and individually signing and encrypting each one, PGP can automatically segment a message into pieces that are small enough to send through all electronic mail systems. And at the other end, PGP can reassemble the pieces into one large message. The segmentation is done during the last step of processing, and does not affect encryption or signing in any way. And the reassembly is done before any decryption or verification.

PGP Public Keys

A PGP public key consists of key components and a userid (generally a name followed by an Internet address). It may also have signatures attached to it.

Each person generates his own public-key/private-key pair. He then has it signed by people he knows. These signatures serve as certifications of the key's validity, and can help convince other people of the fact.

This looks like a small ASCII file. You can treat this file just like any other. You can put it on a disk and give it to someone else. You can send it to someone else over electronic mail. You can post it on a PGP key server or put it in your **.plan** file. You want to distribute your public key as widely as possible; it is what other people will use to send you secure messages.

PGP Public Key "Certification"

Key certification is where PGP really differentiates itself from PEM. Recall that PEM was based on the concept of a common hierarchy of key certifications. Alice knows that Bob's key is valid because she can always find a common trusted individual who certified both her key and his.

PGP does things differently. PGP is based on the idea that trust is a social concept. People trust their friends. Alice has her public key signed by people she knows: people who trust her. Bob has his key signed by people who trust him. If Alice and Bob share a common trusted friend, then they can use that friend to vouch for each other's identity.

When, for example, Bob gets Alice's key, he looks at the signatures on the key. If he trusts any of the people who signed her key, he trusts the key. If he doesn't, then he doesn't trust the key.

Bob can still use Alice's key, even if he doesn't trust it. There is no problem with this. Consider the analogous situation in real life. Bob meets Alice on the street. They have no friends in common; there is no way for either of them to verify each other's identity. They exchange addresses and, later they exchange mail.

In this situation, Bob doesn't know Alice's real identity. Alice could have given Bob a false name, a mail drop for an address, and a convincing story. Bob doesn't know if the person whom he thinks of as "Alice" is actually Alice, but he does know that mail sent to "Alice's" address is answered by "Alice."

In many cases, what we want is not absolute identity, but continuity. If I am corresponding on the net with someone who goes by the name "Cheeseburger," I can be reasonably sure that Cheeseburger also has a real name. Maybe I need to know that real name, but most of the time I don't. What I need to know is that mail sent to Cheeseburger is read only by Cheeseburger. What I need to verify is that mail received from Cheeseburger was actually sent by Cheeseburger, and has not been tampered with by someone else. Cheeseburger's real identity isn't my concern.

The drawback to this system is that any particular PGP user cannot verify the validity of every other PGP key. With PEM, any user can verify every other PEM key. There is only one certification hierarchy with PEM; each pair of users shares at least one person in their certification paths. PGP is not like this. It is possible to have isolated groups of PGP users; a user in such a group might be able to verify the validity of every other key in the group, but not the validity of any key outside the group.

Verifying Another's PGP Key

When you get someone's public key in the mail or off a public key server, how do you verify that it is valid? The easiest way is to see if it is signed by someone you trust. If it is, then you know that it is valid.

This is a very simple notion, but it is very powerful. What it says is that every person has a group of people whom he trusts. These people are allowed to "introduce" him to other people, whom he may not even know.

This mirrors real life. Alice and Bob are friends; Alice trusts Bob. If Alice and Bob are together and Bob introduces Alice to Carol, Alice's trust of Carol depends on her relation with Bob. If, on the other hand, Alice and Bob were not friends, then Alice might not trust his introduction of Carol.

PGP allows you to put people in one of three categories: fully trusted, partially trusted, and unknown. (For the purposes of PGP, unknown equals untrusted—it pays to be paranoid in this business.)

If you receive a key that has been signed by someone you trust, then PGP assumes that it is a trusted key. If you receive a key that has been signed by two people whom you partially trust, then PGP assumes that it is a trusted key. (These parameters can be modified to suit your own paranoia: Either one trusted introducer or two partially-trusted introducers is the default.)

If you receive a key that has not been signed by enough trusted or partially-trusted introducers, then it is not a trusted key. You can still use it to verify signatures and send encrypted messages, but PGP will flag the key as untrusted.

Again, this mirrors real life. If you meet someone on the street with whom you do not share any friends, you have no reason to trust him. But you can still communicate with him, and with PGP, you can still communicate securely with him. Trust is a social relation; in time you might come to trust this person even though you share no friends in common. Then you might even sign his public key directly.

Key Fingerprints

PGP supports a key fingerprinting option. A fingerprint is the MD5 one-way hash value of the public key. This is a 16-byte number that is, for all practical purposes, unique to each key. And given the fingerprint value, it is computationally impossible for someone to generate a public key that hashes to that value.

This fingerprint makes for an easy way to verify a key. If Alice wants to send Bob her public key, she can send it to him via e-mail. When Bob receives it, he needs to verify that it is valid. Assuming that Alice's key is not signed by someone Bob trusts, he can call Alice on the telephone and ask her to recite the fingerprint of her key. Alice does so, and Bob can compare the fingerprint received from Alice with the fingerprint of the public key he received from Alice. If they match, Bob knows that Alice's key has not been tampered with in transmission.

For Eve to successfully tamper with this process, she has to be able to generate a false key with the same key fingerprint. She can't do this. Otherwise, she has to be able to impersonate Alice on the telephone. We have to assume that Alice and Bob can recognize each other on the telephone for this to work. If they can, then key fingerprints will prevent any maliciousness on the part of Eve.

Storing PGP Keys

PGP keys are stored in key rings. A key ring is exactly what you think it is: a bunch of keys. (Actually, it's a file of keys: This is the computer world.)

PGP users store copies of other users' public keys. That is, if Alice communicates securely with Bob regularly, she keeps a copy of Bob's public key on her public key ring. If she wants to send Bob a secure message and doesn't have his public key on her key ring, she goes out and gets it. (Perhaps she asks Bob for a copy; perhaps she gets it from a PGP key server somewhere.) When she gets it, she adds it to her public key ring. Then, she can send him secure messages.

The public key ring is stored unencrypted. This is not a problem; public keys are public. No security is gained by keeping them secret.

PGP actually maintains two key rings: A public key ring which contains all of the public keys that you know, and a secret key ring which contains your secret key (or keys). Your secret keys are protected by a pass phrase.

Names

Unlike PEM, PGP uses a person's Internet address as his name. For example, my PGP key identifies me as:

    schneier@counterpane.com

People can be known under their own name or under an alias. People can have more than one name. People can have multiple keys with the same name. PGP does not put any requirements on identities.

PGP Versions

Every time you turn around, there seems to be a new version of PGP. This is due to the complicated politics surrounding the program, and is likely to calm down now that PGP is using RSAREF. For those keeping track, here is a rundown of some of the recent versions of PGP:

PGP version 2.3a: The last version of PGP that did not use RSAREF.

PGP version 2.4: The original ViaCrypt PGP.

PGP version 2.5: An interim release of PGP with RSAREF.

PGP version 2.6: The current freeware version of PGP.

PGP version 2.7: The current commercial version of PGP, sold by ViaCrypt.

PGP version 2.6 and 2.7 interoperate with each other. All PGP users should have one of those two versions.

PGP version 2.6.1

At the time of this writing, the current version of PGP is version 2.6.2.

PGP version 2.6 and later uses the RSAREF toolkit for public-key cryptography, so it is perfectly legal for personal, noncommercial use. Part of MIT's announcement regarding version 2.6 said:

As part of the release process, MIT commissioned an independent legal review of the intellectual property issues surrounding earlier releases of PGP and PGP keyservers. This review determined that use of PGP 2.3 within the United States infringes a patent licensed by MIT to RSADSI, and that keyservers that primarily accept 2.3 keys are most likely contributing to this infringement.

The following is a policy statement, dated 28 May 1994, from Phil Zimmermann about PGP version 2.6:

On 24 May 1994, the Massachusetts Institute of Technology released PGP (Pretty Good Privacy) version 2.6. PGP is a software package that encrypts electronic mail, using public key cryptography. Over the past three years, PGP has become the worldwide de facto standard for email encryption. PGP 2.6 is being published under the terms of the RSAREF license from RSA Data Security, Inc (RSADSI). This is a significant milestone in PGP's legal development.

Export of this software from the US or Canada may be restricted by the US Government. PGP version 2.6 is being released through a posting on a controlled FTP site maintained by MIT. This site has restrictions and limitations which have been used on other FTP sites to comply with export control requirements with respect to other encryption software such as Kerberos and software from RSA Data Security, Inc. These special mechanisms are intended to preclude export of cryptographic software from the US. The MIT FTP site that carries PGP is net-dist.mit.edu, in the pub/PGP directory.

This new freeware version of PGP is for noncommercial use. For commercial use, you may get ViaCrypt PGP, available on a variety of platforms. ViaCrypt may be contacted at 602-944-0773, or via email at viacrypt@acm.org.

PGP 2.6 is as strong as earlier versions. It contains no back doors. It can read messages, signatures, and keys from PGP versions 2.5, 2.4, 2.3a, and 2.3. Beginning in September, a built-in software timer will trigger PGP 2.6 to begin producing messages, signatures, and keys that cannot be read by earlier versions of PGP. It will still retain its ability to read things from earlier versions after that date, so that users who upgrade to 2.6 will not be inconvenienced, particularly if everyone else upgrades by that time. The reason for the change in format is to grant RSADSI's request to MIT to encourage all users to stop using older versions. ViaCrypt's new products will support the new formats used by PGP 2.6. Details of the compatibility issues and their reasons are outlined in the PGP User's Guide, included in the release package. See also the official statements released by MIT for further details.

Version 2.6 also has some bug fixes and improvements of the version 2.5 released by MIT on 9 May 1994. Both the 2.5 and 2.6 versions were produced in a joint project between myself and MIT. Both versions were released by MIT after extensive review by MIT's administration and their legal counsel. I am told by MIT that MIT's legal counsel believes that both versions 2.5 and 2.6 do not infringe the RSA patents in any way, and they both comply with the terms of the RSAREF licenses that each were released under. But regardless of the noninfringing nature of version 2.5, I urge all PGP users in the US to upgrade to version 2.6, to help move toward eradication of earlier, pre-RSAREF versions of PGP. This will improve the overall political and legal landscape surrounding PGP. MIT will publish details on the simple format change so that earlier European versions of PGP may be independently upgraded by Europeans.

It is illegal to export PGP. Of course, someone already did, and PGP version 2.6 is available on several ftp sites outside the United States.

ViaCrypt PGP (version 2.7)

ViaCrypt sells a commercial implementation of PGP. This version of PGP is fully licensed (ViaCrypt has a license for both RSA and IDEA) and can be used for commercial applications.

ViaCrypt is a division of company called Lemcom Systems, Inc. These guys are traditional IBM mainframe communications people, and licensed the RSA algorithm for a completely different purpose.

In early 1993 ViaCrypt cut a deal with Phil Zimmermann to commercially sell PGP. They already had a patent license for RSADSI, so there were no problems on that front. (I wonder if RSADSI would have given them a license expressly for PGP.) They licensed IDEA from Adscom Tech AG. And they were in business.

The original version of ViaCrypt PGP was version 2.4. The current version is 2.7, which is compatible with the freeware PGP version 2.6. ViaCrypt PGP 2.7 is sort-of compatible with ViaCrypt PGP 2.4, but the company strongly urges everyone to upgrade their program. Following is a policy statement, issued on 27 May 1994, from ViaCrypt about their commercial support of PGP:

> On 24 May 1994, The Massachusetts Institute of Technology began distribution of PGP Version 2.6 which incorporates the RSAREF™ Cryptographic Toolkit and is licensed for personal noncommercial use along with other restrictions. MIT stated that to protect RSADSI's intellectual property rights in public key technology, PGP V2.6 is designed so that messages it creates after 1 September 1994 will be unreadable by earlier versions of PGP, which includes ViaCrypt PGP V2.4. PGP V2.6 will, however, always be able to read messages generated by ViaCrypt PGP V2.4.

> It is ViaCrypt's policy to make ViaCrypt PGP interoperable with both ViaCrypt PGP V2.4 as well as with MIT's release of PGP V2.6. Therefore ViaCrypt will soon release ViaCrypt PGP V2.7 which will contain new features found in PGP V2.6 and will accept messages created by ViaCrypt PGP V2.4 as well as those created by PGP V2.6.

> For messages created by ViaCrypt PGP V2.7, either the present format compatible with ViaCrypt 2.4 or the new format which will be produced by PGP V2.6 after 1 September 1994, can be selected. Because PGP V2.6 is licensed for personal noncommercial use, after 1 September 1994 the new format is expected to come into wide use. ViaCrypt strongly urges all ViaCrypt PGP users to upgrade to ViaCrypt PGP V2.7 and to the new format.

> A ViaCrypt PGP V2.7 upgrade package will be made available to registered users of ViaCrypt PGP V2.4 at a nominal charge of $10 (which includes shipping and handling). Effective the date of this notice and until

ViaCrypt PGP V2.7 begins shipping, all new purchasers of ViaCrypt PGP V2.4 will automatically receive a free ViaCrypt PGP V2.7 upgrade package.

Remember, ViaCrypt PGP is the *only* version of PGP legal for all uses: personal, government, and commercial. Free PGP from MIT (currently, version 2.6.1) is only legal for personal, noncommercial use. And ViaCrypt has pretty good technical support, as well.

ViaCrypt sells PGP for MS-DOS, UNIX, and the Macintosh. A Windows version is currently in development, and may be released by the time this book is published.

ViaCrypt also sells a version of PGP that is integrated with CompuServe's WinCIM and CSNav. It's real easy to use, and I recommend it.

PGP's User Interface

All right, I admit it. Using PGP can be a pain. It's not integrated into your mail program. To send a message, you have to write and save it. Then you have to encrypt it, upload it into your mailer, and finally address the mail message and send it off. To receive a message, you have to save it from your mailer, decrypt it through PGP, and then read it from your favorite word processor or editor. It would be nice if there were a mail program that had PGP built in, so that you could do all this without having to leave your mailer. Maybe someday.

Installing PGP

PGP runs on a variety of platforms: MS-DOS, several varieties of UNIX, VAX VMS, Atari, Amiga, Macintosh, and possibly other systems. The only thing to watch is the version number. Porting is done by hobbyists who are not being paid for their work and the latest version of PGP is not necessarily available on all systems. The Macintosh port doesn't use the Macintosh interface very well, but it does work. Naturally, installation instructions differ depending on your hardware. Separate instructions are provided here for MS-DOS and UNIX.

No matter what the machine you are on, though, read the documentation first. At least read Volume I of the PGP User's Guide. It's Appendix A of this book, so it should be easy to find. Cryptography software is easy to misuse, and if you don't use it properly much of the security you could gain by using it will be lost! Even if you are already familiar with cryptography, it is important that you understand the various security issues associated with using PGP. It may not matter if you read the fine print on a box of breakfast cereal, but it may be crucial to read the label of a prescription drug. Cryptography software has as much dangerous potential as pharmaceuticals—so read the manual!

MS-DOS Installation

PGP is distributed in a compressed archive format, which keeps all the relevant files grouped together, and also saves disk space and transmission time.

The current version, 2.6, is archived with the ZIP utility, and the PGP executable binary release system is in a file named **PGP26.ZIP**. This contains the executable program, the user documentation, and a few keys and signatures. There is also a second file available containing the C and assembly source code, called **PGP26SRC.ZIP**; unless you are a programmer interested in cryptography, it is probably of little interest to you. This file may or may not be available from the source where you get **PGP26.ZIP**; if not, and you want it, see the "Licensing and Distribution" section of the PGP User's Guide in Appendix A.

You will need PKUNZIP version 1.1 or later to uncompress and split the **PGP26.ZIP** archive file into individual files. PKUNZIP is shareware and is widely available for MS-DOS machines.

Create a directory for the PGP files. For this description, let's use the directory **C:\PGP** as an example, but you may substitute your own disk and directory name. Type these commands to make the new directory:

```
c:\
md \pgp
cd \pgp
```

Uncompress the distribution file **PGP26.ZIP** to the directory. For this example, we will assume the file is on floppy drive A:—if not, substitute your own file location.

```
pkunzip -d a:pgp26
```

If you omit the **-d** flag, all the files in the **doc** subdirectory will be deposited in the **PGP** directory. This merely causes clutter.

Next, you can set an MS-DOS environment variable to let PGP know where to find its special files, in case you use it from other than the default PGP directory. Use your favorite text editor to add the following lines to your **AUTOEXEC.BAT** file (usually on your C: drive):

```
SET PGPPATH=C:\PGP
SET PATH=C:\PGP;%PATH%
```

Substitute your own directory name if different from **C:\PGP**.

The **CONFIG.TXT** file contains various preferences. You can change the language PGP operates in, and the character set it uses. The IBM PC's default character set, "Code Page 850," will be used if the line **charset=cp850** appears in the **CONFIG.TXT** file. You probably want to add that line.

Another environmental variable you should set in MS-DOS is **TZ**, which tells MS-DOS what time zone you are in, and helps PGP create GMT timestamps for its keys and signatures. If you properly define **TZ** in **AUTOEXEC.BAT**, then MS-DOS gives you good GMT timestamps, and handles daylight savings time adjustments for you. Here are some sample lines to insert into **AUTOEXEC.BAT**, depending on your time zone:

For Los Angeles: `SET TZ=PST8PDT`
For Denver: `SET TZ=MST7MDT`
For Arizona: `SET TZ=MST7`
(Arizona never uses daylight savings time)
For Chicago: `SET TZ=CST6CDT`
For New York: `SET TZ=EST5EDT`
For London: `SET TZ=GMT0BST`
For Amsterdam: `SET TZ=MET-1DST`
For Moscow: `SET TZ=MSK-3MSD`
For Auckland: `SET TZ=NZT-13`

Now reboot your system to run **AUTOEXEC.BAT**, which will set up **PGP-PATH** and **TZ** for you.

Next, you have to generate your public-key/private-key pair. This is described in more detail in the "RSA Key Generation" section of the *PGP User's Guide*. Remember that your key becomes something like your written signature or your bank card code number or even a house key—keep it secret and keep it secure! Use a long, unguessable pass phrase and remember it. Right after you generate a key, put it on your key ring and copy your secret key ring (**SECRING.PGP**) to a blank floppy and write-protect that floppy.

You might wish to generate a short test key to play around with PGP for a little bit and see how it works, or even more than one so you can pretend to send messages between two people. Since you won't be guarding any secrets, this can be short and have a simple pass phrase. But when you generate your permanent key, the one you intend to give to others so they can send secure messages to you, be much more careful.

After you generate your own key pair, you can add a few more public keys to your key ring. A collection of sample public keys is provided with the release in the file **KEYS.ASC**. See the *PGP User's Guide*, in the section on adding keys to your key ring.

UNIX Installation

You will probably have to compile PGP for your system; to do this, first make sure the unpacked files are in the correct UNIX textfile format (the files in **PGP26SRC.ZIP** are in MS-DOS CRLF format, so for UNIX you must unpack with **unzip -a**; the **tar** file **pgp26.tar.Z** uses normal UNIX line feed conventions). Then copy the file **makefile.unx** in the distribution to **Makefile**.

If you don't have an ANSI C compiler you will need the unproto package written by Wietse Venema. The unproto package was posted to **comp.sources.misc** on Usenet and can be obtained from the various sites that archive that newsgroup (volume 26: v26i012 and v26i013) or **ftp.win.tue.nl** file: **/pub/programming/unproto4.shar.Z**. Read the file **README** in the unproto distribution for instructions on how to use unproto. The UNIX makefile for PGP (**makefile.unx**) contains a few targets for compiling with unproto; these assume you have unpacked unproto in a subdirectory "**unproto** in the PGP **src** directory.

Then type:

`make sungcc`	for Sun with GNU gcc
`make suncc`	for Sun with cc and unproto
`make sysv_386`	for SVR4 386 with asm primitives
`make x286`	for XENIX/286 with asm primitives and unproto
`make ultrix`	for DEC 4.2BSD Ultrix with gcc
`make rs6000`	for RS6000 AIX

There are more targets in **makefile.unx**. If your system doesn't have a target in **makefile.unx** you will have to edit the makefile. Make sure you compile for the correct byte order for your system: Define HIGHFIRST if your system is big-endian (for example, Motorola 68030). There are also some platform-specific parameters included in the file **platform.h**. Some platforms may have to modify this file.

If all goes well, you will end up with an executable file called **pgp**. Before you install **pgp**, run these tests (do not create your real public key yet, this is just for testing):

1. Create a public-key/private-key pair (enter "test" as userid/password):

   `pgp -kg`

2. Add the sample keys from the file **keys.asc** to the public key ring:

   `pgp -ka keys.asc`

   PGP will ask if you want to sign the keys you are adding; answer yes for at least one key.

3. Do a key ring check:

```
pgp -kc
```

4. Encrypt **pgpdoc1.txt**:

```
pgp -e pgpdoc1.txt test -o testfile.pgp
```

5. Decrypt this file:

```
pgp testfile.pgp
```

This should produce the file **testfile**. Compare this file with **pgp-doc1.txt**.

If everything went well, install **pgp** in a **bin** directory.

Place the documentation, **pgpdoc1.txt** and **pgpdoc2.txt**, somewhere where you can easily read it; since it's for you, not the software, the location doesn't really matter.

Place the man page (**pgp.1**) in an appropriate spot. If you don't know anything about how man pages work, you can make the man page look human-readable yourself by typing:

```
nroff -man pgp.1 | more
```

Then you can read **pgp.man**.

Create a subdirectory somewhere in your home directory hierarchy to hold your public and private key rings and anything else PGP might need (like the **language.txt** file). You must set the environment variable PGPPATH to point to this place before you use the system. Copy the files **language.txt**, **config.txt**, and the **.hlp** files from the distribution into this subdirectory.

Tell PGP the character set and language you wish to use in the **config.txt** file. If you have a terminal that only displays 7-bit ASCII, use **charset=ascii** to display an approximation (accents are omitted) of extended characters. This directory cannot be shared! It will contain your personal private keys!

VMS Installation

Read the file **readme.vms** in the **doc** subdirectory

Amiga Installation

The standard distribution does not yet compile directly on an Amiga. If you have SAS C, you might try the **makefile.amy** as a starting place.

Atari Installation

The standard distribution does not yet compile directly on an Atari ST.

PGP Add-Ons

There are numerous PGP add-on programs floating around on the Internet. Some of them are good; some are not so good. All are shareware. What follows is a brief description of some of them.

I admit that I haven't worked with them all. I haven't even tried them all. They're available on the net, somewhere, if you want to find them. Good luck.

Archimedes

PGPwimp is a multi-tasking WIMP front-end for PGP. It requires RISC OS 3. PGPwimp operates on files, and has no hooks to allow integration with mailers/newsreaders.

RNscripts4PGP is a collection of scripts and a small BASIC program which integrates PGP with the ReadNews mailer/newsreader. The scripts provide encryption, decryption, signature and signature verification, and key management capabilities.

DOS and Microsoft Windows

HPACK79 is a PGP-compatible archiver.

Menushell is a PGP menu shell for MS-DOS. It requires either 4DOS or NDOS to run.

PBBS is the Public Bulletin Board System, a privacy-oriented host BBS application designed with the "anonymous movement's" diverse needs in mind. It is designed to work with PGP. Users can send each other private "postcards" or upload and download PGP-encrypted messages to one another's mail boxes. PBBS also contains a comprehensive public message base with anonymous read, write, and reply options. PBBS has a built-in emergency self-destruct sequence for the sysop who desires an extra level of security. The self-destruct option will completely shred (that is, erase per DoD specifications) all PBBS-related files on disk, assuring the sysop that her BBS will not be compromised in any way. PBBS is a compact application at 75K, allowing it to be run from a floppy disk if desired, and it requires no telecommunications experience to operate. The program supports Xmodem,

Ymodem, and Zmodem, and speeds up to 57,600 bps; it includes door support, full ANSI-emulation, and many more features.

PGPBLU17.ZIP is an interface between PGP and the BlueWave offline mail reader.

PGP-Front is an interactive shell for PGP. It features an easy-to-use interface for those who don't want to learn all PGP commands by heart but still want to make use of its versatility. The most-used options of PGP are supported, including most key-management options. An improved version is under development and will feature support for some of the advanced options of PGP and a lot of extra configuration options for PGP-Front itself.

PGP-NG is a Norton Guide database for PGP.

PGPSHELL is a front-end DOS program for use with PGP. PGPShell incorporates easy-to-use, mouse-driven menus and a unique Key Management Screen to easily display all public key ring information in a flash. The program makes using PGP easy: A user can breeze through PGP Userids, Keyids, fingerprints, e-mail addresses, signatures, trust parameters, and PGP's validity ratings all in one screen, at one place, and with a single mouse-click.

PGPUTILS is a collection of BAT-files, and PIF-files for Windows.

PGPWinFront is a Windows front-end for PGP. It has features like automatic message creation, key management, editable command line, and one-button access to PGP documentation.

TAPPKE (TAPcis Public Key Encryption) integrates PGP into TAPCIS, a popular navigator/offline message reader used on PCs to access CompuServe. This program is an interface between TAPCIS message-writing facilities and PGP. When you compose messages in TAPCIS, they get collected into a batch in a **.SND** file along with some control information about where and how the messages are to be posted or mailed; next time you go on-line to CompuServe, TAPCIS processes any messages waiting in its .SND files. The TAPPKE add-on can be run before you do this transmission step. TAPPKE scans messages in a .SND file, and any message that contains a keyword (##PRIVATE## or ##SIGNATURE##) is extracted and just that message is handed to PGP for encryption or signature, then reinserted into the **.SND** file for transmission. All this is a simplified interface to make it more convenient to encrypt and sign messages while still using the normal message composition features of TAPCIS.

PWF12 is a Windows front-end for PGP. Users can access main PGP features more easily than from DOS. This program features a simple file management system, support for your choice of editor to create plaintext files for encryption, a quick way to shell to DOS to access esoteric PGP features, and a command line editor to access the more specialized features of PGP.

UNIX

Emacs Auto-PGP integrates PGPO into your Emacs mailreader. It scans the header of a message to be encrypted to determine the recipients and thus their private keys. Incoming encrypted messages can be decrypted once and then stored as plaintext, but information about the recipient keys of an incoming encrypted message is held encrypted. Incoming signed and encrypted messages are turned into plaintext signed messages.

Mailcrypt.el is an elisp package for encrypting and decrypting mail. It can provide an interface to RIPEM as well as PGP. The program includes VM mailreader support, key management functions, and menu bar support under Emacs 19 and gnus.

PGPPAGER is a pager program for PGP designed to be integrated with the elm mailreader.

Rat-pgp.el is a GNU Emacs interface to the PGP public key system. It lets you easily encrypt, decrypt, and sign messages. It also does signature verification, and it provides a number of other functions.

VAX/VMS

ENCRYPT.COM is a VMS mail script.

Chapter **12**

Comparing PGP and PEM

PGP and PEM are both electronic-mail security programs. They both encrypt messages; they both sign messages. They are both based on public-key cryptography. They have different philosophies, though. At a first cut, the difference can be understood that:

> PEM is based on the concept of a hierarchical organization, while PGP is based on a distributed network of individuals.

Thus, PEM might be more suited for applications in companies, governments, and other organizations. PGP is definitely more suited for people on the Internet.

The following sections compare PGP and PEM in more detail.

Trust Model

PEM assumes a hierarchical distribution of keys. Centralized control comes through a small number of root servers (IRPAs) that are the source of all trust. Trusting these is mandatory. "I know who you are because your CA has signed for you, the relevant PCA has signed for your CA, and the IRPA has signed for the PCA."

PGP assumes a network distribution of trust. "I know who you are because I know (and trust) someone else who believes you are who you say you are." But the users alone decide whom they trust to vouch for other users. They actually need not trust anyone, and can obtain all keys directly. In effect, each user becomes her own source of trust, and each trusted third party becomes a trusted CA. There is no PCA equivalent.

PEM assumes the user trusts the verified certification chain of a signed message, whereas PGP assumes that only the user is qualified to decide whom to trust.

Target Applications

PEM has always been designed specifically to work with electronic mail. Authentication is more important than privacy (it is not possible to send a PEM message that is not authenticated).

PGP considers privacy at least as important as authentication, perhaps even more important. It was originally designed for securing electronic mail, but PGP is also very useful for securing arbitrary binary files. Additionally, PGP compresses binary files before encrypting them. This reduces the size of the radix-64 converted mailable text.

PEM developers were more concerned with identity, and less concerned with degrees of trust. PGP takes a more pragmatic view and has a much more flexible trust model. Sometimes, though, trust and identity are equated.

Encryption

Both PGP and PEM can do encrypted and signed messages; both can do signed but unencrypted messages. Only PGP can encrypt unsigned messages. This is a significant difference: With PEM it is impossible to send a message that is unsigned. PEM users cannot hide behind anonymous remailers. PGP messages can be unsigned and anonymous. Table 12.1 summarizes these differences.

PGP can reduce any message to signed-only (MIC-CLEAR, in PEM talk) if it is to be forwarded. The PEM RFCs also specify that any implementation

TABLE 12.1: PGP and PEM Message Types

Type of Security	PEM Terminology	PGP Command Line Switches
Clear text, signed	MIC-CLEAR	-sta +clearsig=on
Signed only	MIC-ONLY	-sta
Signed and encrypted	ENCRYPTED	-stea
Encrypted only	<none>	-tea

should be able to downgrade the security of messages. However, not all implementations support this feature.

Hiding of Signature Information

It is impossible to verify a PGP signature if the message is still encrypted. It is possible to verify a PEM signature even if the message is encrypted. This is a subtle difference, but it means that anyone can verify who sent a PEM-encrypted message—even someone not authorized to read the message. So not only is it impossible for a PEM user to send an anonymous but encrypted message, it is impossible for a PEM user to send a message that is anonymous to the network but can be authenticated by the valid recipient.

Key Generation

A PGP user generates his own public-key/private-key pair using provided software. The public-key certificate is based on:

1. An arbitrary ASCII string (typically "name <e-mail address>").
2. A random number derived from the typing characteristics analyzed when entering some random text.

The user protects his private key with a pass phrase which has to be entered every time the PGP software accesses the private key. This reduces problems caused by leaving the computer unattended.

The arbitrary ASCII string that you enter is your user name in your public key, and is the means by which other people will refer to your public key. By following the Internet address guidelines it would be guaranteed to be unique, but this is not enforced.

In PEM, X.509 certificates are generated either by the user, by a nominated person, or by a hardware device. The certificate is signed by the user's CA and is stored in a directory server. Details of private-key handling vary depending on the implementation.

The user's public key is referenced using an X.500 distinguished name. This is guaranteed unique, and the standard is designed to be descriptive and scaleable.

Which naming convention will eventually prevail depends on the outcome of a battle of standards. One PGP user expressed his disgust at the attitude of advocates of the PEM X.500 naming scheme: "When the X.500 revolution comes, your name will be lined up against the wall and shot."

PEM is supporting this revolution, while PGP maintains that the current Internet electronic-mail naming convention (the X.400 standard) works just fine. It doesn't try to impose any arbitrary models or standards—it just works.

PEM keys include a validity period, after which they are deemed to have expired. Long validity is discouraged (this is equivalent to changing your computer password frequently), as revocation is needed when compromise is suspected.

It is impossible to revoke PGP keys, as explained below in the section on revocation.

Key Distribution

PGP public keys are typically distributed by e-mail, bulletin boards or e-mail-based key servers. To prevent tampering, keys are signed by third parties. Each PGP user can decide which third parties they trust and which they don't trust (limited trust is also supported). You must obtain the public keys of people you trust by secure means (verification by word of mouth is supported through generation of key signatures).

If you find a public key signed by someone whom you trust then you will trust that public key. The "trusted introducer" is the means by which public keys are propagated.

Trust is not transitive. If Alice trusts Bob and Bob trusts Carol then Alice does not have to trust Carol. It is, of course, possible for Bob to trust Carol so much that Bob is willing to re-sign keys previously signed by Carol, thereby forcing the trust to be transitive.

The PGP version of a "Certifying Authority" is a widely trusted repository of public keys. The notion of a hierarchy of key repositories is mentioned, but is not developed. PGP typically operates in an environment with an arbitrary network of trust rather than a strict hierarchy.

PEM public keys can be distributed by any means, normally by electronic mail or by X.500 directory look-up. The public keys are signed by the private key of the issuing CA, and can be verified by obtaining the corresponding public key. This can be obtained from CAs higher in the hierarchy.

Key Revocation

In PGP, key distribution is ad hoc and largely by word of mouth. This means that it is impossible to guarantee the revocation of a certificate if it is compromised. You can send out a "key revocation certificate," but there are no guarantees it will reach everyone who has your public key on his or her public key ring.

As the key revocation certificate would be signed with your private key, if you lose your private key altogether it is impossible to revoke it, as you can't sign the necessary certificate.

In PEM, Certificate Revocation Lists (CRLs) are held in X.500 directories or in mailboxes maintained by each PCA. Certificates can therefore quickly be revoked, as long as the infrastructure for accessing the CRL database remains intact. The CRL must be distributed to every user who maintains a local cache of certificates.

Whether or not this system will work remains to be seen. There are people who think that CRLs will never work, and that it will in practice be impossible to revoke a certificate. There are people who think that CRLs will work amazingly well, and that a bad certificate will never be accepted. I expect the truth to be somewhere in the middle.

Conclusions

PEM was developed to a carefully written specification. PGP was designed and programmed by a handful of people. (An RFC defining the message format is in preparation.) PEM is just a protocol for message exchange—nothing else is specified, while PGP also includes many functions that you'd find in the user software for a PEM implementation. PGP benefits enormously from the fact that there is one (consistent) set of software that everyone is using and that it is being developed by a small team. PEM is a standard, and hence debated endlessly by standards committees.

One of the design goals of PEM was to make it work for the long term, with hundreds of millions of users and millions of companies. Part of the impediment in deploying PEM is the lack of an infrastructure to support this scaleability.

On the other hand, PGP is easy to deploy. It requires no infrastructure; two people can start using it to communicate securely with each other immediately, and more users can be added to the network quickly and easily.

While this ad hoc scaleability is perfect for the distributed environment of the Internet, it may be less ideal for hierarchical organizations. The following may impede the deployment of PGP in those places:

Lack of a way of expressing certification policies.

Lack of guaranteed certificate revocation.

Lack of rigorous name space management.

The first two will count against PGP in commercial and governmental applications, while the third provides potential scaleability problems.

In short, PGP is a pragmatic practical e-mail security program that will evolve as its limits are found. PEM is sometimes more elegant (or, at least, better adheres to conventional standards and practices), but the infrastructure requirements make it more heavyweight. Each has its own marketplace, and will probably be around for a while. Wouldn't it be nice if the two could interoperate?

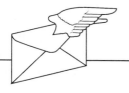

Chapter 13

Attacks Against PGP and PEM

The only secure computer is one that is turned off, locked in a safe, and buried twenty feet down in a secret location—and I'm not completely confident of that one, either. PGP and PEM are real-world security products, and hence have many potential security problems. Here is a brief rundown on the most serious ones.

Cryptanalytic Attacks

Breaking RSA would allow an attacker to find out your private key, in which cases he could read any mail encrypted to you and sign messages with your private key. This isn't very likely: RSA is generally believed to be safe against all standard cryptanalytic techniques. Even a short key length—about 516 bits with RIPEM, 512 bits with PGP—is long enough to render this impractical, barring a huge investment in hardware or a breakthrough in factoring.

Breaking DES would allow an attacker to read any given PEM message, since the message itself is encrypted with DES. It would not allow an attacker to claim to be you. This is probably possible for large governments, but still impractical for most people. DES has only 56 bits in its key, and thus could conceivably be compromised by brute force with sufficient hardware, but few agencies have such money to devote to simply read a message. Since each message has a different DES key, the work for each message would remain significant. RIPEM 1.1 allows triple-DES to be used as an option; it is believed stronger than single-DES and should resist brute-force attacks.

Breaking IDEA would have the same effect on PGP messages. IDEA has a 128-bit key, which makes a brute-force attack impractical, now and probably forever. On the other hand, IDEA is still a new algorithm; it is possible that some clever cryptanalyst will discover a way to break IDEA.

Key Management Attacks

Stealing your private key would provide the same benefits as breaking RSA. To safeguard your private key, it is encrypted with a DES key which is derived from a pass phrase you type in. However, if an attacker can get a copy of your private key file and your pass phrase (by snooping network packets, tapping lines, or whatever) she could break the whole scheme. This is true of both keys.

The main risk is that of transferring either the pass phrase or the private key file across an untrusted link. So don't do that. Run PGP or PEM on a trusted machine, preferably one sitting right in front of you. Ideally, your own machine in your own home (or maybe office) which nobody else has physical access to.

Fooling you into accepting a bogus public key for someone else could allow an adversary to deceive you into sending secret messages to her rather than to the real recipient. If the enemy can fool your intended recipient as well, she could re-encrypt the messages with the other bogus public key and pass them along.

It is important to get the proper public keys of other people. The most common mechanism for this is finger; assuming the adversary has not compromised routers or daemons or such, finger can be given a fair amount of trust. The strongest method of key authentication is to exchange keys in person; however, this is not always practical. PGP solves this problem by establishing a web of trusted introducers. PEM uses a single hierarchy of trust.

Playback Attacks

Even if an adversary cannot break the cryptography, she could still cause trouble. Using PEM as an example, suppose you send a message with MIC-ONLY (a PEM mode which does not provide confidentiality) to Alice which says "OK, let's do that." Your adversary intercepts it, and now re-sends it to Bob, who now has a message which is authenticated as if from you telling him to do that. Of course, he may interpret it in an entirely different context. Or your adversary could transmit the same message to the same recipient much later, figuring it would be seen differently at a later time. Or the adversary could change the **Originator-Name:** to her name, register your public key as hers, and send a message hoping the recipient will send her return mail indicating (perhaps even quoting!) the unknown message.

To defeat playback attacks, the plaintext of each message should include some indication of the sender and recipient, and a unique identifier (typically the date). As a recipient, you should be sure that the **Originator-Name:** header and the sender indicated within the plaintext are the same, that you really are a recipient, and that the message is not an old one.

Local Attacks

Clearly, the security of any electronic-mail security program cannot be greater than the security of the machine where the encryption is performed. For example, under UNIX, a superuser could manage to get at your encrypted mail, although it would take some planning and effort to do something like replace the PGP or PEM executable program with a Trojan horse or to get a copy of the plaintext, depending how it's stored.

In addition, the link between you and the machine running your electronic-mail security program is an extension of that machine. If you decrypt with PGP or PEM on a remote machine to which you are connected via network (or, worse yet, modem), an eavesdropper could see the plaintext (and probably also your pass phrase.)

You should only use your electronic-mail security program on systems you trust, obviously. In the extreme case, you should only use your program on your own machine, which you have total control over and which nobody else has access to, which has only carefully examined software known to be free of viruses, and so on. However, there's a very real trade-off between convenience and security here.

A more moderately cautious user might use her e-mail security program on a UNIX workstation where other people have access (even root access), but increase security by keeping private keys and the executable security program on a floppy disk.

Some people will keep their e-mail security program on a multi-user system, but when dialing in over an insecure line, they will download messages to their own system and perform the PEM or PGP decryption there. However, the security provided by such a mechanism is somewhat illusory; since you presumably type your plaintext password to log in, you've just given away the store. The adversary can now log in as you and install traps in your account to steal your private key next time you use it from a more secure line.

This will likely remain the situation as long as most systems use the rather quaint mechanism of plaintext password authentication.

Untrusted Partners

Encryption will ensure that only a person with the private key corresponding to the public key used to encrypt the data may read the traffic. However, once someone with that key gets the message, she may always make whatever kind of transformations she wishes. No cryptographic barriers prevent a recipient from converting an encrypted message to a plaintext message, readable by anyone.

Including the recipients in the plaintext, as mentioned above, will make it possible for recipients of a redistributed message to be aware of its original nature. Naturally, the security of the cryptography can never be greater than the security of the people using it.

Traffic Analysis

Some attacks are outside the scope of electronic-mail security programs; traffic analysis is a prominent one of these. Neither PGP nor PEM prevents an enemy from potentially discovering whom your traffic is being exchanged with and how often or lengthy these messages are. This can be a problem for some people, though the potential for invasion of privacy may be more a collective than an individual one.

The traditional way to prevent traffic analysis is to throw a lot of bogus traffic into the channel to obscure the real stuff; this could be done but would be detrimental to network load and a burden on bogus message recipients. Trusted third-party remailers that handle aliases can help some, though frequently used aliases can still be analyzed (indeed, traffic analysis might determine which aliases go with which real people).

Final Words

Both PGP and PEM represent the end products of many design decisions and trade-offs. They both provide excellent security; most of the attacks listed above are very complicated, and some are considered impossible with today's technology. While it is prudent to always assume the worst when evaluating a product's security, both PGP and PEM can provide adequate security against most known adversaries.

Appendix A

Pretty Good Privacy

Phil's Pretty Good Software

Presents

PGP™
Pretty Good™ Privacy
Public Key Encryption for the Masses

PGP™ User's Guide
Volume I: Essential Topics
© 1991–1994 by Philip R. Zimmermann

Revised 22 May 94

PGP Version 2.6 – 22 May 94

Software by

Philip Zimmermann, and many others.

Synopsis:

PGP™ uses public-key encryption to protect E-mail and data files. Communicate securely with people you've never met, with no secure channels needed for prior exchange of keys. PGP is well featured and fast, with sophisticated key management, digital signatures, data compression, and good ergonomic design.

Software and documentation© Copyright 1990–1994 Philip Zimmermann.

All rights reserved. For information on PGP licensing, distribution, copyrights, patents, trademarks, liability limitations, and export controls, see the "Legal Issues" section in the "PGP User's Guide, Volume II: Special Topics." Distributed by the Massachusetts Institute of Technology.

*"Whatever you do will be insignificant,
but it is very important that you do it."*

—Mahatma Gandhi

Contents

Quick Overview

Pretty Good™ Privacy (PGP), from Phil's Pretty Good Software, is a high security cryptographic software application for MSDOS, Unix, VAX/VMS, and other computers. PGP allows people to exchange files or messages with privacy, authentication, and convenience. Privacy means that only those intended to receive a message can read it. Authentication means that messages that appear to be from a particular person can only have originated from that person. Convenience means that privacy and authentication are provided without the hassles of managing keys associated with conventional cryptographic software. No secure channels are needed to exchange keys between users, which makes PGP much easier to use. This is because PGP is based on a powerful new technology called "public key" cryptography.

PGP combines the convenience of the Rivest-Shamir-Adleman (RSA) public key cryptosystem with the speed of conventional cryptography, message digests for digital signatures, data compression before encryption, good ergonomic design, and sophisticated key management. And PGP performs the public-key functions faster than most other software implementations. PGP is public key cryptography for the masses.

PGP does not provide any built-in modem communications capability. You must use a separate software product for that.

This document, "Volume I: Essential Topics," only explains the essential concepts for using PGP, and should be read by all PGP users. "Volume II: Special Topics" covers the advanced features of PGP and other special topics, and may be read by more serious PGP users. Neither volume explains the underlying technology details of cryptographic algorithms and data structures.

Why Do You Need PGP?

It's personal. It's private. And it's no one's business but yours. You may be planning a political campaign, discussing your taxes, or having an illicit affair. Or you may be doing something that you feel shouldn't be illegal, but is. Whatever it is, you don't want your private electronic mail (E-mail) or confidential documents read by anyone else. There's nothing wrong with asserting your privacy. Privacy is as apple pie as the Constitution.

Perhaps you think your E-mail is legitimate enough that encryption is unwarranted. If you really are a law-abiding citizen with nothing to hide, then why don't you always send your paper mail on postcards? Why not submit to drug testing on demand? Why require a warrant for police searches of your house? Are you trying to hide something? You must be a subversive or a drug dealer if you hide your mail inside envelopes. Or maybe a paranoid nut. Do law-abiding citizens have any need to encrypt their E-mail?

What if everyone believed that law-abiding citizens should use postcards for their mail? If some brave soul tried to assert his privacy by using an envelope for his mail, it would draw suspicion. Perhaps the authorities would open his mail to see what he's hiding. Fortunately, we don't live in that kind of world, because everyone protects most of their mail with envelopes. So no one draws suspicion by asserting their privacy with an envelope. There's safety in numbers. Analogously, it would be nice if everyone routinely used encryption for all their E-mail, innocent or not, so that no one drew suspicion by asserting their E-mail privacy with encryption. Think of it as a form of solidarity.

Today, if the Government wants to violate the privacy of ordinary citizens, it has to expend a certain amount of expense and labor to intercept and steam open and read paper mail, and listen to and possibly transcribe spoken telephone conversation. This kind of labor-intensive monitoring is not practical on a large scale. This is only done in important cases when it seems worthwhile.

More and more of our private communications are being routed through electronic channels. Electronic mail is gradually replacing conventional paper mail. E-mail messages are just too easy to intercept and scan for interesting keywords. This can be done easily, routinely, automatically, and undetectably on a grand scale. International cablegrams are already scanned this way on a large scale by the NSA.

We are moving toward a future when the nation will be crisscrossed with high capacity fiber optic data networks linking together all our increasingly ubiquitous personal computers. E-mail will be the norm for everyone, not the novelty it is today. The Government will protect our E-mail with Government-designed encryption protocols. Probably most people will acquiesce to that. But perhaps some people will prefer their own protective measures.

Senate Bill 266, a 1991 omnibus anti-crime bill, had an unsettling measure buried in it. If this non-binding resolution had become real law, it would have forced manufacturers of secure communications equipment to insert special "trap doors" in their products, so that the Government can read anyone's encrypted messages. It reads: "It is the sense of Congress that providers of electronic communications services and manufacturers of electronic communications service equipment shall insure that communications systems permit the Government to obtain the plain text contents of voice, data, and other communications when appropriately authorized by law." This measure was defeated after rigorous protest from civil libertarians and industry groups.

In 1992, the FBI Digital Telephony wiretap proposal was introduced to Congress. It would require all manufacturers of communications equipment to build in special remote wiretap ports that would enable the FBI to remotely wiretap all forms of electronic communication from FBI offices. Although it never attracted any sponsors in Congress in 1992 because of citizen opposition, it was reintroduced in 1994.

Most alarming of all is the White House's bold new encryption policy initiative, under development at NSA since the start of the Bush administration, and unveiled 16 April, 1993. The centerpiece of this initiative is a Government-built encryption device, called the "Clipper" chip, containing a new classified NSA encryption algorithm. The Government is encouraging private industry to design it into all their secure communication products, like secure phones, secure FAX, etc. AT&T is now putting the Clipper into their secure voice products. The catch: At the time of manufacture, each Clipper chip will be loaded with its own unique key, and the Government gets to keep a copy, placed in escrow. Not to worry, though—the Government promises that they will use these keys to read your traffic only when duly authorized by law. Of course, to make Clipper completely effective, the next logical step would be to outlaw other forms of cryptography.

If privacy is outlawed, only outlaws will have privacy. Intelligence agencies have access to good cryptographic technology. So do the big arms and drug traffickers. So do defense contractors, oil companies, and other corporate giants. But ordinary people and grassroots political organizations mostly have not had access to affordable "military grade" public key cryptographic technology. Until now.

PGP empowers people to take their privacy into their own hands. There's a growing social need for it. That's why I wrote it.

How it Works

It would help if you were already familiar with the concept of cryptography in general and public key cryptography in particular. Nonetheless, here are a few introductory remarks about public key cryptography.

First, some elementary terminology. Suppose I want to send you a message, but I don't want anyone but you to be able to read it. I can "encrypt," or "encipher" the message, which means I scramble it up in a hopelessly complicated way, rendering it unreadable to anyone except you, the intended recipient of the message. I supply a cryptographic "key" to encrypt the message, and you have to use the same key to decipher or "decrypt" it. At least that's how it works in conventional "single-key" cryptosystems.

In conventional cryptosystems, such as the U.S. Federal Data Encryption Standard (DES), a single key is used for both encryption and decryption. This means that a key must be initially transmitted via secure channels so that both parties can know it before encrypted messages can be sent over insecure channels. This may be inconvenient. If you have a secure channel for exchanging keys, then why do you need cryptography in the first place?

In public key cryptosystems, everyone has two related complementary keys, a publicly revealed key and a secret key. Each key unlocks the code that the other key makes. Knowing the public key does not help you deduce the corresponding secret key. The public key can be published and widely disseminated across a communications network. This protocol provides privacy without the need for the same kind of secure channels that a conventional cryptosystem requires.

Anyone can use a recipient's public key to encrypt a message to that person, and that recipient uses her own corresponding secret key to decrypt that message. No one but the recipient can decrypt it, because no one else has access to that secret key. Not even the person who encrypted the message can decrypt it.

Message authentication is also provided. The sender's own secret key can be used to encrypt a message, thereby "signing" it. This creates a digital signature of a message, which the recipient (or anyone else) can check by using the sender's public key to decrypt it. This proves that the sender was the true originator of the message, and that the message has not been subsequently altered by anyone else, because the sender alone possesses the secret key that made that signature. Forgery of a signed message is infeasible, and the sender cannot later disavow his signature.

These two processes can be combined to provide both privacy and authentication by first signing a message with your own secret key, then encrypting the signed message with the recipient's public key. The recipient reverses these steps by first decrypting the message with her own secret key, then checking the enclosed signature with your public key. These steps are done automatically by the recipient's software.

Because the public key encryption algorithm is much slower than conventional single-key encryption, encryption is better accomplished by using a high-quality fast conventional single-key encryption algorithm to encipher the message. This original unenciphered message is called "plaintext." In a process invisible to the user, a temporary random key, created just for this one "session," is used to conventionally encipher the plaintext file. Then the recipient's public key is used to encipher this temporary random conventional key. This public-key-enciphered conventional "session" key is sent along with the enciphered text (called "ciphertext") to the recipient. The recipient uses her own secret key to recover this temporary session key, and then uses that key to run the fast conventional single-key algorithm to decipher the large ciphertext message.

Public keys are kept in individual "key certificates" that include the key owner's user ID (which is that person's name), a timestamp of when the key pair was generated, and the actual key material. Public key certificates contain the public key material, while secret key certificates contain the secret key material. Each secret key is also encrypted with its own password, in case it gets stolen. A key file, or "key ring" contains one or more of these key certificates. Public key rings contain public key certificates, and secret key rings contain secret key certificates.

The keys are also internally referenced by a "key ID," which is an "abbreviation" of the public key (the least significant 64 bits of the large public key). When this key ID is displayed, only the lower 32 bits are shown for further brevity. While many keys may share the same user ID, for all practical purposes no two keys share the same key ID.

PGP uses "message digests" to form signatures. A message digest is a 128-bit cryptographically strong one-way hash function of the message. It is somewhat analogous to a "checksum" or CRC error checking code, in that it compactly "represents" the message and is used to detect changes in the message. Unlike a CRC, however, it is computationally infeasible for an attacker to devise a substitute message that would produce an identical message digest. The message digest gets encrypted by the secret key to form a signature.

Documents are signed by prefixing them with signature certificates, which contain the key ID of the key that was used to sign it, a secret-key-signed message digest of the document, and a timestamp of when the signature was made.

The key ID is used by the receiver to look up the sender's public key to check the signature. The receiver's software automatically looks up the sender's public key and user ID in the receiver's public key ring.

Encrypted files are prefixed by the key ID of the public key used to encrypt them. The receiver uses this key ID message prefix to look up the secret key needed to decrypt the message. The receiver's software automatically looks up the necessary secret decryption key in the receiver's secret key ring.

These two types of key rings are the principal method of storing and managing public and secret keys. Rather than keep individual keys in separate key files, they are collected in key rings to facilitate the automatic lookup of keys either by key ID or by user ID. Each user keeps his own pair of key rings. An individual public key is temporarily kept in a separate file long enough to send to your friend who will then add it to her key ring.

Installing PGP

The MSDOS PGP 2.6 release comes in a compressed archive file called PGP26.ZIP (each new release will have a name in the form "PGPxy.ZIP" for PGP version number x.y). The archive can be decompressed with the MSDOS shareware decompression utility PKUNZIP, or the Unix utility "unzip." The PGP release package contains a README.DOC file that you should always read before installing PGP. This README.DOC file contains late-breaking news on what's new in this release of PGP, as well as information on what's in all the other files included in the release.

If you already have an earlier version of PGP, you should rename it or delete it, to avoid name conflicts with the new PGP.

To install PGP on your MSDOS system, you just have to copy the compressed archive PGPxx.ZIP file into a suitable directory on your hard disk (like C:\PGP), and decompress it with PKUNZIP. For best results, you will also modify your AUTOEXEC.BAT file, as described elsewhere in this manual, but you can do that later, after you've played with PGP a bit and read more of this manual. If you haven't run PGP before, the first step after installation (and reading this manual) is to run the PGP key generation command "pgp -kg."

Installing on Unix and VAX/VMS is generally similar to installing on MSDOS, but you may have to compile the source code first. A Unix makefile is provided with the source release for this purpose.

For further details on installation, see the separate PGP Installation Guide, in the file SETUP.DOC included with this release. It fully describes how to set up the PGP directory and your AUTOEXEC.BAT file and how to use PKUNZIP to install it.

How to Use PGP

To See a Usage Summary

To see a quick command usage summary for PGP, just type:

```
pgp -h
```

Encrypting a Message

To encrypt a plaintext file with the recipient's public key, type:

```
pgp -e textfile her_userid
```

This command produces a ciphertext file called textfile.pgp. A specific example is:

```
pgp -e letter.txt Alice
```

or:

```
pgp -e letter.txt "Alice S"
```

The first example searches your public key ring file "pubring.pgp" for any public key certificates that contain the string "Alice" anywhere in the user ID field. The second example would find any user IDs that contain "Alice S." You can't use spaces in the string on the command line unless you enclose the whole string in quotes. The search is not case-sensitive. If it finds a matching public key, it uses it to encrypt the plaintext file "letter.txt," producing a ciphertext file called "letter.pgp."

PGP attempts to compress the plaintext before encrypting it, thereby greatly enhancing resistance to cryptanalysis. Thus the ciphertext file will likely be smaller than the plaintext file.

If you want to send this encrypted message through E-mail channels, convert it into printable ASCII "radix-64" format by adding the "-a" option, as described later.

Encrypting a Message to Multiple Recipients

If you want to send the same message to more than one person, you may specify encryption for several recipients, any of whom may decrypt the same ciphertext file. To specify multiple recipients, just add more user IDs to the command line, like so:

```
pgp -e letter.txt Alice Bob Carol
```

This would create a ciphertext file called letter.pgp that could be decrypted by Alice or Bob or Carol. Any number of recipients may be specified.

Signing a Message

To sign a plaintext file with your secret key, type:

```
pgp -s textfile [-u your_userid]
```

Note that [brackets] denote an optional field, so don't actually type real brackets. This command produces a signed file called textfile.pgp. A specific example is:

```
pgp -s letter.txt -u Bob
```

This searches your secret key ring file "secring.pgp" for any secret key certificates that contain the string "Bob" anywhere in the user ID field. Your name is Bob, isn't it? The search is not case-sensitive. If it finds a matching secret key, it uses it to sign the plaintext file "letter.txt," producing a signature file called "letter.pgp."

If you leave off the user ID field, the first key on your secret key ring is used as the default secret key for your signature.

PGP attempts to compress the message after signing it. Thus the signed file will likely be smaller than the original file, which is useful for archival applications. However, this renders the file unreadable to the casual human observer, even if the original message was ordinary ASCII text. It would be nice if you could make a signed file that was still directly readable to a human. This would be particularly useful if you want to send a signed message as E-mail.

For signing E-mail messages, where you most likely do want the result to be human-readable, it is probably most convenient to use the CLEARSIG feature, explained later. This allows the signature to be applied in printable form at the end of the text, and also disables compression of the text. This means the text is still human-readable by the recipient even if the recipient doesn't use PGP to check the signature. This is explained in detail in the section entitled "CLEARSIG-Enable Signed Messages to be Encapsulated as Clear Text," in the Special Topics volume. If you can't wait to read that section of the manual, you can see how an E-mail message signed this way would look, with this example:

```
pgp -sta message.txt
```

This would create a signed message in file "message.asc," comprised of the original text, still human-readable, appended with a printable ASCII signature certificate, ready to send through an E-mail system. This example assumes that you are using the normal settings for enabling the CLEARSIG flag in the config file.

Signing and then Encrypting

To sign a plaintext file with your secret key, and then encrypt it with the recipient's public key:

```
pgp -es textfile her_userid [-u your_userid]
```

Note that [brackets] denote an optional field, so don't actually type real brackets.

This example produces a nested ciphertext file called textfile.pgp. Your secret key to create the signature is automatically looked up in your secret key ring via your user ID. Her public encryption key is automatically looked up in your public key ring via her user ID. If you leave off her user ID field from the command line, you will be prompted for it.

If you leave off your own user ID field, the first key on your secret key ring is to be used as the default secret key for your signature.

Note that PGP attempts to compress the plaintext before encrypting it.

If you want to send this encrypted message through E-mail channels, convert it into printable ASCII "radix-64" format by adding the "-a" option, as described later. Multiple recipients may be specified by adding more user IDs to the command line.

Using Just Conventional Encryption

Sometimes you just need to encrypt a file the old-fashioned way, with conventional single-key cryptography. This approach is useful for protecting archive files that will be stored but will not be sent to anyone else. Since the same person that encrypted the file will also decrypt the file, public key cryptography is not really necessary.

To encrypt a plaintext file with just conventional cryptography, type:

```
pgp -c textfile
```

This example encrypts the plaintext file called textfile, producing a ciphertext file called textfile.pgp, without using public key cryptography, key rings, user IDs, or any of that stuff. It prompts you for a pass phrase to use as a conventional key to encipher the file. This pass phrase need not be (and, indeed, SHOULD not be) the same pass phrase that you use to protect your own secret key. Note that PGP attempts to compress the plaintext before encrypting it.

PGP will not encrypt the same plaintext the same way twice, even if you used the same pass phrase every time.

Decrypting and Checking Signatures

To decrypt an encrypted file, or to check the signature integrity of a signed file:

```
pgp ciphertextfile [-o plaintextfile]
```

Note that [brackets] denote an optional field, so don't actually type real brackets.

The ciphertext file name is assumed to have a default extension of ".pgp." The optional plaintext output file name specifies where to put processed plaintext output. If no name is specified, the ciphertext filename is used, with no extension. If a signature is nested inside of an encrypted file, it is automatically decrypted and the signature integrity is checked. The full user ID of the signer is displayed.

Note that the "unwrapping" of the ciphertext file is completely automatic, regardless of whether the ciphertext file is just signed, just encrypted, or both. PGP uses the key ID prefix in the ciphertext file to automatically find the appropriate secret decryption key on your secret key ring. If there is a nested signature, PGP then uses the key ID prefix in the nested signature to automatically find the appropriate public key on your public key ring to check the signature. If all the right keys are already present on your key rings, no user intervention is required, except that you will be prompted for your password for your secret key if necessary. If the ciphertext file was conventionally encrypted without public key cryptography,

PGP recognizes this and prompts you for the pass phrase to conventionally decrypt it.

Managing Keys

Since the time of Julius Caesar, key management has always been the hardest part of cryptography. One of the principal distinguishing features of PGP is its sophisticated key management.

RSA Key Generation

To generate your own unique public/secret key pair of a specified size, type:

```
pgp -kg
```

PGP shows you a menu of recommended key sizes (low commercial grade, high commercial grade, or "military" grade) and prompts you for what size key you want, up to more than a thousand bits. The bigger the key, the more security you get, but you pay a price in speed.

It also asks for a user ID, which means your name. It's a good idea to use your full name as your user ID, because then there is less risk of other people using the wrong public key to encrypt messages to you. Spaces and punctuation are allowed in the user ID. It would help if you put your E-mail address in <angle brackets> after your name, like so:

```
Robert M. Smith <rms@xyzcorp.com>
```

If you don't have an E-mail address, use your phone number or some other unique information that would help ensure that your user ID is unique.

PGP also asks for a "pass phrase" to protect your secret key in case it falls into the wrong hands. Nobody can use your secret key file without this pass phrase. The pass phrase is like a password, except that it can be a whole phrase or sentence with many words, spaces, punctuation, or anything else you want in it. Don't lose this pass phrase—there's no way to recover it if you do lose it. This pass phrase will be needed later every time you use your secret key. The pass phrase is case-sensitive, and should not be too short or easy to guess. It is never displayed on the screen. Don't leave it written down anywhere where someone else can see it, and don't store it on your computer. If you don't want a pass phrase (You fool!), just press return (or enter) at the pass phrase prompt.

The public/secret key pair is derived from large truly random numbers derived mainly from measuring the intervals between your keystrokes with a fast timer. The software will ask you to enter some random text to help it accumulate some random bits for the keys. When asked, you should provide some keystrokes that are reasonably random in their timing, and it wouldn't hurt to make the actual characters that you type irregular in content as well. Some of the randomness is derived from the unpredictability of the content of what you type. So don't just type repeated sequences of characters.

Note that RSA key generation is a lengthy process. It may take a few seconds for a small key on a fast processor, or quite a few minutes for a large key on an old IBM PC/XT. PGP will visually indicate its progress during key generation.

The generated key pair will be placed on your public and secret key rings. You can later use the -kx command option to extract (copy) your new public key from your public key ring and place it in a separate public key file suitable for distribution to your friends. The public key file can be sent to your friends for inclusion in their public key rings. Naturally, you keep your secret key file to yourself, and you should include it on your secret key ring. Each secret key on a key ring is individually protected with its own pass phrase.

Never give your secret key to anyone else. For the same reason, don't make key pairs for your friends. Everyone should make their own key pair. Always keep physical control of your secret key, and don't risk exposing it by storing it on a remote timesharing computer. Keep it on your own personal computer.

If PGP complains about not being able to find the PGP User's Guide on your computer, and refuses to generate a key pair without it, read the explanation of the NOMANUAL parameter in the section "Setting Configuration Parameters" in the Special Topics volume.

Adding a Key to Your Key Ring

Sometimes you will want to add to your key ring a key provided to you by someone else, in the form of a keyfile.

To add a public or secret key file's contents to your public or secret key ring (note that [brackets] denote an optional field):

```
pgp -ka keyfile [keyring]
```

The keyfile extension defaults to ".pgp." The optional keyring file name defaults to "pubring.pgp" or "secring.pgp," depending on whether the keyfile contains a public or a secret key. You may specify a different key ring file name, with the extension defaulting to ".pgp."

If the key is already on your key ring, PGP will not add it again. All of the keys in the keyfile are added to the key ring, except for duplicates.

Later in the manual, we will explain the concept of certifying keys with signatures. If the key being added has attached signatures certifying it, the signatures are added with the key. If the key is already on your key ring, PGP just merges in any new certifying signatures for that key that you don't already have on your key ring.

PGP was originally designed for handling small personal key rings. If you want to handle really big key rings, see the section on "Handling Large Public Key Rings" in the Special Topics volume.

Removing a Key or User ID from Your Key Ring

To remove a key or a user ID from your public key ring:

```
pgp -kr userid [keyring]
```

This searches for the specified user ID in your key ring, and removes it if it finds a match. Remember that any fragment of the user ID will suffice for a match. The optional key ring file name is assumed to be literally "pubring.pgp." It can be omitted, or you can specify "secring.pgp" if you want to remove a secret key. You may specify a different key ring file name. The default key ring extension is ".pgp."

If more than one user ID exists for this key, you will be asked if you want to remove only the user ID you specified, while leaving the key and its other user IDs intact.

Extracting (Copying) a Key from Your Key Ring

To extract (copy) a key from your public or secret key ring:

```
pgp -kx userid keyfile [keyring]
```

This non-destructively copies the key specified by the user ID from your public or secret key ring to the specified key file. This is particularly useful if you want to give a copy of your public key to someone else.

If the key has any certifying signatures attached to it on your key ring, they are copied off along with the key.

If you want the extracted key represented in printable ASCII characters suitable for E-mail purposes, use the -kxa options.

Viewing the Contents of Your Key Ring

To view the contents of your public key ring:

```
pgp -kv[v] [userid] [keyring]
```

This lists any keys in the key ring that match the specified user ID substring. If you omit the user ID, all of the keys in the key ring are listed. The optional key ring file name is assumed to be "pubring.pgp." It can be omitted, or you can specify "secring.pgp" if you want to list secret keys. If you want to specify a different key ring file name, you can. The default key ring extension is ".pgp."

Later in the manual, we will explain the concept of certifying keys with signatures. To see all the certifying signatures attached to each key, use the -kvv option:

```
pgp -kvv [userid] [keyring]
```

If you want to specify a particular key ring file name, but want to see all the keys in it, try this alternative approach:

```
pgp keyfile
```

With no command options specified, PGP lists all the keys in keyfile.pgp, and also attempts to add them to your key ring if they are not already on your key ring.

How to Protect Public Keys from Tampering

In a public key cryptosystem, you don't have to protect public keys from exposure. In fact, it's better if they are widely disseminated. But it is important to protect public keys from tampering, to make sure that a public key really belongs to whom it appears to belong to. This may be the most important vulnerability of a public-key cryptosystem. Let's first look at a potential disaster, then at how to safely avoid it with PGP.

Suppose you wanted to send a private message to Alice. You download Alice's public key certificate from an electronic bulletin board system (BBS). You encrypt your letter to Alice with this public key and send it to her through the BBS's E-mail facility.

Unfortunately, unbeknownst to you or Alice, another user named Charlie has infiltrated the BBS and generated a public key of his own with Alice's user ID attached to it. He covertly substitutes his bogus key in place of Alice's real public key. You unwittingly use this bogus key belonging to Charlie instead of Alice's public key. All looks normal because this bogus key has Alice's user ID. Now Charlie can decipher the message intended for Alice because he has the matching secret key. He may even re-encrypt the deciphered message with Alice's real public key and send it on to her so that no one suspects any wrongdoing. Furthermore, he can even make apparently good signatures from Alice with this secret key because everyone will use the bogus public key to check Alice's signatures.

The only way to prevent this disaster is to prevent anyone from tampering with public keys. If you got Alice's public key directly from Alice, this is no problem. But that may be difficult if Alice is a thousand miles away, or is currently unreachable.

Perhaps you could get Alice's public key from a mutual trusted friend David who knows he has a good copy of Alice's public key. David could sign Alice's public key, vouching for the integrity of Alice's public key. David would create this signature with his own secret key.

This would create a signed public key certificate, and would show that Alice's key had not been tampered with. This requires you to have a known good copy of David's public key to check his signature. Perhaps David could provide Alice with a signed copy of your public key also. David is thus serving as an "introducer" between you and Alice.

This signed public key certificate for Alice could be uploaded by David or Alice to the BBS, and you could download it later. You could then check the signature via David's public key and thus be assured that this is really Alice's public key. No impostor can fool you into accepting his own bogus key as Alice's because no one else can forge signatures made by David.

A widely trusted person could even specialize in providing this service of "introducing" users to each other by providing signatures for their public key certificates. This trusted person could be regarded as a "key server," or as a "Certifying Authority." Any public key certificates bearing the key server's signature could be trusted as truly belonging to whom they appear to belong to. All users who wanted to participate would need a known good copy of just the key server's public key, so that the key server's signatures could be verified.

A trusted centralized key server or Certifying Authority is especially appropriate for large impersonal centrally controlled corporate or government institutions. Some institutional environments use hierarchies of Certifying Authorities.

For more decentralized grassroots "guerrilla style" environments, allowing all users to act as trusted introducers for their friends would probably work better than a centralized key server. PGP tends to emphasize this organic decentralized non-institutional approach. It better reflects the natural way humans interact on a personal social level, and allows people to better choose who they can trust for key management.

This whole business of protecting public keys from tampering is the single most difficult problem in practical public key applications. It is the Achilles' heel of public key cryptography, and a lot of software complexity is tied up in solving this one problem.

You should use a public key only after you are sure that it is a good public key that has not been tampered with, and actually belongs to the person it claims to. You can be sure of this if you got this public key certificate directly from its owner, or if it bears the signature of someone else that you trust, from whom you already have a good public key. Also, the user ID should have the full name of the key's owner, not just her first name.

No matter how tempted you are—and you will be tempted—never, NEVER give in to expediency and trust a public key you downloaded from a bulletin board, unless it is signed by someone you trust. That uncertified public key could have been tampered with by anyone, maybe even by the system administrator of the bulletin board.

If you are asked to sign someone else's public key certificate, make certain that it really belongs to that person named in the user ID of that public key certificate. This is because your signature on her public key certificate is a promise by you that this public key really belongs to her. Other people who trust you will accept her public key because it bears your signature. It may be ill-advised to rely on hearsay—don't sign her public key unless you have independent firsthand knowledge that it really belongs to her. Preferably, you should sign it only if you got it directly from her.

In order to sign a public key, you must be far more certain of that key's ownership than if you merely want to use that key to encrypt a message. To be convinced of a key's validity enough to use it, certifying signatures from trusted introducers should suffice. But to sign a key yourself, you should require your own independent firsthand knowledge of who owns that key. Perhaps you could call the key's owner on the phone and read the key file to her to get her to confirm that the key you have really is her key—and make sure you really are talking to the right person. See the section called "Verifying a Public Key Over the Phone" in the Special Topics volume for further details.

Bear in mind that your signature on a public key certificate does not vouch for the integrity of that person, but only vouches for the integrity (the ownership) of that person's public key. You aren't risking your credibility by signing the public key of a sociopath, if you were completely confident that the key really belonged to him. Other people would accept that key as belonging to him because you signed it (assuming they trust you), but they wouldn't trust that key's owner. Trusting a key is not the same as trusting the key's owner.

Trust is not necessarily transferable; I have a friend whom I trust not to lie. He's a gullible person who trusts the President not to lie. That doesn't mean I trust the President not to lie. This is just common sense. If I trust Alice's signature on a key, and Alice trusts Charlie's signature on a key, that does not imply that I have to trust Charlie's signature on a key.

It would be a good idea to keep your own public key on hand with a collection of certifying signatures attached from a variety of "introducers," in the hopes that most people will trust at least one of the introducers who vouch for your own public key's validity. You could post your key with its attached collection of certifying signatures on various electronic bulletin boards. If you sign someone else's public key, return it to them with your signature so that they can add it to their own collection of credentials for their own public key.

PGP keeps track of which keys on your public key ring are properly certified with signatures from introducers that you trust. All you have to do is tell PGP which people you trust as introducers, and certify their keys yourself with your own ultimately trusted key. PGP can take it from there, automatically validating any other keys that have been signed by your designated introducers. And of course you may directly sign more keys yourself. More on this later.

Make sure no one else can tamper with your own public key ring. Checking a new signed public key certificate must ultimately depend on the integrity of the trusted public keys that are already on your own public key ring. Maintain physical control of your public key ring, preferably on your own personal computer rather than on a remote timesharing system, just as you would do for your secret key. This is to protect it from tampering, not from disclosure. Keep a trusted backup copy of your public key ring and your secret key ring on write-protected media.

Since your own trusted public key is used as a final authority to directly or indirectly certify all the other keys on your key ring, it is the most important key to protect from tampering. To detect any tampering of your own ultimately trusted public key, PGP can be set up to automatically compare your public key against a backup copy on write-protected media. For details, see the description of the "-kc" key ring check command in the Special Topics volume.

PGP generally assumes you will maintain physical security over your system and your key rings, as well as your copy of PGP itself. If an intruder can tamper with your disk, then in theory he can tamper with PGP itself, rendering moot the safeguards PGP may have to detect tampering with keys.

One somewhat complicated way to protect your own whole public key ring from tampering is to sign the whole ring with your own secret key. You could do this by making a detached signature certificate of the public key ring, by signing the ring with the "-sb" options (see the section called "Separating Signatures from Messages" in the PGP User's Guide, Special Topics volume). Unfortunately, you would still have to keep a separate trusted copy of your own public key around to check the signature you made. You couldn't rely on your own public key stored on your public key ring to check the signature you made for the whole ring, because that is part of what you're trying to check.

How Does PGP Keep Track of Which Keys are Valid?

Before you read this section, be sure to read the above section on "How to Protect Public Keys from Tampering."

PGP keeps track of which keys on your public key ring are properly certified with signatures from introducers that you trust. All you have to do is tell PGP which people you trust as introducers, and certify their keys yourself with your own ultimately trusted key. PGP can take it from there, automatically validating any other keys that have been signed by your designated introducers. And of course you may directly sign more keys yourself.

There are two entirely separate criteria PGP uses to judge a public key's usefulness — don't get them confused:

1. Does the key actually belong to whom it appears to belong? In other words, has it been certified with a trusted signature?

2. Does it belong to someone you can trust to certify other keys?

PGP can calculate the answer to the first question. To answer the second question, PGP must be explicitly told by you, the user. When you supply the answer to question 2, PGP can then calculate the answer to question 1 for other keys signed by the introducer you designated as trusted.

Keys that have been certified by a trusted introducer are deemed valid by PGP. The keys belonging to trusted introducers must themselves be certified either by you or by other trusted introducers.

PGP also allows for the possibility of you having several shades of trust for people to act as introducers. Your trust for a key's owner to act as an introducer does not just reflect your estimation of their personal integrity—it should also reflect how competent you think they are at understanding key management and using good judgment in signing keys. You can designate a person to PGP as unknown, untrusted, marginally trusted, or completely trusted to certify other public keys. This trust information is stored on your key ring with their key, but when you tell PGP to copy a key off your key ring, PGP will not copy the trust information along with the key, because your private opinions on trust are regarded as confidential.

When PGP is calculating the validity of a public key, it examines the trust level of all the attached certifying signatures. It computes a weighted score of validity—two marginally trusted signatures are deemed as credible as one fully trusted signature. PGP's skepticism is adjustable—for example, you may tune PGP to require two fully trusted signatures or three marginally trusted signatures to judge a key as valid.

Your own key is "axiomatically" valid to PGP, needing no introducer's signature to prove its validity. PGP knows which public keys are yours, by looking for the corresponding secret keys on the secret key ring. PGP also assumes you ultimately trust yourself to certify other keys.

As time goes on, you will accumulate keys from other people that you may want to designate as trusted introducers. Everyone else will each choose their own trusted introducers. And everyone will gradually accumulate and distribute with their key a collection of certifying signatures from other people, with the expectation that anyone receiving it will trust at least one or two of the signatures. This will cause the emergence of a decentralized fault-tolerant web of confidence for all public keys.

This unique grass-roots approach contrasts sharply with government standard public key management schemes, such as Internet Privacy Enhanced Mail (PEM), which are based on centralized control and mandatory centralized trust. The standard schemes rely on a hierarchy of Certifying Authorities who dictate whom you must trust. PGP's decentralized probabilistic method for determining public key legitimacy is the centerpiece of its key management architecture. PGP lets you alone choose whom you trust, putting you at the top of your own private certification pyramid. PGP is for people who prefer to pack their own parachutes.

How to Protect Secret Keys from Disclosure

Protect your own secret key and your pass phrase carefully. Really, really carefully. If your secret key is ever compromised, you'd better get the word out quickly to all interested parties (good luck) before someone else uses it to make signatures in your name. For example, they could use it to sign bogus public key certificates, which could create problems for many people, especially if your signature is widely trusted. And of course, a compromise of your own secret key could expose all messages sent to you.

To protect your secret key, you can start by always keeping physical control of your secret key. Keeping it on your personal computer at home is OK, or keep it in your notebook computer that you can carry with you. If you must use an office computer that you don't always have physical control of, then keep your public and secret key rings on a write-protected removable floppy disk, and don't leave it behind when you leave the office. It wouldn't be a good idea to allow your secret key to reside on a remote timesharing computer, such as a remote dial-in Unix system. Someone could eavesdrop on your modem line and capture your pass phrase, and then obtain your actual secret key from the remote system. You should only use your secret key on a machine that you have physical control over.

Don't store your pass phrase anywhere on the computer that has your secret key file. Storing both the secret key and the pass phrase on the same computer is as dangerous as keeping your PIN in the same wallet as your Automatic Teller Machine bank card. You don't want somebody to get their hands on your disk containing both the pass phrase and the secret key file. It would be most secure if you just memorize your pass phrase and don't store it anywhere but your brain. If you feel you must write down your pass phrase, keep it well protected, perhaps even more well protected than the secret key file.

And keep backup copies of your secret key ring—remember, you have the only copy of your secret key, and losing it will render useless all the copies of your public key that you have spread throughout the world.

The decentralized non-institutional approach PGP uses to manage public keys has its benefits, but unfortunately this also means we can't rely on a single centralized list of which keys have been compromised. This makes it a bit harder to contain the damage of a secret key compromise. You just have to spread the word and hope everyone hears about it.

If the worst case happens—your secret key and pass phrase are both compromised (hopefully you will find this out somehow)—you will have to issue a "key compromise" certificate. This kind of certificate is used to warn other people to stop using your public key. You can use PGP to create such a certificate by using the "-kd" command. Then you must somehow send this compromise certificate to everyone else on the planet, or at least to all your friends and their friends, et cetera. Their own PGP software will install this key compromise certificate on their public key rings and will automatically prevent them from accidentally using your public key ever again. You can then generate a new secret/public key pair and publish the new public key. You could send out one package containing both your new public key and the key compromise certificate for your old key.

Revoking a Public Key

Suppose your secret key and your pass phrase are somehow both compromised. You have to get the word out to the rest of the world, so that they will all stop using your public key. To do this, you will have to issue a "key compromise," or "key revocation" certificate to revoke your public key.

To generate a certificate to revoke your own key, use the -kd command:

```
pgp -kd your_userid
```

This certificate bears your signature, made with the same key you are revoking. You should widely disseminate this key revocation certificate as soon as possible. Other people who receive it can add it to their public key rings, and their PGP software then automatically prevents them from accidentally using your old public key ever again. You can then generate a new secret/public key pair and publish the new public key.

You may choose to revoke your key for some other reason than the compromise of a secret key. If so, you may still use the same mechanism to revoke it.

What If You Lose Your Secret Key?

Normally, if you want to revoke your own secret key, you can use the "-kd" command to issue a revocation certificate, signed with your own secret key (see "Revoking a Public Key").

But what can you do if you lose your secret key, or if your secret key is destroyed? You can't revoke it yourself, because you must use your own secret key to revoke it, and you don't have it anymore. A future version of PGP will offer a more secure means of revoking keys in these circumstances, allowing trusted introducers to certify that a public key has been revoked. But for now, you will have to get the word out through whatever informal means you can, asking users to "disable" your public key on their own individual public key rings.

Other users may disable your public key on their own public key rings by using the "-kd" command. If a user ID is specified that does not correspond to a secret key on the secret key ring, the -kd command will look for that user ID on the public key ring, and mark that public key as disabled. A disabled key may not be used to encrypt any messages, and may not be extracted from the key ring with the -kx command. It can still be used to check signatures, but a warning is displayed. And if the user tries to add the same key again to his key ring, it will not work because the disabled key is already on the key ring. These combined features will help curtail the further spread of a disabled key.

If the specified public key is already disabled, the -kd command will ask if you want the key reenabled.

Advanced Topics

Most of the "Advanced Topics" are covered in the "PGP User's Guide, Volume II: Special Topics." But here are a few topics that bear mentioning here.

Sending Ciphertext Through E-mail Channels: Radix-64 Format

Many electronic mail systems only allow messages made of ASCII text, not the 8-bit raw binary data that ciphertext is made of. To get around this problem, PGP supports ASCII radix-64 format for ciphertext messages, similar to the Internet Privacy-Enhanced Mail (PEM) format, as well as the Internet MIME format. This special format represents binary data by using only printable ASCII characters, so it is useful for transmitting binary encrypted data through 7-bit channels or for sending binary encrypted data as normal E-mail text. This format acts as a form of "transport armor," protecting it against corruption as it travels through intersystem gateways on the Internet. PGP also appends a CRC to detect transmission errors.

Radix-64 format converts the plaintext by expanding groups of 3 binary 8-bit bytes into 4 printable ASCII characters, so the file grows by about 33%. But this expansion isn't so bad when you consider that the file probably was compressed more than that by PGP before it was encrypted.

To produce a ciphertext file in ASCII radix-64 format, just add the "a" option when encrypting or signing a message, like so:

```
pgp -esa message.txt her_userid
```

This example produces a ciphertext file called "message.asc" that contains data in a PEM-like ASCII radix-64 format. This file can be easily uploaded into a text editor through 7-bit channels for transmission as normal E-mail on the Internet or any other E-mail network.

Decrypting the radix-64 transport-armored message is no different than a normal decrypt. For example:

```
pgp message
```

PGP automatically looks for the ASCII file "message.asc" before it looks for the binary file "message.pgp." It recognizes that the file is in radix-64 format and converts it back to binary before processing as it normally does, producing as a by-product a ".pgp" ciphertext file in binary form. The final output file is in normal plaintext form, just as it was in the original file "message.txt."

Most Internet E-mail facilities prohibit sending messages that are more than 50,000 bytes long. Longer messages must be broken into smaller chunks that can be mailed separately. If your encrypted message is very large, and you requested radix-64 format, PGP automatically breaks it up into chunks that are each small enough to send via E-mail. The chunks are put into files named with extensions ".as1," ".as2," ".as3," etc. The recipient must concatenate these separate files back together in their proper order into one big file before decrypting it. While decrypting, PGP ignores any extraneous text in mail headers that are not enclosed in the radix-64 message blocks.

If you want to send a public key to someone else in radix-64 format, just add the -a option while extracting the key from your key ring.

If you forgot to use the -a option when you made a ciphertext file or extracted a key, you may still directly convert the binary file into radix-64 format by simply using the -a option alone, without any encryption specified. PGP converts it to a ".asc" file.

If you sign a plaintext file without encrypting it, PGP will normally compress it after signing it, rendering it unreadable to the casual human observer. This is a suitable way of storing signed files in archival applications. But if you want to send the signed message as E-mail, and the original plaintext message is in text (not binary) form, there is a way to send it through an E-mail channel in such a way that the plaintext does not get compressed, and the ASCII armor is applied only to the binary signature certificate, but not to the plaintext message. This makes it possible for the recipient to read the signed message with human eyes, without the aid of PGP. Of course, PGP is still needed to actually check the signature. For further information on this feature, see the explanation of the CLEARSIG parameter in the section "Setting Configuration Parameters:

CONFIG.TXT" in the Special Topics volume.

Environmental Variable for Path Name

PGP uses several special files for its purposes, such as your standard key ring files "pubring.pgp" and "secring.pgp," the random number seed file "randseed.bin," the PGP configuration file "config.txt," and the foreign language string translation file "language.txt." These special files can be kept in any directory, by setting the environmental variable "PGPPATH" to the desired pathname. For example, on MSDOS, the shell command:

```
SET PGPPATH=C:\PGP
```

makes PGP assume that your public key ring filename is "C:\PGP\pubring.pgp." Assuming, of course, that this directory exists. Use your favorite text editor to modify your MSDOS AUTOEXEC.BAT file to automatically set up this variable whenever you start up your system. If PGPPATH remains undefined, these special files are assumed to be in the current directory.

Setting Configuration Parameters: CONFIG.TXT

PGP has a number of user-settable parameters that can be defined in a special configuration text file called "config.txt," in the directory pointed to by the shell environmental variable PGPPATH. Having a configuration file enables the user to define various flags and parameters for PGP without the burden of having to always define these parameters in the PGP command line.

With these configuration parameters, for example, you can control where PGP stores its temporary scratch files, or you can select what foreign language PGP will use to display its diagnostics messages and user prompts, or you can adjust PGP's level of skepticism in determining a key's validity based on the number of certifying signatures it has.

For more details on setting these configuration parameters, see the appropriate section of the PGP User's Guide, Special Topics volume.

Vulnerabilities

No data security system is impenetrable. PGP can be circumvented in a variety of ways. Potential vulnerabilities you should be aware of include compromising your pass phrase or secret key, public key tampering, files that you deleted but are still somewhere on the disk, viruses and Trojan horses, breaches in your physical security, electromagnetic emissions, exposure on multi-user systems, traffic analysis, and perhaps even direct cryptanalysis.

For a detailed discussion of these issues, see the "Vulnerabilities" section in the PGP User's Guide, Special Topics volume.

Beware of Snake Oil

When examining a cryptographic software package, the question always remains, why should you trust this product? Even if you examined the source code yourself, not everyone has the cryptographic experience to judge the security. Even if you are an experienced cryptographer, subtle weaknesses in the algorithms could still elude you.

When I was in college in the early seventies, I devised what I believed was a brilliant encryption scheme. A simple pseudorandom number stream was added to the plaintext stream to create ciphertext. This would seemingly thwart any frequency analysis of the ciphertext, and would be uncrackable even to the most resourceful Government intelligence agencies. I felt so smug about my achievement. So cock-sure.

Years later, I discovered this same scheme in several introductory cryptography texts and tutorial papers. How nice. Other cryptographers had thought of the same scheme. Unfortunately, the scheme was presented as a simple homework assignment on how to use elementary cryptanalytic techniques to trivially crack it. So much for my brilliant scheme.

From this humbling experience I learned how easy it is to fall into a false sense of security when devising an encryption algorithm. Most people don't realize how fiendishly difficult it is to devise an encryption algorithm that can withstand a prolonged and determined attack by a resourceful opponent. Many mainstream software engineers have developed equally naive encryption schemes (often even the very same encryption scheme), and some of them have been incorporated into commercial encryption software packages and sold for good money to thousands of unsuspecting users.

This is like selling automotive seat belts that look good and feel good, but snap open in even the slowest crash test. Depending on them may be worse than not wearing seat belts at all. No one suspects they are bad until a real crash. Depending on weak cryptographic software may cause you to unknowingly place sensitive information at risk. You might not otherwise have done so if you had no cryptographic software at all. Perhaps you may never even discover your data has been compromised.

Sometimes commercial packages use the Federal Data Encryption Standard (DES), a good conventional algorithm recommended by the Government for commercial use (but not for classified information, oddly enough—hmmm). There are several "modes of operation" the DES can use, some of them better than others. The Government specifically recommends not using the weakest simplest mode for messages, the Electronic Codebook (ECB) mode. But they do recommend the stronger and more complex Cipher Feedback (CFB) or Cipher Block Chaining (CBC) modes.

Unfortunately, most of the commercial encryption packages I've looked at use ECB mode. When I've talked to the authors of a number of these implementations, they say they've never heard of CBC or CFB modes, and didn't know anything about the weaknesses of ECB mode. The very fact that they haven't even learned enough cryptography to know these elementary concepts is not reassuring. These same software packages often include a second faster encryption algorithm that can be used instead of the slower DES. The author of the package often thinks his proprietary faster algorithm is as secure as the DES, but after questioning him I usually discover that it's just a variation of my own brilliant scheme from college days. Or maybe he won't even reveal how his proprietary encryption scheme works, but assures me it's a brilliant scheme and I should trust it. I'm sure he believes that his algorithm is brilliant, but how can I know that without seeing it?

In all fairness I must point out that in most cases these products do not come from companies that specialize in cryptographic technology.

There is a company called AccessData (87 East 600 South, Orem, Utah 84058, phone 1-800-658-5199) that sells a package for $185 that cracks the built-in encryption schemes used by WordPerfect, Lotus 1-2-3, MS Excel, Symphony, Quattro Pro, Paradox, and MS Word 2.0. It doesn't simply guess passwords—it does real cryptanalysis. Some people buy it when they forget their password for their own files. Law enforcement agencies buy it too, so they can read files they seize. I talked to Eric Thompson, the author, and he said his program only takes a split second to crack them, but he put in some delay loops to slow it down so it doesn't look so easy to the customer. He also told me that the password encryption feature of PKZIP files can often be easily broken, and that his law enforcement customers already have that service regularly provided to them from another vendor.

In some ways, cryptography is like pharmaceuticals. Its integrity may be absolutely crucial. Bad penicillin looks the same as good penicillin. You can tell if your spreadsheet software is wrong, but how do you tell if your cryptography package is weak? The ciphertext produced by a weak encryption algorithm looks as good as ciphertext produced by a strong encryption algorithm. There's a lot of snake oil out there. A lot of quack cures. Unlike the patent medicine hucksters of old, these software implementors usually don't even know their stuff is snake oil. They may be good software engineers, but they usually haven't even read any of the academic literature in cryptography. But they think they can write good cryptographic software. And why not? After all, it seems intuitively easy to do so. And their software seems to work okay.

Anyone who thinks they have devised an unbreakable encryption scheme either is an incredibly rare genius or is naive and inexperienced.

I remember a conversation with Brian Snow, a highly placed senior cryptographer with the NSA. He said he would never trust an encryption algorithm designed by someone who had not "earned their bones" by first spending a lot of time cracking codes. That did make a lot of sense. I observed that practically no one in the commercial world of cryptography qualified under this criterion. "Yes," he said with a self assured smile, "And that makes our job at NSA so much easier." A chilling thought. I didn't qualify either.

The Government has peddled snake oil too. After World War II, the U.S. sold German Enigma ciphering machines to third world governments. But they didn't tell them that the Allies cracked the Enigma code during the war, a fact that remained classified for many years. Even today many Unix systems worldwide use the Enigma cipher for file encryption, in part because the Government has created legal obstacles against using better algorithms. They even tried to prevent the initial publication of the RSA algorithm in 1977. And they have squashed essentially all commercial efforts to develop effective secure telephones for the general public.

The principal job of the U.S. Government's National Security Agency is to gather intelligence, principally by covertly tapping into people's private communications (see James Bamford's book, "The Puzzle Palace"). The NSA has amassed considerable skill and resources for cracking codes. When people can't get good cryptography to protect themselves, it makes NSA's job much easier. NSA also has the responsibility of approving and recommending encryption algorithms. Some critics charge that this is a conflict of interest, like putting the fox in charge of guarding the hen house. NSA has been pushing a conventional encryption algorithm that they designed, and they won't tell anybody how it works because that's classified. They want others to trust it and use it. But any cryptographer can tell you that a well-designed encryption algorithm does not have to be classified to remain secure. Only the keys should need protection. How does anyone else really know if NSA's classified algorithm is secure? It's not that hard for NSA to design an encryption algorithm that only they can crack, if no one else can review the algorithm. Are they deliberately selling snake oil?

I'm not as certain about the security of PGP as I once was about my brilliant encryption software from college. If I were, that would be a bad sign. But I'm pretty sure that PGP does not contain any glaring weaknesses. The crypto algorithms were developed by people at high levels of civilian cryptographic academia, and have been individually subject to extensive peer review. Source code is available to facilitate peer review of PGP and to help dispel the fears of some users. It's reasonably well researched, and has been years in the making. And I don't work for the NSA. I hope it doesn't require too large a "leap of faith" to trust the security of PGP.

PGP Quick Reference

Here's a quick summary of PGP commands.

To encrypt a plaintext file with the recipient's public key:

```
pgp -e textfile her_userid
```

To sign a plaintext file with your secret key:

```
pgp -s textfile [-u your_userid]
```

To sign a plaintext ASCII text file with your secret key, producing a signed plaintext message suitable for sending via E-mail:

```
pgp -sta textfile [-u your_userid]
```

To sign a plaintext file with your secret key, and then encrypt it with the recipient's public key:

```
pgp -es textfile her_userid [-u your_userid]
```

To encrypt a plaintext file with just conventional cryptography, type:

```
pgp -c textfile
```

To decrypt an encrypted file, or to check the signature integrity of a signed file:

```
pgp ciphertextfile [-o plaintextfile]
```

To encrypt a message for any number of multiple recipients:

```
pgp -e textfile userid1 userid2 userid3
```

Key management commands:

To generate your own unique public/secret key pair:

```
pgp -kg
```

To add a public or secret key file's contents to your public or secret key ring:

```
pgp -ka keyfile [keyring]
```

To extract (copy) a key from your public or secret key ring:

```
pgp -kx userid keyfile [keyring]
```

or:

```
pgp -kxa userid keyfile [keyring]
```

To view the contents of your public key ring:

```
pgp -kv[v] [userid] [keyring]
```

To view the "fingerprint" of a public key, to help verify it over the telephone with its owner:

```
pgp -kvc [userid] [keyring]
```

To view the contents and check the certifying signatures of your public key ring:

```
pgp -kc [userid] [keyring]
```

To edit the user ID or pass phrase for your secret key:

```
pgp -ke userid [keyring]
```

To edit the trust parameters for a public key:

```
pgp -ke userid [keyring]
```

To remove a key or just a user ID from your public key ring:

```
pgp -kr userid [keyring]
```

To sign and certify someone else's public key on your public key ring:

```
pgp -ks her_userid [-u your_userid] [keyring]
```

To remove selected signatures from a user ID on a keyring:

```
pgp -krs userid [keyring]
```

To permanently revoke your own key, issuing a key compromise certificate:

```
pgp -kd your_userid
```

To disable or reenable a public key on your own public key ring:

```
pgp -kd userid
```

Esoteric commands:

To decrypt a message and leave the signature on it intact:

```
pgp -d ciphertextfile
```

To create a signature certificate that is detached from the document:

```
pgp -sb textfile [-u your_userid]
```

To detach a signature certificate from a signed message:

```
pgp -b ciphertextfile
```

Command options

(can be used in combination with other command options—sometimes even spelling interesting words!):

To produce a ciphertext file in ASCII radix-64 format, just add the -a option when encrypting or signing a message or extracting a key:

```
pgp -sea textfile her_userid
```

or:

```
pgp -kxa userid keyfile [keyring]
```

To wipe out the plaintext file after producing the ciphertext file, just add the -w (wipe) option when encrypting or signing a message:

```
pgp -sew message.txt her_userid
```

To specify that a plaintext file contains ASCII text, not binary, and should be converted to recipient's local text line conventions, add the -t (text) option to other options:

```
pgp -seat message.txt her_userid
```

To view the decrypted plaintext output on your screen (like the Unix-style "more" command), without writing it to a file, use the -m (more) option while decrypting:

```
pgp -m ciphertextfile
```

To specify that the recipient's decrypted plaintext will be shown ONLY on her screen and cannot be saved to disk, add the -m option:

```
pgp -steam message.txt her_userid
```

To recover the original plaintext filename while decrypting, add the -p option:

```
pgp -p ciphertextfile
```

To use a Unix-style filter mode, reading from standard input and writing to standard output, add the -f option:

```
pgp -feast her_userid <inputfile >outputfile
```

Legal Issues

For detailed information on PGP™ licensing, distribution, copyrights, patents, trademarks, liability limitations, and export controls, see the "Legal Issues" section in the "PGP User's Guide, Volume II: Special Topics."

PGP uses a public key algorithm claimed by U.S. patent #4,405,829. The exclusive licensing rights to this patent are held by a California company called Public Key Partners, and you may be infringing the patent if you use PGP in the USA without a license. These issues are detailed in the Volume II manual, and in the RSAREF license that comes with the freeware version of PGP. PKP has licensed others to practice the patent, including a company known as ViaCrypt, in Phoenix, Arizona. ViaCrypt sells a fully-licensed version of PGP. ViaCrypt may be reached at 602-944-0773.

PGP is "guerrilla" freeware, and I don't mind if you distribute it widely. Just don't ask me to send you a copy. Instead, you can look for it yourself on many BBS systems and a number of Internet FTP sites. But before you distribute PGP, it is essential that you understand the U.S. export controls on encryption software.

Acknowledgments

Formidable obstacles and powerful forces have been arrayed to stop PGP. Dedicated people are helping to overcome these obstacles. PGP has achieved notoriety as "underground software," and bringing PGP "above ground" as fully licensed freeware has required patience and persistence. I'd especially like to thank Hal Abelson, Jeff Schiller, Brian LaMacchia, and Derek Atkins at MIT for their determined efforts. I'd also like to thank Jim Bruce and David Litster in the MIT administration and Bob Prior and Terry Ehling at the MIT Press. And I'd like to thank my entire legal defense team, whose job is not over yet. I used to tell a lot of lawyer jokes, before I encountered so many positive examples of lawyers in my legal defense team, most of whom work pro bono.

The development of PGP has turned into a remarkable social phenomenon, whose unique political appeal has inspired the collective efforts of an ever-growing number of volunteer programmers. Remember that children's story called "Stone Soup"?

I'd like to thank the following people for their contributions to the creation of Pretty Good Privacy. Although I was the author of PGP version 1.0, major parts of later versions of PGP were implemented by an international collaborative effort involving a large number of contributors, under my design guidance.

Branko Lankester, Hal Finney, and Peter Gutmann all contributed a huge amount of time in adding features for PGP 2.0, and ported it to Unix variants.

Hugh Kennedy ported it to VAX/VMS, Lutz Frank ported it to the Atari ST, and Cor Bosman and Colin Plumb ported it to the Commodore Amiga.

Translation of PGP into foreign languages was done by Jean-loup Gailly in France, Armando Ramos in Spain, Felipe Rodriquez Svensson and Branko Lankester in The Netherlands, Miguel Angel Gallardo in Spain, Hugh Kennedy and Lutz Frank in Germany, David Vincenzetti in Italy, Harry Bush and Maris Gabalins in Latvia, Zygimantas Cepaitis in Lithuania, Peter Suchkow and Andrew Chernov in Russia, and Alexander Smishlajev in Esperantujo. Peter Gutmann offered to translate it into New Zealand English, but we finally decided PGP could get by with U.S. English.

Jean-loup Gailly, Mark Adler, and Richard B. Wales published the ZIP compression code, and granted permission for inclusion into PGP. The MD5 routines were developed and placed in the public domain by Ron Rivest. The IDEA™ cipher was developed by Xuejia Lai and James L. Massey at ETH in Zurich, and is used in PGP with permission from Ascom-Tech AG.

Charlie Merritt originally taught me how to do decent multiprecision arithmetic for public key cryptography, and Jimmy Upton contributed a faster multiply/modulo algorithm. Thad Smith implemented an even faster modmult algorithm. Zhahai Stewart contributed a lot of useful ideas on PGP file formats and other stuff, including having more than one user ID for a key. I heard the idea of introducers from Whit Diffie. Kelly Goen did most of the work for the initial electronic publication of PGP 1.0.

Various contributions of coding effort also came from Colin Plumb, Derek Atkins, and Castor Fu. Other contributions of effort, coding or otherwise, have come from Hugh Miller, Eric Hughes, Tim May, Stephan Neuhaus, and too many others for me to remember right now. Zbigniew Fiedorwicz did a Macintosh port.

Since the release of PGP 2.0, many other programmers have sent in patches and bug fixes and porting adjustments for other computers. There are too many to individually thank here.

Just as in the "Stone Soup" story, it is getting harder to peer through the thick soup to see the stone at the bottom of the pot that I dropped in to start it all off.

About the Author

Philip Zimmermann is a software engineer consultant with 19 years experience, specializing in embedded real-time systems, cryptography, authentication, and data communications. Experience includes design and implementation of authentication systems for financial information networks, network data security, key management protocols, embedded real-time multitasking executives, operating systems, and local area networks.

Custom versions of cryptography and authentication products and public key implementations such as the NIST DSS are available from Zimmermann, as well as custom product development services. His consulting firm's address is:

Boulder Software Engineering
3021 Eleventh Street
Boulder, Colorado 80304 USA

Phone: 303-541-0140 (10:00 am - 7:00 pm Mountain Time)

Fax: arrange by phone

Internet: prz@acm.org

Phil's Pretty Good Software

Presents

PGP™
Pretty Good™ Privacy
Public Key Encryption for the Masses

PGP™ User's Guide
Volume II: Special Topics
by Philip Zimmermann

Revised 22 May 94

PGP Version 2.6 – 22 May 94

Software by

Philip Zimmermann, and many others.

Synopsis:

PGP™ uses public-key encryption to protect E-mail and data files. Communicate securely with people you've never met, with no secure channels needed for prior exchange of keys. PGP is well featured and fast, with sophisticated key management, digital signatures, data compression, and good ergonomic design.

Software and documentation© Copyright 1990–1994 Philip Zimmermann. All rights reserved. For information on PGP licensing, distribution, copyrights, patents, trademarks, liability limitations, and export controls, see the "Legal Issues" section. Distributed by the Massachusetts Institute of Technology.

Contents

Quick Overview

Pretty Good™ Privacy (PGP), from Phil's Pretty Good Software, is a high-security cryptographic software application for MSDOS, Unix, VAX/VMS, and other computers. PGP combines the convenience of the Rivest-Shamir-Adleman (RSA) public key cryptosystem with the speed of conventional cryptography, message digests for digital signatures, data compression before encryption, good ergonomic design, and sophisticated key management.

This volume II of the PGP User's Guide covers advanced topics about PGP that were not covered in the "PGP User's Guide, Volume I: Essential Topics." You should first read the Essential Topics volume, or this manual won't make much sense to you. Reading this Special Topics volume is optional, except for the legal issues section, which everyone should read.

Special Topics

Selecting Keys via Key ID

In all commands that let the user type a user ID or fragment of a user ID to select a key, the hexadecimal key ID may be used instead. Just use the key ID, with a prefix of "0x," in place of the user ID. For example:

```
pgp -kv 0x67F7
```

This would display all keys that had 67F7 as part of their key IDs.

This feature is particularly useful if you have two different keys from the same person, with the same user ID. You can unambiguously pick which key you want by specifying the key ID.

Separating Signatures from Messages

Normally, signature certificates are physically attached to the text they sign. This makes it convenient in simple cases to check signatures. It is desirable in some circumstances to have signature certificates stored separately from the messages they sign. It is possible to generate signature certificates that are detached from the text they sign. To do this, combine the 'b' (break) option with the 's' (sign) option. For example:

```
pgp -sb letter.txt
```

This example produces an isolated signature certificate in a file called "letter.sig." The contents of letter.txt are not appended to the signature certificate.

After creating the signature certificate file (letter.sig in the above example), send it along with the original text file to the recipient. The recipient must have both files to check the signature integrity. When the recipient attempts to process the signature file, PGP notices that there is no text in the same file with the signature and prompts the user for the filename of the text. Only then can PGP properly check the signature integrity. If the recipient knows in advance that the signature is detached from the text file, she can specify both filenames on the command line:

```
pgp letter.sig letter.txt
```

or:

```
pgp letter letter.txt
```

PGP will not have to prompt for the text file name in this case.

A detached signature certificate is useful if you want to keep the signature certificate in a separate certificate log. A detached signature of an executable program is also useful for detecting a subsequent virus infection. It is also useful if more than one party must sign a document such as a legal contract, without nesting signatures. Each person's signature is independent.

If you receive a ciphertext file that has the signature certificate glued to the message, you can still pry the signature certificate away from the message during the decryption. You can do this with the -b option during decrypt, like so:

```
pgp -b letter
```

This decrypts the letter.pgp file and if there is a signature in it, PGP checks the signature and detaches it from the rest of the message, storing it in the file letter.sig.

Decrypting the Message and Leaving the Signature on it

Usually, you want PGP to completely unravel a ciphertext file, decrypting it and checking the nested signature if there is one, peeling away the layers until you are left with only the original plaintext file.

But sometimes you want to decrypt an encrypted file, and leave the inner signature still attached, so that you are left with a decrypted signed message. This may be useful if you want to send a copy of a signed document to a third party, perhaps re-enciphering it. For example, suppose you get a message signed by Charlie, encrypted to you. You want to decrypt it, and, leaving Charlie's signature on it, you want to send it to Alice, perhaps re-enciphering it with Alice's public key. No problem. PGP can handle that.

To simply decrypt a message and leave the signature on it intact, type:

```
pgp -d letter
```

This decrypts letter.pgp, and if there is an inner signature, it is left intact with the decrypted plaintext in the output file.

Now you can archive it, or maybe re-encrypt it and send it to someone else.

Sending ASCII Text Files Across Different Machine Environments

You may use PGP to encrypt any kind of plaintext file, binary 8-bit data or ASCII text. Probably the most common usage of PGP will be for E-mail, when the plaintext is ASCII text.

ASCII text is sometimes represented differently on different machines. For example, on an MSDOS system, all lines of ASCII text are terminated with a carriage return followed by a linefeed. On a Unix system, all lines end with just a linefeed. On a Macintosh, all lines end with just a carriage return. This is a sad fact of life.

Normal unencrypted ASCII text messages are often automatically translated to some common "canonical" form when they are transmitted from one machine to another. Canonical text has a carriage return and a linefeed at the end of each line of text. For example, the popular KERMIT communication protocol can convert text to canonical form when transmitting it to another system. This gets converted back to local text line terminators by the receiving KERMIT. This makes it easy to share text files across different systems.

But encrypted text cannot be automatically converted by a communication protocol, because the plaintext is hidden by encipherment. To remedy this inconvenience, PGP lets you specify that the plaintext should be treated as ASCII text (not binary data) and should be converted to canonical text form before it gets encrypted. At the receiving end, the decrypted plaintext is automatically converted back to whatever text form is appropriate for the local environment.

To make PGP assume the plaintext is text that should be converted to canonical text before encryption, just add the "t" option when encrypting or signing a message, like so:

```
pgp -et message.txt her_userid
```

This mode is automatically turned off if PGP detects that the plaintext file contains what it thinks is non-text binary data.

For PGP users that use non-English 8-bit character sets, when PGP converts text to canonical form, it may convert data from the local character set into the LATIN1 (ISO 8859-1 Latin Alphabet 1) character set, depending on the setting of the CHARSET parameter in the PGP configuration file. LATIN1 is a superset of ASCII, with extra characters added for many European languages.

Leaving No Traces of Plaintext on the Disk

After PGP makes a ciphertext file for you, you can have PGP automatically overwrite the plaintext file and delete it, leaving no trace of plaintext on the disk so that no one can recover it later using a disk block scanning utility. This is useful if the plaintext file contains sensitive information that you don't want to keep around.

To wipe out the plaintext file after producing the ciphertext file, just add the "w" (wipe) option when encrypting or signing a message, like so:

```
pgp -esw message.txt her_userid
```

This example creates the ciphertext file "message.pgp," and the plaintext file "message.txt" is destroyed beyond recovery.

Obviously, you should be careful with this option. Also note that this will not wipe out any fragments of plaintext that your word processor might have created on the disk while you were editing the message before running PGP. Most word processors create backup files, scratch files, or both. Also, it overwrites the file only once, which is enough to thwart conventional disk recovery efforts, but not enough to withstand a determined and sophisticated effort to recover the faint magnetic traces of the data using special disk recovery hardware.

Displaying Decrypted Plaintext on Your Screen

To view the decrypted plaintext output on your screen (like the Unix-style "more" command), without writing it to a file, use the -m (more) option while decrypting:

```
pgp -m ciphertextfile
```

This displays the decrypted plaintext display on your screen one screenful at a time.

Making a Message For Her Eyes Only

To specify that the recipient's decrypted plaintext will be shown ONLY on her screen and will not be saved to disk, add the -m option:

```
pgp -sem message.txt her_userid
```

Later, when the recipient decrypts the ciphertext with her secret key and pass phrase, the plaintext will be displayed on her screen but will not be saved to disk. The text will be displayed as it would if she used the Unix "more" command, one screenful at a time. If she wants to read the message again, she will have to decrypt the ciphertext again.

This feature is the safest way for you to prevent your sensitive message from being inadvertently left on the recipient's disk. This feature was added at the request of a user who wanted to send intimate messages to his lover, but was afraid she might accidentally leave the decrypted messages on her husband's computer.

Note that this feature will not prevent a clever and determined person from finding a way to save the decrypted plaintext to disk—it's to help prevent a casual user from doing it inadvertently.

Preserving the Original Plaintext Filename

Normally, PGP names the decrypted plaintext output file with a name similar to the input ciphertext filename, but dropping the extension. Or, you can override that convention by specifying an output plaintext filename on the command line with the -o option. For most E-mail, this is a reasonable way to name the plaintext file, because you get to decide its name when you decipher it, and your typical E-mail messages often come from useless original plaintext filenames like "to_phil.txt."

But when PGP encrypts a plaintext file, it always saves the original filename and attaches it to the plaintext before it compresses and encrypts the plaintext. Normally, this hidden original filename is discarded by PGP when it decrypts, but you can tell PGP you want to preserve the original plaintext filename and use it as the name of the decrypted plaintext output file. This is useful if PGP is used on files whose names are important to preserve.

To recover the original plaintext filename while decrypting, add the -p option, like so:

```
pgp -p ciphertextfile
```

I usually don't use this option, because if I did, about half of my incoming E-mail would decrypt to the same plaintext filenames of "to_phil.txt" or "prz.txt."

Editing Your User ID or Pass Phrase

Sometimes you may need to change your pass phrase, perhaps because someone looked over your shoulder while you typed it in.

Or you may need to change your user ID, because you got married and changed your name, or maybe you changed your E-mail address. Or maybe you want to add a second or third user ID to your key, because you may be known by more than one name or E-mail address or job title. PGP lets you attach more than one user ID to your key, any one of which may be used to look up your key on the key ring.

To edit your own user ID or pass phrase for your secret key:

```
pgp -ke userid [keyring]
```

PGP prompts you for a new user ID or a new pass phrase.

The optional [keyring] parameter, if specified, must be a public key ring, not a secret key ring. The user ID field must be your own user ID, which PGP knows is yours because it appears on both your public key ring and your secret key ring. Both key rings will be updated, even though you only specified the public key ring.

The -ke command works differently depending on whether you use it on a public or secret key. It can also be used to edit the trust parameters for a public key.

Editing the Trust Parameters for a Public Key

Sometimes you need to alter the trust parameters for a public key on your public key ring. For a discussion on what these trust parameters mean, see the section "How Does PGP Keep Track of Which Keys are Valid?" in the Essential Topics volume of the PGP User's Guide.

To edit the trust parameters for a public key:

```
pgp -ke userid [keyring]
```

The optional [keyring] parameter, if specified, must be a public key ring, not a secret key ring.

Checking If Everything is OK on Your Public Key Ring

Normally, PGP automatically checks any new keys or signatures on your public key ring and updates all the trust parameters and validity scores. In theory, it keeps all the key validity status information up-to-date as material is added to or deleted from your public key ring. But perhaps you may want to explicitly force PGP to perform a comprehensive analysis of your public key ring, checking all the certifying signatures, checking the trust parameters, updating all the validity scores, and checking your own ultimately trusted key against a backup copy on a write-protected floppy disk. It may be a good idea to do this hygienic maintenance periodically to make sure nothing is wrong with your public key ring. To force PGP to perform a full analysis of your public key ring, use the -kc (key ring check) command:

```
pgp -kc
```

You can also make PGP check all the signatures for just a single-selected public key by:

```
pgp -kc userid [keyring]
```

For further information on how the backup copy of your own key is checked, see the description of the BAKRING parameter in the configuration file section of this manual.

Verifying a Public Key Over the Phone

If you get a public key from someone that is not certified by anyone you trust, how can you tell if it's really their key? The best way to verify an uncertified key is to verify it over some independent channel other than the one you received the key through. One convenient way to tell, if you know this person and would recognize them on the phone, is to call them and verify their key over the telephone. Rather than reading their whole tiresome (ASCII-armored) key to them over the phone, you can just read their key's "fingerprint" to them. To see this fingerprint, use the -kvc command:

```
pgp -kvc userid [keyring]
```

This will display the key with the 16-byte digest of the public key components. Read this 16-byte fingerprint to the key's owner on the phone, while she checks it against her own, using the same -kvc command at her end.

You can both verify each other's keys this way, and then you can sign each other's keys with confidence. This is a safe and convenient way to get the key trust network started for your circle of friends.

Note that sending a key fingerprint via E-mail is not the best way to verify the key, because E-mail can be intercepted and modified. It's best to use a different channel than the one that was used to send the key itself. A good combination is to send the key via E-mail, and the key fingerprint via a voice telephone conversation. Some people distribute their key fingerprint on their business cards, which looks really cool.

If you don't know me, please don't call me to verify my key over the phone—I get too many calls like that. Since every PGP user has a copy of my public key, no one could tamper with all the copies that are out there. The discrepancy would soon be noticed by someone who checked it from more than one source, and word would soon get out on the Internet.

Handling Large Public Key Rings

PGP was originally designed for handling small personal key rings for keeping all your friends on, like a personal rolodex. A couple hundred keys is a reasonable size for such a key ring. But as PGP has become more popular, people are now trying to add other large key rings to their own key ring. Sometimes this involves adding thousands of keys to your key ring. PGP, in its present form, cannot perform this operation in a reasonable period of time, while you wait at your keyboard. Not for huge key rings.

You may want to add a huge "imported" key ring to your own key ring, because you are only interested in a few dozen keys on the bigger key ring you are bringing in. If that's all you want from the other key ring, it would be more efficient if you extract the few keys you need from the big foreign key ring, and then add just these few keys to your own key ring. Use the -kx command to extract them from the foreign key ring, specifying the key ring name on the command line. Then add these extracted keys to your own key ring.

The real solution is to improve PGP to use advanced database techniques to manage large key rings efficiently. Until this happens, you will just have to use smaller key rings, or be patient.

Using PGP as a Unix-style Filter

Unix fans are accustomed to using Unix "pipes" to make two applications work together. The output of one application can be directly fed through a pipe to be read as input to another application. For this to work, the applications must be capable of reading the raw material from "standard input" and writing the finished output to "standard output." PGP can operate in this mode. If you don't understand what this means, then you probably don't need this feature.

To use a Unix-style filter mode, reading from standard input and writing to standard output, add the -f option, like so:

```
pgp -feast her_userid <inputfile >outputfile
```

This feature makes it easier to make PGP work with electronic mail applications. When using PGP in filter mode to decrypt a ciphertext file, you may find it useful to use the PGPPASS environmental variable to hold the pass phrase, so that you won't be prompted for it. The PGPPASS feature is explained below.

Suppressing Unnecessary Questions: BATCHMODE

With the BATCHMODE flag enabled on the command line, PGP will not ask any unnecessary questions or prompt for alternate filenames. Here is an example of how to set this flag:

```
pgp +batchmode cipherfile
```

This is useful for running PGP non-interactively from Unix shell scripts or MSDOS batch files. Some key management commands still need user interaction even when BATCHMODE is on, so shell scripts may need to avoid them.

BATCHMODE may also be enabled to check the validity of a signature on a file. If there was no signature on the file, the exit code is 1. If it had a signature that was good, the exit code is 0.

Force "Yes" Answer to Confirmation Questions: FORCE

This command-line flag makes PGP assume "yes" for the user response to the confirmation request to overwrite an existing file, or when removing a key from the key ring via the -kr command. Here is an example of how to set this flag:

```
pgp +force cipherfile
```

or:

```
pgp -kr +force Smith
```

This feature is useful for running PGP non-interactively from a Unix shell script or MSDOS batch file.

PGP Returns Exit Status to the Shell

To facilitate running PGP in "batch" mode, such as from an MSDOS ".bat" file or from a Unix shell script, PGP returns an error exit status to the shell. An exit status code of zero means normal exit, while a nonzero exit status indicates some kind of error occurred. Different error exit conditions return different exit status codes to the shell.

Environmental Variable for Pass Phrase

Normally, PGP prompts the user to type a pass phrase whenever PGP needs a pass phrase to unlock a secret key. But it is possible to store the pass phrase in an environmental variable from your operating system's command shell. The environmental variable PGPPASS can be used to hold the pass phrase that PGP will attempt to use first. If the pass phrase stored in PGPPASS is incorrect, PGP recovers by prompting the user for the correct pass phrase.

For example, on MSDOS, the shell command:

```
SET PGPPASS=zaphod beeblebrox for president
```

would eliminate the prompt for the pass phrase if the pass phrase were indeed "zaphod beeblebrox for president."

This dangerous feature makes your life more convenient if you have to regularly deal with a large number of incoming messages addressed to your secret key, by eliminating the need for you to repeatedly type in your pass phrase every time you run PGP.

I added this feature because of popular demand. However, this is a somewhat dangerous feature, because it keeps your precious pass phrase stored somewhere other than just in your brain. Even worse, if you are particularly reckless, it may even be stored on a disk on the same computer as your secret key. It would be particularly dangerous and stupid if you were to install this command in a batch or script file, such as the MSDOS AUTOEXEC.BAT file. Someone could come along on your lunch hour and steal both your secret key ring and the file containing your pass phrase.

I can't emphasize the importance of this risk enough. If you are contemplating using this feature, be sure to read the sections "Exposure on Multi-user Systems" and "How to Protect Secret Keys from Disclosure" in this volume and in the Essential Topics volume of the PGP User's Guide.

If you must use this feature, the safest way to do it would be to just manually type in the shell command to set PGPPASS every time you boot your machine to start using PGP, and then erase it or turn off your machine when you are done. And you should definitely never do it in an environment where someone else may have access to your machine. Someone could come along and simply ask your computer to display the contents of PGPPASS.

Setting Configuration Parameters: CONFIG.TXT

PGP has a number of user-settable parameters that can be defined in a special configuration text file called "config.txt," in the directory pointed to by the shell environmental variable PGPPATH. Having a configuration file enables the user to define various flags and parameters for PGP without the burden of having to always define these parameters in the PGP command line.

Configuration parameters may be assigned integer values, character string values, or on/off values, depending on what kind of configuration parameter it is. A sample configuration file is provided with PGP, so you can see some examples.

In the configuration file, blank lines are ignored, as is anything following the '#' comment character. Keywords are not case-sensitive.

Here is a short sample fragment of a typical configuration file:

```
# TMP is the directory for PGP scratch files, such as a RAM disk.
TMP = "e:\" # Can be overridden by environment variable TMP.
Armor = on # Use -a flag for ASCII armor whenever applicable.
# CERT_DEPTH is how deeply introducers may introduce introducers.
cert_depth = 3
```

If some configuration parameters are not defined in the configuration file, or if there is no configuration file, or if PGP can't find the configuration file, the values for the configuration parameters default to some reasonable value.

Note that it is also possible to set these same configuration parameters directly from the PGP command line, by preceding the parameter setting with a "+" character. For example, the following two PGP commands produce the same effect:

```
pgp -e +armor=on message.txt smith
```

or:

```
pgp -ea message.txt smith
```

The following is a summary of the various parameters that may be defined in the configuration file.

TMP - Directory Pathname for Temporary Files

Default setting: TMP = ""

The configuration parameter TMP specifies what directory to use for PGP's temporary scratch files. The best place to put them is on a RAM disk, if you have one. That speeds things up quite a bit, and increases security somewhat. If TMP is undefined, the temporary files go in the current directory. If the shell environmental variable TMP is defined, PGP instead uses that to specify where the temporary files should go.

LANGUAGE - Foreign Language Selector

Default setting: LANGUAGE = "en"

PGP displays various prompts, warning messages, and advisories to the user on the screen. For example, messages such as "File not found.," or "Please enter your pass phrase:." These messages are normally in English. But it is possible to get PGP to display its messages to the user in other languages, without having to modify the PGP executable program.

A number of people in various countries have translated all of PGP's display messages, warnings, and prompts into their native languages. These hundreds of translated message strings have been placed in a special text file called "language.txt," distributed with the PGP release. The messages are stored in this file in English, Spanish, Dutch, German, French, Italian, Russian, Latvian, and Lithuanian. Other languages may be added later.

The configuration parameter LANGUAGE specifies what language to display these messages in. LANGUAGE may be set to "en" for English, "es" for Spanish, "de" for German, "nl" for Dutch, "fr" for French, "it" for Italian, "ru" for Russian, "lt3" for Lithuanian, "lv" for Latvian, and "esp" for Esperanto. For example, if this line appeared in the configuration file:

```
LANGUAGE = "fr"
```

PGP would select French as the language for its display messages. The default setting is English.

When PGP needs to display a message to the user, it looks in the "language.txt" file for the equivalent message string in the selected foreign language and displays that translated message to the user. If PGP can't find the language string file, or if the selected language is not in the file, or if that one phrase is not translated into the selected language in the file, or if that phrase is missing entirely from the file, PGP displays the message in English.

To conserve disk space, most foreign translations are not included in the standard PGP release package, but are available separately.

MYNAME - Default User ID for Making Signatures

Default setting: MYNAME = ""

The configuration parameter MYNAME specifies the default user ID to use to select the secret key for making signatures. If MYNAME is not defined, the most recent secret key you installed on your secret key ring will be used. The user may also override this setting by specifying a user ID on the PGP command line with the -u option.

TEXTMODE - Assuming Plaintext is a Text File

Default setting: TEXTMODE = off

The configuration parameter TEXTMODE is equivalent to the -t command line option. If enabled, it causes PGP to assume the plaintext is a text file, not a binary file, and converts it to "canonical text" before encrypting it. Canonical text has a carriage return and a linefeed at the end of each line of text.

This mode will be automatically turned off if PGP detects that the plaintext file contains what it thinks is non-text binary data. If you intend to use PGP primarily for E-mail purposes, you should turn TEXTMODE=ON.

For VAX/VMS systems, the current version of PGP defaults TEXTMODE=ON.

For further details, see the section "Sending ASCII Text Files Across Different Machine Environments."

CHARSET - Specifies Local Character Set for Text Files

Default setting: `CHARSET = NOCONV`

Because PGP must process messages in many non-English languages with non-ASCII character sets, you may have a need to tell PGP what local character set your machine uses. This determines what character conversions are performed when converting plaintext files to and from canonical text format. This is only a concern if you are in a non-English non-ASCII environment.

The configuration parameter CHARSET selects the local character set. The choices are NOCONV (no conversion), LATIN1 (ISO 8859-1 Latin Alphabet 1), KOI8 (used by most Russian Unix systems), ALT_CODES (used by Russian MSDOS systems), ASCII, and CP850 (used by most western European languages on standard MSDOS PCs).

LATIN1 is the internal representation used by PGP for canonical text, so if you select LATIN1, no conversion is done. Note also that PGP treats KOI8 as LATIN1, even though it is a completely different character set (Russian), because trying to convert KOI8 to either LATIN1 or CP850 would be futile anyway. This means that setting CHARSET to NOCONV, LATIN1, or KOI8 are all equivalent to PGP.

If you use MSDOS and expect to send or receive traffic in western European languages, set CHARSET = "CP850." This will make PGP convert incoming canonical text messages from LATIN1 to CP850 after decryption. If you use the -t (textmode) option to convert to canonical text, PGP will convert your CP850 text to LATIN1 before encrypting it.

For further details, see the section "Sending ASCII Text Files Across Different Machine Environments."

ARMOR - Enable ASCII Armor Output

Default setting: `ARMOR = off`

The configuration parameter ARMOR is equivalent to the -a command line option. If enabled, it causes PGP to emit ciphertext or keys in ASCII radix-64 format suitable for transporting through E-mail channels. Output files are named with the ".asc" extension.

If you intend to use PGP primarily for E-mail purposes, you should turn ARMOR=ON.

For further details, see the section "Sending Ciphertext Through E-mail Channels: Radix-64 Format" in the Essential Topics volume.

ARMORLINES - Size of ASCII Armor Multipart Files

Default setting: `ARMORLINES = 720`

When PGP creates a very large ".asc" radix-64 file for sending ciphertext or keys through E-mail, it breaks the file up into separate chunks small enough to send through Internet mail utilities. Normally, Internet mailers prohibit files larger than about 50,000 bytes, which means that if we restrict the number of lines to about 720, we'll be well within the limit. The file chunks are named with suffixes ".as1," ".as2," ".as3," ....

The configuration parameter ARMORLINES specifies the maximum number of lines to make each chunk in a multipart ".asc" file sequence. If you set it to zero, PGP will not break up the file into chunks.

Fidonet E-mail files usually have an upper limit of about 32K bytes, so 450 lines would be appropriate for Fidonet environments.

For further details, see the section "Sending Ciphertext Through E-mail Channels: Radix-64 Format" in the Essential Topics volume.

KEEPBINARY - Keep Binary Ciphertext Files After Decrypting

Default setting: KEEPBINARY = off

When PGP reads a ".asc" file, it recognizes that the file is in radix-64 format and will convert it back to binary before processing as it normally does, producing as a by-product a ".pgp" ciphertext file in binary form. After further processing to decrypt the ".pgp" file, the final output file will be in normal plaintext form.

You may want to delete the binary ".pgp" intermediate file, or you may want PGP to delete it for you automatically. You can still rerun PGP on the original ".asc" file.

The configuration parameter KEEPBINARY enables or disables keeping the intermediate ".pgp" file during decryption.

For further details, see the section "Sending Ciphertext Through E-mail Channels: Radix-64 Format" in the Essential Topics volume.

COMPRESS - Enable Compression

Default setting: COMPRESS = on

The configuration parameter COMPRESS enables or disables data compression before encryption. It is used mainly for debugging PGP. Normally, PGP attempts to compress the plaintext before it encrypts it. Generally, you should leave this alone and let PGP attempt to compress the plaintext.

COMPLETES_NEEDED - Number of Completely Trusted Introducers Needed

Default setting: COMPLETES_NEEDED = 1

The configuration parameter COMPLETES_NEEDED specifies the minimum number of completely trusted introducers required to fully certify a public key on your public key ring. This gives you a way of tuning PGP's skepticism.

For further details, see the section "How Does PGP Keep Track of Which Keys are Valid?" in the Essential Topics volume.

MARGINALS_NEEDED - Number of Marginally Trusted Introducers Needed

Default setting: MARGINALS_NEEDED = 2

The configuration parameter MARGINALS_NEEDED specifies the minimum number of marginally trusted introducers required to fully certify a public key on your public key ring. This gives you a way of tuning PGP's skepticism.

For further details, see the section "How Does PGP Keep Track of Which Keys are Valid?" in the Essential Topics volume.

CERT_DEPTH - How Deep May Introducers Be Nested

Default setting: CERT_DEPTH = 4

The configuration parameter CERT_DEPTH specifies how many levels deep you may nest introducers to certify other introducers to certify public keys on your public key ring. For example, if CERT_DEPTH is set to 1, there may only be one layer of introducers below your own ultimately trusted key. If that were the case, you would be required to directly certify the public keys of all trusted introducers on your key ring. If you set CERT_DEPTH to 0, you could have no introducers at all, and you would have to directly certify each and every key on your public key ring in order to use it. The minimum CERT_DEPTH is 0, the maximum is 8.

For further details, see the section "How Does PGP Keep Track of Which Keys are Valid?" in the Essential Topics volume.

BAKRING - Filename for Backup Secret Key Ring

Default setting: BAKRING = ""

All of the key certification that PGP does on your public key ring ultimately depends on your own ultimately trusted public key (or keys). To detect any tampering of your public key ring, PGP must check that your own key has not been tampered with. To do this, PGP must compare your public key against a backup copy of your secret key on some tamper-resistant media, such as a write-protected floppy disk. A secret key contains all the information that your public key has, plus some secret components. This means PGP can check your public key against a backup copy of your secret key.

The configuration parameter BAKRING specifies what pathname to use for PGP's trusted backup copy of your secret key ring. On MSDOS, you could set it to "a:\secring.pgp" to point it at a write-protected backup copy of your secret key ring on your floppy drive. This check is performed only when you execute the PGP -kc option to check your whole public key ring.

If BAKRING is not defined, PGP will not check your own key against any back-up copy.

For further details, see the sections "How to Protect Public Keys from Tampering" and "How Does PGP Keep Track of Which Keys are Valid?" in the Essential Topics volume.

PUBRING - Filename for Your Public Key Ring

Default setting: PUBRING = "$PGPPATH/pubring.pgp"

You may want to keep your public key ring in a directory separate from your config.txt file in the directory specified by your $PGPPATH environmental variable. You may specify the full path and filename for your public key ring by setting the PUBRING parameter. For example, on an MSDOS system, you might want to keep your public key ring on a floppy disk by:

PUBRING = "a:pubring.pgp"

This feature is especially handy for specifying an alternative key ring on the command line.

SECRING - Filename for Your Secret Key Ring

Default setting: SECRING = "$PGPPATH/secring.pgp"

You may want to keep your secret key ring in a directory separate from your config.txt file in the directory specified by your $PGPPATH environmental variable. This comes in handy for putting your secret key ring in a directory or device that is more protected than your public key ring. You may specify the full path and filename for your secret key ring by setting the SECRING parameter. For example, on an MSDOS system, you might want to keep your secret key ring on a floppy disk by:

SECRING = "a:secring.pgp"

RANDSEED - Filename for Random Number Seed

Default setting: RANDSEED = "$PGPPATH/randseed.bin"

You may want to keep your random number seed file (for generation of session keys) in a directory separate from your config.txt file in the directory specified by your $PGPPATH environmental variable. This comes in handy for putting your random number seed file in a directory or device that is more protected than your public key ring. You may specify the full path and filename for your random seed file by setting the RANDSEED parameter. For example, on an MSDOS system, you might want to keep it on a floppy disk by:

```
RANDSEED = "a:randseed.bin"
```

PAGER - Selects Shell Command to Display Plaintext Output

Default setting: PAGER = ""

PGP lets you view the decrypted plaintext output on your screen (like the Unix-style "more" command), without writing it to a file, if you use the -m (more) option while decrypting. This displays the decrypted plaintext display on your screen one screenful at a time.

If you prefer to use a fancier page display utility, rather than PGP's built-in one, you can specify the name of a shell command that PGP will invoke to display your plaintext output file. The configuration parameter PAGER specifies the shell command to invoke to display the file. For example, on MSDOS systems, you might want to use the popular shareware program "list.com" to display your plaintext message. Assuming you have a copy of "list.com," you may set PAGER accordingly:

```
PAGER = "list"
```

However, if the sender specified that this file is for your eyes only, and may not be written to disk, PGP always uses its own built-in display function.

For further details, see the section "Displaying Decrypted Plaintext on Your Screen."

SHOWPASS - Echo Pass Phrase to User

Default setting: SHOWPASS = off

Normally, PGP does not let you see your pass phrase as you type it in. This makes it harder for someone to look over your shoulder while you type and learn your pass phrase. But some typing-impaired people have problems typing their pass phrase without seeing what they are typing, and they may be typing in the privacy of their own homes. So they asked if PGP can be configured to let them see what they type when they type in their pass phrase.

The configuration parameter SHOWPASS enables PGP to echo your typing during pass phrase entry.

TZFIX - Timezone Adjustment

Default setting: TZFIX = 0

PGP provides timestamps for keys and signature certificates in Greenwich Mean Time (GMT), or Coordinated Universal Time (UTC), which means the same thing for our purposes. When PGP asks the system for the time of day, the system is supposed to provide it in GMT.

But sometimes, because of improperly configured MSDOS systems, the system time is returned in U.S. Pacific Standard Time time plus 8 hours. Sounds weird, doesn't it? Perhaps because of some sort of U.S. west-coast jingoism, MSDOS presumes local time is U.S. Pacific time, and pre-corrects Pacific time to GMT. This adversely affects the behavior of the internal MSDOS GMT time function that PGP calls. However, if your MSDOS environmental variable TZ is already properly defined for your timezone, this corrects the misconception MSDOS has that the whole world lives on the U.S. west coast.

The configuration parameter TZFIX specifies the number of hours to add to the system time function to get GMT, for GMT timestamps on keys and signatures. If the MSDOS environmental variable TZ is defined properly, you can leave TZFIX=0. Unix systems usually shouldn't need to worry about setting TZFIX at all. But if you are using some other obscure operating system that doesn't know about GMT, you may have to use TZFIX to adjust the system time to GMT.

On MSDOS systems that do not have TZ defined in the environment, you should make TZFIX=0 for California, –1 for Colorado, –2 for Chicago, –3 for New York, –8 for London, –9 for Amsterdam. In the summer, TZFIX should be manually decremented from these values. What a mess.

It would be much cleaner to set your MSDOS environmental variable TZ in your AUTOEXEC.BAT file, and not use the TZFIX correction. Then MSDOS gives you good GMT timestamps, and will handle daylight savings time adjustments for you. Here are some sample lines to insert into AUTOEXEC.BAT, depending on your time zone:

For Los Angeles: `SET TZ=PST8PDT`

For Denver: `SET TZ=MST7MDT`

For Arizona: `SET TZ=MST7`

(Arizona never uses daylight savings time)

For Chicago: `SET TZ=CST6CDT`

For New York: `SET TZ=EST5EDT`

For London: `SET TZ=GMT0BST`

For Amsterdam: `SET TZ=MET-1DST`

For Moscow: `SET TZ=MSK-3MSD`

For Aukland: `SET TZ=NZT-13`

CLEARSIG - Enable Signed Messages to be Encapsulated as Clear Text

Default setting: `CLEARSIG = on`

Normally, unencrypted PGP signed messages have a signature certificate prepended in binary form. Also, the signed message is compressed, rendering the message unreadable to casual human eyes, even though the message is not actually encrypted. To send this binary data through a 7-bit E-mail channel, radix-64 ASCII armor is applied (see the ARMOR parameter). Even if PGP didn't compress the message, the ASCII armor would still render the message unreadable to human eyes. The recipient must use PGP to strip the armor off and decompress it before reading the message.

If the original plaintext message is in text (not binary) form, there is a way to send a signed message through an E-mail channel in such a way that the signed message is not compressed and the ASCII armor is applied only to the binary signature certificate, but not to the plaintext message. The CLEARSIG flag provides this useful feature, making it possible to generate a signed message that can be read with human eyes, without the aid of PGP. Of course, you still need PGP to actually check the signature.

The CLEARSIG flag is preset to "on" beginning with PGP version 2.5. To enable the full CLEARSIG behavior, the ARMOR and TEXTMODE flags must also be turned on. Set ARMOR=ON (or use the -a option), and set TEXTMODE=ON (or use the -t option). If your config file has CLEARSIG turned off, you can turn it back on again directly on the command line, like so:

```
pgp -sta +clearsig=on message.txt
```

This message representation is analogous to the MIC-CLEAR message type used in Internet Privacy Enhanced Mail (PEM). It is important to note that since this method only applies ASCII armor to the binary signature certificate, and not to the message text itself, there is some risk that the unarmored message may suffer some accidental molestation while en route. This can happen if it passes through some E-mail gateway that performs character set conversions, or in some cases extra spaces may be added to or stripped from the ends of lines. If this occurs, the signature will fail to verify, which may give a false indication of intentional tampering. But since PEM lives under a similar vulnerability, it seems worth having this feature despite the risks.

Beginning with PGP version 2.2, trailing blanks are ignored on each line in calculating the signature for text in CLEARSIG mode.

VERBOSE - Quiet, Normal, or Verbose Messages

Default setting: VERBOSE = 1

VERBOSE may be set to 0, 1, or 2, depending on how much detail you want to see from PGP diagnostic messages. The settings are:

0 - Display messages only if there is a problem. Unix fans wanted this "quiet mode" setting.

1 - Normal default setting. Displays a reasonable amount of detail in diagnostic or advisory messages.

2 - Displays maximum information, usually to help diagnose problems in PGP. Not recommended for normal use. Besides, PGP doesn't have any problems, right?

INTERACTIVE - Ask for Confirmation for Key Adds

Default Setting: `INTERACTIVE = off`

Enabling this mode will mean that if you add a key file containing multiple keys to your key ring, PGP will ask for confirmation for each key before adding it to your key ring.

NOMANUAL - Let PGP Generate Keys Without the Manual

Default Setting: `NOMANUAL = off`

It is important that the freeware version of PGP not be distributed without the user documentation, which normally comes with it in the standard release package. This manual contains important information for using PGP, as well as important legal notices. But some people have distributed previous versions of PGP without the manual, causing a lot of problems for a lot of people who get it. To discourage the distribution of PGP without the required documentation, PGP has been changed to require the PGP User's Guide to be found somewhere on your computer (like in your PGP directory) before PGP will let you generate a key pair. However, some users like to use PGP on tiny palmtop computers with limited storage capacity, so they like to run PGP without the documentation present on their systems. To satisfy these users, PGP can be made to relax its requirement that the manual be present, by enabling the NOMANUAL flag on the command line during key generation, like so:

```
pgp -kg +nomanual
```

The NOMANUAL flag can only be set on the command line, not in the config file. Since you must read this manual to learn how to do enable this override feature, I hope this will still be effective in discouraging the distribution of PGP without the manual.

A Peek Under the Hood

Let's take a look at a few internal features of PGP.

Random Numbers

PGP uses a cryptographically strong pseudorandom number generator for creating temporary conventional session keys. The seed file for this is called "randseed.bin." It too can be kept in whatever directory is indicated by the PGP-PATH environmental variable. If this random seed file does not exist, it is automatically created and seeded with truly random numbers derived from timing your keystroke latencies.

This generator reseeds the disk file each time it is used by mixing in new key material partially derived with the time of day and other truly random sources. It uses the conventional encryption algorithm as an engine for the random number generator. The seed file contains both random seed material and random key material to key the conventional encryption engine for the random generator.

This random seed file should be at least slightly protected from disclosure, to reduce the risk of an attacker deriving your next or previous session keys. The attacker would have a very hard time getting anything useful from capturing this random seed file, because the file is cryptographically laundered before and after each use. Nonetheless, it seems prudent to at least try to keep it from falling into the wrong hands.

If you feel uneasy about trusting any algorithmically derived random number source however strong, keep in mind that you already trust the strength of the same conventional cipher to protect your messages. If it's strong enough for that, then it should be strong enough to use as a source of random numbers for temporary session keys. Note that PGP still uses truly random numbers from physical sources (mainly keyboard timings) to generate long-term public/secret key pairs.

PGP's Conventional Encryption Algorithm

As described earlier, PGP "bootstraps" into a conventional single-key encryption algorithm by using a public key algorithm to encipher the conventional session key and then switching to fast conventional cryptography. So let's talk about this conventional encryption algorithm. It isn't the DES.

The Federal Data Encryption Standard (DES) used to be a good algorithm for most commercial applications. But the Government never did trust the DES to protect its own classified data, because the DES key length is only 56 bits, short enough for a brute force attack. Also, the full 16-round DES has been attacked with some success by Biham and Shamir using differential cryptanalysis, and by Matsui using linear cryptanalysis.

The most devastating practical attack on the DES was described at the Crypto '93 conference, where Michael Wiener of Bell Northern Research presented a paper on how to crack the DES with a special machine. He has fully designed and tested a chip that guesses 50 million DES keys per second until it finds the right one. Although he has refrained from building the real chips so far, he can get these chips manufactured for $10.50 each, and can build 57,000 of them into a special machine for $1 million that can try every DES key in 7 hours, averaging a solution in 3.5 hours. $1 million can be hidden in the budget of many companies. For $10 million, it takes 21 minutes to crack, and for $100 million, just two minutes. With any major government's budget for examining DES traffic, it can be cracked in seconds. This means that straight 56-bit DES is now effectively dead for purposes of serious data security applications.

A possible successor to DES may be a variation known as "triple DES," which uses two DES keys to encrypt three times, achieving an effective key space of 112 bits. But this approach is three times slower than normal DES. A future version of PGP may support triple DES as an option.

PGP does not use the DES as its conventional single-key algorithm to encrypt messages. Instead, PGP uses a different conventional single-key block encryption algorithm, called IDEA™.

For the cryptographically curious, the IDEA cipher has a 64-bit block size for the plaintext and the ciphertext. It uses a key size of 128 bits. It is based on the design concept of "mixing operations from different algebraic groups." It runs much faster in software than the DES. Like the DES, it can be used in cipher feedback (CFB) and cipher block chaining (CBC) modes. PGP uses it in 64-bit CFB mode.

The IPES/IDEA block cipher was developed at ETH in Zurich by James L. Massey and Xuejia Lai, and published in 1990. This is not a "home-grown" algorithm. Its designers have a distinguished reputation in the cryptologic community. Early published papers on the algorithm called it IPES (Improved Proposed Encryption Standard), but they later changed the name to IDEA (International Data Encryption Algorithm). So far, IDEA has resisted attack much better than other ciphers such as FEAL, REDOC-II, LOKI, Snefru and Khafre. And recent evidence suggests that IDEA is more resistant than the DES to Biham & Shamir's highly successful differential cryptanalysis attack. Biham and Shamir have been examining the IDEA cipher for weaknesses, without success. Academic cryptanalyst groups in Belgium, England, and Germany are also attempting to attack it, as well as the military services from several European countries. As this new cipher continues to attract attack efforts from the most formidable quarters of the cryptanalytic world, confidence in IDEA is growing with the passage of time.

Every once in a while, I get a letter from someone who has just learned the awful truth that PGP does not use pure RSA to encrypt bulk data. They are concerned that the whole package is weakened if we use a hybrid public-key and conventional scheme just to speed things up. After all, a chain is only as strong as its weakest link. They demand an explanation for this apparent "compromise" in the strength of PGP. This may be because they have been caught up in the public's reverence and awe for the strength and mystique of RSA, mistakenly believing that RSA is intrinsically stronger than any conventional cipher. Well, it's not.

People who work in factoring research say that the workload to exhaust all the possible 128-bit keys in the IDEA cipher would equal the factoring workload to crack a 3100-bit RSA key, which is quite a bit bigger than the 1024-bit RSA key size that most people use for high security applications. Given this range of key sizes, and assuming there are no hidden weaknesses in the conventional cipher, the weak link in this hybrid approach is in the public key algorithm, not the conventional cipher.

It is not ergonomically practical to use pure RSA with large keys to encrypt and decrypt long messages. A 1024-bit RSA key would decrypt messages about 4000 times slower than the IDEA cipher. Absolutely no one does it that way in the real world. Many people less experienced in cryptography do not realize that the attraction of public key cryptography is not because it is intrinsically stronger than a conventional cipher—its appeal is because it helps you manage keys more conveniently.

Not only is RSA too slow to use on bulk data, but it even has certain weaknesses that can be exploited in some special cases of particular kinds of messages that are fed to the RSA cipher. These special cases can be avoided by using the hybrid approach of using RSA to encrypt random session keys for a conventional cipher. So the bottom line is this: Using pure RSA on bulk data is the wrong approach, period. It's too slow, it's not stronger, and may even be weaker. If you find a software application that uses pure RSA on bulk data, it probably means the implementor does not understand these issues.

Data Compression

PGP normally compresses the plaintext before encrypting it. It's too late to compress it after it has been encrypted; encrypted data is incompressible. Data compression saves modem transmission time and disk space and more importantly strengthens cryptographic security. Most cryptanalysis techniques exploit redundancies found in the plaintext to crack the cipher. Data compression reduces this redundancy in the plaintext, thereby greatly enhancing resistance to cryptanalysis. It takes extra time to compress the plaintext, but from a security point of view it seems worth it, at least in my cautious opinion.

Files that are too short to compress or just don't compress well are not compressed by PGP.

If you prefer, you can use PKZIP to compress the plaintext before encrypting it. PKZIP is a widely available and effective MSDOS shareware compression utility from PKWare, Inc. Or you can use ZIP, a PKZIP-compatible freeware compression utility on Unix and other systems, available from Jean-loup Gailly. There is some advantage in using PKZIP or ZIP in certain cases, because unlike PGP's built-in compression algorithm, PKZIP and ZIP have the nice feature of compressing multiple files into a single compressed file, which is reconstituted again into separate files when decompressed. PGP will not try to compress a plaintext file that has already been compressed. After decrypting, the recipient can decompress the plaintext with PKUNZIP. If the decrypted plaintext is a PKZIP compressed file, PGP automatically recognizes this and advises the recipient that the decrypted plaintext appears to be a PKZIP file.

For the technically curious readers, the current version of PGP uses the freeware ZIP compression routines written by Jean-loup Gailly, Mark Adler, and Richard B. Wales. This ZIP software uses functionally equivalent compression algorithms as those used by PKWare's new PKZIP 2.0. This ZIP compression software was selected for PGP mainly because of its free portable C source code availability, and because it has a really good compression ratio, and because it's fast.

Peter Gutmann has also written a nice compression utility called HPACK, available for free from many Internet FTP sites. It encrypts the compressed archives, using PGP data formats and key rings. He wanted me to mention that here.

Message Digests and Digital Signatures

To create a digital signature, PGP encrypts with your secret key. But PGP doesn't actually encrypt your entire message with your secret key—that would take too long. Instead, PGP encrypts a "message digest."

The message digest is a compact (128 bit) "distillate" of your message, similar in concept to a checksum. You can also think of it as a "fingerprint" of the message. The message digest "represents" your message, such that if the message were altered in any way, a different message digest would be computed from it. This makes it possible to detect any changes made to the message by a forger. A message digest is computed using a cryptographically strong one-way hash function of the message. It would be computationally infeasible for an attacker to devise a substitute message that would produce an identical message digest. In that respect, a message digest is much better than a checksum, because it is easy to devise a different message that would produce the same checksum. But like a checksum, you can't derive the original message from its message digest.

A message digest alone is not enough to authenticate a message. The message digest algorithm is publicly known, and does not require knowledge of any secret keys to calculate. If all we did was attach a message digest to a message, then a forger could alter a message and simply attach a new message digest calculated from the new altered message. To provide real authentication, the sender has to encrypt (sign) the message digest with his secret key.

A message digest is calculated from the message by the sender. The sender's secret key is used to encrypt the message digest and an electronic timestamp, forming a digital signature, or signature certificate. The sender sends the digital signature along with the message. The receiver receives the message and the digital signature, and recovers the original message digest from the digital signature by decrypting it with the sender's public key. The receiver computes a new message digest from the message, and checks to see if it matches the one recovered from the digital signature. If it matches, then that proves the message was not altered, and it came from the sender who owns the public key used to check the signature.

A potential forger would have to either produce an altered message that produces an identical message digest (which is infeasible), or he would have to create a new digital signature from a different message digest (also infeasible, without knowing the true sender's secret key).

Digital signatures prove who sent the message, and that the message was not altered either by error or design. It also provides nonrepudiation, which means the sender cannot easily disavow his signature on the message.

Using message digests to form digital signatures has other advantages besides being faster than directly signing the entire actual message with the secret key. Using message digests allows signatures to be of a standard small fixed size, regardless of the size of the actual message. It also allows the software to check the message integrity automatically, in a manner similar to using checksums. And it allows signatures to be stored separately from messages, perhaps even in a public archive, without revealing sensitive information about the actual messages, because no one can derive any message content from a message digest.

The message digest algorithm used here is the MD5 Message Digest Algorithm, placed in the public domain by RSA Data Security, Inc. MD5's designer, Ronald Rivest, writes this about MD5:

> "It is conjectured that the difficulty of coming up with two messages having the same message digest is on the order of 2^{64} operations, and that the difficulty of coming up with any message having a given message digest is on the order of 2^{128} operations. The MD5 algorithm has been carefully scrutinized for weaknesses. It is, however, a relatively new algorithm and further security analysis is of course justified, as is the case with any new proposal of this sort. The level of security provided by MD5 should be sufficient for implementing very high security hybrid digital signature schemes based on MD5 and the RSA public-key cryptosystem."

Compatibility with Previous Versions of PGP

PGP version 2.6 can read anything produced by versions 2.3, 2.3a, 2.4, or 2.5. However, because of a negotiated agreement between MIT and RSA Data Security, PGP 2.6 will change its behavior slightly on 1 September 1994, triggered by a built-in software timer. On that date, version 2.6 will start producing a new and slightly different data format for messages, signatures, and keys. PGP 2.6 will still be able to read and process messages, signatures, and keys produced under the old format, but it will generate the new format. This incompatible change is intended to discourage people from continuing to use the older (2.3a and earlier) versions of PGP, which Public Key Partners contends infringes its RSA patent (see the section on Legal Issues). PGP 2.4, distributed by Viacrypt (see the section "Where to Get a Commercial Version of PGP") avoids infringement through Viacrypt's license arrangement with Public Key Partners. PGP 2.5 and 2.6 avoid infringement by using the RSAREF™ Cryptographic Toolkit, under license from RSA Data Security, Inc.

Outside the United States, the RSA patent is not in force, so PGP users there are free to use implementations of PGP that do not rely on RSAREF and its restrictions. Hopefully, implementors of PGP versions outside the U.S. will also switch to the new format, whose detailed description is available from MIT. If everyone upgrades before 1 September 1994, no one will experience any discontinuity in interoperability.

This format change beginning with 2.6 is similar to the process that naturally happens when new features are added, causing older versions of PGP to be unable to read stuff from the newer PGP, while the newer version can still read the old stuff. The only difference is that this is a "legal upgrade," instead of a technical one. It's a worthwhile change, if it can achieve peace in our time.

According to ViaCrypt, which sells a commercial version of PGP, ViaCrypt PGP will evolve to maintain interoperability with new freeware versions of PGP.

There is another change that effects interoperability with earlier versions of PGP. Unfortunately, due to data format limitations imposed by RSAREF, PGP 2.5 and 2.6 cannot interpret any messages or signatures made with PGP version 2.2 or earlier. Since we had no choice but to use the new data formats, because of the legal requirement to switch to RSAREF, we can't do anything about this problem.

Beginning with version 2.4 (which was ViaCrypt's first version) through at least 2.6, PGP does not allow you to generate RSA keys bigger than 1024 bits. The upper limit was always intended to be 1024 bits. But because of a bug in earlier versions of PGP, it was possible to generate keys larger than 1024 bits. These larger keys caused interoperability problems between different older versions of PGP that used different arithmetic algorithms with different native word sizes. On some platforms, PGP choked on the larger keys. In addition to these older key size problems, the 1024-bit limit is now enforced by RSAREF. A 1024-bit key is very likely to be well out of reach of attacks by major governments.

In general, there is compatibility from version 2.0 upwards through 2.4. Because new features are added, older versions may not always be able to handle some files created with newer versions. Because of massive changes to all the algorithms and data structures, PGP version 2.0 (and later) is not even slightly compatible with PGP version 1.0, which no one uses any more anyway.

Vulnerabilities

No data security system is impenetrable. PGP can be circumvented in a variety of ways. In any data security system, you have to ask yourself if the information you are trying to protect is more valuable to your attacker than the cost of the attack. This should lead you to protecting yourself from the cheapest attacks, while not worrying about the more expensive attacks.

Some of the discussion that follows may seem unduly paranoid, but such an attitude is appropriate for a reasonable discussion of vulnerability issues.

Compromised Pass Phrase and Secret Key

Probably the simplest attack is if you leave your pass phrase for your secret key written down somewhere. If someone gets it and also gets your secret key file, they can read your messages and make signatures in your name.

Don't use obvious passwords that can be easily guessed, such as the names of your kids or spouse. If you make your pass phrase a single word, it can be easily guessed by having a computer try all the words in the dictionary until it finds your password. That's why a pass phrase is so much better than a password. A more sophisticated attacker may have his computer scan a book of famous quotations to find your pass phrase. An easy to remember but hard to guess pass phrase can be easily constructed by some creatively nonsensical sayings or very obscure literary quotes.

For further details, see the section "How to Protect Secret Keys from Disclosure" in the Essential Topics volume of the PGP User's Guide.

Public Key Tampering

A major vulnerability exists if public keys are tampered with. This may be the most crucially important vulnerability of a public key cryptosystem, in part because most novices don't immediately recognize it. The importance of this vulnerability, and appropriate hygienic countermeasures, are detailed in the section "How to Protect Public Keys from Tampering" in the Essential Topics volume.

To summarize: When you use someone's public key, make certain it has not been tampered with. A new public key from someone else should be trusted only if you got it directly from its owner, or if it has been signed by someone you trust. Make sure no one else can tamper with your own public key ring. Maintain physical control of both your public key ring and your secret key ring, preferably on your own personal computer rather than on a remote timesharing system. Keep a backup copy of both key rings.

"Not Quite Deleted" Files

Another potential security problem is caused by how most operating systems delete files. When you encrypt a file and then delete the original plaintext file, the operating system doesn't actually physically erase the data. It merely marks those disk blocks as deleted, allowing the space to be reused later. It's sort of like discarding sensitive paper documents in the paper recycling bin instead of the paper shredder. The disk blocks still contain the original sensitive data you wanted to erase, and will probably eventually be overwritten by new data at some point in the future. If an attacker reads these deleted disk blocks soon after they have been de-allocated, he could recover your plaintext.

In fact this could even happen accidentally, if for some reason something went wrong with the disk and some files were accidentally deleted or corrupted. A disk recovery program may be run to recover the damaged files, but this often means some previously deleted files are resurrected along with everything else. Your confidential files that you thought were gone forever could then reappear and be inspected by whomever is attempting to recover your damaged disk. Even while you are creating the original message with a word processor or text editor, the editor may be creating multiple temporary copies of your text on the disk, just because of its internal workings. These temporary copies of your text are deleted by the word processor when it's done, but these sensitive fragments are still on your disk somewhere.

Let me tell you a true horror story. I had a friend, married with young children, who once had a brief and not very serious affair. She wrote a letter to her lover on her word processor, and deleted the letter after she sent it. Later, after the affair was over, the floppy disk got damaged somehow and she had to recover it because it contained other important documents. She asked her husband to salvage the disk, which seemed perfectly safe because she knew she had deleted the incriminating letter. Her husband ran a commercial disk recovery software package to salvage the files. It recovered the files all right, including the deleted letter. He read it, which set off a tragic chain of events.

The only way to prevent the plaintext from reappearing is to somehow cause the deleted plaintext files to be overwritten. Unless you know for sure that all the deleted disk blocks will soon be reused, you must take positive steps to overwrite the plaintext file, and also any fragments of it on the disk left by your word processor. You can overwrite the original plaintext file after encryption by using the PGP -w (wipe) option. You can take care of any fragments of the plaintext left on the disk by using any of the disk utilities available that can overwrite all of the unused blocks on a disk. For example, the Norton Utilities for MSDOS can do this.

Even if you overwrite the plaintext data on the disk, it may still be possible for a resourceful and determined attacker to recover the data. Faint magnetic traces of the original data remain on the disk after it has been overwritten. Special sophisticated disk recovery hardware can sometimes be used to recover the data.

Viruses and Trojan Horses

Another attack could involve a specially-tailored hostile computer virus or worm that might infect PGP or your operating system. This hypothetical virus could be designed to capture your pass phrase or secret key or deciphered messages, and covertly write the captured information to a file or send it through a network to the virus's owner. Or it might alter PGP's behavior so that signatures are not properly checked. This attack is cheaper than cryptanalytic attacks.

Defending against this falls under the category of defending against viral infection generally. There are some moderately capable anti-viral products commercially available, and there are hygienic procedures to follow that can greatly reduce the chances of viral infection. A complete treatment of anti-viral and anti-worm countermeasures is beyond the scope of this document. PGP has no defenses against viruses, and assumes your own personal computer is a trustworthy execution environment. If such a virus or worm actually appeared, hopefully word would soon get around warning everyone.

Another similar attack involves someone creating a clever imitation of PGP that behaves like PGP in most respects, but doesn't work the way it's supposed to. For example, it might be deliberately crippled to not check signatures properly, allowing bogus key certificates to be accepted. This "Trojan horse" version of PGP is not hard for an attacker to create because PGP source code is widely available, so anyone could modify the source code and produce a lobotomized zombie imitation PGP that looks real but does the bidding of its diabolical master. This Trojan horse version of PGP could then be widely circulated, claiming to be from me. How insidious.

You should make an effort to get your copy of PGP from a reliable source, whatever that means. Or perhaps from more than one independent source, and compare them with a file comparison utility.

There are other ways to check PGP for tampering, using digital signatures. If someone you trust signs the executable version of PGP, vouching for the fact that it has not been infected or tampered with, you can be reasonably sure that you have a good copy. You could use an earlier trusted version of PGP to check the signature on a later suspect version of PGP. But this will not help at all if your operating system is infected, nor will it detect if your original copy of PGP.EXE has been maliciously altered in such a way as to compromise its own ability to check signatures. This test also assumes that you have a good trusted copy of the public key that you use to check the signature on the PGP executable.

Physical Security Breach

A physical security breach may allow someone to physically acquire your plaintext files or printed messages. A determined opponent might accomplish this through burglary, trash-picking, unreasonable search and seizure, or bribery, blackmail, or infiltration of your staff. Some of these attacks may be especially feasible against grassroots political organizations that depend on a largely volunteer staff. It has been widely reported in the press that the FBI's COINTELPRO program used burglary, infiltration, and illegal bugging against antiwar and civil rights groups. And look what happened at the Watergate Hotel.

Don't be lulled into a false sense of security just because you have a cryptographic tool. Cryptographic techniques protect data only while it's encrypted— direct physical security violations can still compromise plaintext data or written or spoken information.

This kind of attack is cheaper than cryptanalytic attacks on PGP.

Tempest Attacks

Another kind of attack that has been used by well-equipped opponents involves the remote detection of the electromagnetic signals from your computer. This expensive and somewhat labor-intensive attack is probably still cheaper than direct cryptanalytic attacks. An appropriately instrumented van can park near your office and remotely pick up all of your keystrokes and messages displayed on your computer video screen. This would compromise all of your passwords, messages, etc. This attack can be thwarted by properly shielding all of your computer equipment and network cabling so that it does not emit these signals. This shielding technology is known as "Tempest," and is used by some Government agencies and defense contractors. There are hardware vendors who supply Tempest shielding commercially, although it may be subject to some kind of Government licensing. Now why do you suppose the Government would restrict access to Tempest shielding?

Protecting Against Bogus Timestamps

A somewhat obscure vulnerability of PGP involves dishonest users creating bogus timestamps on their own public key certificates and signatures. You can skip over this section if you are a casual user and aren't deeply into obscure public key protocols.

There's nothing to stop a dishonest user from altering the date and time setting of his own system's clock, and generating his own public key certificates and signatures that appear to have been created at a different time. He can make it appear that he signed something earlier or later than he actually did, or that his public/secret key pair was created earlier or later. This may have some legal or financial benefit to him, for example by creating some kind of loophole that might allow him to repudiate a signature.

A remedy for this could involve some trustworthy Certifying Authority or notary that would create notarized signatures with a trustworthy timestamp. This might not necessarily require a centralized authority. Perhaps any trusted introducer or disinterested party could serve this function, the same way real notary publics do now. A public key certificate could be signed by the notary, and the trusted timestamp in the notary's signature would have some legal significance. The notary could enter the signed certificate into a special certificate log controlled by the notary. Anyone can read this log.

The notary could also sign other people's signatures, creating a signature certificate of a signature certificate. This would serve as a witness to the signature the same way real notaries do now with paper. Again, the notary could enter the detached signature certificate (without the actual whole document that was signed) into a log controlled by the notary. The notary's signature would have a trusted timestamp, which might have greater credibility than the timestamp in the original signature. A signature becomes "legal" if it is signed and logged by the notary.

This problem of certifying signatures with notaries and trusted timestamps warrants further discussion. This can of worms will not be fully covered here now. There is a good treatment of this topic in Denning's 1983 article in IEEE Computer (see references). There is much more detail to be worked out in these various certifying schemes. This will develop further as PGP usage increases and other public key products develop their own certifying schemes.

Exposure on Multi-user Systems

PGP was originally designed for a single-user MSDOS machine under your direct physical control. I run PGP at home on my own PC, and unless someone breaks into my house or monitors my electromagnetic emissions, they probably can't see my plaintext files or secret keys.

But now PGP also runs on multi-user systems such as Unix and VAX/VMS. On multi-user systems, there are much greater risks of your plaintext or keys or passwords being exposed. The Unix system administrator or a clever intruder can read your plaintext files, or perhaps even use special software to covertly monitor your keystrokes or read what's on your screen. On a Unix system, any other user can read your environment information remotely by simply using the Unix "ps" command. Similar problems exist for MSDOS machines connected on a local area network. The actual security risk is dependent on your particular situation. Some multi-user systems may be safe because all the users are trusted, or because they have system security measures that are safe enough to withstand the attacks available to the intruders, or because there just aren't any sufficiently interested intruders. Some Unix systems are safe because they are only used by one user— there are even some notebook computers running Unix. It would be unreasonable to simply exclude PGP from running on all Unix systems.

PGP is not designed to protect your data while it is in plaintext form on a compromised system. Nor can it prevent an intruder from using sophisticated measures to read your secret key while it is being used. You will just have to recognize these risks on multi-user systems, and adjust your expectations and behavior accordingly. Perhaps your situation is such that you should consider running PGP only on an isolated single-user system under your direct physical control. That's what I do, and that's what I recommend.

Traffic Analysis

Even if the attacker cannot read the contents of your encrypted messages, he may be able to infer at least some useful information by observing where the messages come from and where they are going, the size of the messages, and the time of day the messages are sent. This is analogous to the attacker looking at your long distance phone bill to see who you called and when and for how long, even though the actual content of your calls is unknown to the attacker. This is called traffic analysis. PGP alone does not protect against traffic analysis. Solving this problem would require specialized communication protocols designed to reduce exposure to traffic analysis in your communication environment, possibly with some cryptographic assistance.

Cryptanalysis

An expensive and formidable cryptanalytic attack could possibly be mounted by someone with vast supercomputer resources, such as a Government intelligence agency. They might crack your RSA key by using some new secret factoring breakthrough. Perhaps so, but it is noteworthy that the U.S. Government trusts the RSA algorithm enough in some cases to use it to protect its own nuclear weapons, according to Ron Rivest. And civilian academia has been intensively attacking it without success since 1978.

Perhaps the Government has some classified methods of cracking the IDEA™ conventional encryption algorithm used in PGP. This is every cryptographer's worst nightmare. There can be no absolute security guarantees in practical cryptographic implementations.

Still, some optimism seems justified. The IDEA algorithm's designers are among the best cryptographers in Europe. It has had extensive security analysis and peer review from some of the best cryptanalysts in the unclassified world. It appears to have some design advantages over the DES in withstanding differential cryptanalysis, which has been used to crack the DES.

Besides, even if this algorithm has some subtle unknown weaknesses, PGP compresses the plaintext before encryption, which should greatly reduce those weaknesses. The computational workload to crack it is likely to be much more expensive than the value of the message.

If your situation justifies worrying about very formidable attacks of this caliber, then perhaps you should contact a data security consultant for some customized data security approaches tailored to your special needs. Boulder Software Engineering, whose address and phone number are given at the end of this document, can provide such services.

In summary, without good cryptographic protection of your data communications, it may have been practically effortless and perhaps even routine for an opponent to intercept your messages, especially those sent through a modem or E-mail system. If you use PGP and follow reasonable precautions, the attacker will have to expend far more effort and expense to violate your privacy.

If you protect yourself against the simplest attacks, and you feel confident that your privacy is not going to be violated by a determined and highly resourceful attacker, then you'll probably be safe using PGP. PGP gives you Pretty Good Privacy.

Legal Issues

Trademarks, Copyrights, and Warranties

"Pretty Good Privacy," "Phil's Pretty Good Software," and the "Pretty Good" label for computer software and hardware products are all trademarks of Philip Zimmermann and Phil's Pretty Good Software. PGP is © Copyright Philip R. Zimmermann, 1990–1994. All rights reserved. Philip Zimmermann also holds the copyright for the PGP User's Manual, as well as any foreign language translations of the manual or the software, and all derivative works. All rights reserved.

MIT may have a copyright on the particular software distribution package that they distribute from the MIT FTP site. This copyright on the "compilation" of the distribution package in no way implies that MIT has a copyright on PGP itself, or its user documentation.

The author assumes no liability for damages resulting from the use of this software, even if the damage results from defects in this software, and makes no representations concerning the merchantability of this software or its suitability for any specific purpose. It is provided "as is" without express or implied warranty of any kind. Because certain actions may delete files or render them unrecoverable, the author assumes no responsibility for the loss or modification of any data.

Patent Rights on the Algorithms

The RSA public key cryptosystem was developed at MIT, which holds a patent on it (U.S. patent #4,405,829, issued 20 September 1983). A company in California called Public Key Partners (PKP) holds the exclusive commercial license to sell and sub-license the RSA public key cryptosystem. MIT distributes a freeware version of PGP under the terms of the RSAREF license from RSA Data Security, Inc. (RSADSI).

Non-U.S. users of earlier versions of PGP should note that the RSA patent does not apply outside the U.S., and at least at the time of this writing, the author is not aware of any RSA patent in any other country. Federal agencies may use the RSA algorithm, because the Government paid for the development of RSA with grants from the National Science Foundation and the Navy. But despite the fact of Government users having free access to the RSA algorithm, Government use of PGP has additional restrictions imposed by the agreement I have with ViaCrypt, as explained later.

I wrote my PGP software from scratch, with my own independently developed implementation of the RSA algorithm. Before publishing PGP, I got a formal written legal opinion from a patent attorney with extensive experience in software patents. I'm convinced that publishing PGP the way I did does not violate patent law.

Not only did PKP acquire the exclusive patent rights for the RSA cryptosystem, but they also acquired the exclusive rights to three other patents covering other public key schemes invented by others at Stanford University, also developed with federal funding. This essentially gives one company a legal lock in the USA on nearly all practical public key cryptosystems. They even appear to be claiming patent rights on the very concept of public key cryptography, regardless of what clever new original algorithms are independently invented by others. I find such a comprehensive monopoly troubling, because I think public key cryptography is destined to become a crucial technology in the protection of our civil liberties and privacy in our increasingly connected society. At the very least, it places these vital tools at risk by affording to the Government a single pressure point of influence.

Beginning with PGP version 2.5 (distributed by MIT, the holders of the original RSA patent), the freeware version of PGP uses the RSAREF subroutine library to perform its RSA calculations, under the RSAREF license, which allows noncommercial use in the USA. RSAREF is a subroutine package from RSA Data Security, Inc., that implements the RSA algorithm. The RSAREF subroutines are used instead of PGP's original subroutines to implement the RSA functions in PGP. See the RSAREF license for terms and conditions of use of RSAREF applications.

PGP 2.5 was released by MIT for a brief test period in May, 1994 before releasing 2.6. Although 2.5 was released under the 16 March, 1994 RSAREF license, which is a perpetual license, it would be better for users in the United States to upgrade to version 2.6 to facilitate the demise of PGP 2.3a and earlier versions. Also, PGP 2.5 has bugs that are corrected in 2.6, and 2.5 will not read the new data format after 1 September, 1994. (See the section on Compatibility with Previous Versions of PGP.)

The PGP 2.0 release was a joint effort of an international team of software engineers, implementing enhancements to the original PGP with design guidance from me. It was released by Branko Lankester in The Netherlands and Peter Gutmann in New Zealand, out of reach of U.S. patent law. Although released only in Europe and New Zealand, it spontaneously spread to the USA without help from me or the PGP development team.

The IDEA™ conventional block cipher used by PGP is covered by a patent in Europe, held by ETH and a Swiss company called Ascom-Tech AG. The U.S. patent number is US005214703, and the European patent number is EP 0 482 154 B1. IDEA™ is a trademark of Ascom-Tech AG. There is no license fee required for noncommercial use of IDEA. Commercial users of IDEA may obtain licensing details from Dieter Profos, Ascom Tech AG, Teleservices Section, Postfach 151, 4502 Solothurn, Switzerland, Tel +41 65 242885, Fax +41 65 235761.

Ascom-Tech AG has granted permission for the freeware version PGP to use the IDEA cipher in non-commercial uses, everywhere. In the U.S. and Canada, all commercial or Government users must obtain a licensed version from ViaCrypt, who has a license from Ascom-Tech for the IDEA cipher. Ascom-Tech has recently been changing its policies regarding the use of IDEA in PGP for commercial use outside the U.S., and that policy still seems to be in flux.

The ZIP compression routines in PGP come from freeware source code, with the author's permission. I'm not aware of any patents on the compression algorithms used in the ZIP routines, but you're welcome to check into that question yourself.

Licensing and Distribution

In the USA, PGP 2.6 is available from the Massachusetts Institute of Technology, under the terms of the RSAREF license. I have no objection to anyone freely using or distributing the freeware version of PGP, without payment of fees to me, as long as it is for personal non-commercial use. For commercial use, contact ViaCrypt in Phoenix, Arizona (phone 602-944-0773). You must keep the copyright, patent, and trademark notices on PGP and keep all the documentation with it.

NOTE: Regardless of the complexities and partially overlapping restrictions from all the other terms and conditions imposed by the various patent and copyright licenses (RSA, RSAREF, and IDEA) from various third parties, an additional overriding restriction on PGP usage is imposed by my own agreement with ViaCrypt: The freeware version of PGP is only for personal, noncommercial use—

all other users in the USA and Canada must obtain a fully licensed version of PGP from ViaCrypt.

I had to make an agreement with ViaCrypt in the summer of 1993 to license the exclusive commercial rights to PGP, so that there would be a legally safe way for corporations to use PGP without risk of a patent infringement lawsuit from PKP. For PGP to succeed in the long term as a viable industry standard, the legal stigma associated with the RSA patent rights had to be resolved. ViaCrypt had already obtained a patent license from PKP to make, use, and sell products that practice the RSA patents. ViaCrypt offered a way out of the patent quagmire for PGP to penetrate the corporate environment. They could sell a fully-licensed version of PGP, but only if I licensed it to them under these terms. So we entered into an agreement to do that, opening the door for PGP's future in the commercial sector, which was necessary for PGP's long-term political future.

PGP is not shareware, it's freeware. Published as a community service. Giving PGP away for free will encourage far more people to use it, which hopefully will have a greater social impact. This could lead to widespread awareness and use of the RSA public key cryptosystem.

Feel free to disseminate the complete PGP release package as widely as possible, but be careful not to violate U.S. export controls if you live in the USA. Give it to all your friends. If you have access to any electronic Bulletin Boards Systems, please upload the complete PGP executable object release package to as many BBSs as possible. The freeware version of PGP is available in source code form, and you may disseminate the source release package too, if you've got it. NOTE: Under no circumstances should PGP be distributed without the PGP documentation, including this PGP User's Guide and the RSAREF license agreement.

The PGP version 2.6 executable object release package for MSDOS contains the PGP executable software, documentation, RSAREF license, sample key rings including my own public key, and signatures for the software and this manual, all in one PKZIP compressed file called pgp26.zip. The PGP source release package for MSDOS contains all the C source files in one PKZIP compressed file called pgp26src.zip. The filename for the release package is derived from the version number of the release.

The primary release site for PGP is the Massachusetts Institute of Technology, at their FTP site "net-dist.mit.edu," in their /pub/PGP directory. You may obtain free copies or updates to PGP from this site, or any other Internet FTP site or BBS that PGP has spread to. Don't ask me for a copy directly from me, especially if you live outside the U.S. or Canada.

After all this work I have to admit I wouldn't mind getting some fan mail for PGP, to gauge its popularity. Let me know what you think about it and how many of your friends use it. Bug reports and suggestions for enhancing PGP are welcome, too. Perhaps a future PGP release will reflect your suggestions.

This project has not been funded and the project has nearly eaten me alive. This means you can't count on a reply to your mail, unless you only need a short written reply and you include a stamped self-addressed envelope. But I often do reply to E-mail. Please keep it in English, as my foreign language skills are weak. If you call and I'm not in, it's best to just try again later. I usually don't return long distance phone calls, unless you leave a message that I can call you collect. If you need any significant amount of my time, I am available on a paid consulting basis, and I do return those calls.

The most inconvenient mail I get is for some well-intentioned person to send me a few dollars asking me for a copy of PGP. I don't send it to them because I'd rather avoid any legal problems with PKP. Or worse, sometimes these requests are from foreign countries, and I would be risking a violation of U.S. cryptographic export control laws. Even if there were no legal hassles involved in sending PGP to them, they usually don't send enough money to make it worth my time. I'm just not set up as a low-cost low-volume mail order business. I can't just ignore the request and keep the money, because they probably regard the money as a fee for me to fulfill their request. If I return the money, I might have to get in my car and drive down to the post office and buy some postage stamps, because these requests rarely include a stamped self-addressed envelope. I also have to take the time to write a polite reply that I can't do it. If I postpone the reply and set the letter down on my desk, it might be buried within minutes and won't see the light of day again for months. Multiply these minor inconveniences by the number of requests I get, and you can see the problem. Isn't it enough that the software is free? It would be nicer if people could try to get PGP from any of the myriad other sources. If you don't have a modem, ask a friend to get it for you. If you can't find it yourself, I don't mind answering a quick phone call.

If anyone wants to volunteer to improve PGP, please let me know. It could certainly use some more work. Some features were deferred to get it out the door. A number of PGP users have since donated their time to port PGP to Unix on Sun SPARCstations, to Ultrix, to VAX/VMS, to OS/2, to the Amiga, and to the Atari ST. Perhaps you can help port it to some new environments. But please let me know if you plan to port or add enhancements to PGP, to avoid duplication of effort, and to avoid starting with an obsolete version of the source code.

Because so many foreign language translations of PGP have been produced, most of them are not distributed with the regular PGP release package because it would require too much disk space. Separate language translation "kits" are available from a number of independent sources, and are sometimes available separately from the same distribution centers that carry the regular PGP release software. These kits include translated versions of the file LANGUAGE.TXT, PGP.HLP, and the PGP User's Guide. If you want to produce a translation for your own native language, contact me first to get the latest information and standard guidelines, and to find out if it's been translated to your language already. To find out where to get a foreign language kit for your language, you might check on the Internet newsgroups, or get it from Mike Johnson (mpj@csn.org).

If you have access to the Internet, watch for announcements of new releases of PGP on the Internet newsgroups "sci.crypt" and PGP's own newsgroup, "alt.security.pgp." If you want to know where to get PGP, MIT is the primary FTP distribution site (net-dist.mit.edu). Or ask Mike Johnson (mpj@csn.org) for a list of Internet FTP sites and BBS phone numbers.

Future versions of PGP may have to change the data formats for messages, signatures, keys, and key rings, in order to provide important new features. This may cause backward compatibility problems with this version of PGP. Future releases may provide conversion utilities to convert old keys, but you may have to dispose of old messages created with the old PGP.

Export Controls

The U.S. Government has made it illegal in most cases to export good cryptographic technology, and that may include PGP. They regard this kind of software just like they regard munitions. This is determined by volatile State Department, Defense Department, and Commerce Department policies, not fixed laws. I will not export this software out of the U.S. or Canada in cases when it is illegal to do so under U.S. controls, and I urge other people not to export it on their own.

If you live outside the U.S. or Canada, I urge you not to violate U.S. export laws by getting any version of PGP in a way that violates those laws. Since thousands of domestic users got the first version after its initial publication, it somehow leaked out of the U.S. and spread itself widely abroad, like dandelion seeds blowing in the wind.

Starting with PGP version 2.0 through version 2.3a, the release point of the software has been outside the U.S., on publicly accessible computers in Europe. Each release was electronically sent back into the U.S. and posted on publicly accessible computers in the U.S. by PGP privacy activists in foreign countries. There are some restrictions in the U.S. regarding the import of munitions, but I'm not aware of any cases where this was ever enforced for importing cryptographic software into the U.S. I imagine that a legal action of that type would be quite a spectacle of controversy.

ViaCrypt PGP version 2.4 is sold in the United States and Canada and is not for export. The following language was supplied by the U.S. Government to ViaCrypt for inclusion in the ViaCrypt PGP documentation:

> "PGP is export restricted by the Office of Export Administration, United States Department of Commerce and the Offices of Defense Trade Controls and Munitions Control, United States Department of State. PGP cannot be exported or reexported, directly or indirectly, (a) without all export or reexport licenses and governmental approvals required by any applicable laws, or (b) in violation of any prohibition against the export or reexport of any part of PGP."

The Government may take the position that the freeware PGP versions are also subject to those controls.

The freeware PGP versions 2.5 and 2.6 were released through a posting on a controlled FTP site maintained by MIT. This site has restrictions and limitations which have been used on other FTP sites to comply with export control requirements with respect to other encryption software such as Kerberos and software from RSA Data Security, Inc. I urge you not to do anything which would weaken those controls or facilitate any improper export of ViaCrypt PGP or the freeware PGP versions.

Some foreign governments impose serious penalties on anyone inside their country for merely using encrypted communications. In some countries they might even shoot you for that. But if you live in that kind of country, perhaps you need PGP even more.

Philip Zimmermann's Legal Situation

At the time of this writing, I am the target of a U.S. Customs criminal investigation in the Northern District of California. My defense attorney has been told by the Assistant U.S. Attorney that the area of law of interest to the investigation has to do with the export controls on encryption software. The federal mandatory sentencing guidelines for this offense are 41 to 51 months in a federal prison. U.S. Customs appears to be taking the position that electronic domestic publication of encryption software is the same as exporting it. The prosecutor has issued a number of federal grand jury subpoenas. It may be months before a decision is reached on whether to seek indictment. This situation may change at any time, so this description may be out-of-date by the time you read it. Watch the news for further developments. If I am indicted and this goes to trial, it will be a major test case.

I have a legal defense fund set up for this case. So far, no other organization is doing the fundraising for me, so I am depending on people like you to contribute directly to this cause. The fund is run by my lead defense attorney, Phil Dubois, here in Boulder. Please send your contributions to:

Philip Dubois

2305 Broadway

Boulder, Colorado 80304 USA

Phone 303-444-3885

E-mail: dubois@csn.org

You can also phone in your donation and put it on Mastercard or Visa. If you want to be really cool, you can use Internet E-mail to send in your contribution, encrypting your message with PGP so that no one can intercept your credit card number. Include in your E-mail message your Mastercard or Visa number, expiration date, name on the card, and amount of donation. Then sign it with your own key and encrypt it with Phil Dubois's public key (his key is included in the standard PGP distribution package, in the "keys.asc" file). Put a note on the subject line that this is a donation to my legal defense fund, so that Mr. Dubois will decrypt it promptly. Please don't send a lot of casual encrypted E-mail to him—I'd rather he use his valuable time to work on my case.

If you want to read some press stories about this case, see the following references:

1. William Bulkeley, "Cipher Probe," Wall Street Journal, Thursday 28 April, 1994, front page.

2. John Cary, "Spy vs. Computer Nerd: The Fight Over Data Security," Business Week, 4 Oct 1993, page 43.

3. Jon Erickson, "Cryptography Fires Up the Feds," Dr. Dobb's Journal, December 1993, page 6.

4. John Markoff, "Federal Inquiry on Software Examines Privacy Programs," The New York Times, Tuesday 21 September 1993, page C1.

5. Kurt Kleiner, "Punks and Privacy," Mother Jones Magazine, January/February 1994, page 17.

6. John Markoff, "Cyberspace Under Lock and Key," The New York Times, Sunday 13 February 1994.

7. Philip Elmer-DeWitt, "Who Should Keep the Keys," Time, 14 March 1994, page 90.

Where to Get a Commercial Version of PGP

To get a fully licensed version of PGP for use in the USA or Canada, contact:

ViaCrypt
2104 West Peoria Avenue
Phoenix, Arizona 85029
Phone: 602-944-0773
Fax: 602-943-2601
E-mail: viacrypt@acm.org

ViaCrypt has a version of PGP for MSDOS, and a number of Unix platforms. Other versions are under development. If you have a need to use PGP in a commercial or Government setting, and ViaCrypt has a version of PGP for your hardware platform, you should get ViaCrypt PGP.

ViaCrypt has obtained all the necessary licenses from PKP, Ascom-Tech AG, and Philip Zimmermann to sell PGP for use in commercial or Government environments. ViaCrypt PGP is every bit as secure as the freeware PGP, and is entirely compatible in both directions with the freeware version of PGP. ViaCrypt PGP is the perfect way to get a fully-licensed version of PGP into your corporate environment.

Reporting PGP Bugs

Bugs in PGP should be reported via E-mail to MIT, the official distribution site of PGP. The E-mail address for bug reports is pgp-bugs@mit.edu.

Computer-Related Political Groups

PGP is a very political piece of software. It seems appropriate to mention here some computer-related activist groups. Full details on these groups, and how to join them, is provided in a separate document file in the PGP release package.

The Electronic Frontier Foundation (EFF) was founded in 1990 to assure freedom of expression in digital media, with a particular emphasis on applying the principles embodied in the U.S. Constitution and the Bill of Rights to computer-based communication. They can be reached in Washington DC, at (202) 347-5400. Internet E-mail address: eff@eff.org.

Computer Professionals for Social Responsibility (CPSR) empowers computer professionals and computer users to advocate for the responsible use of information technology and empowers all who use computer technology to participate in public policy debates on the impacts of computers on society. They can be reached at: 415-322-3778 in Palo Alto, E-mail address cpsr@csli.stanford.edu.

The League for Programming Freedom (LPF) is a grass-roots organization of professors, students, businessmen, programmers, and users dedicated to bringing back the freedom to write programs. They regard patents on computer algorithms as harmful to the U.S. software industry. They can be reached at (617) 433-7071. E-mail address: lpf@uunet.uu.net.

For more details on these groups, see the accompanying document in the PGP release package.

Recommended Introductory Readings

1. Bruce Schneier, "Applied Cryptography: Protocols, Algorithms, and Source Code in C," John Wiley & Sons, 1993. (This book is a watershed work on the subject.)
2. Dorothy Denning, "Cryptography and Data Security," Addison-Wesley, Reading, MA 1982.
3. Dorothy Denning, "Protecting Public Keys and Signature Keys," IEEE Computer, February 1983.
4. Martin E. Hellman, "The Mathematics of Public-Key Cryptography," Scientific American, August 1979.
5. Steven Levy, "Crypto Rebels," WIRED, May/June 1993, page 54. (This is a "must-read" article on PGP and other related topics.)

Other Readings

6. Ronald Rivest, "The MD5 Message Digest Algorithm," MIT Laboratory for Computer Science, 1991.
7. Xuejia Lai, "On the Design and Security of Block Ciphers," ETH Series on Information Processing (Ed. J. L. Massey), Vol. 1, Hartung-Gorre Verlag, Konstanz, Switzerland, 1992.

8. Philip Zimmermann, "A Proposed Standard Format for RSA Cryptosystems," Advances in Computer Security, Vol. III, edited by Rein Turn, Artech House, 1988.

9. Paul Wallich, "Electronic Envelopes," Scientific American, February 1993, page 30. (This is an article on PGP.)

10. William Bulkeley, "Cipher Probe," Wall Street Journal, 28 April 1994, front page. (This is an article on PGP and Zimmermann.)

To Contact the Author

Philip Zimmermann may be reached at:

Boulder Software Engineering

3021 Eleventh Street

Boulder, Colorado 80304 USA

Internet: prz@acm.org

Phone: 303-541-0140 (voice) (10:00 am – 7:00 pm Mountain Time)

Fax line available, if you arrange it via voice line.

Where to Get PGP

The following describes how to get the freeware public key cryptographic software PGP (Pretty Good Privacy) from an anonymous FTP site on the Internet, or from other sources.

PGP has sophisticated key management, an RSA/conventional hybrid encryption scheme, message digests for digital signatures, data compression before encryption, and good ergonomic design. PGP is well featured and fast, and has excellent user documentation. Source code is free.

The Massachusetts Institute of Technology is the distributor of PGP version 2.6, for distribution in the USA only. It is available from "net-dist.mit.edu," a controlled FTP site that has restrictions and limitations, similar to those used by RSA Data Security, Inc., to comply with export control requirements. The software resides in the directory /pub/PGP.

A reminder: Set mode to binary or image when doing an FTP transfer. And when doing a kermit download to your PC, specify 8-bit binary mode at both ends.

There are two compressed archive files in the standard release, with the file name derived from the release version number. For PGP version 2.6, you must get pgp26.zip which contains the MSDOS binary executable and the PGP User's Guide, and you can optionally get pgp26src.zip which contains all the source code. These files can be decompressed with the MSDOS shareware archive decompression utility PKUNZIP.EXE, version 1.10 or later. For Unix users who lack an implementation of UNZIP, the source code can also be found in the compressed tar file pgp26src.tar.Z.

If you don't have any local BBS phone numbers handy, here is a BBS you might try. The Catacombs BBS, operated by Mike Johnson in Longmont, Colorado, has PGP available for download by people in the U.S. or Canada only. The BBS phone number is 303-772-1062. Mike Johnson's voice phone number is 303-772-1773, and his E-mail address is mpj@csn.org. Mike also has PGP available on an Internet FTP site for users in the U.S. or Canada only; the site name is csn.org, in directory /mpj/, and you must read the README.MPJ file to get it.

To get a fully-licensed version of PGP for use in the USA or Canada, contact ViaCrypt in Phoenix, Arizona. Their phone number is 602-944-0773. ViaCrypt has obtained all the necessary licenses from PKP, Ascom-Tech AG, and Philip Zimmermann to sell PGP for use in commercial or Government environments. ViaCrypt PGP is every bit as secure as the freeware PGP, and is entirely compatible in both directions with the freeware version of PGP. ViaCrypt PGP is the perfect way to get a fully-licensed version of PGP into your corporate or Government environment.

Source and binary distributions of PGP are available from the Canadian Broadcasting Corporation library, which is open to the public. It has branches in Toronto, Montreal, and Vancouver. Contact Max Allen, at +1 416-205-6017 if you have questions.

Here are a few people and their E-mail addresses or phone numbers you can contact in some countries to get information on local PGP availability for versions earlier than 2.5:

Peter Gutmann
pgut1@cs.aukuni.ac.nz
New Zealand

Hugh Kennedy
70042.710@compuserve.com
Germany

Branko Lankester
branko@hacktic.nl
+31 2159 42242
The Netherlands

Miguel Angel Gallardo
gallardo@batman.fi.upm.es
(341) 474 38 09
Spain

Hugh Miller
hmiller@lucpul.it.luc.edu
(312) 508-2727
USA

Colin Plumb
colin@nyx.cs.du.edu
Toronto, Ontario, Canada

Jean-loup Gailly
jloup@chorus.fr
France

Appendix B

Privacy Enhanced Mail

Network Working Group
Request for Comments: 1421
Obsoletes: 1113

J. Linn
IAB IRTF PSRG, IETF PEM WG
February 1993

Privacy Enhancement for Internet Electronic Mail:

Part I
Message Encryption and Authentication Procedures

Status of this Memo

This RFC specifies an IAB standards track protocol for the Internet community, and requests discussion and suggestions for improvements. Please refer to the current edition of the "IAB Official Protocol Standards" for the standardization state and status of this protocol. Distribution of this memo is unlimited.

Acknowledgments

This document is the outgrowth of a series of meetings of the Privacy and Security Research Group (PSRG) of the IRTF and the PEM Working Group of the IETF. I would like to thank the members of the PSRG and the IETF PEM WG, as well as all participants in discussions on the "pem_dev@tis.com" mailing list, for their contributions to this document.

1. Executive Summary

This document defines message encryption and authentication procedures, in order to provide privacy-enhanced mail (PEM) services for electronic mail transfer in the Internet. It is intended to become one member of a related set of four RFCs. The procedures defined in the current document are intended to be compatible with a wide range of key management approaches, including both symmetric (secret-key) and asymmetric (public-key) approaches for encryption of data encrypting keys. Use of symmetric cryptography for message text encryption and/or integrity check computation is anticipated. RFC 1422 specifies supporting key management mechanisms based on the use of public-key certificates. RFC 1423 specifies algorithms, modes, and associated identifiers relevant to the current RFC and to RFC 1422. RFC 1424 provides details of paper and electronic formats and procedures for the key management infrastructure being established in support of these services.

Privacy enhancement services (confidentiality, authentication, message integrity assurance, and nonrepudiation of origin) are offered through the use of end-to-end cryptography between originator and recipient processes at or above the User Agent level. No special processing requirements are imposed on the Message Transfer System at privacy enhancement facilities to be incorporated selectively on a site-by-site or user-by-user basis without impact on other Internet entities. Interoperability among heterogeneous components and mail transport facilities is supported.

The current specification's scope is confined to PEM processing procedures for the RFC-822 textual mail environment, and defines the Content-Domain indicator value "RFC822" to signify this usage. Follow-on work in integration of PEM capabilities with other messaging environments (e.g., MIME) is anticipated and will be addressed in separate and/or successor documents, at which point additional Content-Domain indicator values will be defined.

2. Terminology

For descriptive purposes, this RFC uses some terms defined in the OSI X.400 Message Handling System Model per the CCITT Recommendations. This section replicates a portion of (1984) X.400's Section 2.2.1, "Description of the MHS Model: Overview" in order to make the terminology clear to readers who may not be familiar with the OSI MHS Model.

In the [MHS] model, a user is a person or a computer application. A user is referred to as either an originator (when sending a message) or a recipient (when receiving one). MH Service elements define the set of message types and the capabilities that enable an originator to transfer messages of those types to one or more recipients.

An originator prepares messages with the assistance of his or her User Agent (UA). A UA is an application process that interacts with the Message Transfer System (MTS) to submit messages. The MTS delivers to one or more recipient UAs the messages submitted to it. Functions performed solely by the UA and not standardized as part of the MH Service elements are called local UA functions.

The MTS is composed of a number of Message Transfer Agents (MTAs). Operating together, the MTAs relay messages and deliver them to the intended recipient UAs, which then make the messages available to the intended recipients.

The collection of UAs and MTAs is called the Message Handling System (MHS). The MHS and all of its users are collectively referred to as the Message Handling Environment.

3. Services, Constraints, and Implications

This RFC defines mechanisms to enhance privacy for electronic mail transferred in the Internet. The facilities discussed in this RFC provide privacy enhancement services on an end-to-end basis between originator and recipient processes residing at the UA level or above. No privacy enhancements are offered for message fields which are added or transformed by intermediate relay points between PEM processing components.

If an originator elects to perform PEM processing on an outbound message, all PEM-provided security services are applied to the PEM message's body in its entirety; selective application to portions of a PEM message is not supported. Authentication, integrity, and (when asymmetric key management is employed) nonrepudiation of origin services are applied to all PEM messages; confidentiality services are optionally selectable.

In keeping with the Internet's heterogeneous constituencies and usage modes, the measures defined here are applicable to a broad range of Internet hosts and usage paradigms. In particular, it is worth noting the following attributes:

1. The mechanisms defined in this RFC are not restricted to a particular host or operating system, but rather allow interoperability among a broad range of systems. All privacy enhancements are implemented at the application layer,

and are not dependent on any privacy features at lower protocol layers.

2. The defined mechanisms are compatible with non-enhanced Internet components. Privacy enhancements are implemented in an end-to-end fashion which does not impact mail processing by intermediate relay hosts which do not incorporate privacy enhancement facilities. It is necessary, however, for a message's originator to be cognizant of whether a message's intended recipient implements privacy enhancements, in order that encoding and possible encryption will not be performed on a message whose destination is not equipped to perform corresponding inverse transformations. [Section 4.6.1.1.3 of this RFC describes a PEM message type ("MIC-CLEAR") which represents a signed, unencrypted PEM message in a form readable without PEM processing capabilities yet validatable by PEM-equipped recipients.]

3. The defined mechanisms are compatible with a range of mail transport facilities (MTAs). Within the Internet, electronic mail transport is effected by a variety of SMTP [2] implementations. Certain sites, accessible via SMTP, forward mail into other mail processing environments (e.g., USENET, CSNET, BITNET). The privacy enhancements must be able to operate across the SMTP realm; it is desirable that they also be compatible with protection of electronic mail sent between the SMTP environment and other connected environments.

4. The defined mechanisms are compatible with a broad range of electronic mail user agents (UAs). A large variety of electronic mail user agent programs, with a corresponding broad range of user interface paradigms, is used in the Internet. In order that electronic mail privacy enhancements be available to the broadest possible user community, selected mechanisms should be usable with the widest possible variety of existing UA programs. For purposes of pilot implementation, it is desirable that privacy enhancement processing be incorporable into a separate program, applicable to a range of UAs, rather than requiring internal modifications to each UA with which PEM services are to be provided.

5. The defined mechanisms allow electronic mail privacy enhancement processing to be performed on personal computers (PCs) separate from the systems on which UA functions are implemented. Given the expanding use of PCs and the limited degree of trust which can be placed in UA implementations on many multi-user systems, this attribute can allow many users to process PEM with a higher assurance level than a strictly UA-integrated approach would allow.

6. The defined mechanisms support privacy protection of electronic mail addressed to mailing lists (distribution lists, in ISO parlance).

7. The mechanisms defined within this RFC are compatible with a variety of supporting key management approaches, including (but not limited to) manual predistribution, centralized key distribution based on symmetric

cryptography, and the use of public-key certificates per RFC 1422. Different key management mechanisms may be used for different recipients of a multicast message. For two PEM implementations to interoperate, they must share a common key management mechanism; support for the mechanism defined in RFC 1422 is strongly encouraged.

In order to achieve applicability to the broadest possible range of Internet hosts and mail systems, and to facilitate pilot implementation and testing without the need for prior and pervasive modifications throughout the Internet, the following design principles were applied in selecting the set of features specified in this RFC:

1. This RFC's measures are restricted to implementation at endpoints and are amenable to integration with existing Internet mail protocols at the user agent (UA) level or above, rather than necessitating modifications to existing mail protocols or integration into the message transport system (e.g., SMTP servers).

2. The set of supported measures enhances rather than restricts user capabilities. Trusted implementations, incorporating integrity features protecting software from subversion by local users, cannot be assumed in general. No mechanisms are assumed to prevent users from sending, at their discretion, messages to which no PEM processing has been applied. In the absence of such features, it appears more feasible to provide facilities which enhance user services (e.g., by protecting and authenticating inter-user traffic) than to enforce restrictions (e.g., inter-user access control) on user actions.

3. The set of supported measures focuses on a set of functional capabilities selected to provide significant and tangible benefits to a broad user community. By concentrating on the most critical set of services, we aim to maximize the added privacy value that can be provided with a modest level of implementation effort.

Based on these principles, the following facilities are provided:

1. disclosure protection

2. originator authenticity

3. message integrity measures

4. (if asymmetric key management is used) nonrepudiation of origin

but the following privacy-relevant concerns are not addressed:

1. access control

2. traffic flow confidentiality

3. address list accuracy

4. routing control

5. issues relating to the casual serial reuse of PCs by multiple users

6. assurance of message receipt and non-deniability of receipt

7. automatic association of acknowledgments with the messages to which they refer

8. message duplicate detection, replay prevention, or other stream-oriented services.

4. *Processing of Messages*

4.1 Message Processing Overview

This subsection provides a high-level overview of the components and processing steps involved in electronic mail privacy enhancement processing. Subsequent subsections will define the procedures in more detail.

4.1.1 Types of Keys

A two-level keying hierarchy is used to support PEM transmission:

1. Data Encrypting Keys (DEKs) are used for encryption of message text and (with certain choices among a set of alternative algorithms) for computation of message integrity check (MIC) quantities. In the asymmetric key management environment, DEKs are also used to encrypt the signed representations of MICs in PEM messages to which confidentiality has been applied. DEKs are generated individually for each transmitted message; no predistribution of DEKs is needed to support PEM transmission.

2. Interchange Keys (IKs) are used to encrypt DEKs for transmission within messages. Ordinarily, the same IK will be used for all messages sent from a given originator to a given recipient over a period of time. Each transmitted message includes a representation of the DEK(s) used for message encryption and/or MIC computation, encrypted under an individual IK per named recipient. The representation is associated with Originator-ID and Recipient-ID fields (defined in different forms so as to distinguish symmetric from asymmetric cases), which allow each individual recipient to identify the IK used to encrypt DEKs and/or MICs for that recipient's use. Given an appropriate IK, a recipient can decrypt the corresponding transmitted DEK representation, yielding the DEK required for message text decryption and/or MIC validation. The definition of an IK differs depending on whether symmetric or asymmetric cryptography is used for DEK encryption.

2a.When symmetric cryptography is used for DEK encryption, an IK is a single symmetric key shared between an originator and a recipient. In this case, the same IK is used to encrypt MICs as well as DEKs for transmission. Version/expiration information and IA identification associated with the originator and with the recipient must be concatenated in order to fully qualify a symmetric IK.

2b. When asymmetric cryptography is used, the IK component used for DEK encryption is the public component [8] of the recipient. The IK component used for MIC encryption is the private component of the originator, and therefore only one encrypted MIC representation need be included per message, rather than one per recipient. Each of these IK components can be fully qualified in a Recipient-ID or Originator-ID field, respectively. Alternatively, an originator's IK component may be determined from a certificate carried in an "Originator-Certificate:" field.

4.1.2 Processing Procedures

When PEM processing is to be performed on an outgoing message, a DEK is generated [1] for use in message encryption and (if a chosen MIC algorithm requires a key) a variant of the DEK is formed for use in MIC computation. DEK generation can be omitted for the case of a message where confidentiality is not to be applied, unless a chosen MIC computation algorithm requires a DEK. Other parameters [e.g., Initialization Vectors (IVs)] as required by selected encryption algorithms are also generated.

One or more Originator-ID and/or "Originator-Certificate:" fields are included in a PEM message's encapsulated header to provide recipients with an identification component for the IK(s) used for message processing. All of a message's Originator-ID and/or "Originator- Certificate:" fields are assumed to correspond to the same principal; the facility for inclusion of multiple such fields accomodates the prospect that different keys, algorithms, and/or certification paths may be required for processing by different recipients. When a message includes recipients for which asymmetric key management is employed as well as recipients for which symmetric key management is employed, a separate Originator-ID or "Originator-Certificate:" field precedes each set of recipients.

In the symmetric case, per-recipient IK components are applied for each individually named recipient in preparation of ENCRYPTED, MIC-ONLY, and MIC-CLEAR messages. A corresponding "Recipient-ID-Symmetric:" field, interpreted in the context of the most recent preceding "Originator-ID-Symmetric:" field, serves to identify each IK. In the asymmetric case, per-recipient IK components are applied only for ENCRYPTED messages, are independent of originator-oriented header elements, and are identified by "Recipient-ID-Asymmetric:" fields. Each Recipient-ID field is followed by a "Key-Info:" field, which transfers the message's DEK encrypted under the IK appropriate for the specified recipient.

When symmetric key management is used for a given recipient, the "Key-Info:" field following the corresponding "Recipient-ID-Symmetric:" field also transfers the message's computed MIC, encrypted under the recipient's IK. When asymmetric key management is used, a "MIC-Info:" field associated with an "Originator-ID-Asymmetric:" or "Originator-Certificate:" field carries the message's MIC, asymmetrically signed using the private component of the originator. If the PEM message is of type ENCRYPTED (as defined in Section 4.6.1.1.1 of this

RFC), the asymmetrically signed MIC is symmetrically encrypted using the same DEK, algorithm, encryption mode, and other cryptographic parameters as used to encrypt the message text, prior to inclusion in the "MIC-Info:" field.

4.1.2.1 Processing Steps

A four-phase transformation procedure is employed in order to represent encrypted message text in a universally transmissible form and to enable messages encrypted on one type of host computer to be decrypted on a different type of host computer. A plaintext message is accepted in local form, using the host's native character set and line representation. The local form is converted to a canonical message text representation, defined as equivalent to the inter-SMTP representation of message text. This canonical representation forms the input to the MIC computation step (applicable to ENCRYPTED, MIC-ONLY, and MIC-CLEAR messages) and the encryption process (applicable to ENCRYPTED messages only).

For ENCRYPTED PEM messages, the canonical representation is padded as required by the encryption algorithm, and this padded canonical representation is encrypted. The encrypted text (for an ENCRYPTED message) or the unpadded canonical form (for a MIC-ONLY message) is then encoded into a printable form. The printable form is composed of a restricted character set which is chosen to be universally representable across sites, and which will not be disrupted by processing within and between MTS entities. MIC-CLEAR PEM messages omit the printable encoding step.

The output of the previous processing steps is combined with a set of header fields carrying cryptographic control information. The resulting PEM message is passed to the electronic mail system to be included within the text portion of a transmitted message. There is no requirement that a PEM message comprise the entirety of an MTS message's text portion; this allows PEM-protected information to be accompanied by (unprotected) annotations. It is also permissible for multiple PEM messages (and associated unprotected text, outside the PEM message boundaries) to be represented within the encapsulated text of a higher-level PEM message. PEM message signatures are forwardable when asymmetric key management is employed; an authorized recipient of a PEM message with confidentiality applied can reduce that message to a signed but unencrypted form for forwarding purposes or can re-encrypt that message for subsequent transmission.

When a PEM message is received, the cryptographic control fields within its encapsulated header provide the information required for each authorized recipient to perform MIC validation and decryption of the received message text. For ENCRYPTED and MIC-ONLY messages, the printable encoding is converted to a bitstring. Encrypted portions of the transmitted message are decrypted. The MIC is validated. Then, the recipient PEM process converts the canonical representation to its appropriate local form.

4.1.2.2 Error Cases

A variety of error cases may occur and be detected in the course of processing a received PEM message. The specific actions to be taken in response to such conditions are local matters, varying as functions of user preferences and the type of user interface provided by a particular PEM implementation, but certain general recommendations are appropriate. Syntactically invalid PEM messages should be flagged as such, preferably with collection of diagnostic information to support debugging of incompatibilities or other failures. RFC 1422 defines specific error processing requirements relevant to the certificate-based key management mechanisms defined therein.

Syntactically valid PEM messages which yield MIC failures raise special concern, as they may result from attempted attacks or forged messages. As such, it is unsuitable to display their contents to recipient users without first indicating the fact that the contents' authenticity and integrity cannot be guaranteed and then receiving positive user confirmation of such a warning. MIC-CLEAR messages (discussed in Section 4.6.1.1.3 of this RFC) raise special concerns, as MIC failures on such messages may occur for a broader range of benign causes than are applicable to other PEM message types.

4.2 Encryption Algorithms, Modes, and Parameters

For use in conjunction with this RFC, RFC 1423 defines the appropriate algorithms, modes, and associated identifiers to be used for encryption of message text with DEKs.

The mechanisms defined in this RFC incorporate facilities for transmission of cryptographic parameters [e.g., pseudorandom Initializing Vectors (IVs)] with PEM messages to which the confidentiality service is applied, when required by symmetric message encryption algorithms and modes specified in RFC 1423.

Certain operations require encryption of DEKs, MICs, and digital signatures under an IK for purposes of transmission. A header facility indicates the mode in which the IK is used for encryption. RFC 1423 specifies encryption algorithm and mode identifiers and minimum essential support requirements for key encryption processing.

RFC 1422 specifies asymmetric, certificate-based key management procedures based on CCITT Recommendation X.509 to support the message processing procedures defined in this document. Support for the key management approach defined in RFC 1422 is strongly recommended. The message processing procedures can also be used with symmetric key management, given prior distribution of suitable symmetric IKs, but no current RFCs specify key distribution procedures for such IKs.

4.3 Privacy Enhancement Message Transformations
4.3.1 Constraints

An electronic mail encryption mechanism must be compatible with the transparency constraints of its underlying electronic mail facilities. These constraints are generally established based on expected user requirements and on the characteristics of anticipated endpoint and transport facilities. An encryption mechanism must also be compatible with the local conventions of the computer systems which it interconnects. Our approach uses a canonicalization step to abstract out local conventions and a subsequent encoding step to conform to the characteristics of the underlying mail transport medium (SMTP). The encoding conforms to SMTP constraints. Section 4.5 of RFC 821 [2] details SMTP's transparency constraints.

To prepare a message for SMTP transmission, the following requirements must be met:

1. All characters must be members of the 7-bit ASCII character set.
2. Text lines, delimited by the character pair <CR><LF>, must be no more than 1000 characters long.
3. Since the string <CR><LF>.<CR><LF> indicates the end of a message, it must not occur in text prior to the end of a message.

Although SMTP specifies a standard representation for line delimiters (ASCII <CR><LF>), numerous systems in the Internet use a different native representation to delimit lines. For example, the <CR><LF> sequences delimiting lines in mail inbound to UNIX systems are transformed to single <LF>s as mail is written into local mailbox files. Lines in mail incoming to record-oriented systems (such as VAX VMS) may be converted to appropriate records by the destination SMTP server [3]. As a result, if the encryption process generated <CR>s or <LF>s, those characters might not be accessible to a recipient UA program at a destination which uses different line delimiting conventions. It is also possible that conversion between tabs and spaces may be performed in the course of mapping between inter-SMTP and local format; this is a matter of local option. If such transformations changed the form of transmitted ciphertext, decryption would fail to regenerate the transmitted plaintext, and a transmitted MIC would fail to compare with that computed at the destination.

The conversion performed by an SMTP server at a system with EBCDIC as a native character set has even more severe impact, since the conversion from EBCDIC into ASCII is an information-losing transformation. In principle, the transformation function mapping between inter-SMTP canonical ASCII message representation and local format could be moved from the SMTP server up to the UA, given a means to direct that the SMTP server should no longer perform that transformation. This approach has a major disadvantage: internal file (e.g., mailbox) formats would be incompatible with the native forms used on the systems where they reside. Further, it would require modification to SMTP servers, as mail would be passed to SMTP in a different representation than it is passed at present.

4.3.2 Approach

Our approach to supporting PEM across an environment in which intermediate conversions may occur defines an encoding for mail which is uniformly representable across the set of PEM UAs regardless of their systems' native character sets. This encoded form is used (for specified PEM message types) to represent mail text in transit from originator to recipient, but the encoding is not applied to enclosing MTS headers or to encapsulated headers inserted to carry control information between PEM UAs. The encoding's characteristics are such that the transformations anticipated between originator and recipient UAs will not prevent an encoded message from being decoded properly at its destination.

Four transformation steps, described in the following four subsections, apply to outbound PEM message processing.

4.3.2.1 Step 1: Local Form

This step is applicable to PEM message types ENCRYPTED, MIC-ONLY, and MIC-CLEAR. The message text is created in the system's native character set, with lines delimited in accordance with local convention.

4.3.2.2 Step 2: Canonical Form

This step is applicable to PEM message types ENCRYPTED, MIC-ONLY, and MIC-CLEAR. The message text is converted to a universal canonical form, similar to the inter-SMTP representation [4] as defined in RFC 821 [2] and RFC 822 [5]. The procedures performed in order to accomplish this conversion are dependent on the characteristics of the local form and so are not specified in this RFC.

PEM canonicalization assures that the message text is represented with the ASCII character set and "<CR><LF>" line delimiters, but does not perform the dot-stuffing transformation discussed in RFC 821, Section 4.5.2. Since a message is converted to a standard character set and representation before encryption, a transferred PEM message can be decrypted and its MIC can be validated at any type of destination host computer. Decryption and MIC validation is performed before any conversions which may be necessary to transform the message into a destination-specific local form.

4.3.2.3 Step 3: Authentication and Encryption

Authentication processing is applicable to PEM message types ENCRYPTED, MIC-ONLY, and MIC-CLEAR. The canonical form is input to the selected MIC computation algorithm in order to compute an integrity check quantity for the message. No padding is added to the canonical form before submission to the MIC computation algorithm, although certain MIC algorithms will apply their own padding in the course of computing a MIC.

Encryption processing is applicable only to PEM message type ENCRYPTED. RFC 1423 defines the padding technique used to support encryption of the canonically encoded message text.

4.3.2.4 Step 4: Printable Encoding

This printable encoding step is applicable to PEM message types ENCRYPTED and MIC-ONLY. The same processing is also employed in representation of certain specifically identified PEM encapsulated header field quantities as cited in Section 4.6. Proceeding from left to right, the bit string resulting from step 3 is encoded into characters which are universally representable at all sites, though not necessarily with the same bit patterns (e.g., although the character "E" is represented in an ASCII-based system as hexadecimal 45 and as hexadecimal C5 in an EBCDIC-based system, the local significance of the two representations is equivalent).

A 64-character subset of International Alphabet IA5 is used, enabling 6 bits to be represented per printable character. (The proposed subset of characters is represented identically in IA5 and ASCII.) The character "=" signifies a special processing function used for padding within the printable encoding procedure.

To represent the encapsulated text of a PEM message, the encoding function's output is delimited into text lines (using local conventions), with each line except the last containing exactly 64 printable characters and the final line containing 64 or fewer printable characters. (This line length is easily printable and is guaran-

TABLE 1: Printable Encoding Characters

Value	Encoding	Value	Encoding	Value	Encoding	Value	Encoding
0	A	17	R	34	i	51	z
1	B	18	S	35	j	52	0
2	C	19	T	36	k	53	1
3	D	20	U	37	l	54	2
4	E	21	V	38	m	55	3
5	F	22	W	39	n	56	4
6	G	23	X	40	o	57	5
7	H	24	Y	41	p	58	6
8	I	25	Z	42	q	59	7
9	J	26	a	43	r	60	8
10	K	27	b	44	s	61	9
11	L	28	c	45	t	62	+
12	M	29	d	46	u	63	/
13	N	30	e	47	v		
14	O	31	f	48	w	(pad)	=
15	P	32	g	49	x		
16	Q	33	h	50	y		

teed to satisfy SMTP's 1000-character transmitted line length limit.) This folding requirement does not apply when the encoding procedure is used to represent PEM header field quantities; Section 4.6 discusses folding of PEM encapsulated header fields.

The encoding process represents 24-bit groups of input bits as output strings of 4 encoded characters. Proceeding from left to right across a 24-bit input group extracted from the output of step 3, each 6-bit group is used as an index into an array of 64 printable characters. The character referenced by the index is placed in the output string. These characters, identified in Table 1, are selected so as to be universally representable, and the set excludes characters with particular significance to SMTP (e.g., ".," "<CR>," "<LF>"). Special processing is performed if fewer than 24 bits are available in an input group at the end of a message. A full encoding quantum is always completed at the end of a message. When fewer than 24 input bits are available in an input group, zero bits are added (on the right) to form an integral number of 6-bit groups. Output character positions which are not required to represent actual input data are set to the character "=." Since all canonically encoded output is an integral number of octets, only the following cases can arise: (1) the final quantum of encoding input is an integral multiple of 24 bits; here, the final unit of encoded output will be an integral multiple of 4 characters with no "=" padding, (2) the final quantum of encoding input is exactly 8 bits; here, the final unit of encoded output will be two characters followed by two "=" padding characters, or (3) the final quantum of encoding input is exactly 16 bits; here, the final unit of encoded output will be three characters followed by one "=" padding character.

4.3.2.5 Summary of Transformations

In summary, the outbound message is subjected to the following composition of transformations (or, for some PEM message types, a subset thereof):

Transmit_Form = Encode(Encrypt(Canonicalize(Local_Form)))

The inverse transformations are performed, in reverse order, to process inbound PEM messages:

Local_Form = DeCanonicalize(Decipher(Decode(Transmit_Form)))

Note that the local form and the functions to transform messages to and from canonical form may vary between the originator and recipient systems without loss of information.

4.4 Encapsulation Mechanism

The encapsulation techniques defined in RFC-934 [6] are adopted for encapsulation of PEM messages within separate enclosing MTS messages carrying associated MTS headers. This approach offers a number of advantages relative to a flat approach in which certain fields within a single header are encrypted and/or carry cryptographic control information. As far as the MTS is concerned, the entirety of a PEM message will reside in an MTS message's text portion, not the MTS message's header portion. Encapsulation provides generality and segregates fields with user-to-user significance from those transformed in transit. All fields inserted in the course of encryption/authentication processing are placed in the encapsulated header. This facilitates compatibility with mail handling programs which accept only text, not header fields, from input files or from other programs.

The encapsulation techniques defined in RFC-934 are consistent with existing Internet mail forwarding and bursting mechanisms. These techniques are designed so that they may be used in a nested manner. The encapsulation techniques may be used to encapsulate one or more PEM messages for forwarding to a third party, possibly in conjunction with interspersed (non-PEM) text which serves to annotate the PEM messages.

Two encapsulation boundaries (EB's) are defined for delimiting encapsulated PEM messages and for distinguishing encapsulated PEM messages from interspersed (non-PEM) text. The pre-EB is the string "-----BEGIN PRIVACY-ENHANCED MESSAGE-----," indicating that an encapsulated PEM message follows. The post-EB is either (1) another pre-EB indicating that another encapsulated PEM message follows, or (2) the string "-----END PRIVACY-ENHANCED MESSAGE-----" indicating that any text that immediately follows is non-PEM text. A special point must be noted for the case of MIC-CLEAR messages, the text portions of which may contain lines which begin with the "-" character and which are therefore subject to special processing per RFC-934 forwarding procedures. When the string "- " must be prepended to such a line in the course of a forwarding operation in order to distinguish that line from an encapsulation boundary, MIC computation is to be performed prior to prepending the "- " string. Figure 1 depicts the encapsulation of a single PEM message.

This RFC places no a priori limits on the depth to which such encapsulation may be nested nor on the number of PEM messages which may be grouped in this fashion at a single nesting level for forwarding. An implementation compliant with this RFC must not preclude a user from submitting or receiving PEM messages which exploit this encapsulation capability. However, no specific requirements are levied upon implementations with regard to how this capability is made available to the user. Thus, for example, a compliant PEM implementation is not required to automatically detect and process encapsulated PEM messages.

In using this encapsulation facility, it is important to note that it is inappropriate to forward directly to a third party a message that is ENCRYPTED because recipients of such a message would not have access to the DEK required to decrypt the message. Instead, the user forwarding the message must transform the ENCRYPTED message into a MIC-ONLY or MIC-CLEAR form prior to forwarding. Thus, in order to comply with this RFC, a PEM implementation must provide a facility to enable a user to perform this transformation, while preserving the MIC associated with the original message.

If a user wishes PEM-provided confidentiality protection for transmitted information, such information must occur in the encapsulated text of an ENCRYPTED PEM message, not in the enclosing MTS header or PEM encapsulated header. If a

```
Encapsulated Message
  Pre-Encapsulation Boundary (Pre-EB)
     -----BEGIN PRIVACY-ENHANCED MESSAGE-----
  Encapsulated Header Portion
(Contains encryption control fields inserted in plaintext.
Examples include "DEK-Info:" and "Key-Info:". Note that, although
these control fields have line-oriented representations similar
to RFC 822 header fields, the set of fields valid in this context
is disjoint from those used in RFC 822 processing.)
  Blank Line
(Separates Encapsulated Header from subsequent Encapsulated
Text Portion)
  Encapsulated Text Portion
(Contains message data encoded as specified in Section 4.3.)
  Post-Encapsulation Boundary (Post-EB)
     -----END PRIVACY-ENHANCED MESSAGE-----
```

Figure 1 Encapsulated message format.

user wishes to avoid disclosing the actual subject of a message to unintended parties, it is suggested that the enclosing MTS header contain a "Subject:" field indicating that "Encrypted Mail Follows."

If an integrity-protected representation of information which occurs within an enclosing header (not necessarily in the same format as that in which it occurs within that header) is desired, that data can be included within the encapsulated text portion in addition to its inclusion in the enclosing MTS header. For example, an originator wishing to provide recipients with a protected indication of a message's position in a series of messages could include within the encapsulated text a copy of a timestamp or message counter value possessing end-to-end significance and extracted from an enclosing MTS header field. (Note: mailbox specifiers as entered by end users incorporate local conventions and are subject to modification at intermediaries, so inclusion of such specifiers within encapsulated text should not be regarded as a suitable alternative to the authentication semantics defined in RFC 1422 and based on X.500 Distinguished Names.) The set of header information (if any) included within the encapsulated text of messages is a local matter, and this RFC does not specify formatting conventions to distinguish replicated header fields from other encapsulated text.

4.5 Mail for Mailing Lists

When mail is addressed to mailing lists, two different methods of processing can be applicable: the IK-per-list method and the IK-per-recipient method. Hybrid approaches are also possible, as in the case of IK-per-list protection of a message on its path from an originator to a PEM-equipped mailing list exploder, followed by IK-per-recipient protection from the exploder to individual list recipients.

If a message's originator is equipped to expand a destination mailing list into its individual constituents and elects to do so (IK-per-recipient), the message's DEK (and, in the symmetric key management case, MIC) will be encrypted under each per-recipient IK and all such encrypted representations will be incorporated into the transmitted message. Note that per-recipient encryption is required only for the relatively small DEK and MIC quantities carried in the "Key-Info:" field, not for the message text which is, in general, much larger. Although more IKs are involved in processing under the IK-per-recipient method, the pairwise IKs can be individually revoked and possession of one IK does not enable a successful masquerade of another user on the list.

If a message's originator addresses a message to a list name or alias, use of an IK associated with that name or alias as an entity (IK-per-list), rather than resolution of the name or alias to its constituent destinations, is implied. Such an IK must, therefore, be available to all list members. Unfortunately, it implies an undesirable level of exposure for the shared IK, and makes its revocation difficult. Moreover, use of the IK-per-list method allows any holder of the list's IK to masquerade as another originator to the list for authentication purposes.

Pure IK-per-list key management in the asymmetric case (with a common private key shared among multiple list members) is particularly disadvantageous in the asymmetric environment, as it fails to preserve the forwardable authentication and nonrepudiation characteristics which are provided for other messages in this environment. Use of a hybrid approach with a PEM-capable exploder is therefore particularly recommended for protection of mailing list traffic when asymmetric key management is used; such an exploder would reduce (per discussion in Section 4.4 of this RFC) incoming ENCRYPTED messages to MIC-ONLY or MIC-CLEAR form before forwarding them (perhaps re-encrypted under individual, per-recipient keys) to list members.

4.6 Summary of Encapsulated Header Fields

This section defines the syntax and semantics of the encapsulated header fields to be added to messages in the course of privacy enhancement processing.

The fields are presented in three groups. Normally, the groups will appear in encapsulated headers in the order in which they are shown, though not all fields in each group will appear in all messages. The following figures show the appearance of small example encapsulated messages. Figure 2 assumes the use of symmetric cryptography for key management. Figure 3 illustrates an example encapsulated ENCRYPTED message in which asymmetric key management is used.

```
-----BEGIN PRIVACY-ENHANCED MESSAGE-----
Proc-Type: 4,ENCRYPTED
Content-Domain: RFC822
```

```
DEK-Info: DES-CBC,F8143EDE5960C597
Originator-ID-Symmetric: linn@zendia.enet.dec.com,,
Recipient-ID-Symmetric: linn@zendia.enet.dec.com,ptf-kmc,3
Key-Info: DES-ECB,RSA-MD2,9FD3AAD2F2691B9A,
    B70665BB9BF7CBCDA60195DB94F727D3
Recipient-ID-Symmetric: pem-dev@tis.com,ptf-kmc,4
Key-Info: DES-ECB,RSA-MD2,161A3F75DC82EF26,
    E2EF532C65CBCFF79F83A2658132DB47
LLrHBOeJzyhP+/fSStdW8okeEnv47jxe7SJ/iN72ohNcUk2jHEUSoH1nvNSIWL9M
8tEjmF/zxB+bATMtPjCUWbz8Lr9wloXIkjHU1BLpvXROUrUzYbkNpkOagV2IzUpk
J6UiRRGcDSvzrsoK+oNvqu6z7Xs5Xfz5rDqUcM1K1Z6720dcBWGGsDLpTpSCnpot
dXd/H5LMDWnonNvPCwQUHt==
-----END PRIVACY-ENHANCED MESSAGE-----
```

Figure 2 Example encapsulated message (Symmetric Case).

Figure 4 illustrates an example encapsulated MIC-ONLY message in which asymmetric key management is used; since no per-recipient keys are involved in preparation of asymmetric-case MIC-ONLY messages, this example should be processable for test purposes by arbitrary PEM implementations.

Fully-qualified domain names (FQDNs) for hosts, appearing in the mailbox names found in entity identifier subfields of "Originator-ID-Symmetric:" and "Recipient-ID-Symmetric:" fields, are processed in a case-insensitive fashion. Unless specified to the contrary, other field arguments (including the user name components of mailbox names) are to be processed in a case-sensitive fashion.

In most cases, numeric quantities are represented in header fields as contiguous strings of hexadecimal digits, where each digit is represented by a character from the ranges "0"-"9" or upper case "A"-"F." Since public-key certificates and quantities encrypted

```
-----BEGIN PRIVACY-ENHANCED MESSAGE-----
Proc-Type: 4,ENCRYPTED
Content-Domain: RFC822
DEK-Info: DES-CBC,BFF968AA74691AC1
Originator-Certificate:
MIIB1TCCAScCAWUwDQYJKoZIhvcNAQECBQAwUTELMAkGA1UEBhMCVVMxIDAeBgNV
BAoTF1JTQSBEYXRhIFN1Y3VyaXR5LCBJbmMuMQ8wDQYDVQQLEwZCZXRhIDExDzAN
BgNVBAsTBk5PVEFSWTAeFwO5MTA5MDQxODM4MTdaFwO5MzA5MDMxODM4MTZaMEUx
CzAJBgNVBAYTAlVTMSAwHgYDVQQKExdSU0EgRGFOYSBTZWN1cm10eSwgSW5jLjEU
MBIGA1UEAxMLVGVzdCBVc2VyIDEwWTAKBgRVCAEBAgICAANLADBIAkEAwHZH17i+
```

```
yJcqDtjJCowzTdBJrdAiLAnSC+CnnjOJELyuQiBgkGrgIh3j8/xOfM+YrsyFlu3F
LZPVtzlndhYFJQIDAQABMAOGCSqGSIb3DQEBAgUAAlkACKrOPqphJYwlj+YPtcIq
iWlFPuN5jJ79Khfg7ASFxskYkEMjRNZV/HZDZQEhtVaU7Jxfzs2wfX5byMp2X3U/
5XUXGx7qusDgHQGs7Jk9W8CWlfuSWUgN4w==
Key-Info: RSA,
I3rRIGXUGWAF8js5wCzRTkdhO34PTHdRZY9Tuvm03M+NM7fx6qc5udixps2LngO+
wGrtiUm/ovtKdinz6ZQ/aQ==
Issuer-Certificate:
MIIB3DCCAUgCAQowDQYJKoZIhvcNAQECBQAwTzELMAkGA1UEBhMCVVMxIDAeBgNV
BAoTF1JTQSBEYXRhIFN1Y3VyaXR5LCBJbmMuMQ8wDQYDVQQLEwZCZXRhIDExDTAL
BgNVBAsTBFRMMQOEwHhcNOTEwOTAxMDgwMDAwWhcNOTIwOTAxMDclOTU5WjBRMQsw
CQYDVQQGEwJVUzEgMB4GA1UEChMXUlNBIERhdGEgU2VjdXJpdHksIEluYy4xDzAN
BgNVBAsTBkJldGEgMTEPMAOGA1UECxMGTk9UQVJZMHAwCgYEVQgBAQICArwDYgAw
XwJYCsnp6lQCxYykNlODwutF/jMJ3kL+3PjYyHOwk+/9rLg6X65B/LD4bJHtO5XW
cqAz/7R7XhjYCmOPcqbdzoACZtIlETrKrcJiDYoP+DkZ8klgCk7hQHpbIwIDAQAB
MAOGCSqGSIb3DQEBAgUAA38AAICPv4f9Gx/tY4+p+4DB7MV+tKZnvBoy8zgoMGOx
dD2jMZ/3HsyWKWgSFOeH/AJB3qr9zosG47pyMnTf3aSy2nBO7CMxpUWRBcXUpE+x
EREZd9++32ofGBIXaialnOgVUnOOzSYgugiQO77nJLDUjOhQehCizEs5wUJ35a5h
MIC-Info: RSA-MD5,RSA,
UdFJR8u/TIGhfH65ieewe2lOW4tooa3vZCvVNGBZirf/7nrgzWDABz8w9NsXSexv
AjRFbHoNPzBuxwmOAFeAOHJszL4yBvhG
Recipient-ID-Asymmetric:
MFExCzAJBgNVBAYTAlVTMSAwHgYDVQQKExdSUOEgRGFOYSBTZWN1cmlOeSwgSW5j
LjEPMAOGA1UECxMGQmVOYSAxMQ8wDQYDVQQLEwZOT1RBUlk=,
66
Key-Info: RSA,
O6BSlww9CTyHPtS3bMLD+LOhejdvX6Qv1HK2ds2sQPEaXhX8EhvVphHYTjwekdWv
7x0Z3Jx2vTAhOYHMcqqCjA==
qeWlj/YJ2Uf5ng9yznPbtDOmYloSwIuV9FRYx+gzY+8iXd/NQrXHfi6/MhPfPF3d
jIqCJAxvld2xgqQimUzoSla4r7kQQ5c/Iua4LqKeq3ciFzEv/MbZhA==
-----END PRIVACY-ENHANCED MESSAGE-----
```

Figure 3 Example encapsulated ENCRYPTED message (Asymmetric Case).

using asymmetric algorithms are large in size, use of a more space-efficient encoding technique is appropriate for such quantities, and the encoding mechanism defined in Section 4.3.2.4 of this RFC, representing 6 bits per printed character, is adopted for this purpose.

Encapsulated headers of PEM messages are folded using whitespace per RFC 822 header folding conventions; no PEM-specific conventions are defined for encapsulated header folding. The example shown in Figure 4 shows (in its "MIC-Info:" field) an asymmetrically encrypted quantity in its printably encoded representation, illustrating the use of RFC 822 folding.

In contrast to the encapsulated header representations defined in RFC 1113 and its precursors, the field identifiers adopted in this RFC do not begin with the prefix "X-" (for example, the field previously denoted "X-Key-Info:" is now denoted "Key-Info:") and such prefixes are not to be emitted by implementations conformant to this RFC. To simplify transition and interoperability with earlier implementations, it is suggested that implementations based on this RFC accept incoming encapsulated header fields carrying the "X-" prefix and act on such fields as if the "X-" were not present.

```
-----BEGIN PRIVACY-ENHANCED MESSAGE-----
Proc-Type: 4,MIC-ONLY
Content-Domain: RFC822
Originator-Certificate:
MIIB1TCCAScCAWUwDQYJKoZIhvcNAQECBQAwUTELMAkGA1UEBhMCVVMxIDAeBgNV
BAoTF1JTQSBEYXRhIFN1Y3VyaXR5LCBJbmMuMQ8wDQYDVQQLEwZCZXRhIDExDzAN
BgNVBAsTBk5PVEFSWTAeFw05MTA5MDQxODM4MTdaFw05MzA5MDMxODM4MTZaMEUx
CzAJBgNVBAYTA1VTMSAwHgYDVQQKExdSU0EgRGF0YSBTZWN1cml0eSwgSW5jLjEU
MBIGA1UEAxMLVGVzdCBVc2VyIDEwWTAKBgRVCAEBAgICAANLADBIAkEAwHZH17i+
yJcqDtjJCowzTdBJrdAiLAnSC+CnnjOJELyuQiBgkGrgIh3j8/xOfM+YrsyF1u3F
LZPVtz1ndhYFJQIDAQABMAOGCSqGSIb3DQEBAgUAA1kACKrOPqphJYw1j+YPtcIq
iW1FPuN5jJ79Khfg7ASFxskYkEMjRNZV/HZDZQEhtVaU7Jxfzs2wfX5byMp2X3U/
5XUXGx7qusDgHQGs7Jk9W8CW1fuSWUgN4w==
Issuer-Certificate:
MIIB3DCCAUgCAQowDQYJKoZIhvcNAQECBQAwTzELMAkGA1UEBhMCVVMxIDAeBgNV
BAoTF1JTQSBEYXRhIFN1Y3VyaXR5LCBJbmMuMQ8wDQYDVQQLEwZCZXRhIDExDTAL
BgNVBAsTBFRMQ0EwHhcNOTEwOTAxMDgwMDAwWhcNOTIwOTAxMDc1OTU5WjBRMQsw
CQYDVQQGEwJVUzEgMB4GA1UEChMXU1NBIERhdGEgU2VjdXJpdHksIEluYy4xDzAN
BgNVBAsTBkJldGEgMTEPMA0GA1UECxMGTk9UQVJZMHAwCgYEVQgBAQICArwDYgAw
XwJYCsnp61QCxYykN1ODwutF/jMJ3kL+3PjYyHOwk+/9rLg6X65B/LD4bJHtO5XW
cqAz/7R7XhjYCmOPcqbdzoACZtI1ETrKrcJiDYoP+DkZ8k1gCk7hQHpbIwIDAQAB
MAOGCSqGSIb3DQEBAgUAA38AAICPv4f9Gx/tY4+p+4DB7MV+tKZnvBoy8zgoMGOx
dD2jMZ/3HsyWKWgSFOeH/AJB3qr9zosG47pyMnTf3aSy2nBO7CMxpUWRBcXUpE+x
```

```
EREZd9++32ofGBIXaialnOgVUnOOzSYgugiQO77nJLDUjOhQehCizEs5wUJ35a5h
MIC-Info: RSA-MD5,RSA,
jV2OfH+nnXHU8bnL8kPAad/mSQ1TDZ1bVuxvZAOVRZ5q5+Ej15bQvqNeqOUNQjr6
EtE7K2QDeVMCyXsdJ1A8fA==
LSBBIG11c3NhZ2UgZm9yIHVzZSBpbiBOZXN0aW5nLgOKLSBGb2xsb3dpbmcgaXMg
YSBibGFuayBsaW5lOgOKDQpUaGlzIGlzIHRoZSB1bmQuDQo=
-----END PRIVACY-ENHANCED MESSAGE-----
```

Figure 4 Example encapsulated MIC-ONLY message (Asymmetric Case).

4.6.1 Per-Message Encapsulated Header Fields

This group of encapsulated header fields contains fields which occur no more than once in a PEM message, generally preceding all other encapsulated header fields.

4.6.1.1 Proc-Type Field

The "Proc-Type:" encapsulated header field, required for all PEM messages, identifies the type of processing performed on the transmitted message. Only one "Proc-Type:" field occurs in a message; the "Proc-Type:" field must be the first encapsulated header field in the message.

The "Proc-Type:" field has two subfields, separated by a comma. The first subfield is a decimal number which is used to distinguish among incompatible encapsulated header field interpretations which may arise as changes are made to this standard. Messages processed according to this RFC will carry the subfield value "4" to distinguish them from messages processed in accordance with prior PEM RFCs. The second subfield assumes one of a set of string values, defined in the following subsections.

4.6.1.1.1 ENCRYPTED

The "ENCRYPTED" specifier signifies that confidentiality, authentication, integrity, and (given use of asymmetric key management) nonrepudiation of origin security services have been applied to a PEM message's encapsulated text. ENCRYPTED messages require a "DEK-Info:" field and individual Recipient-ID and "Key- Info:" fields for all message recipients.

4.6.1.1.2 MIC-ONLY

The "MIC-ONLY" specifier signifies that all of the security services specified for ENCRYPTED messages, with the exception of confidentiality, have been applied to a PEM message's encapsulated text. MIC-ONLY messages are encoded (per Section 4.3.2.4 of this RFC) to protect their encapsulated text against modifications at message transfer or relay points.

Specification of MIC-ONLY, when applied in conjunction with certain combinations of key management and MIC algorithm options, permits certain fields which are superfluous in the absence of encryption to be omitted from the encapsulated header. In particular, when a keyless MIC computation is employed for recipients for whom asymmetric cryptography is used, "Recipient-ID-Asymmetric:" and "Key-Info:" fields can be omitted. The "DEK-Info:" field can be omitted for all "MIC-ONLY" messages.

4.6.1.1.3 MIC-CLEAR

The "MIC-CLEAR" specifier represents a PEM message with the same security service selection as for a MIC-ONLY message. The set of encapsulated header fields required in a MIC-CLEAR message is the same as that required for a MIC-ONLY message.

MIC-CLEAR message processing omits the encoding step defined in Section 4.3.2.4 of this RFC to protect a message's encapsulated text against modifications within the MTS. As a result, a MIC-CLEAR message's text can be read by recipients lacking access to PEM software, even though such recipients cannot validate the message's signature. The canonical encoding discussed in Section 4.3.2.2 is performed, so interoperation among sites with different native character sets and line representations is not precluded so long as those native formats are unambiguously translatable to and from the canonical form. (Such interoperability is feasible only for those characters which are included in the canonical representation set.)

Omission of the printable encoding step implies that MIC-CLEAR message MICs will be validatable only in environments where the MTS does not modify messages in transit, or where the modifications performed can be determined and inverted before MIC validation processing. Failed MIC validation on a MIC-CLEAR message does not, therefore, necessarily signify a security-relevant event; as a result, it is recommended that PEM implementations reflect to their users (in a suitable local fashion) the type of PEM message being processed when reporting a MIC validation failure.

A case of particular relevance arises for inbound SMTP processing on systems which delimit text lines with local native representations other than the SMTP-conventional <CR><LF>. When mail is delivered to a UA on such a system and presented for PEM processing, the <CR><LF> has already been translated to local form. In order to validate a MIC-CLEAR message's MIC in this situation, the PEM module must recanonicalize the incoming message in order to determine the inter-SMTP representation of the canonically encoded message (as defined in Section 4.3.2.2 of this RFC), and must compute the reference MIC based on that representation.

4.6.1.1.4 CRL

The "CRL" specifier indicates a special PEM message type, used to transfer one or more Certificate Revocation Lists. The format of PEM CRLs is defined in RFC

1422. No user data or encapsulated text accompanies an encapsulated header specifying the CRL message type; a correctly formed CRL message's PEM header is immediately followed by its terminating message boundary line, with no blank line intervening.

Only three types of fields are valid in the encapsulated header comprising a CRL message. The "CRL:" field carries a printable representation of a CRL, encoded using the procedures defined in Section 4.3.2.4 of this RFC. "CRL:" fields may (as an option) be followed by no more than one "Originator-Certificate:" field and any number of "Issuer-Certificate:" fields. The "Originator-Certificate:" and "Issuer-Certificate:" fields refer to the most recently previous "CRL:" field, and provide certificates useful in validating the signature included in the CRL. "Originator-Certificate:" and "Issuer-Certificate:" fields' contents are the same for CRL messages as they are for other PEM message types.

4.6.1.2 Content-Domain Field

The "Content-Domain:" encapsulated header field describes the type of content which is represented within a PEM message's encapsulated text. It carries one string argument, whose value is defined as "RFC822" to indicate processing of RFC-822 mail as defined in this specification. It is anticipated that additional "Content-Domain:" values will be defined subsequently, in additional or successor documents to this specification. Only one "Content-Domain:" field occurs in a PEM message; this field is the PEM message's second encapsulated header field, immediately following the "Proc-Type:" field.

4.6.1.3 DEK-Info Field

The "DEK-Info:" encapsulated header field identifies the message text encryption algorithm and mode, and also carries any cryptographic parameters (e.g., IVs) used for message encryption. No more than one "DEK-Info:" field occurs in a message; the field is required for all messages specified as "ENCRYPTED" in the "Proc-Type:" field.

The "DEK-Info:" field carries either one argument or two arguments separated by a comma. The first argument identifies the algorithm and mode used for message text encryption. The second argument, if present, carries any cryptographic parameters required by the algorithm and mode identified in the first argument. Appropriate message encryption algorithms, modes and identifiers and corresponding cryptographic parameters and formats are defined in RFC 1423.

4.6.2 Encapsulated Header Fields Normally Per-Message

This group of encapsulated header fields contains fields which ordinarily occur no more than once per message. Depending on the key management option(s) employed, some of these fields may be absent from some messages.

4.6.2.1 Originator-ID Fields

Originator-ID encapsulated header fields identify a message's originator and provide the originator's IK identification component. Two varieties of Originator-ID fields are defined, the "Originator- ID-Asymmetric:" and "Originator-ID-Symmetric:" field. An "Originator-ID-Symmetric:" header field is required for all PEM messages employing symmetric key management. The analogous "Originator-ID-Asymmetric:" field, for the asymmetric key management case, is used only when no corresponding "Originator-Certificate:" field is included.

Most commonly, only one Originator-ID or "Originator-Certificate:" field will occur within a message. For the symmetric case, the IK identification component carried in an "Originator-ID-Symmetric:" field applies to processing of all subsequent "Recipient-ID-Symmetric:" fields until another "Originator-ID-Symmetric:" field occurs. It is illegal for a "Recipient-ID-Symmetric:" field to occur before a corresponding "Originator-ID-Symmetric:" field has been provided. For the asymmetric case, processing of "Recipient-ID-Asymmetric:" fields is logically independent of preceding "Originator-ID-Asymmetric:" and "Originator-Certificate:" fields.

Multiple Originator-ID and/or "Originator-Certificate:" fields may occur in a message when different originator-oriented IK components must be used by a message's originator in order to prepare a message so as to be suitable for processing by different recipients. In particular, multiple such fields will occur when both symmetric and asymmetric cryptography are applied to a single message in order to process the message for different recipients.

Originator-ID subfields are delimited by the comma character (","), optionally followed by whitespace. Section 5.2, Interchange Keys, discusses the semantics of these subfields and specifies the alphabet from which they are chosen.

4.6.2.1.1 Originator-ID-Asymmetric Field

The "Originator-ID-Asymmetric:" field contains an Issuing Authority subfield, and then a Version/Expiration subfield. This field is used only when the information it carries is not available from an included "Originator-Certificate:" field.

4.6.2.1.2 Originator-ID-Symmetric Field

The "Originator-ID-Symmetric:" field contains an Entity Identifier subfield, followed by an (optional) Issuing Authority subfield, and then an (optional) Version/Expiration subfield. Optional "Originator-ID-Symmetric:" subfields may be omitted only if rendered redundant by information carried in subsequent "Recipient-ID-Symmetric:" fields, and will normally be omitted in such cases.

4.6.2.2 Originator-Certificate Field

The "Originator-Certificate:" encapsulated header field is used only when asymmetric key management is employed for one or more of a message's recipients. To facilitate processing by recipients (at least in advance of general directory server availability), inclusion of this field in all messages is strongly recommended. The field transfers an originator's certificate as a numeric quantity, comprised of the certificate's DER encoding, represented in the header field with the encoding mechanism defined in Section 4.3.2.4 of this RFC. The semantics of a certificate are discussed in RFC 1422.

4.6.2.3 MIC-Info Field

The "MIC-Info:" encapsulated header field, used only when asymmetric key management is employed for at least one recipient of a message, carries three arguments, separated by commas. The first argument identifies the algorithm under which the accompanying MIC is computed. The second argument identifies the algorithm under which the accompanying MIC is signed. The third argument represents a MIC signed with an originator's private key.

For the case of ENCRYPTED PEM messages, the signed MIC is, in turn, symmetrically encrypted using the same DEK, algorithm, mode and cryptographic parameters as are used to encrypt the message's encapsulated text. This measure prevents unauthorized recipients from determining whether an intercepted message corresponds to a predetermined plaintext value.

Appropriate MIC algorithms and identifiers, signature algorithms and identifiers, and signed MIC formats are defined in RFC 1423.

A "MIC-Info:" field will occur after a sequence of fields beginning with an "Originator-ID-Asymmetric:" or "Originator-Certificate:" field and followed by any associated "Issuer-Certificate:" fields. A "MIC-Info:" field applies to all subsequent recipients for whom asymmetric key management is used, until and unless overridden by a subsequent "Originator-ID-Asymmetric:" or "Originator-Certificate:" and corresponding "MIC-Info:."

4.6.3 Encapsulated Header Fields with Variable Occurrences

This group of encapsulated header fields contains fields which will normally occur variable numbers of times within a message, with numbers of occurrences ranging from zero to non-zero values which are independent of the number of recipients.

4.6.3.1 Issuer-Certificate Field

The "Issuer-Certificate:" encapsulated header field is meaningful only when asymmetric key management is used for at least one of a message's recipients. A typical "Issuer-Certificate:" field would contain the certificate containing the public component used to sign the certificate carried in the message's "Originator-Certificate:" field, for recipients' use in chaining through that certificate's certification path. Other "Issuer-Certificate:" fields, typically representing higher points in a certification path, also may be included by an originator. It is recommended that the "Issuer-Certificate:" fields be included in an order corresponding to successive points in a certification path leading from the originator to a common point shared with the message's recipients (i.e., the Internet Certification Authority (ICA), unless a lower Policy Certification Authority (PCA) or CA is common to all recipients.) More information on certification paths can be found in RFC 1422.

The certificate is represented in the same manner as defined for the "Originator-Certificate:" field (transporting an encoded representation of the certificate in X.509 [7] DER form), and any "Issuer-Certificate:" fields will ordinarily follow the "Originator-Certificate:" field directly. Use of the "Issuer-Certificate:" field is optional even when asymmetric key management is employed, although its incorporation is strongly recommended in the absence of alternate directory server facilities from which recipients can access issuers' certificates.

4.6.4 Per-Recipient Encapsulated Header Fields

The encapsulated header fields in this group appear for each of an ENCRYPTED message's named recipients. For MIC-ONLY and MIC-CLEAR messages, these fields are omitted for recipients for whom asymmetric key management is employed in conjunction with a keyless MIC algorithm but the fields appear for recipients for whom symmetric key management or a keyed MIC algorithm is employed.

4.6.4.1 Recipient-ID Fields

A Recipient-ID encapsulated header field identifies a recipient and provides the recipient's IK identification component. One Recipient-ID field is included for each of a message's named recipients. Section 5.2, Interchange Keys, discusses the semantics of the subfields and specifies the alphabet from which they are chosen. Recipient-ID subfields are delimited by the comma character (","), optionally followed by whitespace.

For the symmetric case, all "Recipient-ID-Symmetric:" fields are interpreted in the context of the most recent preceding "Originator-ID-Symmetric:" field. It is illegal for a "Recipient-ID-Symmetric:" field to occur in a header before the occurrence of a corresponding "Originator-ID-Symmetric:" field. For the asymmetric case, "Recipient-ID-Asymmetric:" fields are logically independent of a message's "Originator-ID-Asymmetric:" and "Originator-Certificate:" fields. "Recipient-ID-Asymmetric:" fields, and their associated "Key-Info:" fields, are included following a header's originator-oriented fields.

4.6.4.1.1 Recipient-ID-Asymmetric Field

The "Recipient-ID-Asymmetric:" field contains, in order, an Issuing Authority subfield and a Version/Expiration subfield.

4.6.4.1.2 Recipient-ID-Symmetric Field

The "Recipient-ID-Symmetric:" field contains, in order, an Entity Identifier subfield, an (optional) Issuing Authority subfield, and an (optional) Version/Expiration subfield.

4.6.4.2 Key-Info Field

One "Key-Info:" field is included for each of a message's named recipients. In addition, it is recommended that PEM implementations support (as a locally selectable option) the ability to include a "Key-Info:" field corresponding to a PEM message's originator, following an Originator-ID or "Originator-Certificate:" field and before any associated Recipient-ID fields, but inclusion of such a field is not a requirement for conformance with this RFC.

Each "Key-Info:" field is interpreted in the context of the most recent preceding Originator-ID, "Originator-Certificate:," or Recipient-ID field; normally, a "Key-Info:" field will immediately follow its associated predecessor field. The "Key-Info:" field's argument(s) differ depending on whether symmetric or asymmetric key management is used for a particular recipient.

4.6.4.2.1 Symmetric Key Management

When symmetric key management is employed for a given recipient, the "Key-Info:" encapsulated header field transfers four items, separated by commas: an IK Use Indicator, a MIC Algorithm Indicator, a DEK and a MIC. The IK Use Indicator identifies the algorithm and mode in which the identified IK was used for DEK and MIC encryption for a particular recipient. The MIC Algorithm Indicator identifies the MIC computation algorithm used for a particular recipient. The DEK and MIC are symmetrically encrypted under the IK identified by a preceding "Recipient-ID-Symmetric:" field and/or prior "Originator-ID-Symmetric:" field.

Appropriate symmetric encryption algorithms, modes and identifiers, MIC computation algorithms and identifiers, and encrypted DEK and MIC formats are defined in RFC 1423.

4.6.4.2.2 Asymmetric Key Management

When asymmetric key management is employed for a given recipient, the "Key-Info:" field transfers two quantities, separated by a comma. The first argument is an IK Use Indicator identifying the algorithm and mode in which the DEK is asymmetrically encrypted. The second argument is a DEK, asymmetrically encrypted under the recipient's public component.

Appropriate asymmetric encryption algorithms and identifiers, and encrypted DEK formats are defined in RFC 1423.

5. Key Management

Several cryptographic constructs are involved in supporting the PEM message processing procedure. A set of fundamental elements is assumed. Data Encrypting Keys (DEKs) are used to encrypt message text and (for some MIC computation algorithms) in the message integrity check (MIC) computation process. Interchange Keys (IKs) are used to encrypt DEKs and MICs for transmission with messages. In a certificate-based asymmetric key management architecture, certificates are used as a means to provide entities' public components and other information in a fashion which is securely bound by a central authority. The remainder of this section provides more information about these constructs.

5.1 Data Encrypting Keys (DEKs)

Data Encrypting Keys (DEKs) are used for encryption of message text and (with some MIC computation algorithms) for computation of message integrity check quantities (MICs). In the asymmetric key management case, they are also used for encrypting signed MICs in ENCRYPTED PEM messages. It is strongly recommended that DEKs be generated and used on a one-time, per-message, basis. A transmitted message will incorporate a representation of the DEK encrypted under an appropriate interchange key (IK) for each of the named recipients.

DEK generation can be performed either centrally by key distribution centers (KDCs) or by endpoint systems. Dedicated KDC systems may be able to implement stronger algorithms for random DEK generation than can be supported in endpoint systems. On the other hand, decentralization allows endpoints to be relatively self-sufficient, reducing the level of trust which must be placed in components other than those of a message's originator and recipient. Moreover, decentralized DEK generation at endpoints reduces the frequency with which originators must make real-time queries of (potentially unique) servers in order to send mail, enhancing communications availability.

When symmetric key management is used, one advantage of centralized KDC-based generation is that DEKs can be returned to endpoints already encrypted under the IKs of message recipients rather than providing the IKs to the originators. This reduces IK exposure and simplifies endpoint key management requirements. This approach has less value if asymmetric cryptography is used for key management, since per-recipient public IK components are assumed to be generally available and per-originator private IK components need not necessarily be shared with a KDC.

5.2 Interchange Keys (IKs)

Interchange Key (IK) components are used to encrypt DEKs and MICs. In general, IK granularity is at the pairwise per-user level except for mail sent to address lists comprising multiple users. In order for two principals to engage in a useful exchange of PEM using conventional cryptography, they must first possess common IK components (when symmetric key management is used) or complementary IK components (when asymmetric key management is used). When symmetric cryptography is used, the IK consists of a single component, used to encrypt both DEKs and MICs. When asymmetric cryptography is used, a recipient's public component is used as an IK to encrypt DEKs (a transformation invertible only by a recipient possessing the corresponding private component), and the originator's private component is used to encrypt MICs (a transformation invertible by all recipients, since the originator's certificate provides all recipients with the public component required to perform MIC validation).

This RFC does not prescribe the means by which interchange keys are made available to appropriate parties; such means may be centralized (e.g., via key management servers) or decentralized (e.g., via pairwise agreement and direct distribution among users). In any case, any given IK component is associated with a responsible Issuing Authority (IA). When certificate-based asymmetric key management, as discussed in RFC 1422, is employed, the IA function is performed by a Certification Authority (CA).

When an IA generates and distributes an IK component, associated control information is provided to direct how it is to be used. In order to select the appropriate IK(s) to use in message encryption, an originator must retain a correspondence between IK components and the recipients with which they are associated. Expiration date information must also be retained, in order that cached entries may be invalidated and replaced as appropriate.

Since a message may be sent with multiple IK components identified, corresponding to multiple intended recipients, each recipient's UA must be able to determine that recipient's intended IK component. Moreover, if no corresponding IK component is available in the recipient's database when a message arrives, the recipient must be able to identify the required IK component and identify that IK component's associated IA. Note that different IKs may be used for different messages between a pair of communicants. Consider, for example, one message sent from A to B and another message sent (using the IK-per-list method) from A to a mailing list of which B is a member. The first message would use IK components associated individually with A and B, but the second would use an IK component shared among list members.

When a PEM message is transmitted, an indication of the IK components used for DEK and MIC encryption must be included. To this end, Originator-ID and Recipient-ID encapsulated header fields provide (some or all of) the following data:

1. Identification of the relevant Issuing Authority (IA subfield)
2. Identification of an entity with which a particular IK component is associated (Entity Identifier or EI subfield)
3. Version/Expiration subfield

In the asymmetric case, all necessary information associated with an originator can be acquired by processing the certificate carried in an "Originator-Certificate:" field; to avoid redundancy in this case, no "Originator-ID-Asymmetric:" field is included if a corresponding "Originator-Certificate:" appears.

The comma character (",") is used to delimit the subfields within an Originator-ID or Recipient-ID. The IA, EI, and version/expiration subfields are generated from a restricted character set, as prescribed by the following BNF (using notation as defined in RFC 822, Sections 2 and 3.3):

```
IKsubfld := 1*ia-char
ia-char := DIGIT / ALPHA / "'" / "+" / "(" / ")" /
                   "." / "/" / "=" / "?" / "-" / "@" /
                   "%" / "!" / '"' / "-" / "<" / ">"
```

An example Recipient-ID field for the symmetric case is as follows:

```
Recipient-ID-Symmetric: linn@zendia.enet.dec.com,ptf-kmc,2
```

This example field indicates that IA "ptf-kmc" has issued an IK component for use on messages sent to "linn@zendia.enet.dec.com," and that the IA has provided the number 2 as a version indicator for that IK component.

An example Recipient-ID field for the asymmetric case is as follows:

```
Recipient-ID-Asymmetric:

MFExCzAJBgNVBAYTAlVTMSAwHgYDVQQKExdSU0EgRGF0YSBTZWN1cml0eSwgSW5j
LjEPMAOGA1UECxMGQmVOYSAxMQ8wDQYDVQQLEwZOT1RBUlk=,66
```

This example field includes the printably encoded BER representation of a certificate's issuer distinguished name, along with the certificate serial number 66 as assigned by that issuer.

5.2.1 Subfield Definitions

The following subsections define the subfields of Originator-ID and Recipient-ID fields.

5.2.1.1 Entity Identifier Subfield

An entity identifier (used only for "Originator-ID-Symmetric:" and "Recipient-ID-Symmetric:" fields) is constructed as an IKsubfld. More restrictively, an entity identifier subfield assumes the following form:

```
<user>@<domain-qualified-host>
```

In order to support universal interoperability, it is necessary to assume a universal form for the naming information. For the case of installations which transform local host names before transmission into the broader Internet, it is strongly recommended that the host name as presented to the Internet be employed.

5.2.1.2 Issuing Authority Subfield

An IA identifier subfield is constructed as an IKsubfld. This RFC does not define this subfield's contents for the symmetric key management case. Any prospective IAs which are to issue symmetric keys for use in conjunction with this RFC must coordinate assignment of IA identifiers in a manner (centralized or hierarchic) which assures uniqueness.

For the asymmetric key management case, the IA identifier subfield will be formed from the ASN.1 BER representation of the distinguished name of the issuing organization or organizational unit. The distinguished encoding rules specified in Clause 8.7 of Recommendation X.509 ("X.509 DER") are to be employed in generating this representation. The encoded binary result will be represented for inclusion in a transmitted header using the procedure defined in Section 4.3.2.4 of this RFC.

5.2.1.3 Version/Expiration Subfield

A version/expiration subfield is constructed as an IKsubfld. For the symmetric key management case, the version/expiration subfield format is permitted to vary among different IAs, but must satisfy certain functional constraints. An IA's version/expiration subfields must be sufficient to distinguish among the set of IK components issued by that IA for a given identified entity. Use of a monotonically increasing number is sufficient to distinguish among the IK components provided for an entity by an IA; use of a timestamp additionally allows an expiration time or date to be prescribed for an IK component.

For the asymmetric key management case, the version/expiration subfield's value is the hexadecimal serial number of the certificate being used in conjunction with the originator or recipient specified in the "Originator-ID-Asymmetric:" or "Recipient-ID-Asymmetric:" field in which the subfield occurs.

5.2.2 IK Cryptoperiod Issues

An IK component's cryptoperiod is dictated in part by a tradeoff between key management overhead and revocation responsiveness. It would be undesirable to delete an IK component permanently before receipt of a message encrypted using that IK component, as this would render the message permanently undecipherable. Access to an expired IK component would be needed, for example, to process mail received by a user (or system) which had been inactive for an extended period of time. In order to enable very old IK components to be deleted, a message's recipient desiring encrypted local long term storage should transform the DEK used for message text encryption via re-encryption under a locally maintained IK, rather than relying on IA maintenance of old IK components for indefinite periods.

6. User Naming

Unique naming of electronic mail users, as is needed in order to select corresponding keys correctly, is an important topic and one which has received (and continues to receive) significant study. For the symmetric case, IK components are identified in PEM headers through use of mailbox specifiers in traditional Internet-wide form ("user@domain-qualified-host"). Successful operation in this mode relies on users (or their PEM implementations) being able to determine the universal-form names corresponding to PEM originators and recipients. If a PEM implementation operates in an environment where addresses in a local form differing from the universal form are used, translations must be performed in order to map between the universal form and that local representation.

The use of user identifiers unrelated to the hosts on which the users' mailboxes reside offers generality and value. X.500 distinguished names, as employed in the certificates of the recommended key management infrastructure defined in RFC 1422, provide a basis for such user identification. As directory services become more pervasive, they will offer originators a means to search for desired recipients which is based on a broader set of attributes than mailbox specifiers alone. Future work is anticipated in integration with directory services, particularly the mechanisms and naming schema of the Internet OSI directory pilot activity.

7. Example User Interface and Implementation

In order to place the mechanisms and approaches discussed in this RFC into context, this section presents an overview of a hypothetical prototype implementation. This implementation is a stand alone program which is invoked by a user, and lies above the existing UA sublayer. In the UNIX system, and possibly in other environments as well, such a program can be invoked as a "filter" within an electronic mail UA or a text editor, simplifying the sequence of operations which must be performed by the user. This form of integration offers the advantage that the program can be used in conjunction with a range of UA programs, rather than being compatible only with a particular UA.

When a user wishes to apply privacy enhancements to an outgoing message, the user prepares the message's text and invokes the standalone program, which in turn generates output suitable for transmission via the UA. When a user receives a PEM message, the UA delivers the message in encrypted form, suitable for decryption and associated processing by the standalone program.

In this prototype implementation, a cache of IK components is maintained in a local file, with entries managed manually based on information provided by originators and recipients. For the asymmetric key management case, certificates are acquired for a user's PEM correspondents; in advance and/or in addition to retrieval of certificates from directories, they can be extracted from the "Originator-Certificate," fields of received PEM messages.

The IK/certificate cache is, effectively, a simple database indexed by mailbox names. IK components are selected for transmitted messages based on the originator's identity and on recipient names, and corresponding Originator-ID, "Originator-Certificate:," and Recipient-ID fields are placed into the message's encapsulated header. When a message is received, these fields are used as a basis for a lookup in the database, yielding the appropriate IK component entries.

DEKs and cryptographic parameters (e.g., IVs) are generated dynamically within the program.

Options and destination addresses are selected by command line arguments to the standalone program. The function of specifying destination addresses to the privacy enhancement program is logically distinct from the function of specifying the corresponding addresses to the UA for use by the MTS. This separation results from the fact that, in many cases, the local form of an address as specified to a UA differs from the Internet global form as used in "Originator-ID-Symmetric:" and "Recipient-ID-Symmetric:" fields.

8. Minimum Essential Requirements

This section summarizes particular capabilities which an implementation must provide for full conformance with this RFC.

RFC 1422 specifies asymmetric, certificate-based key management procedures to support the message processing procedures defined in this document; PEM implementation support for these key management procedures is strongly encouraged. Implementations supporting these procedures must also be equipped to display the names of originator and recipient PEM users in the X.500 DN form as authenticated by the procedures of RFC 1422.

The message processing procedures defined here can also be used with symmetric key management techniques, though no RFCs analogous to RFC 1422 are currently available to provide correspondingly detailed description of suitable symmetric key management procedures. A complete PEM implementation must support at least one of these asymmetric and/or symmetric key management modes.

A full implementation of PEM is expected to be able to send and receive ENCRYPTED, MIC-ONLY, and MIC-CLEAR messages, and to receive CRL messages. Some level of support for generating and processing nested and annotated PEM messages (for forwarding purposes) is to be provided, and an implementation should be able to reduce ENCRYPTED messages to MIC-ONLY or MIC-CLEAR for forwarding. Fully conformant implementations must be able to emit Certificate and Issuer-Certificate fields, and to include a Key-Info field corresponding to the originator, but users or configurers of PEM implementations may be allowed the option of deactivating those features.

9. Descriptive Grammar

This section provides a grammar describing the construction of a PEM message.

```
; PEM BNF representation, using RFC 822 notation.
; imports field meta-syntax (field, field-name, field-body,
; field-body-contents) from RFC-822, sec. 3.2
; imports DIGIT, ALPHA, CRLF, text from RFC-822
```

```
; Note: algorithm and mode specifiers are officially defined
; in RFC 1423
<pemmsg> ::= <preeb>
        <pemhdr>
        [CRLF <pemtext>] ; absent for CRL message
        <posteb>
<preeb> ::= "-----BEGIN PRIVACY-ENHANCED MESSAGE-----" CRLF
<posteb> ::= "-----END PRIVACY-ENHANCED MESSAGE-----" CRLF /
<preeb>
<pemtext> ::= <encbinbody> ; for ENCRYPTED or MIC-ONLY messages
    / *(<text> CRLF) ; for MIC-CLEAR
<pemhdr> ::= <normalhdr> / <crlhdr>
<normalhdr> ::= <proctype>
    <contentdomain>
    [<dekinfo>]  ; needed if ENCRYPTED
    (1*(<origflds> *<recipflds>)) ; symmetric case --
                ; recipflds included for all proc types
    / ((1*<origflds>) *(<recipflds>)) ; asymmetric case --
                ; recipflds included for ENCRYPTED proc type
<crlhdr> ::= <proctype>
    1*(<crl> [<cert>] *(<issuercert>))
<asymmorig> ::= <origid-asymm> / <cert>
<origflds> ::= <asymmorig> [<keyinfo>] *(<issuercert>)
        <micinfo>   ; asymmetric
        / <origid-symm> [<keyinfo>] ; symmetric
<recipflds> ::= <recipid> <keyinfo>
; definitions for PEM header fields
<proctype> ::= "Proc-Type" ":" "4" "," <pemtypes> CRLF
<contentdomain> ::= "Content-Domain" ":" <contentdescrip> CRLF
<dekinfo> ::= "DEK-Info" ":" <dekalgid> [ "," <dekparameters> ]
CRLF
<symmid> ::= <IKsubfld> "," [<IKsubfld>] "," [<IKsubfld>]
<asymmid> ::= <IKsubfld> "," <IKsubfld>
<origid-asymm> ::= "Originator-ID-Asymmetric" ":" <asymmid> CRLF
<origid-symm> ::= "Originator-ID-Symmetric" ":" <symmid> CRLF
<recipid> ::= <recipid-asymm> / <recipid-symm>
```

```
<recipid-asymm> ::= "Recipient-ID-Asymmetric" ":" <asymmid> CRLF
<recipid-symm> ::= "Recipient-ID-Symmetric" ":" <symmid> CRLF
<cert> ::= "Originator-Certificate" ":" <encbin> CRLF
<issuercert> ::= "Issuer-Certificate" ":" <encbin> CRLF
<micinfo> ::= "MIC-Info" ":" <micalgid> "," <ikalgid> ","
          <asymsignmic> CRLF
<keyinfo> ::= "Key-Info" ":" <ikalgid> "," <micalgid> ","
          <symencdek> "," <symencmic> CRLF ; symmetric case
          / "Key-Info" ":" <ikalgid> "," <asymencdek>
          CRLF    ; asymmetric case
<crl> ::= "CRL" ":" <encbin> CRLF
<pemtypes> ::= "ENCRYPTED" / "MIC-ONLY" / "MIC-CLEAR" / "CRL"
<encbinchar> ::= ALPHA / DIGIT / "+" / "/" / "="
<encbingrp> ::= 4*4<encbinchar>
<encbin> ::= 1*<encbingrp>
<encbinbody> ::= *(16*16<encbingrp> CRLF) [1*16<encbingrp> CRLF]
<IKsubfld> ::= 1*<ia-char>
; Note: "," removed from <ia-char> set so that Orig-ID and
Recip-ID
; fields can be delimited with commas (not colons) like all
other
; fields
<ia-char> ::= DIGIT / ALPHA / "'" / "+" / "(" / ")" /
          "." / "/" / "=" / "?" / "-" / "@" /
          "%" / "!" / '"' / "-" / "<" / ">"
<hexchar> ::= DIGIT / "A" / "B" / "C" / "D" / "E" / "F"
                                  ; no lower case
; This specification defines one value ("RFC822") for
; <contentdescrip>: other values may be defined in future in
; separate or successor documents
;
<contentdescrip> ::= "RFC822"
; The following items are defined in RFC 1423
; <dekalgid>
; <dekparameters>
; <micalgid>
```

```
;  <ikalgid>
;  <asymsignmic>
;  <symencdek>
;  <symencmic>
;  <asymencdek>
```

Notes

[1] Key generation for MIC computation and message text encryption may either be performed by the sending host or by a centralized server. This RFC does not constrain this design alternative. Section 5.1 identifies possible advantages of a centralized server approach if symmetric key management is employed.

[2] Postel, J., "Simple Mail Transfer Protocol", STD 10, RFC 821, August 1982.

[3] This transformation should occur only at an SMTP endpoint, not at an intervening relay, but may take place at a gateway system linking the SMTP realm with other environments.

[4] Use of a canonicalization procedure similar to that of SMTP was selected because its functions are widely used and implemented within the Internet mail community, not for purposes of SMTP interoperability with this intermediate result.

[5] Crocker, D., "Standard for the Format of ARPA Internet Text Messages," STD 11, RFC 822, August 1982.

[6] Rose, M. T. and Stefferud, E. A., "Proposed Standard for Message Encapsulation," RFC 934, January 1985.

[7] CCITT Recommendation X.509 (1988), "The Directory - Authentication Framework."

[8] Throughout this RFC we have adopted the terms "private component" and "public component" to refer to the quantities which are, respectively, kept secret and made publicly available in asymmetric cryptosystems. This convention is adopted to avoid possible confusion arising from use of the term "secret key" to refer to either the former quantity or to a key in a symmetric cryptosystem.

Patent Statement

This version of Privacy Enhanced Mail (PEM) relies on the use of patented public key encryption technology for authentication and encryption. The Internet Standards Process as defined in RFC 1310 requires a written statement from the Patent holder that a license will be made available to applicants under reasonable terms and conditions prior to approving a specification as a Proposed, Draft or Internet Standard.

The Massachusetts Institute of Technology and the Board of Trustees of the Leland Stanford Junior University have granted Public Key Partners (PKP) exclusive sub-licensing rights to the following patents issued in the United States, and all of their corresponding foreign patents:

Cryptographic Apparatus and Method
("Diffie-Hellman")................................ No. 4,200,770

Public Key Cryptographic Apparatus and Method
("Hellman-Merkle")..................... No. 4,218,582

Cryptographic Communications System and Method
("RSA").................................... No. 4,405,829

Exponential Cryptographic Apparatus and Method
("Hellman-Pohlig").................... No. 4,424,414

These patents are stated by PKP to cover all known methods of practicing the art of Public Key encryption, including the variations collectively known as ElGamal.

Public Key Partners has provided written assurance to the Internet Society that parties will be able to obtain, under reasonable, nondiscriminatory terms, the right to use the technology covered by these patents. This assurance is documented in RFC 1170 titled "Public Key Standards and Licenses." A copy of the written assurance dated April 20, 1990, may be obtained from the Internet Assigned Number Authority (IANA).

The Internet Society, Internet Architecture Board, Internet Engineering Steering Group and the Corporation for National Research Initiatives take no position on the validity or scope of the patents and patent applications, nor on the appropriateness of the terms of the assurance. The Internet Society and other groups mentioned above have not made any determination as to any other intellectual property rights which may apply to the practice of this standard. Any further consideration of these matters is the user's own responsibility.

Security Considerations

This entire document is about security.

Author's Address

John Linn
E-Mail: 104-8456@mcimail.com

Network Working Group
Request for Comments: 1422
Obsoletes: 1114
Reproduced with permission
February 1993

S. Kent
BBN
IAB IRTF PSRG, IETF PEM
Stephen T. Kent All Rights Reserved

Privacy Enhancement for Internet Electronic Mail:

Part II
Certificate-Based Key Management

Status of this Memo

This RFC specifies an IAB standards track protocol for the Internet community, and requests discussion and suggestions for improvements. Please refer to the current edition of the "IAB Official Protocol Standards" for the standardization state and status of this protocol. Distribution of this memo is unlimited.

Acknowledgments

This memo is the outgrowth of a series of meetings of the Privacy and Security Research Group of the Internet Research Task Force (IRTF) and the Privacy-Enhanced Electronic Mail Working Group of the Internet Engineering Task Force (IETF). I would like to thank the members of the PSRG and the PEM WG for their comments and contributions at the meetings which led to the preparation of this document. I also would like to thank contributors to the PEM-DEV mailing list who have provided valuable input which is reflected in this memo.

1. Executive Summary

This is one of a series of documents defining privacy enhancement mechanisms for electronic mail transferred using Internet mail protocols. RFC 1421 [6] prescribes protocol extensions and processing procedures for RFC-822 mail messages, given that suitable cryptographic keys are held by originators and recipients as a necessary precondition. RFC 1423 [7] specifies algorithms, modes and associated identifiers for use in processing privacy-enhanced messages, as called for in RFC 1421 and this document. This document defines a supporting key management architecture and infrastructure, based on public-key certificate techniques, to provide keying information to message originators and recipients. RFC 1424 [8] provides additional specifications for services in conjunction with the key management infrastructure described herein.

The key management architecture described in this document is compatible with the authentication framework described in CCITT 1988 X.509 [2]. This document goes beyond X.509 by establishing procedures and conventions for a key management infrastructure for use with Privacy Enhanced Mail (PEM) and with other protocols, from both the TCP/IP and OSI suites, in the future. There are several motivations for establishing these procedures and conventions (as opposed to relying only on the very general framework outlined in X.509):

It is important that a certificate management infrastructure for use in the Internet community accommodate a range of clearly articulated certification policies for both users and organizations in a well-architected fashion. Mechanisms must be provided to enable each user to be aware of the policies governing any certificate which the user may encounter. This requires the introduction and standardization of procedures and conventions that are outside the scope of X.509.

The procedures for authenticating originators and recipient in the course of message submission and delivery should be simple, automated and uniform despite the existence of differing certificate management policies. For example, users should not have to engage in careful examination of a complex set of certification relationships in order to evaluate the credibility of a claimed identity.

The authentication framework defined by X.509 is designed to operate in the X.500 directory server environment. However X.500 directory servers are not expected to be ubiquitous in the Internet in the near future, so some conventions are adopted to facilitate operation of the key management infrastructure in the near term.

Public key cryptosystems are central to the authentication technology of X.509 and those which enjoy the most widespread use are patented in the U.S. Although this certification management scheme is compatible with the use of different digital signature algorithms, it is anticipated that the RSA cryptosystem will be used as the primary signature algorithm in establishing the Internet certification hierarchy. Special license arrangements have been made to facilitate the use of this algorithm in the U.S. portion of Internet environment.

The infrastructure specified in this document establishes a single root for all certification within the Internet, the Internet Policy Registration Authority (IPRA). The IPRA establishes global policies, described in this document, which apply to all certification effected under this hierarchy. Beneath IPRA root are Policy Certification Authorities (PCAs), each of which establishes and publishes (in the form of an informational RFC) its policies for registration of users or organizations. Each PCA is certified by the IPRA. (It is desirable that there be a relatively small number of PCAs, each with a substantively different policy, to facilitate user familiarity with the set of PCA policies. However there is no explicit requirement that the set of PCAs be limited in this fashion.) Below PCAs, Certification Authorities (CAs) will be established to certify users and subordinate organizational entities (e.g., departments, offices, subsidiaries, etc.). Initially, we expect the majority of users will be registered via organizational affiliation, consistent with current practices for how most user mailboxes are provided. In this sense the registration is analogous to the issuance of a university or company ID card.

Some CAs are expected to provide certification for residential users in support of users who wish to register independent of any organizational affiliation. Over time, we anticipate that civil government entities which already provide analogous identification services in other contexts, e.g., driver's licenses, may provide this service. For users who wish anonymity while taking advantage of PEM privacy facilities, one or more PCAs will be established with policies that allow for registration of users, under subordinate CAs, who do not wish to disclose their identities.

2. Overview of Approach

This document defines a key management architecture based on the use of public-key certificates, primarily in support of the message encipherment and authentication procedures defined in RFC 1421. The concept of public-key certificates is defined in X.509 and this architecture is a compliant subset of that envisioned in X.509.

Briefly, a (public-key) certificate is a data structure which contains the name of a user (the "subject"), the public component (this document adopts the terms "private component" and "public component" to refer to the quantities which are, respectively, kept secret and made publicly available in asymmetric cryptosystems. This convention is adopted to avoid possible confusion arising from use of the term "secret key" to refer to either the former quantity or to a key in a symmetric cryptosystem) of that user, and the name of an entity (the "issuer") which vouches that the public component is bound to the named user. This data, along with a time interval over which the binding is claimed to be valid, is cryptographically signed by the issuer using the issuer's private component. The subject and issuer names in certificates are Distinguished Names (DNs) as defined in the directory system (X.500).

Once signed, certificates can be stored in directory servers, transmitted via non-secure message exchanges, or distributed via any other means that make certificates easily accessible to message system users, without regard for the security of the transmission medium. Certificates are used in PEM to provide the originator of a message with the (authenticated) public component of each recipient and to provide each recipient with the (authenticated) public component of the originator. The following brief discussion illustrates the procedures for both originator and recipients.

Prior to sending an encrypted message (using PEM), an originator must acquire a certificate for each recipient and must validate these certificates. Briefly, validation is performed by checking the digital signature in the certificate, using the public component of the issuer whose private component was used to sign the certificate. The issuer's public component is made available via some out of band means (for the IPRA) or is itself distributed in a certificate to which this validation procedure is applied recursively. In the latter case, the issuer of a user's certificate becomes the subject in a certificate issued by another certifying authority (or a PCA), thus giving rise to a certification hierarchy. The validity interval for each certificate is checked and Certificate Revocation Lists (CRLs) are checked to ensure that none of the certificates employed in the validation process has been revoked by an issuer.

Once a certificate for a recipient is validated, the public component contained in the certificate is extracted and used to encrypt the data encryption key (DEK), which, in turn, is used to encrypt the message itself. The resulting encrypted DEK is incorporated into the Key-Info field of the message header. Upon receipt of an encrypted message, a recipient employs his private component to decrypt this field, extracting the DEK, and then uses this DEK to decrypt the message.

In order to provide message integrity and data origin authentication, the originator generates a message integrity code (MIC), signs (encrypts) the MIC using the private component of his public-key pair, and includes the resulting value in the message header in the MIC-Info field. The certificate of the originator is (optionally) included in the header in the Certificate field as described in RFC 1421. This is done in order to facilitate validation in the absence of ubiquitous directory services. Upon receipt of a privacy enhanced message, a recipient validates the originator's certificate (using the IPRA public component as the root of a certification path), checks to ensure that it has not been revoked, extracts the public component from the certificate, and uses that value to recover (decrypt) the MIC. The recovered MIC is compared against the locally calculated MIC to verify the integrity and data origin authenticity of the message.

3. Architecture
3.1 Scope and Restrictions

The architecture described below is intended to provide a basis for managing public-key cryptosystem values in support of privacy enhanced electronic mail in the Internet environment. The architecture describes procedures for registering certification authorities and users, for generating and distributing certificates, and for generating and distributing CRLs. RFC 1421 describes the syntax and semantics of header fields used to transfer certificates and to represent the DEK and MIC in this public-key context. Definitions of the algorithms, modes of use and associated identifiers are separated in RFC 1423 to facilitate the adoption of additional algorithms in the future. This document focuses on the management aspects of certificate-based, public-key cryptography for privacy enhanced mail.

The proposed architecture imposes conventions for the certification hierarchy which are not strictly required by the X.509 recommendation nor by the technology itself. These conventions are motivated by several factors, primarily the need for authentication semantics compatible with automated validation and the automated determination of the policies under which certificates are issued.

Specifically, the architecture proposes a system in which user (or mailing list) certificates represent the leaves in a certification hierarchy. This certification hierarchy is largely isomorphic to the X.500 directory naming hierarchy, with two exceptions: the IPRA forms the root of the tree (the root of the X.500 DIT is not instantiated as a node), and a number of Policy Certification Authorities (PCAs) form the "roots" of subtrees, each of which represents a different certification policy.

Not every level in the directory hierarchy need correspond to a certification authority. For example, the appearance of geographic entities in a distinguished name (e.g., countries, states, provinces, localities) does not require that various governments become certifying authorities in order to instantiate this architecture. However, it is anticipated that, over time, a number of such points in the hierarchy will be instantiated as CAs in order to simplify later transition of management to appropriate governmental authorities.

These conventions minimize the complexity of validating user certificates, e.g., by making explicit the relationship between a certificate issuer and the user (via the naming hierarchy). Note that in this architecture, only PCAs may be certified by the IPRA, and every CA's certification path can be traced to a PCA, through zero or more CAs. If a CA is certified by more than one PCA, each certificate issued by a PCA for the CA must contain a distinct public component. These conventions result in a certification hierarchy which is a compatible subset of that permitted under X.509, with respect to both syntax and semantics.

Although the key management architecture described in this document has been designed primarily to support privacy enhanced mail, this infrastructure also may, in principle, be used to support X.400 mail security facilities (as per 1988 X.411) and X.500 directory authentication facilities. Thus, establishment of this infrastructure paves the way for use of these and other OSI protocols in the Internet in the future. In the future, these certificates also may be employed in the provision of security services in other protocols in the TCP/IP and OSI suites as well.

3.2 Relation to X.509 Architecture

CCITT 1988 Recommendation X.509, "The Directory—Authentication Framework," defines a framework for authentication of entities involved in a distributed directory service. Strong authentication, as defined in X.509, is accomplished with the use of public-key cryptosystems. Unforgeable certificates are generated by certification authorities; these authorities may be organized hierarchically, though such organization is not required by X.509. There is no implied mapping between a certification hierarchy and the naming hierarchy imposed by directory system naming attributes.

This document interprets the X.509 certificate mechanism to serve the needs of PEM in the Internet environment. The certification hierarchy proposed in this document in support of privacy enhanced mail is intentionally a subset of that allowed under X.509. This certification hierarchy also embodies semantics which are not explicitly addressed by X.509, but which are consistent with X.509 precepts. An overview of the rationale for these semantics is provided in Section 1.

3.3 Certificate Definition

Certificates are central to the key management architecture for X.509 and PEM. This section provides an overview of the syntax and a description of the semantics of certificates. See ASN.1 Syntax for Certificates and CRLs. A certificate includes the following contents:

1. version
2. serial number
3. signature (algorithm ID and parameters)
4. issuer name
5. validity period
6. subject name
7. subject public key (and associated algorithm ID)

3.3.1 Version Number

The version number field is intended to facilitate orderly changes in certificate formats over time. The initial version number for certificates used in PEM is the X.509 default which has a value of zero (0), indicating the 1988 version. PEM implementations are encouraged to accept later versions as they are endorsed by CCITT/ISO.

3.3.2 Serial Number

The serial number field provides a short form, unique identifier for each certificate generated by an issuer. An issuer must ensure that no two distinct certificates with the same issuer DN contain the same serial number. (This requirement must be met even when the certification function is effected on a distributed basis and/or when the same issuer DN is certified under two different PCAs. This is especially critical for residential CAs certified under different PCAs.) The serial number is used in CRLs to identify revoked certificates, as described in Section 3.4.3.4. Although this attribute is an integer, PEM UA processing of this attribute need not involve any arithmetic operations. All PEM UA implementations must be capable of processing serial numbers at least 128 bits in length, and size-independent support serial numbers is encouraged.

3.3.3 Signature

This field specifies the algorithm used by the issuer to sign the certificate, and any parameters associated with the algorithm. (The certificate signature is appended to the data structure, as defined by the signature macro in X.509. This algorithm identification information is replicated with the signature.) The signature is validated by the UA processing a certificate, in order to determine that the integrity of its contents have not been modified subsequent to signing by a CA (IPRA, or PCA). In this context, a signature is effected through the use of a Certificate Integrity Check (CIC) algorithm and a public-key encryption algorithm. RFC 1423 contains the definitions and algorithm IDs for signature algorithms employed in this architecture.

3.3.4 Subject Name

A certificate provides a representation of its subject's identity in the form of a Distinguished Name (DN). The fundamental binding ensured by the key management architecture is that between the public component and the user's identity in this form. A distinguished name is an X.500 directory system concept and if a user is already registered in an X.500 directory, his distinguished name is defined via that registration. Users who are not registered in a directory should keep in mind likely directory naming structure (schema) when selecting a distinguished name for inclusion in a certificate.

3.3.5 Issuer Name

A certificate provides a representation of its issuer's identity, in the form of a Distinguished Name. The issuer identification is used to select the appropriate issuer public component to employ in performing certificate validation. (If an issuer (CA) is certified by multiple PCAs, then the issuer DN does not uniquely identify the public component used to sign the certificate. In such circumstances it may be necessary to attempt certificate validation using multiple public components, from certificates held by the issuer under different PCAs. If the 1992 version of a certificate is employed, the issuer may employ distinct issuer UIDs in the certificates it issues, to further facilitate selection of the right issuer public component.) The issuer is the certifying authority (IPRA, PCA or CA) who vouches for the binding between the subject identity and the public key contained in the certificate.

3.3.6 Validity Period

A certificate carries a pair of date and time indications, indicating the start and end of the time period over which a certificate is intended to be used. The duration of the interval may be constant for all user certificates issued by a given CA or it might differ based on the nature of the user's affiliation. For example, an organization might issue certificates with shorter intervals to temporary employees versus permanent employees. It is recommended that the UTCT (Coordinated Universal Time) values recorded here specify granularity to no more than the minute, even though finer granularity can be expressed in the format. (Implementors are warned that no DER is defined for UTCT in X.509, thus transformation between local and transfer syntax must be performed carefully, e.g., when computing the hash value for a certificate. For example, a UTCT value which includes explicit, zero values for seconds would not produce the same hash value as one in which the seconds were omitted.) It also recommended that all times be expressed as Greenwich Mean Time (Zulu), to simplify comparisons and avoid confusion relating to daylight savings time. Note that UTCT expresses the value of a year modulo 100 (with no indication of century), hence comparisons involving dates in different centuries must be performed with care.

The longer the interval, the greater the likelihood that compromise of a private component or name change will render it invalid and thus require that the certificate be revoked. Once revoked, the certificate must remain on the issuer's CRL (see Section 3.4.3.4) until the validity interval expires. PCAs may impose restrictions on the maximum validity interval that may be elected by CAs operating in their certification domain.

3.3.7 Subject Public Key

A certificate carries the public component of its associated subject, as well as an indication of the algorithm, and any algorithm parameters, with which the public component is to be used. This algorithm identifier is independent of that which is specified in the signature field described above. RFC 1423 specifies the algorithm identifiers which may be used in this context.

3.4 Roles and Responsibilities

One way to explain the architecture proposed by this document is to examine the roles which are defined for various entities in the architecture and to describe what is required of each entity in order for the proposed system to work properly. The following sections identify four types of entities within this architecture: users and user agents, the Internet Policy Registration Authority, Policy Certification Authorities, and other Certification Authorities. For each type of entity, this document specifies the procedures which the entity must execute as part of the architecture and the responsibilities the entity assumes as a function of its role in the architecture.

3.4.1 Users and User Agents

The term User Agent (UA) is taken from CCITT X.400 Message Handling Systems (MHS) Recommendations, which define it as follows: "In the context of message handling, the functional object, a component of MHS, by means of which a single direct user engages in message handling." In the Internet environment, programs such as rand mh and Gnu emacs rmail are UAs. UAs exchange messages by calling on a supporting Message Transfer Service (MTS), e.g., the SMTP mail relays used in the Internet.

3.4.1.1 Generating and Protecting Component Pairs

A UA process supporting PEM must protect the private component of its associated entity (e.g., a human user or a mailing list) from disclosure, though the means by which this is effected is a local matter. It is essential that the user take all available precautions to protect his private component as the secrecy of this value is central to the security offered by PEM to that user. For example, the private component might be stored in encrypted form, protected with a locally managed symmetric encryption key (e.g., using DES). The user would supply a password or passphrase which would be employed as a symmetric key to decrypt the private component when required for PEM processing (either on a per message or per session basis). Alternatively, the private component might be stored on a diskette which would be inserted by the user whenever he originated or received PEM messages. Explicit zeroing of memory locations where this component transiently resides could provide further protection. Other precautions, based on local operating system security facilities, also should be employed.

It is recommended that each user employ ancillary software (not otherwise associated with normal UA operation) or hardware to generate his personal public-key component pair. Software for generating user component pairs will be available as part of the reference implementation of PEM distributed freely in the U.S. portion of the Internet. It is critically important that the component pair generation procedure be effected in as secure a fashion as possible, to ensure that the resulting private component is unpredictable. Introduction of adequate randomness into the component pair generation procedure is potentially the most difficult aspect of this process and the user is advised to pay particular attention to this aspect. (Component pairs employed in public-key cryptosystems tend to be large integers which must be "randomly" selected subject to mathematical constraints imposed by the cryptosystem. Input(s) used to seed the component pair generation process must be as unpredictable as possible. An example of a poor random number selection technique is one in which a pseudo-random number generator is seeded solely with the current date and time. An attacker who could determine approximately when a component pair was generated could easily regenerate candidate component pairs and compare the public component to the user's public component to detect when the corresponding private component had been found.)

There is no requirement imposed by this architecture that anyone other than the user, including any certification authority, have access to the user's private component. Thus a user may retain his component pair even if his certificate changes, e.g., due to rollover in the validity interval or because of a change of certifying authority. Even if a user is issued a certificate in the context of his employment, there is generally no requirement that the employer have access to the user's private component. The rationale is that any messages signed by the user are verifiable using his public component. In the event that the corresponding private component becomes unavailable, any ENCRYPTED messages directed to the user would be indecipherable and would require retransmission.

Note that if the user stores messages in ENCRYPTED form, these messages also would become indecipherable in the event that the private component is lost or changed. To minimize the potential for loss of data in such circumstances messages can be transformed into MIC-ONLY or MIC-CLEAR form if cryptographically-enforced confidentiality is not required for the messages stored within the user's computer. Alternatively, these transformed messages might be forwarded in ENCRYPTED form to a (trivial) distribution list which serves in a backup capacity and for which the user's employer holds the private component.

A user may possess multiple certificates which may embody the same or different public components. For example, these certificates might represent a current and a former organizational user identity and a residential user identity. It is recommended that a PEM UA be capable of supporting a user who possess multiple certificates, irrespective of whether the certificates associated with the user contain the same or different DNs or public components.

3.4.1.2 User Registration

Most details of user registration are a local matter, subject to policies established by the user's CA and the PCA under which that CA has been certified. In general a user must provide, at a minimum, his public component and distinguished name to a CA, or a representative thereof, for inclusion in the user's certificate.

(The user also might provide a complete certificate, minus the signature, as described in RFC 1424.) The CA will employ some means, specified by the CA in accordance with the policy of its PCA, to validate the user's claimed identity and to ensure that the public component provided is associated with the user whose distinguished name is to be bound into the certificate. (In the case of PERSONA certificates, described below, the procedure is a bit different.) The certifying authority generates a certificate containing the user's distinguished name and public component, the authority's distinguished name and other information (see Section 3.3) and signs the result using the private component of the authority.

3.4.1.3 CRL Management

Mechanisms for managing a UA certificate cache are, in typical standards parlance, a local matter. However, proper maintenance of such a cache is critical to the correct, secure operation of a PEM UA and provides a basis for improved performance. Moreover, use of a cache permits a PEM UA to operate in the absence of directories (and in circumstances where directories are inaccessible). The following discussion provides a paradigm for one aspect of cache management, namely the processing of CRLs, the functional equivalent of which must be embodied in any PEM UA implementation compliant with this document. The specifications for CRLs used with PEM are provided in Section 3.5.

X.500 makes provision for the storage of CRLs as directory attributes associated with CA entries. Thus, when X.500 directories become widely available, UAs can retrieve CRLs from directories as required. In the interim, the IPRA will coordinate with PCAs to provide a robust database facility which will contain CRLs issued by the IPRA, by PCAs, and by all CAs. Access to this database will be provided through mailboxes maintained by each PCA. Every PEM UA must provide a facility for requesting CRLs from this database using the mechanisms defined in RFC 1424. Thus the UA must include a configuration parameter which specifies one or more mailbox addresses from which CRLs may be retrieved. Access to the CRL database may be automated, e.g., as part of the certificate validation process (see Section 3.6) or may be user directed. Responses to CRL requests will employ the PEM header format specified in RFC 1421 for CRL propagation. As noted in RFC 1421, every PEM UA must be capable of processing CRLs distributed via such messages. This message format also may be employed to support a "push" (versus a "pull") model of CRL distribution, i.e., to support unsolicited distribution of CRLs.

CRLs received by a PEM UA must be validated (A CRL is validated in much the same manner as a certificate, i.e., the CIC (see RFC 1113) is calculated and compared against the decrypted signature value obtained from the CRL. See Section 3.6 for additional details related to validation of certificates.) prior to being processed against any cached certificate information. Any cache entries which match CRL entries should be marked as revoked, but it is not necessary to delete cache entries marked as revoked nor to delete subordinate entries. In processing a CRL against the cache it is important to recall that certificate serial numbers are unique only for each issuer and that multiple, distinct CRLs may be issued under the same CA DN (signed using different private components), so care must be exercised in effecting this cache search. (This situation may arise either because an organizational CA is certified by multiple PCAs, or because multiple residential CAs are certified under different PCAs.)

This procedure applies to cache entries associated with PCAs and CAs, as well as user entries. The UA also must retain each CRL to screen incoming messages to detect use of revoked certificates carried in PEM message headers. Thus a UA must be capable of processing and retaining CRLs issued by the IPRA (which will list revoked PCA certificates), by any PCA (which will list revoked CA certificate issued by that PCA), and by any CA (which will list revoked user or subordinate CA certificates issued by that CA).

3.4.1.4 Facilitating Interoperation

In the absence of ubiquitous directory services or knowledge (acquired through out-of-band means) that a recipient already possesses the necessary issuer certificates, it is recommended that an originating (PEM) UA include sufficient certificates to permit validation of the user's public key. To this end every PEM UA must be capable of including a full (originator) certification path, i.e., including the user's certificate (using the "Originator-Certificate" field) and every superior (CA/PCA) certificate (using "Issuer-Certificate" fields) back to the IPRA, in a PEM message. A PEM UA may send less than a full certification path, e.g., based on analysis of a recipient list, but a UA which provides this sort of optimization must also provide the user with a capability to force transmission of a full certification path.

Optimization for the transmitted originator certification path may be effected by a UA as a side effect of the processing performed during message submission. When an originator submits an ENCRYPTED message (as per RFC 1421, his UA must validate the certificates of the recipients (see Section 3.6). In the course of performing this validation the UA can determine the minimum set of certificates which must be included to ensure that all recipients can process the received message. Submission of a MIC-ONLY or MIC-CLEAR message (as per RFC 1421) does not entail validation of recipient certificates and thus it may not be possible for the originator's UA to determine the minimum certificate set as above.

3.4.2 The Internet Policy Registration Authority (IPRA)

The IPRA acts as the root of the certification hierarchy for the Internet community. The public component of the IPRA forms the foundation for all certificate validation within this hierarchy. The IPRA will be operated under the auspices of the Internet Society, an international, non-profit organization. The IPRA certifies all PCAs, ensuring that they agree to abide by the Internet-wide policy established by the IPRA. This policy, and the services provided by the IPRA, are detailed below.

3.4.2.1 PCA Registration

The IPRA certifies only PCAs, not CAs or users. Each PCA must file with the IPRA a description of its proposed policy. This document will be published as an informational RFC. A copy of the document, signed by the IPRA (in the form of a PEM MIC-ONLY message) will be made available via electronic mail access by the IPRA. This convention is adopted so that every Internet user has a reference point for determining the policies associated with the issuance of any certificate which he may encounter. The existence of a digitally signed copy of the document ensures the immutability of the document. Authorization of a PCA to operate in the Internet hierarchy is signified by the publication of the policy document, and the issuance of a certificate to the PCA, signed by the IPRA. An outline for PCA policy statements is contained in Section 3.4.3 of this document.

As part of registration, each PCA will be required to execute a legal agreement with the IPRA, and to pay a fee to defray the costs of operating the IPRA. Each a PCA must specify its distinguished name. The IPRA will take reasonable precautions to ensure that the distinguished name claimed by a PCA is legitimate, e.g., requiring the PCA to provide documentation supporting its claim to a DN. However, the certification of a PCA by the IPRA does not constitute an endorsement of the PCA's claim to this DN outside of the context of this certification system.

3.4.2.2 Ensuring the Uniqueness of Distinguished Names

A fundamental requirement of this certification scheme is that certificates are not issued to distinct entities under the same distinguished name. This requirement is important to the success of distributed management for the certification hierarchy. The IPRA will not certify two PCAs with the same distinguished name and no PCA may certify two CAs with the same DN. However, since PCAs are expected to certify organizational CAs in widely disjoint portions of the directory namespace, and since X.500 directories are not ubiquitous, a facility is required for coordination among PCAs to ensure the uniqueness of CA DNs. (This architecture allows multiple PCAs to certify residential CAs and thus multiple, distinct residential CAs with identical DNs may come into existence, at least until such time as civil authorities assume responsibilities for such certification. Thus, on an interim basis, the architecture explicitly accommodates the potential for duplicate residential CA DNs.)

In support of the uniqueness requirement, the IPRA will establish and maintain a database to detect potential, unintended duplicate certification of CA distinguished names. This database will be made accessible to all PCAs via an e-mail interface. Each entry in this database will consist of a 4-tuple. The first element in each entry is a hash value, computed on a canonical, ASN.1 encoded representation of a CA distinguished name. The second element contains the subjectPublicKey that appears in the CA's certificate. The third element is the distinguished name of the PCA which registered the entry. The fourth element consists of the date and time at which the entry was made, as established by the

IPRA. This database structure provides a degree of privacy for CAs registered by PCAs, while providing a facility for ensuring global uniqueness of CA DNs certified in this scheme.

In order to avoid conflicts, a PCA should query the database using a CA DN hash value as a search key, prior to certifying a CA. The database will return any entries which match the query, i.e., which have the same CA DN. The PCA can use the information contained in any returned entries to determine if any PCAs should be contacted to resolve possible DN conflicts. If no potential conflicts appear, a PCA can then submit a candidate entry, consisting of the first three element values, plus any entries returned by the query. The database will register this entry, supplying the time and date stamp, only if two conditions are met: (1) the first two elements (the CA DN hash and the CA subjectPublicKey) of the candidate entry together must be unique and, (2) any other entries included in the submission must match what the current database would return if the query corresponding to the candidate entry were submitted.

If the database detects a conflicting entry (failure of case 1 above), or if the submission indicates that the PCA's perception of possible conflicting entries is not current (failure of case 2), the submission is rejected and the database will return the potential conflicting entry (entries). If the submission is successful, the database will return the timestamped new entry. The database does not, in itself, guarantee uniqueness of CA DNs as it allows for two DNs associated with different public components to be registered. Rather, it is the responsibility of PCAs to coordinate with one another whenever the database indicates a potential DN conflict and to resolve such conflicts prior to certification of CAs. Details of the protocol used to access the database will be provided in another document.

As noted earlier, a CA may be certified under more than one PCA, e.g., because the CA wants to issue certificates under two different policies. If a CA is certified by multiple different PCAs, the CA must employ a different public key pair for each PCA. In such circumstances the certificate issued to the CA by each PCA will contain a different subjectPublicKey and thus will represent a different entry in this database. The same situation may arise if multiple, equivalent residential CAs are certified by different PCAs.

To complete the strategy for ensuring uniqueness of DNs, there is a DN subordination requirement levied on CAs. In general, CAs are expected to sign certificates only if the subject DN in the certificate is subordinate to the issuer (CA) DN. This ensures that certificates issued by a CA are syntactically constrained to refer to subordinate entities in the X.500 directory information tree (DIT), and this further limits the possibility of duplicate DN registration. CAs may sign certificates which do not comply with this requirement if the certificates are "cross-certificates" or "reverse certificates" (see X.509) used with applications other than PEM.

The IPRA also will establish and maintain a separate database to detect potential duplicate certification of (residential) user distinguished names. Each entry in this database will consist of 4-tuple as above, but the first components is the hash of a residential user DN and the third component is the DN of the residential CA DN which registered the user. This structure provides a degree of privacy for users registered by CAs which service residential users while providing a facility for ensuring global uniqueness of user DNs certified under this scheme. The same database access facilities are provided as described above for the CA database. Here it is the responsibility of the CAs to coordinate whenever the database indicates a potential conflict and to resolve the conflict prior to (residential) user certification.

3.4.2.3 Accuracy of Distinguished Names

As noted above, the IPRA will make a reasonable effort to ensure that PCA DNs are accurate. The procedures employed to ensure the accuracy of a CA distinguished name, i.e., the confidence attached to the DN/public component binding implied by a certificate, will vary according to PCA policy. However, it is expected that every PCA will make a good faith effort to ensure the legitimacy of each CA DN certified by the PCA. Part of this effort should include a check that the purported CA DN is consistent with any applicable national standards for DN assignment, e.g., NADF recommendations within North America [5,9].

3.4.2.4 Distinguished Name Conventions

A few basic DN conventions are included in the IPRA policy. The IPRA will certify PCAs, but not CAs nor users. PCAs will certify CAs, but not users. These conventions are required to allow simple certificate validation within PEM, as described later. Certificates issued by CAs (for use with PEM) will be for users or for other CAs, either of which must have DNs subordinate to that of the issuing CA.

The attributes employed in constructing DNs will be specified in a list maintained by the IANA, to provide a coordinated basis for attribute identification for all applications employing DNs. This list will initially be populated with attributes taken from X.520. This document does not impose detailed restrictions on the attributes used to identify different entities to which certificates are issued, but PCAs may impose such restrictions as part of their policies. PCAs, CAs and users are urged to employ only those DN attributes which have printable representations, to facilitate display and entry.

3.4.2.5 CRL Management

Among the procedures articulated by each PCA in its policy statement are procedures for the maintenance and distribution of CRLs by the PCA itself and by its subordinate CAs. The frequency of issue of CRLs may vary according to PCA-specific policy, but every PCA and CA must issue a CRL upon inception to provide a basis for uniform certificate validation procedures throughout the Internet hierarchy. The IPRA will maintain a CRL for all the PCAs it certifies and this CRL will be updated monthly. Each PCA will maintain a CRL for all of the CAs which it certifies and these CRLs will be updated in accordance with each PCA's policy. The format for these CRLs is that specified in Section 3.5.2 of the document.

In the absence of ubiquitous X.500 directory services, the IPRA will require each PCA to provide, for its users, robust database access to CRLs for the Internet hierarchy, i.e., the IPRA CRL, PCA CRLs, and CRLs from all CAs. The means by which this database is implemented is to be coordinated between the IPRA and PCAs. This database will be accessible via e-mail as specified in RFC 1424, both for retrieval of (current) CRLs by any user, and for submission of new CRLs by CAs, PCAs and the IPRA. Individual PCAs also may elect to maintain CRL archives for their CAs, but this is not required by this policy.

3.4.2.6 Public Key Algorithm Licensing Issues

This certification hierarchy is architecturally independent of any specific digital signature (public key) algorithm. Some algorithms, employed for signing certificates and validating certificate signatures, are patented in some countries. The IPRA will not grant a license to any PCA for the use of any signature algorithm in conjunction with the management of this certification hierarchy. The IPRA will acquire, for itself, any licenses needed for it to sign certificates and CRLs for PCAs, for all algorithms which the IPRA supports. Every PCA will be required to represent to the IPRA that the PCA has obtained any licenses required to issue (sign) certificates and CRLs in the environment(s) which the PCA will serve.

For example, the RSA cryptosystem is patented in the United States and thus any PCA operating in the U.S. and using RSA to sign certificates and CRLs must represent that it has a valid license to employ the RSA algorithm in this fashion. In contrast, a PCA employing RSA and operating outside of the U.S. would represent that it is exempt from these licensing constraints.

3.4.3 Policy Certification Authorities

The policy statement submitted by a prospective PCA must address the topics in the following outline. Additional policy information may be contained in the statement, but PCAs are requested not to use these statements as advertising vehicles.

1. PCA Identity—The DN of the PCA must be specified. A postal address, an Internet mail address, and telephone (and optional fax) numbers must be provided for (human) contact with the PCA. The date on which this statement is effective, and its scheduled duration must be specified.

2. PCA Scope—Each PCA must describe the community which the PCA plans to serve. A PCA should indicate if it will certify organizational, residential, and/or PERSONA CAs. There is not a requirement that a single PCA serve only one type of CA, but if a PCA serves multiple types of CAs, the policy statement must specify clearly how a user can distinguish among these classes. If the PCA will operate CAs to directly serve residential or PERSONA users, it must so state.

3. PCA Security & Privacy—Each PCA must specify the technical and procedural security measures it will employ in the generation and protection of its component pair. If any security requirements are imposed on CAs certified by the PCA these must be specified as well. A PCA also must specify what measures it will take to protect the privacy of any information collected in the course of certifying CAs. If the PCA operates one or more CAs directly, to serve residential or PERSONA users, then this statement on privacy measures applies to these CAs as well.

4. Certification Policy—Each PCA must specify the policy and procedures which govern its certification of CAs and how this policy applies transitively to entities (users or subordinate CAs) certified by these CAs. For example, a PCA must state what procedure is employed to verify the claimed identity of a CA, and the CA's right to use a DN. Similarly, if any requirements are imposed on CAs to validate the identity of users, these requirements must be specified. Since all PCAs are required to cooperate in the resolution of potential DN conflicts, each PCA is required to specify the procedure it will employ to resolve such conflicts. If the PCA imposes a maximum validity interval for the CA certificates it issues, and/or for user (or subordinate CA) certificates issued by the CAs it certifies, then these restrictions must be specified.

5. CRL Management—Each PCA must specify the frequency with which it will issue scheduled CRLs. It also must specify any constraints it imposes on the frequency of scheduled issue of CRLs by the CAs it certifies, and by subordinate CAs. Both maximum and minimum constraints should be specified. Since the IPRA policy calls for each CRL issued by a CA to be forwarded to the cognizant PCA, each PCA must specify a mailbox address to which CRLs are to be transmitted. The PCA also must specify a mailbox address for CRL queries. If the PCA offers any additional CRL management services, e.g., archiving of old CRLs, then procedures for invoking these services must be specified. If the PCA requires CAs to provide any additional CRL management services, such services must be specified here.

6. Naming Conventions—If the PCA imposes any conventions on DNs used by the CAs it certifies, or by entities certified by these CAs, these conventions must be specified. If any semantics are associated with such conventions, these semantics must be specified.

7. Business Issues—If a legal agreement must be executed between a PCA and the CAs it certifies, reference to that agreement must be noted, but the agreement itself ought not be a part of the policy statement. Similarly, if any fees are charged by the PCA this should be noted, but the fee structure per se ought not be part of this policy statement.

8. Other—Any other topics the PCA deems relevant to a statement of its policy can be included. However, the PCA should be aware that a policy statement is considered to be an immutable, long lived document and thus consider-

able care should be exercised in deciding what material is to be included in the statement.

3.4.4 Certification Authorities

In X.509 the term "certification authority" is defined as "an authority trusted by one or more users to create and assign certificates." X.509 imposes few constraints on CAs, but practical implementation of a worldwide certification system requires establishment of technical and procedural conventions by which all CAs are expected to abide. Such conventions are established throughout this document. All CAs are required to maintain a database of the DNs which they have certified and to take measures to ensure that they do not certify duplicate DNs, either for users or for subordinate CAs.

It is critical that the private component of a CA be afforded a high level of security, otherwise the authenticity guarantee implied by certificates signed by the CA is voided. Some PCAs may impose stringent requirements on CAs within their purview to ensure that a high level of security is afforded the certificate signing process, but not all PCAs are expected to impose such constraints.

3.4.4.1 Organizational CAs

Many of the CAs certified by PCAs are expected to represent organizations. A wide range of organizations are encompassed by this model: commercial, governmental, educational, non-profit, professional societies, etc. The common thread is that the entities certified by these CAs have some form of affiliation with the organization. The object classes for organizations, organizational units, organizational persons, organizational roles, etc., as defined in X.521, form the models for entities certified by such CAs. The affiliation implied by organizational certification motivates the DN subordination requirement cited in Section 3.4.2.4.

As an example, an organizational user certificate might contain a subject DN of the form: C = "US" SP = "Massachusetts" L = "Cambridge" O = "Bolt Beranek and Newman" OU = "Communications Division" CN = "Steve Kent." The issuer of this certificate might have a DN of the form: C = "US" SP = "Massachusetts" L = "Cambridge" O= "Bolt Beranek and Newman." Note that the organizational unit attribute is omitted from the issuer DN, implying that there is no CA dedicated to the "Communications Division."

3.4.4.2 Residential CAs

Users may wish to obtain certificates which do not imply any organizational affiliation but which do purport to accurately and uniquely identify them. Such users can be registered as residential persons and the DN of such a user should be consistent with the attributes of the corresponding X.521 object class. Over time we anticipate that such users will be accommodated by civil government entities who will assume electronic certification responsibility at geographically designated points in the naming hierarchy. Until civil authorities are prepared to issue certificates of this form, residential user CAs will accommodate such users.

Because residential CAs may be operated under the auspices of multiple PCAs, there is a potential for the same residential CA DN to be assumed by several distinct entities. This represents the one exception to the rule articulated throughout this document that no two entities may have the same DN. This conflict is tolerated so as to allow residential CAs to be established offering different policies. Two requirements are levied upon residential CAs as a result: (1) residential CAs must employ the residential DN conflict detection database maintained by the IPRA, and (2) residential CAs must coordinate to ensure that they do not assign duplicate certificate serial numbers.

As an example, a residential user certificate might include a subject name of the form: C = "US" SP = "Massachusetts" L = "Boston" PA = "19 North Square" CN = "Paul Revere." The issuer of that certificate might have a DN of the form: C = "US" SP = "Massachusetts" L = "Boston." Note that the issuer DN is superior to the subject DN, as required by the IPRA policy described earlier.

3.4.4.3 PERSONA CAs

One or more CAs will be established to accommodate users who wish to conceal their identities while making use of PEM security features, e.g., to preserve the anonymity offered by "arbitrary" mailbox names in the current mail environment. In this case the certifying authority is explicitly NOT vouching for the identity of the user. All such certificates are issued under a PERSONA CA, subordinate to a PCA with a PERSONA policy, to warn users explicitly that the subject DN is NOT a validated user identity. To minimize the possibility of syntactic confusion with certificates which do purport to specify an authenticated user identity, a PERSONA certificate is issued as a form of organizational user certificate, not a residential user certificate. There are no explicit, reserved words used to identify PERSONA user certificates.

A CA issuing PERSONA certificates must institute procedures to ensure that it does not issue the same subject DN to multiple users (a constraint required for all certificates of any type issued by any CA). There are no requirements on an issuer of PERSONA certificates to maintain any other records that might bind the true identity of the subject to his certificate. However, a CA issuing such certificates must establish procedures (not specified in this document) in order to allow the holder of a PERSONA certificate to request that his certificate be revoked (i.e., listed on a CRL).

As an example, a PERSONA user certificate might include a subject DN of the form: C = "US" SP = "Massachusetts" L = "Boston" O = "Pseudonyms R US" CN = "Paul Revere." The issuer of this certificate might have a DN of the form: C = "US" SP = "Massachusetts" L = "Boston" O = "Pseudonyms R US." Note the differences between this PERSONA user certificate for "Paul Revere" and the corresponding residential user certificate for the same common name.

3.4.4.4 CA Responsibilities for CRL Management

As X.500 directory servers become available, CRLs should be maintained and accessed via these servers. However, prior to widespread deployment of X.500 directories, this document adopts some additional requirements for CRL management by CAs and PCAs. As per X.509, each CA is required to maintain a CRL (in the format specified by this document in ASN.1 Syntax for Certificates and CRLs) which contains entries for all certificates issued and later revoked by the CA. Once a certificate is entered on a CRL it remains there until the validity interval expires. Each PCA is required to maintain a CRL for revoked CA certificates within its domain. The interval at which a CA issues a CRL is not fixed by this document, but the PCAs may establish minimum and maximum intervals for such issuance.

As noted earlier, each PCA will provide access to a database containing CRLs issued by the IPRA, PCAs, and all CAs. In support of this requirement, each CA must supply its current CRL to its PCA in a fashion consistent with CRL issuance rules imposed by the PCA and with the next scheduled issue date specified by the CA (see Section 3.5.1). CAs may distribute CRLs to subordinate UAs using the CRL processing type available in PEM messages (see RFC 1421). CAs also may provide access to CRLs via the database mechanism described in RFC 1424 and alluded to immediately above.

3.5 Certificate Revocation
3.5.1 X.509 CRLs

X.509 states that it is a CA's responsibility to maintain: "a time-stamped list of the certificates it issued which have been revoked." There are two primary reasons for a CA to revoke a certificate, i.e., suspected compromise of a private component (invalidating the corresponding public component) or change of user affiliation (invalidating the DN). The use of Certificate Revocation Lists (CRLs) as defined in X.509 is one means of propagating information relative to certificate revocation, though it is not a perfect mechanism. In particular, an X.509 CRL indicates only the age of the information contained in it; it does not provide any basis for determining if the list is the most current CRL available from a given CA.

The proposed architecture establishes a format for a CRL in which not only the date of issue, but also the next scheduled date of issue is specified. Adopting this convention, when the next scheduled issue date arrives a CA (Throughout this section, when the term "CA" is employed, it should be interpreted broadly, to include the IPRA and PCAs as well as organizational, residential, and PERSONA CAs.) will issue a new CRL, even if there are no changes in the list of entries. In this fashion each CA can independently establish and advertise the frequency with which CRLs are issued by that CA. Note that this does not preclude CRL issuance on a more frequent basis, e.g., in case of some emergency, but no system-wide mechanisms are architected for alerting users that such an unscheduled issuance has taken place. This scheduled CRL issuance convention allows users (UAs) to determine whether a given CRL is "out of date," a facility not available from the (1988) X.509 CRL format.

The description of CRL management in the text and the format for CRLs specified in X.509 (1988) are inconsistent. For example, the latter associates an issuer distinguished name with each revoked certificate even though the text states that a CRL contains entries for only a single issuer (which is separately specified in the CRL format). The CRL format adopted for PEM is a (simplified) format consistent with the text of X.509, but not identical to the accompanying format. The ASN.1 format for CRLs used with PEM is provided in ASN.1 Syntax for Certificates and CRLs.

X.509 also defines a syntax for the "time-stamped list of revoked certificates representing other CAs." This syntax, the "AuthorityRevocationList" (ARL) allows the list to include references to certificates issued by CAs other than the list maintainer. There is no syntactic difference between these two lists except as they are stored in directories. Since PEM is expected to be used prior to widespread directory deployment, this distinction between ARLs and CRLs is not syntactically significant. As a simplification, this document specifies the use the CRL format defined below for revocation both of user and of CA certificates.

3.5.2 PEM CRL Format

Appendix A contains the ASN.1 description of CRLs specified by this document. This section provides an informal description of CRL components analogous to that provided for certificates in Section 3.3.

1. signature (signature algorithm ID and parameters)
2. issuer
3. last update
4. next update
5. revoked certificates

The "signature" is a data item completely analogous to the signature data item in a certificate. Similarly, the "issuer" is the DN of the CA which signed the CRL. The "last update" and "next update" fields contain time and date values (UTCT format) which specify, respectively, when this CRL was issued and when the next CRL is scheduled to be issued. Finally, "revoked certificates" is a sequence of ordered pairs, in which the first element is the serial number of the revoked certificate and the second element is the time and date of the revocation for that certificate.

The semantics for this second element are not made clear in X.509. For example, the time and date specified might indicate when a private component was thought to have been compromised or it may reflect when the report of such compromise was reported to the CA.

For uniformity, this document adopts the latter convention, i.e., the revocation date specifies the time and date at which a CA formally acknowledges a report of a compromise or a change or DN attributes. As with certificates, it is recommended that the UTCT values be of no finer granularity than minutes and that all values be stated in terms of Zulu.

3.6 Certificate Validation
3.6.1 Validation Basics

Every UA must contain the public component of the IPRA as the root for its certificate validation database. Public components associated with PCAs must be identified as such, so that the certificate validation process described below can operate correctly. Whenever a certificate for a PCA is entered into a UA cache, e.g., if encountered in a PEM message encapsulated header, the certificate must NOT be entered into the cache automatically. Rather, the user must be notified and must explicitly direct the UA to enter any PCA certificate data into the cache. This precaution is essential because introduction of a PCA certificate into the cache implies user recognition of the policy associated with the PCA.

Validating a certificate begins with verifying that the signature affixed to the certificate is valid, i.e., that the hash value computed on the certificate contents matches the value that results from decrypting the signature field using the public component of the issuer. In order to perform this operation the user must possess the public component of the issuer, either via some integrity-assured channel, or by extracting it from another (validated) certificate. In order to rapidly terminate this recursive validation process, we recommend each PCA sign certificates for all CAs within its domain, even CAs which are certified by other, superior CAs in the certification hierarchy.

The public component needed to validate certificates signed by the IPRA is made available to each user as part of the registration or via the PEM installation process. Thus a user will be able to validate any PCA certificate immediately. CAs are certified by PCAs, so validation of a CA certificate requires processing a validation path of length two. User certificates are issued by CAs (either immediately subordinate to PCAs or subordinate to other CAs), thus validation of a user certificate may require three or more steps. Local caching of validated certificates by a UA can be used to speed up this process significantly.

Consider the situation in which a user receives a privacy enhanced message from an originator with whom the recipient has never previously corresponded, and assume that the message originator includes a full certification path in the PEM message header. First the recipient can use the IPRA's public component to validate a PCA certificate contained in an Issuer-Certificate field. Using the PCA's public component extracted from this certificate, the CA certificate in an Issuer-Certificate field also can be validated. This process can be repeated until the certificate for the originator, from the Originator-Certificate field, is validated.

Having performed this certificate validation process, the recipient can extract the originator's public component and use it to decrypt the content of the MIC-Info field. By comparing the decrypted contents of this field against the MIC computed locally on the message the user verifies the data origin authenticity and integrity of the message. It is recommended that implementations of privacy enhanced mail cache validated public components (acquired from incoming mail) to speed up this process. If a message arrives from an originator whose public component is held in the recipient's cache (and if the cache is maintained in a fashion that ensures timely incorporation of received CRLs), the recipient can immediately employ that public component without the need for the certificate validation process described here. (For some digital signature algorithms, the processing required for certificate validation is considerably faster than that involved in signing a certificate. Use of such algorithms serves to minimize the computational burden on UAs.)

3.6.2 Display of Certificate Validation Data

PEM provides authenticated identities for message recipients and originators expressed in the form of distinguished names. Mail systems in which PEM is employed may employ identifiers other than DNs as the primary means of identifying recipients or originators. Thus, in order to benefit from these authentication facilities, each PEM implementation must employ some means of binding native mail system identifiers to distinguished names in a fashion which does not undermine this basic PEM functionality.

For example, if a human user interacts directly with PEM, then the full DN of the originator of any message received using PEM should be displayed for the user. Merely displaying the PEM-protected message content, containing an originator name from the native mail system, does not provide equivalent security functionality and could allow spoofing. If the recipient of a message is a forwarding agent such as a list exploder or mail relay, display of the originator's DN is not a relevant requirement. In all cases the essential requirement is that the ultimate recipient of a PEM message be able to ascertain the identity of the originator based on the PEM certification system, not on unauthenticated identification information, e.g., extracted from the native message system.

Conversely, for the originator of an ENCRYPTED message, it is important that recipient identities be linked to the DNs as expressed in PEM certificates. This can be effected in a variety of ways by the PEM implementation, e.g., by display of recipient DNs upon message submission or by a tightly controlled binding between local aliases and the DNs. Here too, if the originator is a forwarding process this linkage might be effected via various mechanisms not applicable to direct human interaction. Again, the essential requirement is to avoid procedures which might undermine the authentication services provided by PEM.

As described above, it is a local matter how and what certification information is displayed for a human user in the course of submission or delivery of a PEM message. Nonetheless all PEM implementations must provide a user with the ability to display a full certification path for any certificate employed in PEM upon demand. Implementors are urged to not overwhelm the user with certification path information which might confuse him or distract him from the critical information cited above.

3.6.3 Validation Procedure Details

Every PEM implementation is required to perform the following validation steps for every public component employed in the submission of an ENCRYPTED PEM message or the delivery of an ENCRYPTED, MIC-ONLY, or MIC-CLEAR PEM message. Each public component may be acquired from an internal source, e.g., from a (secure) cache at the originator/recipient or it may be obtained from an external source, e.g., the PEM header of an incoming message or a directory. The following procedures applies to the validation of certificates from either type of source.

Validation of a public component involves constructing a certification path between the component and the public component of the IPRA. The validity interval for every certificate in this path must be checked. PEM software must, at a minimum, warn the user if any certificate in the path fails the validity interval check, though the form of this warning is a local matter. For example, the warning might indicate which certificate in the path had expired. Local security policy may prohibit use of expired certificates.

Each certificate also must be checked against the current CRL from the certificate's issuer to ensure that revoked certificates are not employed. If the UA does not have access to the current CRL for any certificate in the path, the user must be warned. Again, the form of the warning is a local matter. For example, the warning might indicate whether the CRL is unavailable or, if available but not current, the CRL issue date should be displayed. Local policy may prohibit use of a public component which cannot be checked against a current CRL, and in such cases the user should receive the same information provided by the warning indications described above.

If any revoked certificates are encountered in the construction of a certification path, the user must be warned. The form of the warning is a local matter, but it is recommended that this warning be more stringent than those previously alluded to above. For example, this warning might display the issuer and subject DNs from the revoked certificate and the date of revocation, and then require the user to provide a positive response before the submission or delivery process may proceed. In the case of message submission, the warning might display the identity of the recipient affected by this validation failure and the user might be provided with the option to specify that this recipient be dropped from recipient list processing without affecting PEM processing for the remaining recipients. Local policy may prohibit PEM processing if a revoked certificate is encountered in the course of constructing a certification path.

Note that in order to comply with these validation procedures, a certificate cache must maintain all of the information contained in a certificate, not just the DNs and the public component. For example the serial number and validity interval must be associated with the cache entry to comply with the checks described above. Also note that these procedures apply to human interaction in message submission and delivery and are not directly applicable to forwarding processes. When non-human interaction is involved, a compliant PEM implementation must provide parameters to enable a process to specify whether certificate validation will succeed or fail if any of the conditions arise which would result in warnings to a human user.

Finally, in the course of validating certificates as described above, one additional check must be performed: the subject DN of every certificate must be subordinate to the certificate issuer DN, except if the issuer is the IPRA or a PCA (hence another reason to distinguish the IPRA and PCA entries in a certificate cache). This requirement is levied upon all PEM implementations as part of maintaining the certification hierarchy constraints defined in this document. Any certificate which does not comply with these requirements is considered invalid and must be rejected in PEM submission or delivery processing. The user must be notified of the nature of this fatal error.

A. ASN.1 Syntax for Certificates and CRLs
A.1 Certificate Syntax

The X.509 certificate format is defined by the following ASN.1 syntax:

```
Certificate ::= SIGNED SEQUENCE{
    version [0] Version DEFAULT v1988,
    serialNumber CertificateSerialNumber,
    signature AlgorithmIdentifier,
    issuer  Name,
    validity Validity,
    subject  Name,
    subjectPublicKeyInfo SubjectPublicKeyInfo}
Version ::= INTEGER {v1988(0)}
CertificateSerialNumber ::= INTEGER
Validity ::= SEQUENCE{
    notBefore UTCTime,
    notAfter UTCTime}
SubjectPublicKeyInfo ::= SEQUENCE{
    algorithm  AlgorithmIdentifier,
    subjectPublicKey BIT STRING}
AlgorithmIdentifier ::= SEQUENCE{
    algorithm OBJECT IDENTIFIER,
    parameters ANY DEFINED BY algorithm OPTIONAL}
```

The components of this structure are defined by ASN.1 syntax defined in the X.500 Series Recommendations. RFC 1423 provides references for and the values of AlgorithmIdentifiers used by PEM in the subjectPublicKeyInfo and the signature data items. It also describes how a signature is generated and the results represented. Because the certificate is a signed data object, the distinguished encoding rules (see X.509, section 8.7) must be applied prior to signing.

A.2 Certificate Revocation List Syntax

The following ASN.1 syntax, derived from X.509 and aligned with the suggested format in recently submitted defect reports, defines the format of CRLs for use in the PEM environment.

```
CertificateRevocationList ::= SIGNED SEQUENCE{
    signature AlgorithmIdentifier,
    issuer   Name,
    lastUpdate UTCTime,
    nextUpdate UTCTime,
    revokedCertificates
                SEQUENCE OF CRLEntry OPTIONAL}
CRLEntry ::= SEQUENCE{
    userCertificate SerialNumber,
    revocationDate UTCTime}
```

References

1 CCITT Recommendation X.411 (1988), "Message Handling Systems: Message Transfer System: Abstract Service Definition and Procedures."

2 CCITT Recommendation X.509 (1988), "The Directory - Authentication Framework."

3 CCITT Recommendation X.520 (1988), "The Directory - Selected Attribute Types."

4 NIST Special Publication 500-183, "Stable Agreements for Open Systems Interconnection Protocols," Version 4, Edition 1, December 1990.

5 North American Directory Forum, "A Naming Scheme for c=US," RFC 1255, NADF, September 1991.

6 Linn, J., "Privacy Enhancement for Internet Electronic Mail: Part I: Message Encryption and Authentication Procedures," RFC 1421, DEC, February 1993.

7 Balenson, D., "Privacy Enhancement for Internet Electronic Mail: Part III: Algorithms, Modes, and Identifiers," RFC 1423, TIS, February 1993.

8 Balaski, B., "Privacy Enhancement for Internet Electronic Mail: Part IV: Notary, Co-Issuer, CRL-Storing and CRL-Retrieving Services," RFC 1424, RSA Laboratories, February 1993.

9 North American Directory Forum, "NADF Standing Documents: A Brief Overview," RFC 1417, NADF, February 1993.

Patent Statement

This version of Privacy Enhanced Mail (PEM) relies on the use of patented public key encryption technology for authentication and encryption. The Internet

Standards Process as defined in RFC 1310 requires a written statement from the Patent holder that a license will be made available to applicants under reasonable terms and conditions prior to approving a specification as a Proposed, Draft or Internet Standard.

The Massachusetts Institute of Technology and the Board of Trustees of the Leland Stanford Junior University have granted Public Key Partners (PKP) exclusive sub-licensing rights to the following patents issued in the United States, and all of their corresponding foreign patents:

Cryptographic Apparatus and Method
("Diffie-Hellman").............................. No. 4,200,770
Public Key Cryptographic Apparatus and Method
("Hellman-Merkle").................... No. 4,218,582
Cryptographic Communications System and Method
("RSA")................................. No. 4,405,829
Exponential Cryptographic Apparatus and Method
("Hellman-Pohlig").................... No. 4,424,414

These patents are stated by PKP to cover all known methods of practicing the art of Public Key encryption, including the variations collectively known as ElGamal.

Public Key Partners has provided written assurance to the Internet Society that parties will be able to obtain, under reasonable, nondiscriminatory terms, the right to use the technology covered by these patents. This assurance is documented in RFC 1170 titled "Public Key Standards and Licenses". A copy of the written assurance dated April 20, 1990, may be obtained from the Internet Assigned Number Authority (IANA).

The Internet Society, Internet Architecture Board, Internet Engineering Steering Group and the Corporation for National Research Initiatives take no position on the validity or scope of the patents and patent applications, nor on the appropriateness of the terms of the assurance. The Internet Society and other groups mentioned above have not made any determination as to any other intellectual property rights which may apply to the practice of this standard. Any further consideration of these matters is the user's own responsibility.

Security Considerations

This entire document is about security.

Author's Address

Steve Kent
BBN Communications
50 Moulton Street
Cambridge, MA 02138
Phone: (617) 873-3988
E-Mail: kent@BBN.CO

Network Working Group
Request for Comments: 1423
Obsoletes: 1115
February 1993

D. Balenson
TIS
IAB IRTF PSRG, IETF PEM WG

Privacy Enhancement for Internet Electronic Mail:

Part III
Algorithms, Modes, and Identifiers

Status of This Memo

This RFC specifies an IAB standards track protocol for the Internet community, and requests discussion and suggestions for improvements. Please refer to the current edition of the "IAB Official Protocol Standards" for the standardization state and status of this protocol. Distribution of this memo is unlimited.

Abstract

This document provides definitions, formats, references, and citations for cryptographic algorithms, usage modes, and associated identifiers and parameters used in support of Privacy Enhanced Mail (PEM) in the Internet community. It is intended to become one member of the set of related PEM RFCs. This document is organized into four primary sections, dealing with message encryption algorithms, message integrity check algorithms, symmetric key management algorithms, and asymmetric key management algorithms (including both asymmetric encryption and asymmetric signature algorithms).

Some parts of this material are cited by other documents and it is anticipated that some of the material herein may be changed, added, or replaced without affecting the citing documents. Therefore, algorithm-specific material has been placed into this separate document.

Use of other algorithms and/or modes will require case-by-case study to determine applicability and constraints. The use of additional algorithms may be documented first in Prototype or Experimental RFCs. As experience is gained, these protocols may be considered for incorporation into the standard. Additional algorithms and modes approved for use in PEM in this context will be specified in successors to this document.

Acknowledgments

This specification was initially developed by the Internet Research Task Force's Privacy and Security Research Group (IRTF PSRG) and subsequently refined based on discussion in the Internet Engineering Task Force's Privacy Enhanced Mail Working Group (IETF PEM WG). John Linn contributed significantly to the predecessor of this document (RFC 1115). I would like to thank the members of the PSRG and PEM WG, as well as all participants in discussions on the "pem-dev@tis.com" mailing list, for their contributions to this document.

Table of Contents

1. Message Encryption Algorithms

This section identifies the alternative message encryption algorithms and modes that shall be used to encrypt message text and, when asymmetric key management is employed in an ENCRYPTED PEM message, for encryption of message signatures. Character string identifiers are assigned and any parameters required by the message encryption algorithm are defined for incorporation in an encapsulated "DEK- Info:" header field.

Only one alternative is currently defined in this category.

1.1 DES in CBC Mode (DES-CBC)

Message text and, if required, message signatures are encrypted using the Data Encryption Standard (DES) algorithm in the Cipher Block Chaining (CBC) mode of operation. The DES algorithm is defined in FIPS PUB 46-1 [1], and is equivalent to the Data Encryption Algorithm (DEA) provided in ANSI X3.92-1981 [2]. The CBC mode of operation of DES is defined in FIPS PUB 81 [3], and is equivalent to those provided in ANSI X3.106 [4] and in ISO IS 8372 [5]. The character string "DES-CBC" within an encapsulated PEM header field indicates the use of this algorithm/mode combination.

The input to the DES CBC encryption process shall be padded to a multiple of 8 octets, in the following manner. Let n be the length in octets of the input. Pad the input by appending 8-(n mod 8) octets to the end of the message, each having the value 8-(n mod 8), the number of octets being added. In hexadecimal, the possible paddings are: 01, 0202, 030303, 04040404, 0505050505, 060606060606, 07070707070707, and 0808080808080808. All input is padded with 1 to 8 octets to produce a multiple of 8 octets in length. The padding can be removed unambiguously after decryption.

The DES CBC encryption process requires a 64-bit cryptographic key. A new, pseudorandom key shall be generated for each ENCRYPTED PEM message. Of the 64 bits, 56 are used directly by the DES CBC process, and 8 are odd parity bits, with one parity bit occupying the right-most bit of each octet. When symmetric key management is employed, the setting and checking of odd parity bits is encouraged, since these bits could detect an error in the decryption of a DES key encrypted under a symmetric key management algorithm (e.g., DES ECB). When asymmetric key management is employed, the setting of odd parity bits is encouraged, but the checking of odd parity bits is discouraged, in order to facilitate interoperability, and since an error in the decryption of a DES key can be detected by other means (e.g., an incorrect PKCS #1 encryption-block format). In all cases, the encrypted form of a DES key shall carry all 64 bits of the key, including the 8 parity bits, though those bits may have no meaning.

The DES CBC encryption process also requires a 64-bit Initialization Vector (IV). A new, pseudorandom IV shall be generated for each ENCRYPTED PEM message. Section 4.3.1 of [7] provides rationale for this requirement, even given the fact that individual DES keys are generated for individual messages. The IV is transmitted with the message within an encapsulated PEM header field.

When this algorithm/mode combination is used for message text encryption, the "DEK-Info:" header field carries exactly two arguments. The first argument identifies the DES CBC algorithm/mode using the character string defined above. The second argument contains the IV, represented as a contiguous string of 16 ASCII hexadecimal digits.

When symmetric key management is employed with this algorithm/mode combination, a symmetrically encrypted DES key will be represented in the third argument of a "Key-Info:" header field as a contiguous string of 16 ASCII hexadecimal digits (corresponding to a 64-bit key).

To avoid any potential ambiguity regarding the ordering of the octets of a DES key that is input as a data value to another encryption process (e.g., RSAEncryption), the following holds true. The first (or left-most displayed, if one thinks in terms of a key's "print" representation) (for purposes of discussion in this document, data values are normalized in terms of their "print" representation. For an octet stream, the "first" octet would appear as the one on the "left," and the "last" octet would appear on the "right") octet of the key (i.e., bits 1-8 per FIPS PUB 46-1), when considered as a data value, has numerical weight 2^{56}. The last (or right-most displayed) octet (i.e., bits 57-64 per FIPS PUB 46-1) has numerical weight 2^{0}.

2. Message Integrity Check Algorithms

This section identifies the alternative algorithms that shall be used to compute Message Integrity Check (MIC) values for PEM messages. Character string identifiers and ASN.1 object identifiers are assigned for incorporation in encapsulated "MIC-Info:" and "Key- Info:" header fields to indicate the choice of MIC algorithm employed.

A compliant PEM implementation shall be able to process all of the alternative MIC algorithms defined here on incoming messages. It is a sender option as to which alternative is employed on an outbound message.

2.1 RSA-MD2 Message Digest Algorithm

The RSA-MD2 message digest is computed using the algorithm defined in RFC 1319 [9]. (An error has been identified in RFC 1319. The statement in the text of Section 3.2 which reads "Set C[j] to S[c xor L]" should read "Set C[j] to S[c xor L] xor C[j]." Note that the C source code in the appendix of RFC 1319 is correct.) The character string "RSA-MD2" within an encapsulated PEM header field indicates the use of this algorithm. Also, as defined in RFC 1319, the ASN.1 object identifier

```
md2 OBJECT IDENTIFIER ::= {
    iso(1) member-body(2) US(840) rsadsi(113549)
```

```
    digestAlgorithm(2) 2
  }
```

identifies this algorithm. When this object identifier is used with the ASN.1 type AlgorithmIdentifier, the parameters component of that type is the ASN.1 type NULL.

The RSA-MD2 message digest algorithm accepts as input a message of any length and produces as output a 16-octet quantity. When symmetric key management is employed, an RSA-MD2 MIC is encrypted by splitting the MIC into two 8-octet halves, independently encrypting each half, and concatenating the results.

When symmetric key management is employed with this MIC algorithm, the symmetrically encrypted MD2 message digest is represented in a the fourth argument of a "Key-Info:" header field as a contiguous string of 32 ASCII hexadecimal digits (corresponding to a 128-bit MD2 message digest).

To avoid any potential ambiguity regarding the ordering of the octets of an MD2 message digest that is input as a data value to another encryption process (e.g., RSAEncryption), the following holds true. The first (or left-most displayed, if one thinks in terms of a digest's "print" representation) octet of the digest (i.e., digest[0] as specified in RFC 1319), when considered as an RSA data value, has numerical weight 2^{120}. The last (or right-most displayed) octet (i.e., digest[15] as specified in RFC 1319) has numerical weight 2^0.

2.2 RSA-MD5 Message Digest Algorithm

The RSA-MD5 message digest is computed using the algorithm defined in RFC 1321 [10]. The character string "RSA-MD5" within an encapsulated PEM header field indicates the use of this algorithm. Also, as defined in RFC 1321, the object identifier

```
md5 OBJECT IDENTIFIER ::= {
    iso(1) member-body(2) US(840) rsadsi(113549)
    digestAlgorithm(2) 5 }
```

identifies this algorithm. When this object identifier is used with the ASN.1 type AlgorithmIdentifier, the parameters component of that type is the ASN.1 type NULL.

The RSA-MD5 message digest algorithm accepts as input a message of any length and produces as output a 16-octet quantity. When symmetric key management is employed, an RSA-MD5 MIC is encrypted by splitting the MIC into two 8-octet halves, independently encrypting each half, and concatenating the results.

When symmetric key management is employed with this MIC algorithm, the symmetrically encrypted MD5 message digest is represented in the fourth argument of a "Key-Info:" header field as a contiguous string of 32 ASCII hexadecimal digits (corresponding to a 128-bit MD5 message digest).

To avoid any potential ambiguity regarding the ordering of the octets of a MD5 message digest that is input as an RSA data value to the RSA encryption process, the following holds true. The first (or left-most displayed, if one thinks in terms of a digest's "print" representation) octet of the digest (i.e., the low-order octet of A as specified in RFC 1321), when considered as an RSA data value, has numerical weight 2^{120}. The last (or right-most displayed) octet (i.e., the high-order octet of D as specified in RFC 1321) has numerical weight 2^0.

3. Symmetric Key Management Algorithms

This section identifies the alternative algorithms and modes that shall be used when symmetric key management is employed, to encrypt data encryption keys (DEKs) and message integrity check (MIC) values. Character string identifiers are assigned for incorporation in encapsulated "Key-Info:" header fields to indicate the choice of algorithm employed.

All alternatives presently defined in this category correspond to different usage modes of the DES algorithm, rather than to other algorithms.

When symmetric key management is employed, the symmetrically encrypted DEK and MIC, carried in the third and fourth arguments of a "Key-Info:" header field, respectively, are each represented as a string of contiguous ASCII hexadecimal digits. The manner in which to use the following symmetric encryption algorithms and the length of the symmetrically encrypted DEK and MIC may vary depending on the length of the underlying DEK and MIC. Section 1, Message Encryption Algorithms, and Section 2, Message Integrity Check Algorithms, provide information on the proper manner in which a DEK and MIC, respectively, are symmetrically encrypted when the size of the DEK or MIC is not equal to the symmetric encryption algorithm's input block size. These sections also provide information on the proper format and length of the symmetrically encrypted DEK and MIC, respectively.

3.1 DES in ECB Mode (DES-ECB)

The DES algorithm in Electronic Codebook (ECB) mode [1][3] is used for DEK and MIC encryption when symmetric key management is employed. The character string "DES-ECB" within an encapsulated PEM header field indicates use of this algorithm/mode combination.

A compliant PEM implementation supporting symmetric key management shall support this algorithm/mode combination.

3.2 DES in EDE Mode (DES-EDE)

The DES algorithm in Encrypt-Decrypt-Encrypt (EDE) multiple encryption mode, as defined by ANSI X9.17 [6] for encryption and decryption with pairs of 64-bit keys, may be used for DEK and MIC encryption when symmetric key management is employed. The character string "DES-EDE" within an encapsulated PEM header field indicates use of this algorithm/mode combination.

A compliant PEM implementation supporting symmetric key management may optionally support this algorithm/mode combination.

4. Asymmetric Key Management Algorithms

This section identifies the alternative asymmetric keys and the alternative asymmetric key management algorithms with which those keys shall be used, namely the asymmetric encryption algorithms with which DEKs and MICs are encrypted, and the asymmetric signature algorithms with which certificates and certificate revocation lists (CRLs) are signed.

4.1 Asymmetric Keys

This section describes the asymmetric keys that shall be used with the asymmetric encryption algorithms and the signature algorithms described later. ASN.1 object identifiers are identified for incorporation in a public-key certificate to identify the algorithm(s) with which the accompanying public key is to be employed.

4.1.1 RSA Keys

An RSA asymmetric key pair is comprised of matching public and private keys.

An RSA public key consists of an encryption exponent e and an arithmetic modulus n, which are both public quantities typically carried in a public-key certificate. For the value of e, Annex C to X.509 suggests the use of Fermat's Number F4 (65537 decimal, or $1+2^{16}$) as a value "common to the whole environment in order to reduce transmission capacity and complexity of transformation," i.e., the value can be transmitted as 3 octets and at most seventeen (17) multiplications are required to effect exponentiation. As an alternative, the number three (3) can be employed as the value for e, requiring even less octets for transmission and yielding even faster exponentiation. For purposes of PEM, the value of e shall be either F4 or the number three (3). The use of the number three (3) for the value of e is encouraged, to permit rapid certificate validation.

An RSA private key consists of a decryption exponent d, which should be kept secret, and the arithmetic modulus n. Other values may be stored with a private key to facilitate efficient private key operations (see PKCS #1 [11]).

For purposes of PEM, the modulus n may vary in size from 508 to 1024 bits.

Two ASN.1 object identifiers have been defined to identify RSA public keys. In Annex H of X.509 [8], the object identifier

```
rsa OBJECT IDENTIFIER ::= {
    joint-iso-ccitt(2) ds(5) algorithm(8)
    encryptionAlgorithm(1) 1
}
```

is defined to identify an RSA public key. A single parameter, KeySize, the length of the public key modulus in bits, is defined for use in conjunction with this object identifier. When this object identifier is used with the ASN.1 type AlgorithmIdentifier, the parameters component of that type is the number of bits in the modulus, ASN.1 encoded as an INTEGER.

Alternatively, in PKCS #1 [11], the ASN.1 object identifier

```
rsaEncryption OBJECT IDENTIFIER ::= {
    iso(1) member-body(2) US(840) rsadsi(113549) pkcs(1)
    pkcs-1(1) 1
}
```

is defined to identify both an RSA public key and the RSAEncryption process. There are no parameters defined in conjunction with this object identifier, hence, when it is used with the ASN.1 type AlgorithmIdentifier, the parameters component of that type is the ASN.1 type NULL.

A compliant PEM implementation may optionally generate an RSA public-key certificate that identifies the enclosed RSA public key (within the SubjectPublicKeyInformation component) with either the "rsa" or the "rsaEncryption" object identifier. Use of the "rsa" object identifier is encouraged, since it is, in some sense, more generic in its identification of a key, without indicating how the key will be used. However, to facilitate interoperability, a compliant PEM implementation shall accept RSA public-key certificates that identify the enclosed RSA public key with either the "rsa" or the "rsaEncryption" object identifier. In all cases, an RSA public key identified in an RSA public-key certificate with either the "rsa" or "rsaEncryption" object identifier, shall be used according to the procedures defined below for asymmetric encryption algorithms and asymmetric signature algorithms.

4.2 Asymmetric Encryption Algorithms

This section identifies the alternative algorithms that shall be used when asymmetric key management is employed, to encrypt DEKs and MICs. Character string identifiers are assigned for incorporation in "MIC-Info:" and "Key-Info:" header fields to indicate the choice of algorithm employed.

Only one alternative is presently defined in this category.

4.2.1 RSAEncryption

The RSAEncryption public-key encryption algorithm, defined in PKCS #1 [11], is used for DEK and MIC encryption when asymmetric key management is employed. The character string "RSA" within a "MIC-Info:" or "Key-Info:" header field indicates the use of this algorithm.

All PEM implementations supporting asymmetric key management shall support this algorithm.

As described in PKCS #1, all quantities input as data values to the RSAEncryption process shall be properly justified and padded to the length of the modulus prior to the encryption process. In general, an RSAEncryption input value is formed by concatenating a leading NULL octet, a block type BT, a padding string PS, a NULL octet, and the data quantity D, that is,

RSA input value = 0x00 ‖ BT ‖ PS ‖ 0x00 ‖ D.

To prepare a DEK for RSAEncryption, the PKCS #1 "block type 02" encryption-block formatting scheme is employed. The block type BT is a single octet containing the value 0x02 and the padding string PS is one or more octets (enough octets to make the length of the complete RSA input value equal to the length of the modulus) each containing a pseudorandomly generated, non-zero value. For multiple recipient messages, a different, pseudorandom padding string should be used for each recipient. The data quantity D is the DEK itself, which is right-justified within the RSA input such that the last (or rightmost displayed, if one thinks in terms of the "print" representation) octet of the DEK is aligned with the rightmost, or least-significant, octet of the RSA input. Proceeding to the left, each of the remaining octets of the DEK, up through the first (or left-most displayed) octet, are each aligned in the next more significant octet of the RSA input.

To prepare a MIC for RSAEncryption, the PKCS #1 "block type 01" encryption-block formatting scheme is employed. The block type BT is a single octet containing the value 0x01 and the padding string PS is one or more octets (enough octets to make the length of the complete RSA input value equal to the length of the modulus) each containing the value 0xFF. The data quantity D is comprised of the MIC and the MIC algorithm identifier which are ASN.1 encoded as the following sequence.

```
SEQUENCE {
    digestAlgorithm AlgorithmIdentifier,
    digest OCTET STRING
}
```

The ASN.1 type AlgorithmIdentifier is defined in X.509 as follows.

```
AlgorithmIdentifier ::= SEQUENCE {
    algorithm OBJECT IDENTIFIER,
    parameters ANY DEFINED BY algorithm OPTIONAL
}
```

An RSA input block is encrypted using the RSA algorithm with the first (or left-most) octet taken as the most significant octet, and the last (or right-most) octet taken as the least significant octet. The resulting RSA output block is interpreted in a similar manner.

When RSAEncryption is used to encrypt a DEK, the second argument in a "MIC-Info:" header field, an asymmetrically encrypted DEK, is represented using the printable encoding technique defined in Section 4.3.2.4 of RFC 1421 [12].

When RSAEncryption is used to sign a MIC, the third argument in a "MIC-Info:" header field, an asymmetrically signed MIC, is represented using the printable encoding technique defined in Section 4.3.2.4 of RFC 1421.

4.3 Asymmetric Signature Algorithms

This section identifies the alternative algorithms which shall be used to asymmetrically sign certificates and certificate revocation lists (CRLs) in accordance with the SIGNED macro defined in Annex G of X.509. ASN.1 object identifiers are identified for incorporation in certificates and CRLs to indicate the choice of algorithm employed.

Only one alternative is presently defined in this category.

4.3.1 md2WithRSAEncryption

The md2WithRSAEncryption signature algorithm is used to sign certificates and CRLs. The algorithm is defined in PKCS #1 [11]. It combines the RSA-MD2 message digest algorithm described here in Section 2.2 with the RSAEncryption asymmetric encryption algorithm described here in Section 4.2.1. As defined in PKCS #1, the ASN.1 object identifier

```
md2WithRSAEncryption OBJECT IDENTIFIER ::= {
    iso(1) member-body(2) US(840) rsadsi(113549) pkcs(1)
    pkcs-1(1) 2
}
```

identifies this algorithm. When this object identifier is used with the ASN.1 type AlgorithmIdentifier, the parameters component of that type is the ASN.1 type NULL.

There is some ambiguity in X.509 regarding the definition of the SIGNED macro and, in particular, the representation of a signature in a certificate or a CRL. The interpretation selected for PEM requires that the data to be signed (in our case, an MD2 message digest) is first ASN.1 encoded as an OCTET STRING and the result is encrypted (in our case, using RSAEncryption) to form the signed quantity, which is then ASN.1 encoded as a BIT STRING.

5. Descriptive Grammar

```
; Addendum to PEM BNF representation, using RFC 822 notation
; Provides specification for official PEM cryptographic algo-
rithms,
; modes, identifiers and formats.
; Imports <hexchar> and <encbin> from RFC [1421]
<dekalgid> ::= "DES-CBC"
<ikalgid> ::= "DES-EDE" / "DES-ECB" / "RSA"
<sigalgid> ::= "RSA"
```

```
<micalgid> ::= "RSA-MD2" / "RSA-MD5"
<dekparameters> ::= <DESCBCparameters>
<DESCBCparameters> ::= <IV>
<IV> ::= <hexchar16>
<symencdek> ::= <DESECBencDESCBC> / <DESEDEencDESCBC>
<DESECBencDESCBC> ::= <hexchar16>
<DESEDEencDESCBC> ::= <hexchar16>
<symencmic> ::= <DESECBencRSAMD2> / <DESECBencRSAMD5>
<DESECBencRSAMD2> ::= 2*2<hexchar16>
<DESECBencRSAMD5> ::= 2*2<hexchar16>
<asymsignmic> ::= <RSAsignmic>
<RSAsignmic> ::= <encbin>
<asymencdek> ::= <RSAencdek>
<RSAencdek> ::= <encbin>
<hexchar16> ::= 16*16<hexchar>
```

References

[1] Federal Information Processing Standards Publication (FIPS PUB) 46-1, Data Encryption Standard, Reaffirmed 1988 January 22 (supersedes FIPS PUB 46, 1977 January 15).

[2] ANSI X3.92-1981, American National Standard Data Encryption Algorithm, American National Standards Institute, Approved 30 December 1980.

[3] Federal Information Processing Standards Publication (FIPS PUB) 81, DES Modes of Operation, 1980 December 2.

[4] ANSI X3.106-1983, American National Standard for Information Systems—Data Encryption Algorithm—Modes of Operation, American National Standards Institute, Approved 16 May 1983.

[5] ISO 8372, Information Processing Systems: Data Encipherment: Modes of Operation of a 64-bit Block Cipher.

[6] ANSI X9.17-1985, American National Standard, Financial Institution Key Management (Wholesale), American Bankers Association, April 4, 1985, Section 7.2.

[7] Voydock, V. L. and Kent, S. T., "Security Mechanisms in High—Level Network Protocols," ACM Computing Surveys, Vol. 15, No. 2, June 1983, pp. 135-171.

[8] CCITT Recommendation X.509, "The Directory—Authentication Framework," November 1988, (Developed in collaboration, and technically aligned, with ISO 9594-8).

[9] Kaliski, B., "The MD2 Message-Digest Algorithm," RFC 1319, RSA Laboratories, April 1992.

[10] Rivest, R., "The MD5 Message-Digest Algorithm," RFC 1321, MIT Laboratory for Computer Science and RSA Data Security, Inc., April 1992.

[11] PKCS #1: RSA Encryption Standard, Version 1.4, RSA Data Security, Inc., June 3, 1991.

[12] Linn, J., "Privacy Enhancement for Internet Electronic Mail: Part I: Message Encryption and Authentication Procedures," RFC 1421, DEC, February 1993.

[13] Kent, S., "Privacy Enhancement for Internet Electronic Mail: Part II: Certificate-Based Key Management," RFC 1422, BBN, February 1993.

[14] Kaliski, B., "Privacy Enhancement for Internet Electronic Mail: Part IV: Key Certification and Related Services," RFC 1424, RSA Laboratories, February 1993.

Patent Statement

This version of Privacy Enhanced Mail (PEM) relies on the use of patented public key encryption technology for authentication and encryption. The Internet Standards Process as defined in RFC 1310 requires a written statement from the Patent holder that a license will be made available to applicants under reasonable terms and conditions prior to approving a specification as a Proposed, Draft or Internet Standard.

The Massachusetts Institute of Technology and the Board of Trustees of the Leland Stanford Junior University have granted Public Key Partners (PKP) exclusive sub-licensing rights to the following patents issued in the United States, and all of their corresponding foreign patents:

Cryptographic Apparatus and Method ("Diffie-Hellman") ....No. 4,200,770

Public Key Cryptographic Apparatus and Method
("Hellman-Merkle")...No. 4,218,582

Cryptographic Communications System and
Method ("RSA")..No. 4,405,829

Exponential Cryptographic Apparatus and Method
("Hellman-Pohlig") ....No. 4,424,414

These patents are stated by PKP to cover all known methods of practicing the art of Public Key encryption, including the variations collectively known as ElGamal.

Public Key Partners has provided written assurance to the Internet Society that parties will be able to obtain, under reasonable, nondiscriminatory terms, the right to use the technology covered by these patents. This assurance is documented in RFC 1170 titled "Public Key Standards and Licenses." A copy of the written assurance dated April 20, 1990, may be obtained from the Internet Assigned Number Authority (IANA).

The Internet Society, Internet Architecture Board, Internet Engineering Steering Group and the Corporation for National Research Initiatives take no position on the validity or scope of the patents and patent applications, nor on the appropriateness of the terms of the assurance. The Internet Society and other groups mentioned above have not made any determination as to any other intellectual property rights which may apply to the practice of this standard. Any further consideration of these matters is the user's own responsibility.

Security Considerations

This entire document is about security.

Author's Address

David Balenson
Trusted Information Systems
3060 Washington Road
Glenwood, Maryland 21738
Phone: 301-854-6889
E-Mail: balenson@tis.com

Network Working Group
Request for Comments: 1424
February 1993

B. Kaliski
RSA Laboratories

Privacy Enhancement for Internet Electronic Mail:

Part IV
Key Certification and Related Services

Status of this Memo

This RFC specifies an IAB standards track protocol for the Internet community, and requests discussion and suggestions for improvements. Please refer to the current edition of the "IAB Official Protocol Standards" for the standardization state and status of this protocol. Distribution of this memo is unlimited.

Acknowledgments

This document is the product of many discussions at RSA Data Security, at Trusted Information Systems, and on the <pem-dev@tis.com> mailing list. Contributors include Dave Balenson, Jim Bidzos, Pat Cain, Vint Cerf, Pam Cochrane, Steve Dusse, Jeff Fassett, Craig Finseth, Jim Galvin, Mike Indovina, Bob Jueneman, Steve Kent, John Lowry, Paul McKenney, Jeff Thompson, and Charles Wu. This document is the product of the Privacy-Enhanced Electronic Mail Working Group.

1. Executive Summary

This document describes three types of service in support of Internet Privacy-Enhanced Mail (PEM) [1-3]: key certification, certificate-revocation list (CRL) storage, and CRL retrieval. Such services are among those required of an RFC 1422 [2] certification authority. Other services such as certificate revocation and certificate retrieval are left to the certification authority to define, although they may be based on the services described in this document.

Each service involves an electronic-mail request and an electronic-mail reply. The request is either an RFC 1421 [1] privacy-enhanced message or a message with a new syntax defined in this document. The new syntax follows the general RFC 1421 syntax but has a different process type, thereby distinguishing it from ordinary privacy-enhanced messages. The reply is either an RFC 1421 privacy-enhanced message, or an ordinary unstructured message.

Replies that are privacy-enhanced messages can be processed like any other privacy-enhanced message, so that the new certificate or the retrieved CRLs can be inserted into the requestor's database during normal privacy-enhanced mail processing.

Certification authorities may also require non-electronic forms of request and may return non-electronic replies. It is expected that descriptions of such forms, which are outside the scope of this document, will be available through a certification authority's "information" service.

2. Overview of Services

This section describes the three services in general terms.

The electronic-mail address to which requests are sent is left to the certification authority to specify. It is expected that certification authorities will advertise their addresses as part of an "information" service. Replies are sent to the address in the "Reply-To:" field of the request, and if that field is omitted, to the address in the "From:" field.

2.1 Key Certification

The key-certification service signs a certificate containing a specified subject name and public key. The service takes a certification request (see Section 3.1), signs a certificate constructed from the request, and returns a certification reply (see Section 3.2) containing the new certificate.

The certification request specifies the requestor's subject name and public key in the form of a self-signed certificate. The certification request contains two signatures, both computed with the requestor's private key:

1. The signature on the self-signed certificate, having the cryptographic purpose of preventing a requestor from requesting a certificate with another party's public key. (See Section 4.)

2. A signature on some encapsulated text, having the practical purpose of allowing the certification authority to construct an ordinary RFC 1421 privacy-enhanced message as a reply, with user-friendly encapsulated text. (RFC 1421 does not provide for messages with certificates but no encapsulated text; and the self- signed certificate is not "user friendly" text.) The text should be something innocuous like "Hello world!"

A requestor would typically send a certification request after generating a public-key/private-key pair, but may also do so after a change in the requestor's distinguished name.

A certification authority signs a certificate only if both signatures in the certification request are valid.

The new certificate contains the subject name and public key from the self-signed certificate, and an issuer name, serial number, validity period, and signature algorithm of the certification authority's choice. (The validity period may be derived from the self-signed certificate.) Following RFC 1422, the issuer may be any whose distinguished name is superior to the subject's distinguished name, typically the one closest to the subject. The certification authority signs the certificate with the issuer's private key, then transforms the request into a reply containing the new certificate (see Section 3.2 for details).

The certification reply includes a certification path from the new certificate to the RFC 1422 Internet certification authority. It may also include other certificates such as cross-certificates that the certification authority considers helpful to the requestor.

2.2 CRL Storage

The CRL storage service stores CRLs. The service takes a CRL-storage request (see Section 3.3) specifying the CRLs to be stored, stores the CRLs, and returns a CRL-storage reply (see Section 3.4) acknowledging the request.

The certification authority stores a CRL only if its signature and certification path are valid, following concepts in RFC 1422 (Although a certification path is not required in a CRL-storage request, it may help the certification authority validate the CRL.)

2.3 CRL Retrieval

The CRL retrieval service retrieves the latest CRLs of specified certificate issuers. The service takes a CRL-retrieval request (see Section 3.5), retrieves the latest CRLs the request specifies, and returns a CRL-retrieval reply (see Section 3.6) containing the CRLs.

There may be more than one "latest" CRL for a given issuer, if that issuer has more than one public key (see RFC 1422 for details).

The CRL-retrieval reply includes a certification path from each retrieved CRL to the RFC 1422 Internet certification authority. It may also include other certificates such as cross-certificates that the certification authority considers helpful to the requestor.

3. Syntax

This section describes the syntax of requests and replies for the three services, giving simple examples.

3.1 Certification request

A certification request is an RFC 1421 MIC-ONLY or MIC-CLEAR privacy-enhanced message containing a self-signed certificate. There is only one signer.

The fields of the self-signed certificate (which has type Certificate, as in RFC 1422) are as follows:

version is 0

serialNumber is arbitrary; the value 0 is suggested unless the certification authority specifies otherwise

signature is the algorithm by which the self-signed certificate is signed; it need not be the same as the algorithm by which the requested certificate is to be signed

issuer is the requestor's distinguished name

validity is arbitrary; the value with start and end both at 12:00 am GMT, January 1, 1970, is suggested unless the certification authority specifies otherwise

subject is the requestor's distinguished name

subjectPublicKeyInfo is the requestor's public key

The requestor's MIC encryption algorithm must be asymmetric (e.g., RSA) and the MIC algorithm must be keyless (e.g., RSA-MD2, not MAC), so that anyone can verify the signature.

Example:

```
To: cert-service@ca.domain
From: requestor@host.domain
-----BEGIN PRIVACY-ENHANCED MESSAGE-----
Proc-Type: 4,MIC-ONLY
Content-Domain: RFC822
Originator-Certificate: <requestor's self-signed certificate>
MIC-Info: RSA,RSA-MD2,<requestor's signature on text>
<text>
-----END PRIVACY-ENHANCED MESSAGE-----
```

3.2 Certification reply

A certification reply is an RFC 1421 MIC-ONLY or MIC-CLEAR privacy-enhanced message containing a new certificate, its certification path to the RFC 1422 Internet certification authority, and possibly other certificates. There is only one signer. The "MIC-Info:" field and encapsulated text are taken directly from the certification request. The reply has the same process type (MIC-ONLY or MIC-CLEAR) as the request.

Since the reply is an ordinary privacy-enhanced message, the new certificate can be inserted into the requestor's database during normal privacy-enhanced mail processing. The requestor can forward the reply to other requestors to disseminate the certificate.

Example:

```
To: requestor@host.domain
From: cert-service@ca.domain
-----BEGIN PRIVACY-ENHANCED MESSAGE-----
Proc-Type: 4,MIC-ONLY
Content-Domain: RFC822
Originator-Certificate: <requestor's new certificate>
Issuer-Certificate: <issuer's certificate>
MIC-Info: RSA,RSA-MD2,<requestor's signature on text>
<text>
-----END PRIVACY-ENHANCED MESSAGE-----
```

3.3 CRL-storage request

A CRL-storage request is an RFC 1421 CRL-type privacy-enhanced message containing the CRLs to be stored and optionally their certification paths to the RFC 1422 Internet certification authority.

Example:

```
To: cert-service@ca.domain
From: requestor@host.domain
-----BEGIN PRIVACY-ENHANCED MESSAGE-----
Proc-Type: 4,CRL
CRL: <CRL to be stored>
Originator-Certificate: <CRL issuer's certificate>
CRL: <another CRL to be stored>
Originator-Certificate: <other CRL issuer's certificate>
-----END PRIVACY-ENHANCED MESSAGE-----
```

3.4 CRL-storage reply

A CRL-storage reply is an ordinary message acknowledging the storage of CRLs. No particular syntax is specified.

3.5 CRL-retrieval request

A CRL-retrieval request is a new type of privacy-enhanced message, distinguished from RFC 1421 privacy-enhanced messages by the process type CRL-RETRIEVAL-REQUEST.

The request has two or more encapsulated header fields: the required "Proc-Type:" field and one or more "Issuer:" fields. The fields must appear in the order just described. There is no encapsulated text, so there is no blank line separating the fields from encapsulated text.

Each "Issuer:" field specifies an issuer whose latest CRL is to be retrieved. The field contains a value of type Name specifying the issuer's distinguished name. The value is encoded as in an RFC 1421 "Originator-ID-Asymmetric:" field (i.e., according to the Basic Encoding Rules, then in ASCII).

Example:

```
To: cert-service@ca.domain
From: requestor@host.domain
-----BEGIN PRIVACY-ENHANCED MESSAGE-----
Proc-Type: 4,CRL-RETRIEVAL-REQUEST
Issuer: <issuer whose latest CRL is to be retrieved>
```

```
Issuer: <another issuer whose latest CRL is to be retrieved>
-----END PRIVACY-ENHANCED MESSAGE-----
```

3.6 CRL-retrieval reply

A CRL-retrieval reply is an RFC 1421 CRL-type privacy-enhanced message containing retrieved CRLs, their certification paths to the RFC 1422 Internet certification authority, and possibly other certificates.

Since the reply is an ordinary privacy-enhanced message, the retrieved CRLs can be inserted into the requestor's database during normal privacy-enhanced mail processing. The requestor can forward the reply to other requestors to disseminate the CRLs.

Example:

```
To: requestor@host.domain
From: cert-service@ca.domain
-----BEGIN PRIVACY-ENHANCED MESSAGE-----
Proc-Type: 4,CRL
CRL: <issuer's latest CRL>
Originator-Certificate: <issuer's certificate>
CRL: <other issuer's latest CRL>
Originator-Certificate: <other issuer's certificate>
-----END PRIVACY-ENHANCED MESSAGE-----
```

Patent Statement

This version of Privacy Enhanced Mail (PEM) relies on the use of patented public key encryption technology for authentication and encryption. The Internet Standards Process as defined in RFC 1310 requires a written statement from the Patent holder that a license will be made available to applicants under reasonable terms and conditions prior to approving a specification as a Proposed, Draft or Internet Standard.

The Massachusetts Institute of Technology and the Board of Trustees of the Leland Stanford Junior University have granted Public Key Partners (PKP) exclusive sub-licensing rights to the following patents issued in the United States, and all of their corresponding foreign patents:

Cryptographic Apparatus and Method ("Diffie-Hellman") ....No. 4,200,770

Public Key Cryptographic Apparatus and Method
("Hellman-Merkle")...No. 4,218,582

Cryptographic Communications System and Method ("RSA") ....No. 4,405,829

Exponential Cryptographic Apparatus and Method

("Hellman-Pohlig") ....No. 4,424,414

These patents are stated by PKP to cover all known methods of practicing the art of Public Key encryption, including the variations collectively known as ElGamal.

Public Key Partners has provided written assurance to the Internet Society that parties will be able to obtain, under reasonable, nondiscriminatory terms, the right to use the technology covered by these patents. This assurance is documented in RFC 1170 titled "Public Key Standards and Licenses." A copy of the written assurance dated April 20, 1990, may be obtained from the Internet Assigned Number Authority (IANA).

The Internet Society, Internet Architecture Board, Internet Engineering Steering Group and the Corporation for National Research Initiatives take no position on the validity or scope of the patents and patent applications, nor on the appropriateness of the terms of the assurance. The Internet Society and other groups mentioned above have not made any determination as to any other intellectual property rights which may apply to the practice of this standard. Any further consideration of these matters is the user's own responsibility.

Security Considerations

The self-signed certificate (Section 3.1) prevents a requestor from requesting a certificate with another party's public key. Such an attack would give the requestor the minor ability to pretend to be the originator of any message signed by the other party. This attack is significant only if the requestor does not know the message being signed, and the signed part of the message does not identify the signer. The requestor would still not be able to decrypt messages intended for the other party, of course.

References

[1] Linn, J., "Privacy Enhancement for Internet Electronic Mail: Part I: Message Encryption and Authentication Procedures," RFC 1421, DEC, February 1993.

[2] Kent, S., "Privacy Enhancement for Internet Electronic Mail: Part II: Certificate-Based Key Management," RFC 1422, BBN, February 1993.

[3] Balenson, D., "Privacy Enhancement for Internet Electronic Mail: Part III: Algorithms, Modes, and Identifiers," RFC 1423, TIS, February 1993.

Author's Address

Burton S. Kaliski, Jr.
RSA Laboratories (a division of RSA Data Security, Inc.)
10 Twin Dolphin Drive
Redwood City, CA 94065
Phone: (415) 595-7703
FAX: (415) 595-4126
E-Mail: burt@rsa.com

RIPEM User's Guide

for RIPEM version 1.1
written by Mark Riordan
mrr@scss3.cl.msu.edu
June 1993

Introduction

What is RIPEM?

RIPEM (Riordan's Internet Privacy-Enhanced Mail, pronounced RYE- pehm) is a public key encryption program oriented toward use with electronic mail. It allows you to generate your own public key pairs, and to encrypt and decrypt messages based on your key and the keys of your correspondents. RIPEM is free, but each user is required to agree to a license agreement which places some limitations on its use.

This document is meant to instruct new users on the basic use of RIPEM. It does not replace the Unix man page ripem.man, also distributed with RIPEM. The man page describes all RIPEM options in reference format; some obscure options are discussed only in the man page. See also the Usenet newsgroup alt.security.ripem.

Public Key Encryption

Public key encryption, a fairly recent concept, is an encryption scheme in which messages are encrypted and decrypted with pairs of keys. One component of a user's keypair is used for encryption; the other is used for decryption. Thus, public key cryptography is sometimes referred to as asymmetric cryptography. Though both halves of the keypair are computed at the same time, neither can be derived from the other.

This arrangement allows each correspondent to publish one half of his keypair (the encryption key, public key, or public component), keeping secret only the decryption half, or private component. Users wishing to send a message to, say, Alice, simply consult a non-secret directory of public components to find Alice's public key component. They encrypt their messages to Alice using her public key. Because only Alice knows her private component, only she can decrypt any of these messages to her. And none of the users corresponding with Alice need ever have first exchanged any secret information with her.

Each user needs to keep secret only his/her own private component. Contrast this with traditional secret-key, or symmetric, cryptography. In a group of N correspondents, each user must keep track of $N-1$ secret keys. Furthermore, the total number of secret keys required for traditional cryptography is $(N)*(N-1)/2$, much larger than the N keys required by public key cryptography. Thus, public key cryptography's value lies in improved key management, especially for large numbers of correspondents. However, for the value of public key cryptography to be realized, there must be an effective way for individual users to widely advertise their public key components.

Privacy-Enhanced Mail

RIPEM provides capabilities very similar to Privacy-Enhanced Mail (PEM), as described by Internet RFC's 1113–1115. However, RIPEM lacks the concept of a certificate, a document which guarantees that you have the correct public key of a correspondent. RIPEM does implement a simple public key server, but this is much less secure than the certificate-based key management described in those RFC's. Because RIPEM does not implement certificates, it is not compliant with these Internet PEM RFC's. However, RIPEM is as compliant as is possible without implementing certificates.

As specified in the PEM RFC's, RIPEM generates a pseudo-random message key, and uses this key to encipher the message using a traditional symmetric-key encryption algorithm. In the current implementation of RIPEM, the DES (Data Encryption Standard) algorithm in one of two different modes. RIPEM then enciphers the message key using the RSA (Rivest-Shamir-Adleman) public key algorithm, and includes the enciphered message key with the message. Although the actual message text is never enciphered with a public key algorithm, the effect is the same. The advantage of this hybrid approach is performance-related: DES and other typical symmetric cryptosystems are typically thousands of times faster than public key systems.

RIPEM also "signs" the message by computing a checksum or hash function of the message plaintext, and encrypting this hash value with the sender's private key component. (Private RSA key components are usually used for decryption of messages encrypted with the public component, but in fact the reverse process also works.) Rivest's MD5 message digest algorithm is used for the hash function. This signature is verified by the recipient, to ensure that the message really was from the purported sender. The recipient computes her own message digest of the message after decrypting the message. The recipient then decrypts the encrypted message digest using the sender's public key and checks it against the recomputed digest. If the two match, the message must have been encrypted by the sender, since only the sender knows his private component.

The results of these computations—the encrypted message key, the encrypted message, the signature (encrypted hash value), and various pieces of control information—are formatted into lines of ASCII text suitable for inclusion into an electronic mail message.

About RIPEM
Platforms Supported

RIPEM runs on MS-DOS, Macintosh, OS/2, Windows NT, and a variety of Unix systems, including NeXTStep, SunOS, Sun Solaris 2.1, DEC ULTRIX, IBM AIX, HP/UX,

SGI Irix, MIPS RISC/os, Motorola System V/88, Apollo, SCO Unix, Jolitz's 386BSD, Linux, ESIX, and others. Ports to other platforms are anticipated. Some ports of RIPEM do not have all the functionality of the Unix version; in particular, some versions do not implement direct network access to the RIPEM key server.

Licensing

The source code to RIPEM itself is in the public domain. However, because RIPEM was developed using RSA Data Security's RSAREF toolkit, use of RIPEM requires an RSAREF license. A copy of this license is included in RIPEM distributions, and users of RIPEM should read this license before running the program. The author of RIPEM believes that the current RSAREF license allows free personal use of RIPEM by citizens of the United States and Canada. Commercial use is forbidden. However, this personal interpretation has no legal standing, and RIPEM users are urged to read the RSAREF license agreement themselves. Note: persons wishing to redistribute RIPEM should consider relevent U.S. Government export restrictions.

How to Obtain RIPEM

RIPEM is distributed via anonymous FTP from rsa.com. RIPEM's home base, on which the most recent version can always be found, is the site ripem.msu.edu. RIPEM is distributed via non-anonymous FTP from this site. To comply with export restrictions, cryptology-related files on this server cannot be obtained via anonymous FTP. To apply for FTP access to ripem.msu.edu, send an e-mail message to ripem@ripem.msu.edu. State your citizenship (must be USA or Canadian) and your willingness to comply with relevant export laws and software licenses. Also state the "canonical" Internet domain name of your host, and the country in which your host resides.

If you are not absolutely certain of the primary name of your host, FTP to ripem.msu.edu under user anonymous. The FTP server will inform you of your hostname. This is extremely important—experience distributing RIPEM to date has shown that many users do not know the canonical Internet hostname of their computer.

Here's a sample e-mail message you might send:

```
To: ripem@ripem.msu.edu
Subject: FTP Access to ripem.msu.edu
```

Please give me access to ripem.msu.edu. I am an American citizen, and I agree to comply with crypto export laws and RSAREF license terms. My hostname is hobbit.egr.bigu.edu. This host is located in the United States.

After you have sent your request, you'll receive a special FTP username and password by return e-mail. (There may be some delay, because I need to actually read your message before creating a username and password.) This username will work only from the hostname you specified in your message.

Once you have retrieved RIPEM, you are free to redistribute it, subject to export restrictions and RSAREF license terms. The complex distribution mechanism described above applies only to the site ripem.msu.edu, due to local site restrictions.

Caveats

Text files only. RIPEM encrypts only text-based messages; "binary" messages must be printably encoded (for instance, with uuencode) before being encrypted.

1023-character lines. The lines of text in plaintext messages processed by RIPEM must be less than 1024 characters long. (This restriction is borrowed from Internet RFC's on electronic mail and privacy-enhanced mail.)

Message size limits. Due to the nature of the RSAREF toolkit, RIPEM can encipher only messages which can fit entirely into the central memory of your computer. This is unlikely to be a problem on most workstations and larger computers, but may be a problem for some PC users. The vanilla MS-DOS version of RIPEM restricts messages to less than 48,000 characters.

Simple "filter" only. RIPEM acts only as a "filter": it simply reads an input source and produces output. RIPEM is not capable of formatting or delivering electronic mail messages. In fact, although RIPEM has some features to facilitate its use with electronic mail, it need not be used in conjunction with electronic mail at all. For use with electronic mail, RIPEM requires an external mail program; for instance, the Unix mail program.

No guarantees. As RIPEM is free software, it should not be surprising that it comes with no guarantees of any type.

Credits

RIPEM was written primarily by Mark Riordan, but nearly all of the cryptographic technology comes from the RSAREF toolkit by RSA Data Security, Inc. Much-appreciated contributions were made by Mark Henderson, Richard Outerbridge, Greg Onufer, Marc VanHeyningen, Mark Windsor, and others. The Macintosh version of RIPEM was written by Ray Lau.

Using RIPEM
Usage Overview

Using RIPEM generally requires the following steps: generating a keypair, communicating the public component of your key to correspondents, encrypting messages, and decrypting messages.

RIPEM has a bewildering array of command line options. However, most of them are not needed for ordinary use. Also, RIPEM looks at certain environment variables to determine what to do in the absence of certain command line options. Environment variables are named entities attached to your session which have values which you can set, either interactively or, more commonly, automatically at login time. For instance, a Unix user running the C Shell might include a line like

```
setenv RIPEM-SERVER-NAME ripem.msu.edu
```

in his/her .cshrc file, while an MS-DOS user would accomplish the same thing by including

```
set RIPEM-SERVER-NAME=ripem.msu.edu
```

in the AUTOEXEC.BAT file.

For discussion of individual environment variables, see the sections below and the RIPEM man pages. However, there is one environment variable of general interest: the variable RIPEM_ARGS can be given the value of options using exactly the same syntax as used in command line parameters. Conflicts between parameters specified both in RIPEM_ARGS and on the command line are resolved in favor of the command line.

Here is a quick, simplified run-through of sample RIPEM usage:

To generate a keypair, placing the public component in mypublic and the private component in mysecret:

```
ripem -g -P mypublic -S mysecret -R eks
```

Assume at this point that you have collected a number of correspondents' public components in the file bigpubkeyfile by concatenating a number of individual -P files.

To encrypt a message to recipient@bighost.edu, whose public key can be found in bigpubkeyfile, assuming my private component is in mysecret, the input message is in mymessage, and the encrypted output is to be placed in cipher.out:

```
ripem -e -r recipient@bighost.edu -p bigpubkeyfile -s mysecret
 -i mymessage -o cipher.out
```

To decrypt a message to you, reading from the file cipher.out and placing the decrypted message in the file plain.out, given my private component is in the file mysecret:

```
ripem -d -s mysecret -i cipher.out -o plain.out
```

Generating a Keypair

Before you can use RIPEM, you must generate your own keypair. To do this, you must run RIPEM with the -g (for generate) option, and specify sources of pseudo-random information that RIPEM can use to create a unique keypair for you. RIPEM can obtain pseudo-random information from the running system, from characters you type at the keyboard, from a file, and from the command line. The first two options are generally the most useful.

You must also specify two special output files: one for the public component of the keypair and one for the private component.

Because keypairs are typically left unchanged for long periods of time—a year or more—it is very important that the private component of your keypair be kept secret. For this reason, RIPEM stores private key components only in encrypted form. (The key is encrypted using DES in CBC mode, with a pseudo-random "salt" added to the key.) When generating a keypair, RIPEM asks you for a key to be used to encrypt the private key component. This secondary key will be needed whenever you use RIPEM subsequently. It is critical that this key-to-a-key be chosen carefully, and that you remember it. If you forget the key to your private key component, your public key is worthless and unusable. The key to your private key can be up to 255 characters long. (This length limitation is an arbitrary implementation detail; RIPEM takes a hash function of the password you type before actually using it to encrypt the private component.)

A typical invocation of RIPEM to generate a keypair is:

```
ripem -g -u fred@snark.edu -P mypublickey -S mysecretkey -R eks
```

This call requests RIPEM to generate a keypair (-g). It identifies you (-u) as fred@snark.edu; this information is placed in the output files. The public component (-P) is placed in the file mypublickey. The private (or secret) component (-S) is placed in the file mysecretkey. RIPEM will prompt you (twice) for an encryption password before writing to this file. The -R eks option means that to obtain a pseudo-random data for key generation, RIPEM will use the entire command line, will prompt you at the keyboard for a pseudo-random string, and will also query the system for pseudo-random information before generating the keypair.

RIPEM identifies your key by your electronic mail address, which is specified by the -u option. If you omit the -u option, RIPEM will attempt to determine your e-mail address by taking the value of the environment variable RIPEM_USER_NAME or, if that is not present, by querying the running system. It is best to identify your key in a form that others will be able to use as an e-mail address. For instance, in the above example, fred@snark.edu is a better key identifier than just fred, because it is more readily used by correspondents on other hosts. If your host is known on the network by several different names, or if you ordinarily use several different computers interchangeably, it may be safer to explicitly specify your e-mail address to RIPEM, rather than have it to figure out the address from the running system.

By default, RIPEM generates keypairs roughly 516 bits in size. The author of RIPEM believes that this size is more than adequate for most purposes. However, the -b parameter is available for users who wish to generate larger keys. Specify - b bitsize to generate a key of size bitsize bits; bitsize must be between 512 and 1024, inclusive. Large keys are slower to generate as well as to subsequently use for encryption.

Generating a keypair is much slower than encryption or decryption. On a 386 PC-class computer, be prepared to wait several minutes for the key generation to complete.

Note that the first several bytes of all RIPEM keys are the same. This is due to RIPEM's use of OSI Distinguished Encoding Rules and associated key identifying strings to encode keys. It does not mean that the public keys generated are numerically similar.

Managing Keys

Once you have generated a keypair, you must publicize the public component so that others can use it to send messages to you. Also, you must obtain access to the keys of other users. Key distribution can be by:

- Internet key server (requires Internet access for key lookup, but not for publication)
- The finger protocol (requires Internet access for key lookup and publication)
- Flat files (can be used with little or no network access)

You can choose the techniques that RIPEM uses to find a key by setting the -Y command line option. The -Y option takes an argument which is a string of one or more of the characters s, g, and f, which stand for Server, finGer, and File. For each correspondent, when necessary, RIPEM will attempt to learn the correspondent's public key by consulting these sources in the order specified until the key is obtained.

The default value of the -Y option is "sf," which means that RIPEM first attempts to look up a public key via an Internet key server. If it is unsuccessful, it attempts to look up the key in a flat file. Read the discussion below for details on other related command line options.

Key Distribution via the RIPEM Internet Key Server
Key Server Description and Limitations

If you have Internet access, you can communicate your key to others by registering the key on an Internet RIPEM key server. Currently, there is an "experimental" RIPEM key server running on the host ripem.msu.edu. This host is experimental in that it is an unofficial service which may have to be terminated with little or no advance notice.

This RIPEM key server acts as a central repository for public keys, saving users the effort of distributing their keys individually to all potential correspondents. This key server is not an especially secure mechanism. The level of security present in the key protocols is much less than that provided, for instance, by the Privacy Enhanced Mail certificate mechanism specified in the Internet PEM RFC's. The authenticity of keys maintained on the server is not guaranteed. The RIPEM key server is simply a means for RIPEM users to conveniently exchange keys.

Registering a Key via the Key Server

To allow the maximum number of users to publicize their keys via this mechanism, the RIPEM key server accepts key registration requests by electronic mail. Although the RIPEM key server itself is connected only to the Internet, users of non-Internet networks such as CompuServe, BITNET, and so on can register their keys by sending their key registration requests via an appropriate network gateway.

To register your key, send the public component (the output file from the -P option) to the e-mail address

```
ripem-register-keys@ripem.msu.edu
```

On a Unix system, for instance, you can register your key by a command like:

```
mail ripem-register-keys@ripem.msu.edu <mypublickey
```

The key server will register your public key in its database and will send you a confirming message. The key is identified by the e-mail address specified during the generation of the key, but the confirming message is sent to the address from which the key file was sent.

If you read electronic mail on several different hosts but wish to use the same public key on all of them, you can register the key under multiple names. You can do this by editing the key file before sending it to the server, and adding additional User: lines. (See the separate document on file formats.) Or, you can register the key under different names via separate e-mail messages.

To subsequently delete your key from the server, encrypt a message starting with the string

```
RemoveKey
```

with the -m mic-only command line option and send the encrypted message to the address:

```
ripem-remove-keys@ripem.msu.edu
```

The message must have been encrypted by the owner of the key being removed.

To change your key on the server, generate a new keypair and encrypt the public component (the file from RIPEM's -P option) with the -m mic-only command line option. Send the result to the address:

```
ripem-change-keys@ripem.msu.edu
```

The message must have been encrypted by the owner of the key being changed.

Obtaining Keys from the Key Server: Live Access

Real-time "live" queries to the RIPEM key server are made directly by RIPEM using the UDP IP network protocol. "Live" queries are possible if your computer is connected to the Internet, your copy of RIPEM has been compiled for network access, and your computer is running the right network software. This is often true of Unix computers but is generally not true of other computers. At this writing, for instance, the MS-DOS version of RIPEM supports only the PC/TCP network software from FTP Software, Inc.

In order to access the key server, RIPEM needs to know its Internet address. You can tell RIPEM the address of the server in two ways: you can set the environment variable RIPEM-SERVER-NAME to the name of the server, or you can specify the server name with the -y command line option. In either case, you can specify more than one server name, separating the server names with commas (and no blank spaces). If you specify a list of server names in this way, when querying servers RIPEM will query the servers in the order listed until it obtains the desired public key, or exhausts the list.

Obtaining Keys from the Key Server: E-mail-Only Access

For users for whom live UDP network access to the RIPEM key server is not possible or not feasible, electronic mail access to the key server has been implemented. To obtain a copy of the complete database of registered RIPEM keys via e-mail, send a message to the address:

```
ripem-get-keys@ripem.msu.edu
```

The subject and content of the message are ignored by the server, and hence can be left blank.

The return e-mail message will contain a flat file of public keys, readable directly by RIPEM. This same file can be gotten by anonymous FTP to the host ripem.msu.edu. This file can be used as described below in the section discussing flat files.

Key Distribution via the Internet Finger Program

Another means of distributing keys over the Internet is via the finger mechanism. Finger is a simple protocol which allows a user to publish personal information that can be accessed across a TCP/IP network. For the most part, only Unix users can publish their keys using this mechanism. The advantage of finger over a RIPEM key server is that it relies only upon the correct operation of the sender's and receiver's computers, and upon the link between them. If the RIPEM key server is unavailable due to hardware, networking, or human errors, finger will be a more reliable choice. In general, though, key lookup using finger is slower than the RIPEM key server.

To set up your Unix account to give out your public key, include your public component in a file named .plan, located in your home directory. Your computer must be set up to run the fingerd finger daemon, which is normally the case on most Unix computers. Your computer must be up and running on the network for a correspondent to be able to access your key via the finger mechanism.

In no case do you need the finger program itself; RIPEM contains its own implementation of the finger protocol sufficient for the purpose of looking up keys. Hence, in some cases you can use the finger mechanism to look up someone else's key even if you are unable to publish your own key via finger due to the lack of a fingerd server program on your computer. For instance, an MS-DOS version of RIPEM is available that can look up keys via finger on PC's running the PC/TCP network implementation from FTP Software, Inc.

Aside from the -Y g command line option, there are no RIPEM command line options specific to the use of the finger mechanism.

Key Distribution via Flat Files

The key files generated by the -g option are ordinary text files formatted in such a way that a database of public keys can be created simply concatenating a collection of separate public key files. RIPEM is capable of scanning such flat files. It looks up a user's key based upon e-mail address, so there is no ambiguity even if a flat file of keys contains keys for a large number of individuals from different sites.

The best way of obtaining a flat file containing keys is from the RIPEM key server, via e-mail or FTP as described above.

When RIPEM uses a flat key for public key lookup, it determines the file's name in one of three ways:

- By using the value of the -p (for public key component) command line argument. If you specify -p mypubfile on the RIPEM command line, RIPEM will use mypubfile as the flat file of public keys.

- In the absence of -p, by using the value of the RIPEM_PUBLIC_KEY_FILE environment variable.

- If neither of the above is specified, by using a default file name. On Unix systems, this file name is the fixed name /usr/local/etc/rpubkeys. On MS-DOS systems, it is the name \RIPEMPUB.

It is possible to specify multiple public key files by specifying the -p option more than once. This allows you, for instance, to specify a common key file shared by a group of people, plus a separate key file for your personal correspondents.

Automatic Key Distribution via RIPEM Headers

One final way of distributing your public key component is automatic: RIPEM includes your public key in the PEM headers inside every message you encrypt. RIPEM takes advantage of this fact when deciphering, as follows:

When you are deciphering a message, RIPEM needs to find the sender's public component in order to verify the signature on the message. If RIPEM cannot find the public key of the sender via the mechanisms described above, it resorts to looking in the PEM headers that immediately precede the ciphertext in any RIPEM-enciphered message. If RIPEM finds the sender's public component in the header, it will use this key in attempting to verify the signature. It will also issue a warning message, since if the message is fake, the key inside the message is probably fake as well.

If RIPEM does not find the sender's key, it exits with an error message.

If the -P option has been specified, RIPEM, under these conditions, will append the sender's public key to the file specified by -P. You should be cautious about trusting keys obtained in this manner.

Managing Private Key Components

Unlike public key components, private key components are stored in flat files only. Typically, a given user will have only one RIPEM key, and its private component will be kept by itself in the file originally specified by the -S option during key generation.

During encryption and decryption, RIPEM will need to consult this file to determine your private key component. RIPEM determines the file's name in one of three ways:

- By using the value of the -s (for secret key component) command line argument. If you specify -s myprivatekey on the RIPEM command line, RIPEM will use myprivatekey as the flat file of private keys.
- In the absence of -s, by using the value of the RIPEM_PRIVATE_KEYFILE environment variable.
- If neither of the above is specified, by using a default file name. On Unix systems, this file name is the fixed name .ripemprv in your home directory. On MS-DOS systems, it is the name \RIPEMPRV.

Because the private key component file generated by ripem -g identifies your key by your e-mail address, it is possible to create a database of private keys by concatenating the -S files created by RIPEM. RIPEM uses only the private component that corresponds to your currently-specified e-mail address. This may be useful if, for some reason, you wish to maintain multiple public keys, identified by different e-mail aliases. Also, because the private key components are encrypted, it is possible to maintain a publicly accessible file of private key components without great loss of security. However, it is generally best for each user to have exactly one public key, and for its private component to be kept in its own file, reasonably secured against access by others.

Changing the Key to Your Private Key

You can change the key to your private component by using the -c option. This tells RIPEM to read your current private key file, decrypt it with your current key, prompt you for a new key, reencrypt your private component with the new key-to-the-key, and write out a new private component file. The old private key file is specified as described above. The modified private key file to be created is specified via the -S option. Thus, the sequence:

```
$ ripem -c -s mysecret -S newsecret
```

```
Enter password to private key:
Enter new password to private key:
Enter again to verify:
```

reads the encrypted private key from mysecret and creates a new file, newsecret, with the same private component encrypted with a new key.

Note that the -c option changes neither the private component nor the public component of your public key. If you believe that the key to your private component has been compromised, it is probably better to change your public key (by creating a new one) than to simply change the key to your private key.

Encrypting a Message

The -e option specifies that RIPEM is encrypting a message.

In encryption mode, RIPEM understands the -u, -p, -s, -y, -Y, and -R options described above. The following options are also important:

Specifying Input and Output Files (-i and -o)

By default, RIPEM reads its input from standard input, and writes its output on standard output. If standard input and output are files, this is written as <infile and >outfile on most systems. Alternatively, an input file can be specified via the -i option, and an output file via the -o option: -i infile -o outfile.

Specifying Recipients and Processing Mail Headers (-r and -h)

The recipient(s) of a message can be specified in two ways: on the command line, or via message headers in the input plaintext.

To specify recipients explicitly on the command line, use the -r option: -r recipient_addr. Recipient_addr must be the recipient's e-mail address, in a form which RIPEM can use to look up the recipient's public key. For instance, suppose your recipient has valid e-mail addresses bob@egr.biguniv.edu and bob@biguniv.BIT-NET. If Bob has registered his RIPEM public key only as bob@egr.biguniv.edu, then the address bob@biguniv.BITNET will not be adequate for RIPEM's purposes, even if it is a valid e-mail address.

The -r option can be used multiple times for multiple recipients.

If the message plaintext has been prepared by a mail program, it may already contain mail headers which state the recipients' e-mail addresses in "To:" and "cc:" lines. To take advantage of this situation, you can use the -h option. The -h option tells RIPEM how to handle plaintext input that contains mail headers. "Mail headers" are defined to be all the lines at the beginning of a message, up to the first blank line.

The syntax is: -h header_opts, where header_opts is one or more of the letters i, p, and r. i tells RIPEM to include the headers as part of the message to be encrypted. p tells RIPEM to prepend the headers to the encrypted output. r tells RIPEM to examine the message headers, looking for "To:" and "cc:" lines. Any recipients named on those lines are included as recipients to RIPEM's encryption.

The default is "-h i," which causes message headers to be included in the plaintext being encrypted, but no other header processing is done. This is equivalent to treating the message as if it does not contain mail headers at all.

A useful combination is "-h pr," which extracts recipients' names from the mail headers at the beginning of the input, copies the mail headers unmodified and unencrypted to the beginning of the output, and then discards the headers before encrypting the rest of the message. This combination is suitable for instances if RIPEM is being used to encrypt a message after it has been prepared by a mail program but before it has been sent.

Decrypting a Message

The -d option specifies that RIPEM is decrypting a message.

During decryption, RIPEM looks at the values of the -i, -o, -u, -p, -s, -P, -y, and -Y options discussed above.

If RIPEM cannot decrypt the input message, or if the input message fails the signature check, RIPEM will generate no output in the -o file or on standard output. Instead, it will issue an error message on the standard error device, which is usually your terminal. In addition, RIPEM returns a value of zero to the operating system if the message decrypts properly, and it returns a non-zero value if there are problems. This is typical behavior for programs under Unix and MS-DOS and allows you to write command scripts which check to see whether decryption proceeded properly.

If RIPEM does decrypt the message properly, it will write the decrypted plaintext to the -o file or to standard output. The output contains only the original plaintext (subject to any modifications performed by the -h option used by the sender of the message). It does not include any mail headers or other superfluous text added to the encrypted message—for instance, by a mail system—after the encryption.

Advanced Usage

Specifying Encryption Algorithm (-A)

By default, RIPEM encrypts messages using DES in Cipher Block Chaining (CBC) mode. This is the data encryption algorithm and mode used by Internet PEM-conformant software.

Although DES has proven quite resistant to theoretical attacks of cryptanalysts for 16 years, many cryptologists have expressed concern over DES's relatively small keyspace, which leaves it potentially vulnerable to brute-force attack by a well-funded opponent. (DES keys are 56 bits long.) One obvious solution to the keyspace problem is to use multiple passes of DES.

A few years ago, IBM suggested a particular multi-pass usage of DES called Encrypt-Decrypt-Encrypt (EDE). In EDE usage (sometimes called Triple-DES), each 64-bit block is encrypted with a 56-bit key we'll call key1. The result of that encryption is decrypted with a second 56-bit key called key2. Finally, the 64-bit result of that decryption is encrypted with key1. This use of DES results in a dramatic increase of keyspace from 2^{56} keys to 2^{112} keys.

RIPEM implements this use of DES, with Cipher Block Chaining applied after each triple encryption, and refers to it as DES- EDE-CBC. When encrypting, specify -A des-ede-cbc to select this mode. When decrypting, RIPEM automatically detects the encryption algorithm used and decrypts appropriately.

DES-EDE has not been widely adopted by the cryptographic community. In particular, DES-EDE encryption is not conformant with Internet PEM as of this writing. Therefore, use the default mode (which can also be explicitly requested via -A des-cbc) for all but your most critical messages. In addition, consider that there is some performance degradation associated with Triple-DES.

Specifying Debug Mode (-D and -Z)

Users experiencing problems with RIPEM, or simply wishing to examine the inner workings of the program, can use the -D option to cause RIPEM to print informative messages while it executes. Debugging options were originally implemented in RIPEM for development purposes, but have been left in place for the benefit of curious users. Specify -D debuglevel to turn on debug messages. Debuglevel is an integer specifying the amount of debug output desired. 0 specifies no debug output, while 4 is the maximum value currently implemented.

Debug messages are normally written to the standard error output, which is usually your terminal screen. To write debug messages to a file, use the -Z debug-file option.

Specifying Encryption Mode (-m)

By default, in encryption (-e) mode RIPEM encrypts a message, encodes it to printable ASCII characters, and signs the message. This processing corresponds to the -m encrypted command line option. With non-default values for the -m option, RIPEM can perform other types of processing in -e mode.

-m mic-clear specifies that the message is signed, but not encrypted. The body of the message is left in plaintext, so that the recipient can read it without decryption software of any sort. If the recipient wishes to verify the signature, however, he/she will have to use RIPEM in -d mode as usual.

-m mic-only also specifies that the message is signed, but not encrypted. However, the body of the message is printably encoded into ASCII characters as per RFC 1113. This encoding expands the size of the message by about 33% and adds no security; it simply helps guarantee that the message will survive hostile mail software verbatim. In practice, mic-only mode is infrequently used.

Specifying Your Username (E-mail Address) (-u)

As described above, you can specify your username (or more correctly, your e-mail address) via the -u option or via the environment variable IPEM_USER_NAME. The default is for RIPEM to attempt to determine your e-mail address from the running system.

RIPEM makes use of this information in all three modes: key generation, encryption, and decryption. If you have a number of e-mail addresses that you wish to be regarded as equivalent, you can specify your username as a list of comma-separated e-mail addresses. During key generation and encryption, RIPEM will use the first name in the list as your username. During decryption, RIPEM will search your private key file for your private component under each one of the comma-separated names until it succeeds in finding a matching key in the file.

These features make it easier to use RIPEM if you have mail forwarded to a primary mail account from a number of other e-mail addresses. To make use of the multiple username capability, you must edit your private key file to include multiple User: lines.

Specifying the Key to Your Private Component (-k)

By default, RIPEM prompts you interactively when it needs to know the key to the private component of your public key. However, with some loss in security, it is possible to inform RIPEM of this key by other means. This capability may be useful for instances when RIPEM is invoked by another program, or for when you are testing or benchmarking.

You can specify the key to your private key via the -k option; specify -k keytokey on the command line. As a special case, you can specify -k-. Specifying - as your password on the command line causes RIPEM to read the password as the first line from standard input.

If -k is not specified, RIPEM will check the value of the environment variable RIPEM_KEY_TO_PRIVATE_KEY. If this variable exists and has a non-null value, its value will be used as the key to the private key; otherwise, RIPEM will prompt you on your terminal for this key.

Specifying the key to your private key via -k or via the environment variable is generally less secure than typing it interactively. Although RIPEM erases its command line arguments shortly after startup, there is a brief window of time during which other users on a Unix system could view your command line arguments by using the ps command. Likewise, other users could determine the value of your RIPEM_KEY_TO_PRIVATE_KEY variable by various means, especially if they had physical access to your terminal. Therefore, these options should be used with caution, if at all.

Using UNIX Mail Programs and Utilities

This section suggests techniques for using RIPEM in conjunction with popular Unix mail programs. Use of the C-Shell is assumed.

It is possible, of course, to compose a message in a text editor, save the message to a file, run RIPEM to encrypt the message, start your mailer, insert the encrypted file into a message, and then send the message. In fact, the encryption and mailing can be done on separate systems, with appropriate file transfers. However, on most Unix systems it is possible to eliminate several of these tedious steps.

Setting Up Your Environment

It is recommended that Internet-connected Unix users include the following in their .cshrc file:

```
setenv RIPEM_SERVER_NAME    ripem.msu.edu
setenv RIPEM_PRIVATE_KEY_FILE ~/.ripemprv
setenv RIPEM_PUBLIC_KEY_FILE ~/ripempub
setenv RIPEM_USER_NAME    (Your email address; e.g.,
smith@bigu.edu)
```

Create a shell script to encrypt RIPEM messages. Place the following lines in a file named ripem-encrypt, put this file in a directory mentioned in your path, and give it execute permission. (This file is available in the RIPEM distribution, in the util directory.)

```
#!/bin/sh
tempfile=/tmp/msg_`whoami`
ripem -e -h pr -i $1 -o $tempfile
cp $tempfile $1
rm $tempfile
```

Create a shell script to decrypt RIPEM messages. As above, place these lines in the file ripemd:

```
ripem -d | more
```

Create a shell script to help reply to encrypted RIPEM messages. Place this in ripemr:

```
ripem -d -h pr | quote -h
```

Include the following lines in the file .mailrc in your home directory. (A sample .mailrc can be found in the RIPEM distribution, in the util directory.)

```
set editheaders
set EDITOR=ripem-encrypt
```

Creating a RIPEM Public Key

The initial generation of keys can procede something like this:

```
cd ~
ripem -g -S .ripemprv -P ripempub -R eks
```

Type random garbage at the keyboard when prompted.
Type in a secret password when prompted for the password to your private key.
Type it again when prompted for verification.
Now register the key:

```
mail ripem-register-keys@ripem.msu.edu <ripempub
```

Encrypting an E-mail Message Using "mail"

If you are using the "mail" package that comes with many Unix systems, you can use the following procedure to compose, encrypt, and send a message. In this example, your input is in bold.

```
$ mail smith@bigu.edu
Subject: Greetings
This is a test message
~e
Enter password to private key: (Type your password here.)
(Type Control-D)
$
```

The ~e command to mail was originally designed to edit the message being composed. Nowadays, however, it is rarely used (in favor of the ~v visual edit command). The tricks described above effectively turn ~e into an "encrypt" command on SunOS and some other Unix systems. On some Unix systems, however, the mail command does not interpret the editheaders option. On those systems, you need to use a different approach, which requires you to type the recipient's address twice:

```
$ mail smith@bigu.edu
Subject: Greetings
This is a test message
~| ripem -e -r smith@bigu.edu
Enter password to private key: (Type your password here.)
(continue)
(Type Control-D)
$
```

Decrypting an E-mail Message Using "mail"

```
$ mail
Mail version ......
"/usr/spool/mail/jones": 1 message 1 new
>N 1 smith@bigu.edu   Wed Sep 30 22:38 29/1119
Greetings
& pipe ripemd
Pipe to: "ripemd"
Enter password to private key: (Type your password here.)
(The plaintext message is displayed.)
"ripemd" 29/1119
& q
$
```

Encrypting an E-mail Message Using "Mush"

Mush is a mail package that is compatible with mail, but provides additional capabilities. The procedure described above for encrypting messages with mail also works with mush.

Decrypting an E-mail Message Using "Mush"

The procedures described for mail also work with mush. However, mush's greater power allows you to configure it to be easier to use than mail, especialy in curses mode. Configure mush by creating a file named .mushrc in your home directory and placing the following lines in it:

```
set edit_hdrs
set editor=/home/scss3/mrr/bin/ripem-encrypt
set visual=/usr/ucb/vi
bind-macro D :pipe ripemd\n
bind-macro R r~f\n~\|ripemr\n~v\n
```

To decrypt and display a message in curses mode, simply type the letter D while the cursor is positioned on the corresponding message index line:

```
56 U Mark Riordan <mrr@cl-next Nov 3, (13/460) "test"
(press D)
:pipe ripemd (This is generated automatically by the mush
macro.)
Enter password to private key: (Type the password.)
```

```
(The plaintext is displayed.)
56 Mark Riordan <mrr@cl-next Nov 3, (13/460) "test"

    mrr 56: ...continue...
```

To reply to an encrypted message, type R while the cursor is positioned on the corresponding message line. The R macro decrypts the message, quotes the text of the message with the traditional "> " line prefix, and enters a visual editor. For this procedure to work, you must have compiled the quote program—located in the ripem/util directory—and installed it in a directory on your path.

```
56 U Mark Riordan <mrr@cl-next Nov 3, (13/460) "test"
(press R)
To: mrr@museum.cl.msu.edu
Subject: Re: test 5
~f
Including message 56 ... (30 lines)
(continue editing letter)
~|ripemr (All of this is generated automatically by the
macro.)
Enter password to private key: (Type the password, to decrypt
the message.)
(Mush calls up a visual editor on a quoted copy of the plain-
text of the message to you. Compose your reply and exit the edi-
tor. To exit vi, for instance, type ZZ.)
(continue editing letter)
~e  (Type this to encrypt your reply)
Enter password to private key: (Type the password, to encrypt
your reply.)
(continue editing letter)
(Type control-D to finish the outgoing letter and have mush
send it.)
```

Using RIPEM with ELM's MIME Features

The popular Unix mailer Elm has recently been extended to provide MIME (Multipurpose Internet Mail Extension) capabilities. (MIME is not particular to Elm, and MIME support is or will soon be available in other mailers as well.) RIPEM can be used with Elm's MIME support, though somewhat awkwardly. Below are preliminary instructions for interfacing RIPEM with Elm.

Edit your local or system mailcap file to add the following lines:

```
# This entry is for reading a mail message encoded by RIPEM
application/ripem;   ripem -d ; copiousoutput
```

This is necessary only on the receiving end.
On the sending end:

- Compose the message and encode it, saving the result in a temporary file, say, mymsg.
- Start the mail message in Elm and include the temporary file as a MIME message with a line of the form: [include mymsg application/ripem]
- Send the message.

Upon receipt, Elm will recognize it as a MIME message and start RIPEM to decode it. If the receiving mailer does not understand MIME, the usual methods of decrypting RIPEM messages can be used.

Using RIPEM with the MH Mailer

The RIPEM source distribution contains two Perl scripts that facilitate reading and sending encrypted messages with RIPEM. display-ripem decrypts and displays RIPEM messages; send-ripem encrypts and sends messages. These utilities, written by Marc VanHeyningen, can be found in the ripem/util directory. See the source code for documentation.

Using RIPEM with EMACS

Jeff Thompson has written functions for the powerful EMACS editor to facilitate use of RIPEM. These functions are in the file ripem/util/ripem.el in the RIPEM source distribution. To enable the use of these functions, edit your ~/.emacs file and add to it a line like:

```
(load "/home/local/ripem/util/emacs/ripem.el")
```

(Modify the file name in quotes to be the correct path to the ripem.el file.)
To encrypt a message, enter the message, including the To: and
cc: lines, into an EMACS buffer and type:

```
Esc x ripem-encrypt
```

To decrypt a message, load it into an EMACS buffer and type:

```
Esc x ripem-receive
```

Online help is available by typing:

```
Ctrl-h f function-name
```

where function-name is one of: ripem-encrypt, ripem-sign, ripem-receive, or ripem-list-users.

RIPEM(1)   UNIX Programmer's Manual   RIPEM(1)

Name

ripem - RSAREF-based Internet Privacy Enhanced Mail, version 1.1.
Enciphers and deciphers messages using a public key encryption system,
and formats them for embedding in electronic mail messages. Also generates
RSA public keys.

Synopsis

ripem { -e | -d | -g | -c }
[-r recipient(s)] [-b # of bits] [-A enc-alg]
[-m { encrypted | mic-only | mic-clear }]
[-u myusername] [-h ipr] [-T amn]
[-p publickey infile] [-s privatekey infile]
[-k {key to private key\-}]
[-P publickey outfile] [-S privatekey outfile]
[-y pub key server name] [-Y fs]
[-i infile] [-o outfile]
[-D debug level] [-Z debug file]
[-R cfkms] [-F random file] [-C random string]
<in >out

Options

-e (encipher) means apply the transformations specified by the "-m" option
to the input, writing to output an encapsulated message suitable for inclusion in an electronic mail message.

-d (decipher) means produce plaintext from the input file, which is expected
to contain an encapsulated PEM-style message. Depending upon the headers
in the message, this may not actually require decryption. Also check the
message signature, if present.

-g (generate) means generate an RSA key. The private component will be
written to the file specified by the "- S" option. The public component will
be written to the file specified by the "-P" option. Take care not to accidentally overwrite your public key database. Note: key generation can be a time-
consuming process.

-c (change) means change the key to your private key. The reencrypted private componenet will be written to the file specified by the "-S" option. The
public component is not touched.

-r (recipient) specifies the user to whom the message is being sent. Used only
with the "-e" option. The recipient name is usually specified as a complete
e-mail address. The recipient name is used to lookup the recipient's public

key component. Multiple recipients can be specified, each with a separate "-r" option.

-b (bits) specifies the number of bits desired in the public key being created. Used only with the "-g" option. Must be in the range 508 to 1024. The default is a pseudo-random number of bits between 512 and 523.

-A (Algorithm) specifies the data encryption algorithm. Used only with "-e." The legal values are "des-cbc," which is the default well-known DES in Cipher Block Chaining mode, and "des-ede-cbc." The latter specifies Encrypt-Decrypt-Encrypt "Triple-DES" as suggested by IBM a few years ago. Each 64-bit block is enciphered with one 56-bit key, deciphered with a second 56-bit key, and enciphered again with the first 56-bit key. Cipher Block Chaining is applied only after all three operations have been done. The result is effectively a 112-bit key, much more difficult to exhaustively search than single-DES.

Note that EDE-CBC mode is not widely used, and that there is even some disagreement as to just what crypto-graphic operations should be implied by this appellation. Use EDE-CBC mode only when data security is much more important than compatibility, as EDE-CBC is not yet a PEM standard.

-R (random) specifies the source(s) of pseudo-random input used by RIPEM to generate message keys, initialization vectors, and RSA keys. Used only with the "-e" and "- g" options. Following -R must be a string of option letters selected from below:

c

(command) means use information from the command-line "-C" option.

e

(entire) means use information from the entire command line.

f

(file) means read information from a file; see the "-F" option.

k

(keyboard) means prompt the user for a string typed at the keyboard.

m

(message) means take characters from the input plaintext message as pseudo-random input. (For -e only.)

s

(system) means query the system for system-dependent information. The type and "randomness" of this information depend upon both the specific computer and the port of RIPEM that you are using.

Default is "efms," but command line and file data are not used if the "-C" and "-F" arguments are not present.

-m (mode) specifies the mode of the outgoing encrypted message. Used only with the "-e" option.

"encrypted" specifies that the message is to be encrypted using DES in CBC mode, and that the message is to be "signed" computing a message digest of the input message, encrypting the digest with the sender's private key, and including the result in the outgoing message. The encrypted text of the message is encoded in RFC 1113 printable form and included in the output. (RFC 1113 printable form is similar to the well-known "uuencoding" format, but differs in a few details.) The MD5 message digest is always used upon output, but incoming messages using the MD2 algorithm can be processed correctly.

"mic-only" specifies that the message is to be signed as described above, but not encrypted. The text of the message is encoded in RFC 1113 form. This option provides authentication but no confidentiality.

"mic-clear" specifies that the message is to be signed as described above. The text of the message is neither encrypted nor printably encoded, so the text of the message can be read by anyone with any standard mail program.

-h (header) specifies options for enciphering messages that contain mail headers. Used only with the "-e" option. Following -h must be a string of option letters selected from below:

i

(include) means include the message headers as part of the plaintext message—that is, encipher them.

p

(prepend) means place the unenciphered message headers at the beginning of the enciphered output, before the first Privacy Enhanced Message Boundary. This option is useful when using RIPEM as a filter for messages that will be fed directly to a mailer.

r

(recipients) means scan the message headers for "To:" and "cc:" lines, and add these recipients to the recipient list.

-T (recipienT options) specifies options related to the processing of recipients. Following -T must be a string of option letters selected from below:

a

(abort) specifies that RIPEM should unconditionally abort if, while in -e mode, it is unable to find the public key of one or more recipients. The default is to prompt the user for what to do.

m

(me) specifies that RIPEM should include the user as a recipient if encrypting in "-m encrypted" mode.

n

(none) specifies that RIPEM should clear the conditions that would be specified by "a" and "m" above.

-k (key) specifies the key used to encrypt the RSA private key that resides in the file referenced by the "-s" option. If the "-k" option is not used, RIPEM looks for a non-empty environment variable named "RIPEM KEY TO PRIVATE KEY"; if it is found, its value is used as the key to decrypt the private component of the user's public key. If neither the "-k" option nor the environment variable can be found, RIPEM prompts the user interactively for the private key. Use of the "-k" option on a multiuser system is discouraged, as it increases the chances that another user can discover the key to your private key.

As a special case, if the key is specified as "-" RIPEM will read the first line from standard input and use it as the key the the private key. This capability is intended for use by programs that invoke RIPEM.

-s (secret key) specifies the file containing the secret (or private) component of the RSA public key. Read when the "-d" or "-e" options are used. If -s is not specified, the program looks for an environment vari- able named RIPEM PRIVATE KEY FILE; if found, its value is used as the file name; otherwise, the name defaults to "~/.ripemprv" for Unix or "RIPEMPRV" for MS-DOS.

-p (public key) specifies a file containing the public components of users' RSA public keys, indexed by user name. Read when the "-e" or "-d" options are used. If -p is not specified, the program looks for an environment variable named RIPEM PUBLIC KEY FILE; if found, its value is used as the file name; otherwise, the name defaults to "/usr/local/etc/rpubkeys" for Unix, or RIPEMPUB for MS-DOS.

Multiple values can be specified; RIPEM will search these public key files in the order specified until a desired key is found.

-S (secret key output) specifies the file name to which the encrypted secret key should be written. Used only by the "-g" option. To prevent inadvertant overwriting of existing files, there is no default for this argument.

-P (public key output) specifies the file name to which a public key should be written. Used by the "-g" option, and by "-d" when RIPEM extracts public keys from the headers of messages being decrypted. (It does this only when it cannot find a record of the public key elsewhere.) To prevent inadvertant overwriting of existing files, there is no default for this argument. When this file is written to in "-d" mode, it is appended to; in "-g" mode, it is overwritten.

-y (server) specifies the domain name of an Internet RIPEM key server. Depending upon the value of the -Y option, RIPEM may try to contact this server to obtain public keys. The default server port is 1611; to override this, follow the name of the server with a ":" followed by the server port number in decimal. This feature may be disabled on some platforms, depending upon the development and networking environment. If -y is not specified, the value of the environment variable RIPEM SERVER NAME, if any, is used. There is no default value.

If -y is specified as a comma-separated list of servers, when consulting a key server RIPEM will try the servers in the order listed until the desired key is obtained.

-Y (key sources) specifies the source(s) RIPEM should use to obtain public keys. Following -Y must be a string of option letters selected from below. The sources are contacted in the order given; if a key cannot be obtained from the first source, the second source, if any, is used. Default is "sf."

f specifies that RIPEM should look in the public key file; see the -p option.

s specifies that RIPEM should contact a network RIPEM key server; see the -y option.

g specifies that RIPEM should attempt to contact the recipient's host via "finger" to obtain the public key. The recipient must have included the -P output from "ripem -g" in his/her ".plan" file.

-u (username) specifies your username—actually, your e-mail address. For encipherment, the username is simply placed in the message header to inform the recipient of the sender's username. For decipherment, the message header is searched for the username so that RIPEM will know which version of the message key to decrypt.

If "-u" is not specified, RIPEM uses the value of the environment variable RIPEM USER NAME, if non-empty. Otherwise, the username defaults to <login-name>@<hostname> or "me" under MS-DOS and most other operating systems.

The username can be specified as a comma-separated list of names. In this case, the first name in the list is used as your username for -g and -e. For -d, RIPEM will look for a recipient line that matches any of the names specified in the list. This is useful if you have several e-mail addresses that you wish RIPEM to regard as equivalent.

-i (input) specifies input file. Used by the "-e" and "-d" options. Default is standard input.

-o (output) specifies output file. Used by the "-e" and "-d" options. Default is standard output.

-D (debug) specifies the debug level. 0 disables debug output; larger values (up to about 4) specify increasing amounts of debug output. The output is written to the destination specified by the "-Z" option. The default level is 0.

-Z (debug output) specifies the file to which debug output, if any, should be written. The default is standard error.

-F (file) specifies the name of a file containing pseudo-random information. Used only for the "-e" and "-g" options. A pseudo-random amount of data from this file, selected from pseudo-random locations in the file, will be used as a source of pseudo-random initializing data for message keys and so on. The file is used only if the "f" suboption of the "-R" option is specified.

-C (command line) specifies that the remainder of the command line consists of pseudo-random strings to be used to construct message keys and so on. This option must be the last option on the command line, as any arguments following it will be used only as pseudo-random data.

The "-C" option should be used, when possible, with the command substitution capabilities of command shells such as Unix's C Shell. The sequence "-C `ps -aux` `finger` `df`" would generate a reasonable amount of pseudo-random data on many Unix systems.

If the environment variable RIPEM ARGS is present, ripem uses its value to obtain additional command-line options. Any conflicts are resolved in favor of the actual command-line arguments.

Description

RIPEM implements a filter to process messages as part of a public key (asymmetric) cryptography privacy-enhanced mail system.

RIPEM is expected to be used primarily to encrypt and decrypt text to be embedded in electronic mail messages. However, it also has two "sign-only" modes in which an authentication check is added to the message, but no encryption of the message itself takes place. RIPEM can also be used to generate RSA public keypairs.

The techniques and data formats used by RIPEM are as compatible as possible with Privacy-Enhanced Mail Internet RFCs 1113, 1114, and 1115. However, there is no support for "certificates," so RIPEM is not really compatible with PEM as described in those documents.

Briefly, messages are encrypted using a traditional private key (symmetric) cipher (DES in CBC mode) with a message key generated pseudo-randomly, enciphered using the RSA public key (asymmetric) system, and included with the ciphertext of the message. A checksum or "message digest" of the plaintext is computed, encrypted with public key cryptography, and included in the ciphertext of the message. For more information, read the RFCs (available at many Internet sites) and the Public-Key Cryptography Standards (available from rsa.com as "pkcs" files).

When RIPEM exits, it returns a status of 0 indicating successful completion, else a non-zero error code indicating that a problem occurred. In the latter case, an error message is written to standard error.

Files

RIPEM uses:

An input file or stream containing a message to process (i.e., encipher / decipher / verify signature).

An output file or stream from the processing.

A file containing the user's encrypted private RSA key.

A file containing the unencrypted public keys of potentially many users.

Bugs

Due to the nature of RSAREF, RIPEM must keep the entire message and its encrypted version in memory at the same time. This may place an uncomfortable upper limit on the size of messages on some platforms.

History

Written in May – July 1992, with subsequent revisions. Uses RSAREF 1.0, which was released in March 1992.

RIPEM itself is in the public domain. However, it requires the RSAREF toolkit from RSA Data Security, Inc. RSAREF is distributed freely for personal use within the USA, but is not in the public domain. Contact RSA Data Security for terms and conditions.

Authors:

Mark Riordan   mrr@scss3.cl.msu.edu

Principal author; wrote most of the non-cryptographic routines, based in part on earlier work by the same author.

Send comments here.

RSA Data Security rsaref-info@rsa.com

Wrote and distributed RSAREF 1.0, the cryptographic toolkit used here. Also, separately, designed and implemented the MD5 message digest algorithm.

Raymond Lau raylau@mit.edu

Wrote the Macintosh version of RIPEM. This document does not apply to the Macintosh version.

Mark Henderson, Richard Outerbridge, Marc VanHeyningen, Greg Onufer, Mark Windsor, and many others also contributed.

Index

Note: *For topics as they pertain specifically to PEM, PGP, and RIPEM, see those headings. For information on use of PEM, PGP, and RIPEM, see PEM Use, PGP Use, and RIPEM Use.*